Unwilling to Quit

UNWILLING TO QUIT

THE LONG UNWINDING
OF AMERICAN INVOLVEMENT
IN VIETNAM

DAVID L. PRENTICE

Copyright © 2023 by The University Press of Kentucky

Scholarly publisher for the Commonwealth,
serving Bellarmine University, Berea College, Centre
College of Kentucky, Eastern Kentucky University,
The Filson Historical Society, Georgetown College,
Kentucky Historical Society, Kentucky State University,
Morehead State University, Murray State University,
Northern Kentucky University, Spalding University,
Transylvania University, University of Kentucky,
University of Louisville, University of Pikeville, and
Western Kentucky University.
All rights reserved.

Editorial and Sales Offices: The University Press of Kentucky
663 South Limestone Street, Lexington, Kentucky 40508-4008
www.kentuckypress.com

Library of Congress Cataloging-in-Publication Data

Names: Prentice, David L., author.
Title: Unwilling to quit : the long unwinding of American involvement in
  Vietnam / David L. Prentice.
Other titles: Long unwinding of American involvement in Vietnam
Description: Lexington : University Press of Kentucky, [2023] | Includes
  bibliographical references and index.
Identifiers: LCCN 2023007292 | ISBN 9780813197760 (hardcover) | ISBN
  9780813197777 (pdf) | ISBN 9780813197784 (epub)
Subjects: LCSH: Vietnam War, 1961–1975—Diplomatic history. | Vietnam War,
  1961–1975—Public opinion. | Vietnam War, 1961–1975—Political
  aspects—United States.
Classification: LCC DS557.7 .P74 2023 | DDC 959.704/3373—dc23/eng/20230222
LC record available at https://lccn.loc.gov/2023007292

This book is printed on acid-free paper meeting
the requirements of the American National Standard
for Permanence in Paper for Printed Library Materials.

Manufactured in the United States of America.

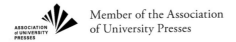

Member of the Association
of University Presses

For my parents

Contents

Abbreviations   ix

Introduction: The Beginning of an Ending   1

1. Good Times, Bad Times: What Nixon Inherited   9
2. Only the Strong Survive: Nixon and Kissinger's Escalation of the War   31
3. My Way: Laird and Vietnamization   53
4. Going Up the Country: Vietnamization, Duck Hook, and the Nixon Doctrine in the Global Context   74
5. Come Together: The Decision against Duck Hook and for Vietnamization   102
6. Give Me Just a Little More Time: The New Optimists   124
7. It's Too Late: Vietnamization's Frailties   143
8. Alone Again, Naturally: The Collapse of the Second Republic   168

Conclusion   180

Acknowledgments   189

Notes   191

Bibliography   249

Index   257

Illustrations follow page 94

Abbreviations

ABM	anti-ballistic missile
ARVN	Army of the Republic of Vietnam
CIA	Central Intelligence Agency
COSVN	Central Office of South Vietnam
DMZ	Demilitarized Zone
DRV	Democratic Republic of Vietnam
GOP	Grand Old Party
GVN	Government of Vietnam
HAK	Henry A. Kissinger
JCS	Joint Chiefs of Staff
JFK	John F. Kennedy
LBJ	Lyndon Baines Johnson
MACV	US Military Assistance Command, Vietnam
NATO	North Atlantic Treaty Organization
NLF	National Liberation Front for the Liberation of Southern Vietnam
NVA	North Vietnamese Army
NSC	National Security Council
PAVN	People's Army of Vietnam
PF	Popular Forces
POW	Prisoner of War
PRC	People's Republic of China
PRG	Provisional Revolutionary Government
PSDF	Popular Self-Defense Forces
RF	Regional Forces
RN	Richard Nixon
RVN	Republic of Vietnam

x Abbreviations

RVNAF	Republic of Vietnam Armed Forces
SALT	Strategic Arms Limitation Talks
SDS	Students for a Democratic Society
SVN	South Vietnam
VC	Vietcong
VSSG	Vietnam Special Studies Group

Introduction

The Beginning of an Ending

Vietnam was America's longest twentieth-century war. The US role there began long before 1965, but Lyndon Johnson's commitment of large numbers of US combat troops that year—the conflict's Americanization—shook the nation's politics, society, and economy and damaged its diplomatic standing abroad. After three years of intense fighting and thousands of casualties, an increasing number of people wanted the United States out of Vietnam. Still, most Americans (and many Vietnamese) remained unwilling to quit.

America's exit proved as contingent, complicated, and agonizing as its decision to intervene on behalf of its ally, the Republic of Vietnam (RVN). Yet, no work adequately explains Richard Nixon's decisions to approve and then continue US troop reductions. Drawing on newly declassified documents and international archives, this manuscript weaves together the domestic and foreign contexts that framed the 1969–1971 decision to end American participation in the Vietnam War. Both are necessary for understanding when and how the United States began to extricate itself from Vietnam.

I argue that there was no teleological winding down of America's war in Vietnam. Vietnamization—the strategy of replacing US soldiers with South Vietnamese forces—was neither a holdover from the Johnson administration nor a foreordained process. The temptation to terminate the conflict with military force remained strong. Only the influence of Secretary of Defense Melvin Laird can explain how Nixon came to accept unilateral troop withdrawals. The president's negotiations and bouts of escalation overshadowed—and at times challenged—Vietnamization, but ultimately Laird's strategy determined the pace and totality of America's exit.

Once on the long road of Vietnamization, Nixon recognized there would be no turning back. Historians who focus on the president and National Security Advisor Henry Kissinger's diplomacy after 1971 are looking at the wrong period. The decisions made from 1969 through 1971 were decisive on the war's outcome. American forces would come home; a residual presence would not be left behind. Whether or not Nixon delayed the final withdrawals by a year to improve his political chances in 1972 and effect a decent interval between the US exit and South Vietnam's fall made little difference.[1] America's ground war would end after the last US soldier departed. And despite overseeing the culmination of the peace talks Johnson had started, Nixon forfeited the means to enforce any agreement. His brittle relations with Congress (also a product of actions taken from 1969 through 1971) and the Watergate scandal denied the president recourse to US airpower. The American war was over.

The Vietnamese read the writing on the wall. They anticipated, challenged, and complicated US decision-making. Still reeling from the disastrous 1968 Tet offensives, Hanoi faced serious challenges from Nixon's coercive diplomacy and expansion of the war in Cambodia and Laos. It chose to persevere. So did Saigon.

I contend that rather than being an unwilling and narrow-minded participant, the Republic's president, Nguyen Van Thieu, understood America's internal concerns, recognized that the US war would soon end, and *embraced* troop withdrawals. By leading on Vietnamization, he hoped to gain the time, autonomy, foreign assistance, and stability necessary to make the strategy work. From 1969 through 1971, Thieu and his officials shared a sense of military progress and increasing national cohesion. There was no foreordained line that ran from Vietnamization to South Vietnam's collapse. But, as in America, Vietnamese decisions taken in this period set in motion events that would see Hanoi triumph.

This book, then, explains when, why, and how the United States curtailed its involvement in Vietnam and how Hanoi and Saigon interpreted and influenced that disengagement. Getting out of a war without a clear victory is more difficult than getting into one. Presidents Nixon and Thieu defied domestic and international pressures as often as they bowed to them. Still, the Americanization of the war was reversed. Having decided that Vietnamization was the only viable path forward, they interpreted signs of military and political progress as proof their strategy was working. Drawing on

Introduction   3

the same, many pundits and scholars concluded the war was all but won or at least winnable during Nixon's first term. But rather than creating a better war, as some writers have argued, the war simply continued while both Thieu and Nixon failed to build a stable consensus for their policies.[2] The war would end not with a self-sufficient Republic of Vietnam but an abject defeat that still lingers over US foreign policy and politics.

Finding and Surviving an American Exit

American policymakers had searched for an acceptable ending to the Vietnam conflict for years. Presidents Harry Truman and Dwight Eisenhower hoped to establish a noncommunist state in Indochina, backed the French in the region's anticolonial struggle, and deepened America's involvement. John Kennedy sought a solution that would enable South Vietnam's survival and reduce America's military commitment. Instead, he significantly expanded it while finding his Vietnamese allies no closer to achieving political stability or military success. Each man fretted over possible military, political, or diplomatic setbacks even as he rejected or postponed decisions to curtail US involvement.[3]

Lyndon Johnson approached Vietnam with the same trepidation and the hope that a little more time and a lot more resources and American men could solve the riddle. He sensed the dangers of sliding into a larger, Americanized conflict. "It's damned easy to get in a war but it's gonna be awfully hard to ever extricate yourself if you get in," he acknowledged.[4] Despite public ignorance of Vietnam and his landslide electoral victory in 1964, losing South Vietnam proved too great a risk. As the head of the State Department's Bureau of Intelligence and Research, Thomas Hughes, recalled, "The one thing that the policy makers of 1965 were incapable of accepting was the idea that there was no positive way out. There had to be some road to victory."[5] By 1969, the costs of an ever-escalating, endless conflict proved too great.

Like LBJ, Melvin Laird understood that "wars are easy to enter into" and "very difficult to get out of."[6] When the American conflict expanded in the mid-1960s, the Wisconsin Republican was among its loudest champions. His actions and his hawkish rhetoric reinforced Johnson's perception that he must enter the Vietnamese conflict or face dire political consequences at home. But as the war's social, material, and human costs grew, Laird, ever the politician, sought an exit that would preserve his party's and his country's credibility and offer the Republic of Vietnam a chance at long-term survival. While Nixon and Kissinger groped for a military or diplomatic solution, the secretary of defense fixed on US troop withdrawals.

Laird consequently played a fundamental role in shaping Nixon's early foreign policy. Most of the scholarship depicts the president and his national security advisor as titans with near absolute control over America's Vietnam strategy.[7] Kissinger liked to boast of his power and influence, but even he had to concede that the secretary of defense got the best of him. "I might be the director of this play," he candidly admitted, "but I am an actor in some other play whose plot Laird hasn't told me yet."[8] Indeed, Laird excelled at waging and winning bureaucratic battles. Although he told only his closest aides, his goal in early 1969 was to have all US military personnel out by 1973 whether there was a diplomatic settlement or not. The military and the White House considered this unthinkable, but he gradually bent both to his will.

Laird's Vietnamization ended America's presence in Vietnam, something an emphasis on the Paris peace negotiations overlooks, but it was a hard sell.[9] Given the faltering home front and the advantage of hindsight, it is too easy to see Vietnamization as foreordained or at least overdetermined.[10] Instead, the president considered a range of options, with Vietnamization often consigned to the bottom of the list. All the while, he was hoping that with enough time, force, great power diplomacy, and aid, he could give the Republic a decent chance of surviving.

Nixon sought peace with honor and the preservation of noncommunist South Vietnam, and he desperately searched for a solution that would accomplish these aims. He at times escalated and expanded the conflict. While other scholars have explored Nixon and Kissinger's coercive diplomacy, they generally overemphasize psychology and realism in the pair's preference for a decisive, military blow against the communist Democratic Republic of Vietnam (DRV).[11] Their temperaments and geopolitical philosophies guided their actions, but they never took their eyes off domestic politics.[12]

This study demonstrates the primacy of US domestic considerations in the administration's decision to Vietnamize the war. Only they adequately explain why Nixon—one of the war's most consistent hawks—adopted policies of de-escalation. Policymakers and politicians always watched the home front. In postwar America, politics was supposed to stop at the water's edge of foreign policy. It seldom did.[13] Beyond politics and partisanship, the rising

Introduction 5

antiwar and conservative movements as well as economic concerns shaped important foreign policy debates. "Political grand strategy fashioned in Washington trumped military strategy conceived and implemented in South Vietnam," military historian Gregory Daddis has rightly noted.[14]

All three men—Laird, Kissinger, and Nixon—worried about the home front. This perception centered on antiwar unrest, growing public antipathy to the war, and especially vocal dissent in Congress. Despite Nixon's claims to the contrary, congressional doves had significant influence on the White House. They lacked the numbers to pass any meaningful antiwar legislation in 1969, but their presence and rhetoric convinced him that time was short. Administration discussions centered on the lack of "time" (as measured in congressional and popular support) to thwart North Vietnamese will or make the South Vietnamese self-sufficient. Archival research confirms that the savage bombing campaign proposed for November 1969—Operation Duck Hook—was part of a year-long plan to end the war before patience ran out at home. It proved too big a political gamble to take. When the president came to the decisive moment of choosing escalation or Vietnamization, Laird prevailed. Nixon publicly admitted in early 1970 that Vietnamization was "irreversible." The spring 1970 incursion into Cambodia and the resulting congressional backlash confirmed his lack of room to maneuver. The withdrawals would continue. That Laird and Vietnamization won out speaks to the power of domestic political considerations.

This book looks beyond American perspectives, though. Despite a growing body of research on the interconnectedness of local and foreign actions, historians have devoted scarce attention to the international aspects of Nixon's Vietnamization policy.[15] Here, the Vietnamese share the stage with their American counterparts and rivals.

Excellent works like Pierre Asselin's *Vietnam's American War* and Lien-Hang Nguyen's *Hanoi's War* have done much to develop the North Vietnamese perspective, and this manuscript supplements their scholarship. The Democratic Republic anticipated Vietnamization and adapted its strategy accordingly. At times, Hanoi feared that Nixon and Thieu might succeed, but it resolved to keep fighting despite the enormous human costs of an increasingly fratricidal war. With America's war ending, its leaders felt victory was at last within their grasp.

Using Vietnamese archival sources, this manuscript complements the recent "South Vietnamese turn in Vietnam War historiography."[16] Indicative of this turn, historians have published outstanding books on the first South Vietnamese president, Ngo Dinh Diem.[17] But Saigon's side of the story remains woefully unexplored and misunderstood. For too long, it has either been ignored or dismissed as a kleptocracy that sought only to perpetuate its undemocratic rule and the wealth of its elites. Little wonder then that Thieu, South Vietnam's president from 1967 to 1975, has received scant attention, though George Veith's *Drawn Swords* is an impressive recent contribution. My book, then, is one of the first to explain Thieu. Vietnamese sources show a complex and enigmatic figure who, along with Melvin Laird, loomed large over events. They also reveal a surprising insight: the Republic embraced (rather than fought) the strategy of unilateral US troop reductions.

Historical references abound as to how Nixon imposed the detestable US withdrawals on the Republic. Looking back on the war after Saigon fell in 1975, some South Vietnamese bitterly remembered Vietnamization. Former vice president and air force general Nguyen Cao Ky called it a "gigantic con trick foisted on American public opinion." General Tran Van Don compared it to "walking blindfolded through a minefield," with the South Vietnamese uncertain of US intentions and the Americans using Vietnamization to cover their retreat. The Republic's ambassador to the United States, Bui Diem, went further: "The manner in which the United States took its leave was more than a mistake; it was an act unworthy of a great power, one that I believe will be remembered long after such unfortunate misconceptions as the search and destroy strategy have been consigned to footnotes." A sense of betrayal thus pervades postwar South Vietnamese memoirs.[18]

Contemporaneous accounts show that this pessimism did not exist at the time. Most South Vietnamese officials anticipated and even privately encouraged the Vietnamization of the war. Thieu advocated for it, and in doing so he attempted to influence the White House. Believing that American will was disintegrating, he concluded that US troop reductions could head off a precipitate allied exit or a disastrous peace deal. He also assumed he could exchange American soldiers for greater US financial aid and developmental assistance. From the start of the 1968 Tet Offensive to the June 1969 announcement of troop reductions, he exhorted Americans to begin a withdrawal program. His general mobilization of South Vietnamese manpower prepared the path for the US decision to withdraw from the ground war. He was confident his nation could stand on its own, but he acknowledged that he needed time and US aid to expand and modernize his military.

Introduction 7

All the while, Thieu's leadership enabled the Republic to weather Vietnamization. When modest withdrawals did begin, the noncommunist nationalists accepted them as appropriate, given American internal problems and perceived allied military gains in the South. They reacted to Thieu and Nixon's strategy with the tentative hope that the Republic could fight and win the war on its own. They also launched ambitious political and economic reforms while expanding government control of the countryside. Without this political stability, Nixon might have been able to justify abandoning South Vietnam in 1969 or, more likely, might not have felt confident enough to begin removing American soldiers. In time, though, Thieu's personal, political, and strategic failures undermined the regime's survival.

Additional foreign archives supplement what is a Vietnamese and American story. This book takes a practical approach to international history, using a range of sources to fill in gaps and better understand alliance politics and the war. British, Australian, Canadian, and others' interactions with top officials offer glimpses into what they were thinking and how they were handling allied diplomacy and cooperation. Wary of both his fellow nationalists and his US partners, Thieu found an outlet with foreign diplomats. His voice is largely absent from Vietnamese and American archives, but he laid out his hopes, frustrations, intentions, political maneuvers, and grand strategy with friendly third parties. Moreover, the views and actions of non-American, non-Vietnamese actors further develop the context. For instance, their reports of the political and military situation in Vietnam provide alternative assessments by which we can judge combatants' appraisals. At times, other nations also influenced events. Significantly, key allies urged American policymakers to achieve peace with honor and not pull out or abandon South Vietnam precipitously. They understood the domestic forces driving Vietnamization and hoped to arrest a global US retreat.

Yet, it was not just that domestic politics shaped the conduct of the war but that the war's continuation fundamentally changed US politics and society.[19] Nixon's actions and rhetoric catalyzed the birth of law-and-order politics, polarization, the rise of the conservative movement, and the shift of the American South toward the Republican Party. It also led him to exceed his constitutional limits, precipitating an institutional crisis that culminated with the Watergate scandal. Public trust in US institutions and leaders has never recovered from Vietnam and Watergate. Prolonging the end of America's Vietnam War left lasting scars in both Vietnam and the United States.

A longer war hastened the unraveling of the American century—that optimistic age of US primacy and global leadership that was supposed to follow World War II.[20] The United States suffered a crisis of confidence and economic travails as the continuation of the Vietnam War eroded the psychological and economic foundations of its might. It also spurred fears of neoisolationism. Grappling with an unending war abroad and dissent at home, Nixon pursued détente and strategic retrenchment to prevent that from happening. The Vietnam War stood at the nexus of these events. Ultimately, Vietnamization neither healed American divisions nor secured South Vietnam. That state's collapse in 1975 failed to free America of its burden. Recriminations over this event and whether the Nixon administration almost won a better war or effected little more than a decent interval continue to the present. America may have ended its fighting in Vietnam, but in too many ways that conflict remains the "war that never ends."

1

Good Times, Bad Times

What Nixon Inherited

The War to January 20, 1969

American presidents often spoke of Vietnam as a bad inheritance: a commitment made, a debt owed, a legacy of mistakes and missed opportunities. Harry Truman faulted French colonialism. Dwight Eisenhower criticized the French and Truman, and on it went through John Kennedy and Lyndon Johnson. Despite gnawing doubts, each man expanded America's commitment to and military presence in South Vietnam.[1] Meanwhile, the war's escalation ravaged the Vietnamese countryside and cities as well as American politics and society.

At his January 20 inauguration, Richard Nixon inherited circumstances not of his making: resolute enemies and suspicious allies, Johnson's limited and stalemated war, and a war-weary home front, fraying within and yet opposed to defeat in Vietnam. The conflict had matured by 1969, with rival Vietnamese states and an American troop commitment that exceeded half a million men. This context framed the new administration's early decisions, but the incoming president was not a novice swimmer cast into the lake of Vietnam's dilemmas.

Nixon had contributed to and at times influenced the conduct of the war. He brought into the White House firm beliefs on the Cold War, American credibility, the conduct of statecraft and warfare, and the critical dynamic between diplomacy and democracy. He doubted that abandoning Vietnam was warranted or even possible. But like his predecessors, he struggled over how to adapt to American and Vietnamese realities.

Nixon also inherited some flexibility. Events were far more fluid than they were often portrayed. Johnson chose to stabilize or level off the war, not end it. As he had intended, his successor could escalate or de-escalate it. The public was equally indecisive. Most people hoped for peace but remained unwilling to accept defeat. America's exit was by no means foreordained in January 1969.

Enemies, Allies, and Johnson's War

Of all the presidents, Lyndon Johnson complained the most about being given a mess in Vietnam. "Well, if they'd say I *inherited* [it], I'll be lucky. But they'll all say I *created* it," he lamented as he raised the US commitment.[2] Yet, it was he who transformed the Vietnam crisis into not just a major American conflict but also one of the most consequential in US history.

To be fair to Johnson, the timing of his presidency could not have been worse. John F. Kennedy's assassination had come only a few weeks after the military coup against South Vietnamese president Ngo Dinh Diem. Political instability and military setbacks followed. Hoping to win before the United States could intervene, Hanoi decided to increase the flow of men and matériel south. Communist forces boldly raided South Vietnamese and American base camps. The National Front for the Liberation of Southern Vietnam (NLF)—the Hanoi-backed southern insurgent and political group—claimed more and more territory from the Government of Vietnam (GVN).[3] An escalating number of terrorist acts against civilian venues like theaters extended the war into South Vietnamese towns and cities.

As the Saigon government crumbled, LBJ confronted his 1964 election campaign and his ambitious agenda for domestic reform. America, he believed, needed sweeping antipoverty measures, urban renewal, and civil rights legislation to solve its internal problems. Vietnam must wait. Besides, the president reasoned, North Vietnam's leader, Ho Chi Minh, would be as reasonable as the Southern segregationists in Congress.[4]

The US government and news media assumed that Ho Chi Minh, the legendary nationalist and affable communist, ran the Democratic Republic of Vietnam. Mistaking who was in charge of North Vietnam and what he wanted, Johnson thought that the right offer (or the right amount of force) would end the Northern-backed and increasingly Northern-fought war against the U.S.-backed government of South Vietnam. Compromise should be possible.

In truth, Johnson faced the intractable Le Duan. To outsiders, the former insurgent seemed "bland"—a political and bureaucratic figure of little consequence. The Central Intelligence Agency (CIA) judged him "the best qualified middle-roader" in the Politburo.[5] They could not have been more wrong. Years of French repression and a full-fledged embrace of communism had created an indefatigable and relentless enemy. Before being recalled to Hanoi in 1957, he had fought the French in the south and subsequently organized resistance to Diem's southern Republic of Vietnam. After displacing Ho in the early 1960s, he would commit North Vietnam and its southern allies to a total war for reunification under a communist state. Hoping to destroy the South Vietnamese army and spark revolution in the cities, Le Duan ordered a sharp upsurge of operations in 1964 and 1965.[6]

Reacting to these stunning reverses in South Vietnam, Johnson began what became the American war. Losing Vietnam, he judged, would be too costly to his political agenda and too risky to American national security. Rather than accept defeat, he escalated the conflict. He began bombing North Vietnam. He upped the number of US military personnel from Kennedy's 16,300 to 23,300 in 1964 before deciding that only a major increase of US ground troops could provide the shield to save South Vietnam. He continued this escalation until there were nearly 550,000 American servicemen (alongside 65,761 other allied forces) in Vietnam and US aircraft were continually bombing targets in Laos, North Vietnam, and South Vietnam. Success remained elusive. The United States and the South Vietnamese government struggled to control the countryside and build a state capable of earning the peoples' support.[7]

After Diem's assassination, South Vietnam found itself on a merry-go-round of regimes. While Hanoi and Washington locked themselves into an ever-escalating military stalemate, Saigon wrestled with its legitimacy and internal dissent. In 1966 and 1967, a military junta agreed to the drafting of a constitution and the formation of a constitutional government. The 1967 birth of the Second Republic, with its courts, bicameral legislature, and president, gave noncommunist and anticommunist Vietnamese hope that greater reform and military success were imminent. Even pessimists conceded that "in the midst of the current political chaos, having something in hand is better than void and nothingness."[8]

Nguyen Van Thieu, the Second Republic's first (and essentially only) president, reflected his country's hopes and fears. Born along Vietnam's south-central coast on April 5, 1923, he came from modest origins. His father was a small farmer, merchant, and part-time fisherman. Although he initially joined the nationalist Viet Minh, Thieu left their ranks after he saw that communists dominated the group. In 1948, he joined the French-created Vietnamese National Army. He fought against the Viet Minh and experimented with pacification in the Red River Delta. A committed anti-communist with political aspirations, he quietly and determinedly rose in the Army of the Republic of Vietnam (ARVN). He played a role in the coup against Diem even as he opposed his murder. Seeing the president's bloodied corpse sickened him, but not enough to dampen his ambition or slow his intrigue. He steadily outflanked his rivals, appointing or promoting officers, provincial chiefs, and district officials loyal to him. Without a runoff provision in the constitution, he won the September 1967 presidential election with 34 percent of the vote. He understood that his election did not guarantee his survival.[9]

Secrecy and caution were Thieu's chief attributes. His nicknames fit his personality: *"Mot Ga Mai"* ("Hen Face") for his inscrutable, silent demeanor, *"Le Grand Louvoyeur"* ("The Great Tacker") for his deft ability to advance even when the winds of fortune seemed against him, and "Sly Fox" for his soft-spoken cunning. Quiet and uncomfortable in public, he preferred explanatory speeches over charismatic leadership, though he could rise to the occasion. His cautious nature proved more problematic. His father imparted this attribute to his children, admonishing them to arrive early at train stations despite the mosquitos and stifling humidity: "People wait for trains. Trains do not wait for people." Yet, events were not trains. Thieu would often move too slowly. It was appropriate that the flamboyant air force commander and politico Nguyen Cao Ky, who Thieu displaced, was nicknamed "The Cowboy" and enjoyed cockfighting. Thieu preferred fishing. His circumspection and passive resistance would frustrate US policymakers. It was fitting that for most of his tenure his American counterpart, Richard Nixon, was also an introvert and schemer. One American official observed that Thieu "has no close friends. He takes no one into his confidence." "What's his passion?" a foreign diplomat who knew him wondered. "I don't know, unless it's suspicion—plotting people out, if that can be a passion."[10]

For Thieu, the plotting began immediately. The lack of a truly free and fair election hurt his legitimacy. The military's decision to make him share the ticket with Ky and not a civilian compounded his political problems. A different running mate would have broadened his appeal and made it harder for the generals to replace him. He denied that his presidency represented a continuation of military rule while seeking the junta's blessing for his actions. And Diem's death hung over his political moves. Owing to his over-cautious, even paranoid nature, he worried that Ky's loyalists could mount another coup. In the weeks after the election, his friends implored him to use his talent for political machinations to embrace the constitution, build a broad noncommunist coalition, and thereby outmaneuver the generals and Ky. Thieu's fears proved too great.[11]

Rather than move toward the center, Thieu shifted rightward. He believed the South Vietnamese military was "the only cohesive force holding the country together." He acknowledged it was also his "major political supporter." He owed his presidency to the secret military council that had given him the top slot in exchange for his promise to get their approval on major decisions.[12] But he also worked at carving out a broader base of support. He would minimize political dissent, using a combination of bribes and compromises to win over Ky's backers and National Assembly hardliners. Buddhists' underrepresentation in the National Assembly further encouraged Thieu to tack toward the right. Their ambivalent stand on the elections meant unwavering anticommunists like northern Catholic refugees won significant influence. As the legislative branch of the Second Republic, the Assembly wielded considerable political power. It could be both a source of legitimacy for the Thieu government and an impediment to his agenda. By the end of 1967, he had created a large bloc of support in the Assembly. The following year, Ky suffered shattering political blows: allies died while others were marginalized or joined Thieu. Still, the tempestuous nature of Saigon politics meant that Thieu never felt safe, especially in a year like 1968.[13]

1968: "A Year of Testing"

Americans and Vietnamese weathered few years as violent, uncertain, and challenging as 1968. The US ambassador to South Vietnam, Ellsworth Bunker, called it "a year of trial" and "a year of testing."[14] It was the bloodiest year of the war, with the Tet Offensive coming to symbolize the endless death and destruction. It was also a year of new hopes as Johnson leveled off the American troop commitment, paused the bombing of North Vietnam, and opened peace talks in Paris. Yet, he was merely reacting to events in Vietnam and America.[15]

Le Duan's 1967 decision to launch attacks throughout South Vietnam would usher in a new era of the war even as his bold initiatives failed to accomplish his aims. A series of offensives in 1968 and 1969, beginning with the Tet Offensive (and collectively referred to as the Tet offensives in this book), sought to destroy the ARVN, spark mass procommunist uprisings in the cities, and ultimately topple the Republic. At great cost, North Vietnamese and NLF forces relentlessly assailed allied soldiers, but they failed to deliver a knockout blow. Battered, Hanoi would play for time and respite from US bombing by engaging in negotiations and deceptively suggesting that peace was at hand. Le Duan never wavered—his tactics changed, his goal did not.[16]

The Tet offensives demonstrated North Vietnam's commitment. The CIA estimated that from January through May the communists—the People's Army of Vietnam (PAVN) regulars and the NLF guerillas—had lost 32,000 men *per month* (the United States and South Vietnam lost 14,589 and 27,915 men respectively *for the entire year*). In the months that followed, allied officials concluded that the Tet offensives had nearly wiped out the NLF. Yet, as the CIA well understood, North Vietnam could replace these losses almost indefinitely. Nor was there any indication that the war's staggering human toll had swayed Hanoi toward compromise.[17]

Things were different in Washington. Even before the Tet Offensive, a growing number of US policymakers had suggested a new strategy of diplomacy and military stabilization. They argued the president should level off the American troop commitment, stop the bombing of North Vietnam, and make every effort to negotiate with Hanoi. Johnson rejected such advice. He believed, and publicly touted, that the allies were making progress in Vietnam. More than one senior official boasted they could see "the light at the end of the tunnel."[18] When the Tet Offensive obscured that light, administration doves offered a way out of the darkness. They convinced Johnson to implement a partial bombing halt over North Vietnam, pursue negotiations, and place a ceiling on America's troop commitment. Looking at the unraveling of American society, the president further decided that he could not hold the country together while running for reelection and pursuing peace. On March 31, he announced, along with the partial bombing halt and a new emphasis on diplomacy, that he would not seek another term in office. He became a lame duck, mindful of his legacy and his growing impotence to achieve lasting peace in Vietnam.

The military offensives, a burgeoning refugee crisis, and uncertainty over American intentions took their toll on South Vietnam. Despite enormous casualties, the Republic of Vietnam Armed Forces (RVNAF) persevered. The nation survived the trials of 1968, finding new unity and confidence. But Johnson's March 31 address, the opening of the peace talks in Paris in May, and the upcoming US presidential election raised worrisome questions about American resolve.

Thieu remained calm, arguing that the allies had dealt Hanoi and the NLF grave blows. Conversely, he thought that the Republic was stronger than ever. To build on this strength, the National Assembly mobilized the country's population for war. This general mobilization drafted every male between seventeen and forty-five.[19] Thieu believed that this step, along with grants of modern arms and equipment, would enable US soldiers to begin returning home in 1968, certainly by 1969. He reasoned that this bold de-Americanization would buy American patience and provide the resources his country needed to outlast Hanoi. His people were war-weary but increasingly confident they could carry the burden and reverse the Americanization of the war.[20]

Thieu's rule remained contingent. Coup rumors proliferated in Saigon, as did talk of a sellout in the negotiations. The National Assembly and South Vietnamese hawks protested even the hint of American unilateralism in Paris. They opposed allied concessions, particularly those regarding a coalition government in the South or recognition of the NLF. Thieu understood that to accept the NLF as equals in the negotiations would undermine his popular support, give the Front an international platform for propaganda, and perhaps encourage further US concessions.[21]

That summer and fall, Thieu demanded that Hanoi negotiate directly with Saigon and that there be no allied recognition—explicit or implicit—of the NLF. With the preliminary talks between North Vietnam and the United States deadlocked over the continued American bombing and Saigon's participation in the negotiations, the South Vietnamese president doubted a diplomatic breakthrough would occur. Then, with breathtaking speed in October, the situation changed. Assured by the Soviets that a deal was within reach and hoping he could achieve peace before he left office, Johnson announced on October 31 that he was ending the bombing of North Vietnam and expected formal negotiations between both sides to begin shortly. Thieu judged that the inclusion of the NLF on Hanoi's side was a potentially fatal concession for South Vietnam. On November 2, he publicly broke with the Johnson administration and refused to join the talks, a move that may have stalled Democrat Hubert Humphrey's surging momentum in the US presidential election. Humphrey barely lost to Nixon days later. Thieu's decision owed to South Vietnamese domestic political and diplomatic considerations, but he was content to let Nixon believe that the Republicans owed him a great debt. Meanwhile, his defiance led to an outpouring of support from Saigon's anticommunist politicians and officials. For many, he had become a legitimate nationalist and a savior of the Republic.[22]

The Thieu government was riding high in November. The president's stand had strengthened the regime's popularity nationwide, creating a "spirit of excitement and strong support" among the people. He had harnessed latent anti-Americanism and gotten the Americans to follow his lead. That the Johnson administration had postponed the talks rather than start without Saigon encouraged the South Vietnamese. Foreign news media attention to the "spirit of unity" also gave officials hope that they could contend with the NLF for legitimacy in the court of global opinion. GVN officials sought to "exploit this political triumph" at home and abroad while preparing the people for the long war and talks they believed lay ahead. "Progressing to self-improvement" would be critical.[23]

Nixon's narrow victory at the polls reassured the South Vietnamese, though most still believed American troops would soon be leaving. "Determined to win" became the catchphrase of progovernment groups to describe their and Nixon's resolve. The British embassy noted that "de-Americanization" had become the "catch-word" around Saigon. Johnson's 1968 policies and crumbling US public support for the war suggested that the South Vietnamese would soon be responsible for their own survival. As one senator put it in early November, the conflict would be "Viet-Namised" regardless of who was US president. As more and more Americans soured on the war, Saigon believed it must bolster its reputation and devise a negotiating and Vietnamization strategy before the new administration betrayed them.[24]

From Washington, Ambassador Bui Diem warned Thieu that greater tests lay ahead. A quiet critic of Thieu and Saigon politics, the urbane diplomat prided himself on his ability to stand apart from the day's passions and provide the analysis his president needed. Thieu must convince Nixon to accept a policy beneficial to the Republic before the "American bureaucratic machinery" settled on a direction. With Congress and the press turning against the war, Diem argued, Saigon must win "hearts and minds" in America and worldwide by accepting US troop reductions and the Paris talks. On the latter, he explained that Americans did not see Saigon's procedural concerns over the status of the NLF as important. Instead, they blamed South Vietnam for holding up the peace talks. The incoming president was no doubt already looking toward the 1972 campaign. "Nixon needs to have enough time and patience to keep the Communists from winning," he concluded. Given the importance of "U.S. public opinion," it "all depends on Vietnam's actions." Diem's cable circulated throughout Thieu's government, which took the ambassador's views more seriously than he thought at the time.[25]

From November 1 through mid-January 1969, South Vietnam obstructed the talks in Paris. Thieu's government recognized it was playing a dangerous game. In a high-level meeting at the Independence Palace on November 5, Thieu explained that the Republic could not be "too excessive" in "kicking America." It needed US cooperation and time. "We have to utilize the time so that under any situation, we can still win," he continued. He rejected four-party talks, instead seeking a two-sided arrangement that made clear Hanoi controlled the NLF delegation.[26] Ideally, the Republic would lead the allied delegation, with American officials acting alongside them. Thieu's delay and insistence prompted the Johnson administration to reiterate that it would not accept a coalition government. Saigon then sent a delegation to Paris, but procedural issues continued to hold up the onset of formal negotiations.[27]

Neither Hanoi nor Saigon wanted to do anything that would raise the stature of the other. The arrangement of tables and the delegations' flags mattered in this new theater of diplomacy: Saigon wanted a rectangular table with the two sides across from one another; Hanoi favored a square table with each party given its own side. All this talk of tables occluded the reality that neither side sought peace. As much as Thieu wanted to deny the NLF a role in Paris, he understood by early 1969 that he had lost that battle. A circular table at last proved amenable to all sides. On January 25, formal talks with all parties began. Peace remained elusive.[28]

With the Paris negotiations entering a new phase, Saigon concluded that the battle over "hearts and minds" extended beyond the Vietnamese countryside: The Republic sought *war and peace Vietnamization* to take control of the war, negotiations, and propaganda. In search of a Vietnamized peace, the government hoped that the talks would raise its stature abroad and attract international support and alliances. Many of these efforts, including those by politicians and labor leaders, were spontaneous as they too decided that the talks presented a new opportunity to make their voices heard. Their ambition exceeded their resources. South Vietnamese citizens and officials often lacked the language skills to communicate with foreign audiences. They found the international environment more challenging than they had anticipated. While pro-Thieu demonstrations in Saigon attracted media attention in November 1968, the NLF increasingly won the lion's share of coverage. They were better at public diplomacy. The Republic hoped "War Vietnamization" would prove easier.[29]

Thieu continued to be out in front on Vietnamization. He had advocated this policy to LBJ in mid-1968 to alleviate US domestic pressures, only to be rebuffed. With the impending change in the White House, he spent December and January discussing reductions with US officials while preparing his people for them. His New Year's Eve address expressed hope. He argued that the Republic was increasingly able to defend itself and that American troop reductions could begin in 1969. But only US policymakers could give the order to bring men home. Thieu again urged Americans to start withdrawing some forces to bolster their home front.[30]

His partners in this early planning were General Creighton Abrams and Ambassador Ellsworth Bunker. Having replaced William Westmoreland as the head of the US Military Assistance Command, Vietnam (MACV) the previous summer, Abrams projected tough determination. His talk of a "one war" strategy that combined the attrition of enemy forces, Vietnamization, and pacification—the control of the countryside—meshed well with Thieu's views and the perennial American hope that victory could be snatched from the jaws of defeat.[31] Bunker spoke similarly, but with language that reflected his elite East Coast upbringing and dignified manner. Bui Diem humorously recalled that his "cool," aristocratic "demeanor had earned him the nickname Old Man Refrigerator among the Vietnamese." Behind the visage, though, was a diplomat who tirelessly managed the fraught relationship between two allies prone to misunderstanding each other.[32]

On January 17, the three met to discuss troop withdrawals. Thieu outlined his "three pillars" strategy for the first three months of 1969. Confident of the military and political situation in South Vietnam, he would, if possible, pursue negotiations that included direct, albeit secret, talks with the NLF. The Republic could accept their political participation if only they would lay down their arms and abide by the constitution; perhaps this offer would lure insurgents away from the communists. Pessimistic about such entreaties, he would continue to emphasize pacification, and he would build up ARVN forces so that America could reduce its military presence in Vietnam. Thieu was "serious about Allied troop withdrawals," Bunker noted, and wanted South Vietnam "to carry its own burden." By advocating unilateral withdrawals, he intended "to give the U.S. Government an assist, particularly in its relations with the American public, so that it may be able to maintain its program of assistance to South Vietnam and not undertake any precipitous withdrawal." He wanted it known publicly that de-Americanization was a Vietnamese initiative, which it had been. Elsewhere, Thieu explained that by proposing specific numbers he hoped "that this might act as a form of brake on [the] incoming USA admins' thinking on this crucial issue." Thieu and the Vietnamese saw withdrawals as inevitable. By leading on the issue, they hoped to buy time and goodwill from the American public. It was also sound leadership, easing popular fears and preparing the South Vietnamese for America's exit.[33]

Thieu and his staff worked with Abrams, often independently of Washington, to plan the anticipated withdrawals. After the US election, MACV officials and Australian military experts quietly drew up contingency plans and timetables for troop reductions while the South Vietnamese did the same. Abrams and Thieu believed that ARVN modernization and expansion, along with progress in pacification, justified redeployments. Thieu suggested they announce the withdrawal of two divisions rather than one to increase the effect on American opinion. Abrams agreed they should present the reductions as a product of South Vietnamese strength to maximize the public impact, but he thought it premature to remove this many troops. He instead proposed that Washington remove the 9th Division (approximately 18,000 men) in July.[34]

There was no corresponding policy development stateside. Secretary of Defense Clark Clifford pleaded with Johnson to announce, or at least plan, US withdrawals. Such actions would start America's exit from Vietnam and pad the president's legacy. Johnson refused. He wanted an honorable peace based on the mutual withdrawal of North Vietnamese and US forces. He adamantly opposed unilateral reductions. "We're not going to pull out," he affirmed. "If [the North Vietnamese] think we're getting ready to bring troops home why they'll continue" fighting. And yet, that was precisely what happened. Looking beyond Johnson's tenure, both the North and South Vietnamese judged that not even Richard Nixon could resist the growing pressure for withdrawals.[35]

Speculation regarding these reductions was rampant in Saigon, but so was tentative optimism. Many South Vietnamese were proud they had weathered the storms of 1968 and believed they could begin taking over the war. "We have walked a tight rope, politically, internationally, and are still on top," reflected the editors at the *Saigon Post*. "Forward to 1969 with something stronger than hope, forward with a will and a strength born of success during our toughest test—our test of '68." Other South Vietnamese newspapers agreed, stressing the new confidence and unity of the people. American officials and soldiers in Saigon shared this optimism. "Hell, we lost the guerilla war in 1964," one noted. "But this is now a new war and we could win it." Analysts believed that the Tet Offensive had decimated the insurgents' numbers and appeal; they estimated that less than 15 percent of the population backed the NLF in early 1969. Thieu's office announced in mid-January that it was working out plans for US troop reductions. Vietnamese reports speculated that 60,000 Americans could leave in 1969. The South Vietnamese public agreed that, should this progress continue, allied soldiers should begin returning home. The darkest cloud on the horizon remained the US home front, and they hoped reductions could convince Americans that their nation was worthy of continued support.[36]

The North Vietnamese and NLF agreed that, despite allied military gains in 1968, the American people would insist that Nixon de-escalate the war. Hanoi had followed the American elections. Its leaders had preferred Humphrey, but they recognized that the Democrats still controlled both houses of Congress and would make it difficult for Nixon to prolong the war.

Meanwhile, LBJ's October 31 total bombing halt improved North Vietnamese morale, economy, and living standards. Although the people hoped peace might be imminent, the bombing halt and America's internal difficulties gave the regime a significant boost as it prepared for continued war. A mid-December memo by the Central Office of South Vietnam (COSVN) encouraged southern cadre and argued that US withdrawals would be forthcoming in the New Year. According to the weekly North Vietnamese paper the *Vietnam Courier*, America was "dog-tired, out of breath, but obstinate." It warned that "de-Americanization" would allow the White House to manage dissent and so prolong the war. The newspaper of the armed forces, *Quan doi Nhan dan,* observed, "Nixon enters the White House in the situation of a US in plenty of troubles and difficulties." Hanoi sought to exploit those difficulties to hasten the presumed withdrawals.[37]

The Politburo cabled its Paris diplomats fresh instructions on January 1, 1969. With US troop reductions inevitable, they should demand a complete American exit while appearing cooperative so that the talks would not break down and the bombing resume. They should use the talks to buy time to improve their battlefield position and press on in their war against the Republic. Negotiations also held the promise of legitimizing the NLF and further dividing Saigon and Washington. Surveying captured documents, Vietnamese prisoners' testimonies, and North Vietnamese military moves, the State Department's Thomas Hughes understood their strategy. He warned Secretary of State Dean Rusk that the North Vietnamese would concede just enough "to keep alive American convictions that negotiations are of value, will eventually bring the war to an end, and therefore must be continued" even as they violated the secret "understandings" that produced the talks.[38] Hanoi would stall in Paris while launching military offensives in South Vietnam.[39]

Lyndon Johnson did not achieve the peace he had yearned for, but his choices in 1968 shaped the domestic and international situations his successor inherited. His administration had capped the number of American soldiers in South Vietnam; no American politician or official would contemplate raising this ceiling.[40] The beginning of the Paris talks and what became a total bombing halt of North Vietnam also raised public expectations about peace and further de-escalation. Dashing such hopes carried enormous political risks. Yet, Johnson had stuck with South Vietnam. Even as he refused to countenance any reduction in American forces, he supported the modernization and mobilization programs necessary to begin handing military responsibility back to the South Vietnamese.

LBJ convinced himself that he was leaving his successor a better war than the one he received in 1963. As was his custom, he had not leveled with the American people that the bombing halt was conditional and that there were limits to his patience. In his final two months in office, he felt Hanoi was taking advantage of his concessions and he considered resuming the bombing. He left that decision to his successor, though his secrecy regarding the October breakthrough meant that any escalation would hurt Nixon politically. Still, he later boasted that Nixon inherited "an ally that was stronger than ever before; an enemy weakened and beaten in every major engagement; and a working forum for peace."[41] The bombing could be resumed and the American war machine was reaching its peak strength. To borrow one of the Texan's metaphors, the United States had two fists—diplomacy and military strength—swinging at Ho Chi Minh's jaw.[42] Johnson believed that his successor would have the means to win the war.

The situation in early 1969 might have been the basis for a better war, but, if anything, the tests of 1968 indicated only that a longer and deadlier war lay ahead. The offensives had decimated the NLF, and allied forces were rapidly pacifying the countryside. The Republic was growing stronger politically and militarily. But Hanoi remained unwilling to quit, America had stopped its bombing of the North, and the talks had devolved into a forum for posturing and propaganda. It was a recipe for strategic confusion, and the faltering US domestic front added another volatile ingredient to the mix.

The American Home Front

While the situation in Vietnam was decidedly better than it had been in November 1963, the same could not be said of the United States. By 1969, Johnson's war had exacted an unexpected and enormous domestic toll. Over 30,000 Americans had died in Vietnam. The loss of loved ones rippled through communities nationwide. Many prowar politicians softened their stand upon learning of the death of a friend's son in Vietnam.[43] Anguish spread in 1968. So did outrage.

The rising voices of antiwar protests and social unrest spoke to the escalating war at home. "The entire world shook in 1968," according to historian Jeremi Suri. "Across cultures, people of all generations recognized the significance of the moment. A global wave of urban protests produced a crisis of authority in nearly every society."[44]

For its centuries of slavery and segregation, the United States was a tinderbox of racial frustration poised to ignite. As Johnson drafted his March 31 speech, civil rights leader Martin Luther King Jr. planned the Poor People's Campaign to address poverty, unemployment, and housing. Striking sanitation workers drew him to Memphis, where he spoke, prayed, and organized nonviolent protests. There, he was gunned down on April 4. Demonstrations in more than 120 cities followed. Chicago and Washington burned, requiring federal troops to restore order. The destruction came within blocks of the

Capitol. Smoke penetrated the White House. Surveying the carnage, General Westmoreland remarked that it "looked worse than Saigon did at the height of the Tet Offensive."[45] There was little doubt among many Americans that a reckoning had arrived and that, when viewed alongside that crisis, Vietnam scarcely mattered.

Many university students agreed. Righteous anger at injustice—whether the war in Vietnam, racism, or poverty—comingled with their idealism and frustration at the sterile, bureaucratic nature of college life. In late April, they occupied several buildings at Columbia University. Photographs of scraggly students smoking in the president's office reinforced the sense among their elders that the old world was being thrown out. At the same time, young men and women energized the dark horse candidacies of Democrats Eugene McCarthy and Robert F. Kennedy. The latter's assassination in June killed their youthful innocence, leaving cynicism and despair in its place. When protestors clashed with police outside the Democratic National Convention that August, they shouted "the whole world is watching." Looking on, "many Americans [concluded] that their society was in the throes of a major, perhaps irrevocable breakdown," political historian Alan Brinkley noted.[46] Or as Ambassador Bunker put it on a trip back home in 1968, "It's just like Vietnam."[47]

The right rose alongside the left in 1968. Social and political divisions hardened. The backlash law and order politics of George Wallace and Richard Nixon spoke to the disaffected. The "silent center," Nixon called them that year. "The millions of people in the middle of the American political spectrum who do not demonstrate, who do not picket or protest loudly."[48] The politicians might promise victory in Vietnam or peace with honor, but they understood that the war competed with domestic needs.

Thus, Washington elites saw a society on the brink of social collapse. *Time* magazine described it as "a virus of internal dissent."[49] For all officials knew, 1969 might be worse than 1968. Even if social disintegration represented the worst-case scenario, they had to admit that events had reduced public support for the war.

Contemporary polling made clear that the American public was deeply divided on Vietnam. An October 7, 1968, Harris poll showed that 48 percent wanted de-escalation, whereas 43 percent opposed.[50] Other polls showed that a solid majority of Americans opposed a bombing halt and a coalition government in South Vietnam that included the NLF. "In other words," the Canadian ambassador in Washington rightly observed, "although a majority of

Americans oppose the way the war is conducted, a majority also oppose the only alternatives which currently seem to be available." And yet, Americans loved politicians' "vague promises of USA withdrawal." Few Americans called for an immediate exit, but the national mood favored troop reductions.[51]

Economic factors also seemed to demand retrenchment. America's global commitments and the war's financial burden nearly undermined the dollar's parity with gold in 1968. Its value held, but more than 200 tons of gold changed hands in mid-March as nations and speculators exchanged dollars for gold. "The biggest gold rush in history," exclaimed the press. Given the outflow of American money and resources to Vietnam, officials feared another run on the dollar could occur at any moment.[52]

The cost of the war and of Johnson's Great Society reforms had also created a sizeable federal budget deficit. The president pushed for a temporary tax surcharge to close the gap. In exchange, liberals demanded reduced military spending and troop reductions worldwide while conservatives insisted on cuts to domestic spending. LBJ managed to get the surtax through Congress with minimal damage to either cause, but a new era of US limits had arrived. Together, the federal budget and national balance-of-payments deficits forced politicians and policymakers to reconsider America's role in Vietnam and the world.

That debate played out in the US Congress. There, representatives and senators expressed concern over domestic unrest, the economy, and foreign relations. Vietnam weighed on these issues. Compounding matters, Johnson's brusque treatment of the Democratic doves on foreign affairs had soured relations between the two branches of government. It was time "to take off the kid gloves" when questioning officials about Vietnam, Senator J. William Fulbright's assistant argued.[53] Deference to the executive, especially on Vietnam, would be in short supply.

The same could be said of the news media. Journalists had listened to Pentagon and White House statements of progress in Vietnam for too long. The shock of the Tet Offensive exposed the gap between administration pronouncements and reality. Vietnam had tarnished the public's and the press's trust in the presidency.[54]

It was little wonder then that the president-elect was less than grateful for what Johnson left behind. One political cartoon from the period depicted a battered LBJ leaving Nixon in a boxing ring full of domestic and foreign enemies; another showed an ebullient Nixon about to be clobbered by Vietnam, congressional Democrats, and civil rights.[55] He understood that the home front, not a favorable military situation on the battlefield, had convinced his predecessor to stabilize the war and pursue negotiations. As tempting as expansion of the war might be, domestic considerations would restrain his hand just as they had his predecessor's.

Richard Nixon and Vietnam

Richard Nixon was no stranger to American politics or Vietnam. His 1960 loss to Kennedy and 1962 defeat in California's gubernatorial race seemed to mark his political demise, but he emerged in the late 1960s as the one Republican who could unite moderates and conservatives. Alongside his ambition, though, lay his assumptions about the Cold War and foreign policy. He had been thinking, writing, and speaking about Vietnam for decades. On the one hand, he stressed the importance of the American commitment and the ability of coercive diplomacy and US firepower to bring Hanoi to heel.[56] On the other hand, he acknowledged Americans' impatience with limited wars and emphasized South Vietnamese responsibility. Politics and geopolitics ran in opposite directions, meaning there would be no easy solution. Thus, despite a great deal of talking and thinking, he had no plan for how to end the war.

Born in 1913, Nixon was the second child of a deeply religious mother and a hardworking California grocer. His childhood was neither privileged nor impoverished. He absorbed his father's work ethic and passion for politics and his mother's Quaker values of tolerance and distaste for showing emotion. He acquired an abiding respect for law and order along with a self-righteous attitude toward those who would use their freedoms as a license for disorder or apathy. These values formed the crucible from which his staunch anticommunism emerged.[57]

Beginning in 1946, Nixon increasingly focused on the communist menace at home and abroad. As a newly elected member of Congress, he toured Europe in 1947, where he met individuals disfigured by communist terror and torture. His conversations with Eastern European leaders confirmed in his mind their allegiance to Moscow as well as the need to counter communism with determination and forceful diplomacy. On returning home, the young representative sought to move the public in favor of President Harry Truman's Cold War policies despite facing reticence and at times opposition from his constituents. He supported US foreign aid programs and the containment strategy in Europe, but he insisted that the president fight communism in Asia as well. At the same time, he exploited popular fears of communist subversion to propel his career. His investigations and proposed anticommunist legislation facilitated his rise from representative to senator to vice president. For Nixon, communism posed a global threat to international stability and democratic development. It also provided numerous political opportunities for the red-baiting Republican.[58]

In the 1950s, Nixon advocated a worldwide defense against communism, and the decade's Third World challenges set powerful precedents for future policy. The Korean War demonstrated to him that Americans could not stomach limited wars and that threats backed by US airpower could end communist aggression. The crisis in French Indochina further proved that without a legitimate nationalist government supported by its own army, America had few options.

As Dwight Eisenhower's vice president, Nixon believed the United States should back French efforts to defeat the Viet Minh and create a pro-Western state in Vietnam. He was often the administration's foremost advocate of a greater US commitment. In his private notes, tours of Indochina, and speeches, he emphasized Vietnam's significance. He believed its rice, natural resources, and trade made it critical to regional allies like Japan. Its loss would be a grave psychological blow to its noncommunist neighbors and would encourage communist aggression elsewhere. The dominoes would fall. After traveling throughout Asia (six days in Indochina alone) in late 1953, Nixon wrote, "I believe that this area is so important that if there is any question at all of adequate equipment, doubts should be resolved in providing what the people on the ground believe is needed."[59]

He also grappled with the thornier question of how to preserve a noncommunist Vietnam. France's will crumbled, prompting its exit in 1954–1955, but after Korea, Americans had no appetite for another war. The vice president had recommended sending US ground forces to Indochina in 1954 to back the French, but after the Geneva accords temporarily ended the fighting, he championed local responsibility. The developing nations themselves must resist communist insurgencies. *If people are for revolt* [against colonial or noncommunist rulers]—*we can't win*," he concluded. America should encourage legitimate, friendly regimes and promise them that "we *will make you strong*." He argued that the newly formed Republic of Vietnam should

Good Times, Bad Times   27

have all the US aid and advisers it needed so that the RVNAF could grow to defend its country. Beyond this assistance, the United States should defend South Vietnam by using air and naval firepower, not its soldiers.[60]

As the conflict in Vietnam escalated in the early 1960s, Nixon took a close interest in South Vietnam's survival. He believed that defeat in Vietnam would jeopardize American credibility. He feared that the potential geostrategic and diplomatic consequences of US failure outweighed the risks of continuing or escalating the war.[61]

To save South Vietnam, Nixon, from 1964 through 1967, supported air attacks against the communist border sanctuaries in Laos and Cambodia and a naval blockade and bombing of North Vietnam to destroy Hanoi's capacity and will to fight. Even as he came around to backing Johnson's Americanization of the war, he was clear: "We must put Vietnamese in front or we stay forever." A Vietnamized ground war backed by US airpower could enable the Republic of Vietnam's survival. Individual responsibility was a cardinal Nixon principle. As early as 1966, his personal notes recorded what he called the "RN Doctrine"—"We should help people fight but never fight war for them." Of course, to implement this strategy Nixon would have to win an election.[62]

Though narrowly defeated by Kennedy in 1960, Nixon never abandoned his quest for the White House. Foreign policy, particularly Vietnam, provided a springboard back into politics. He constantly attacked Democrats for not doing more to win in Indochina—both by building up local forces and bombing the North Vietnamese into submission. These attacks served the political interests of the "chronic campaigner." Yet his commitment went beyond politics and national interest.

Nixon visited Vietnam seven times during his vice presidential and wilderness years. When he purchased his San Clemente, California, villa in 1969, he adorned it with Vietnamese lacquer paintings. By saving coins, poor refugees had purchased and presented the artwork to him during an official visit. That one of these paintings hung over his bed at the San Clemente "Western White House" was symbolic of his commitment.[63]

For Nixon, then, the war and its outcome were political, strategic, and personal. His emphasis remained on bombing North Vietnam and building up South Vietnamese forces to deal with the NLF. This formula did not guarantee political success in 1968.

The public's reaction to Tet changed Nixon's political calculus on the war. Henceforth, the training and expansion of South Vietnamese forces, rather than increased bombing of North Vietnam, received top billing. He contemplated a diplomatic solution that sought Soviet mediation to pressure Hanoi into a settlement, but he staunchly opposed any bombing pause or US withdrawals, much less a coalition government.[64] On the campaign trail, Nixon made clear his administration would be as committed to the Republic as Johnson's. Privately, he had reservations. "I'm not trying to be coy or political," he admitted, but "it's vital to get out in an honorable way."[65] He realized that placing the onus on the South Vietnamese allowed him to attack Johnson's gradualism without trumpeting the need to escalate the American commitment. And it worked. In February 1968, he tested his line about developing ARVN forces, and audiences loved it. He suggested (and his audience accepted) that improved South Vietnamese strength was the magical formula for success that Johnson's Americanized war had missed. Nixon had been emphasizing indigenous training and defense for fifteen years, but in the tumultuous days after the Tet Offensive, even the old could appear new.[66]

By March, Nixon was unambiguous about the need to build up and train the South Vietnamese military. Speaking to students at Washington and Lee University, he lambasted Johnson for having "wasted our air and sea and land power in the conduct of that war." LBJ had ignored Korea's lesson on the danger of American land wars in Asia by "failing to train until very recently on an adequate basis the South Vietnamese so that they could take over the major share of protecting their country against guerillas." While campaigning in New Hampshire, he told a reporter, "Let me just sum it up in a word: For us to win simply a military victory over North Vietnam would not mean that we could get out. Because until the South Vietnamese are in a position that they can defend themselves," the United States could not guarantee that nation's survival.[67] Nixon was not proposing a unilateral US exit but rather a systematic effort to build up ARVN forces while marshaling America's nonmilitary resources to "end the war and win the peace in the Pacific."[68]

His longtime Republican colleague and informal adviser Wisconsin representative Melvin Laird urged the candidate to go further by turning South Vietnamese military improvement into a plan to reduce the number of US troops in Vietnam. Laird had been one of the most powerful Republicans in the House and a vocal hawk.[69] His balding, domed head and militant rhetoric made him an easy target for political cartoonists, but his views were always more nuanced than the bomb-headed caricatures implied.[70] In the early 1960s, he had demanded that Kennedy and Johnson defend South Vietnam with US

Good Times, Bad Times 29

air and naval power, not American soldiers. Nevertheless, in 1965, he chose Johnson's Americanization over a diplomatic solution. By 1968, Laird worried about the Republic's capacity for self-defense, the ability to break North Vietnamese determination, faltering will at home, and the prospect of increasingly violent antiwar protests. Unwilling to let South Vietnam go, he arrived at a political and military strategy based on de-Americanization: the United States would provide all the equipment and aid the South Vietnamese needed to take over the burden of fighting and thus allow US troop reductions. This process, which he would rename Vietnamization in 1969, would go beyond Johnson's efforts to strengthen the South Vietnamese military. It coupled American withdrawals with this improvement. It would take years to complete, but surveying the domestic unrest as well as the slackening public and congressional support for the war, Laird concluded that de-Americanization was the only tenable path. It was also smart politics. Running as the peace candidate was the surest ticket to victory at the ballot box, and he urged the Republican frontrunner accordingly.[71]

Otherwise, Laird believed Nixon was headed for political and strategic defeat. He worried that the candidate's pledge to "end the war" would prove impossible in his first term. He should instead promise to *"end American participation in the war"* by withdrawing US soldiers as ARVN forces took over the fighting. It was no coincidence then that speaking before a crowd in Laird's hometown on March 14, Nixon asserted that America should aid the South Vietnamese but "not fight [the war] for them." "If they do not assume the majority of the burden in their own defense, they cannot be saved." After Nixon won the April 2 Wisconsin primary, Laird publicly endorsed him while pushing him to pledge at the Republican Convention that he would de-Americanize the war.[72]

The Republicans indeed adopted a party platform that promised American troop reductions. They pledged to implement "a strategy permitting a progressive de-Americanization of the war, both military and civilian." South Vietnamese strength was necessary for these withdrawals, and so they promised policies that would "enable and induce the South Vietnamese to assume increasing responsibility." At a moment when Democrats were viciously fighting over Johnson's war, the Republican nominee offered the American people what they wanted: an end to American participation in the Vietnamese ground war.[73]

Despite Nixon's post-Tet emphasis on diplomacy and South Vietnamese self-defense, his penchant for coercion remained. He sought a negotiated end to

North Vietnamese aggression and believed that US airpower could compel and then enforce any agreement. "Real leadership in this field, which has been lacking, uses the threat of military power as a diplomatic weapon," he declared in February.[74] Nixon believed President Eisenhower had secured an armistice in Korea with a similar gamble. As he remembered it, the communists did not begin substantive talks until that administration intimated "that Ike would take stronger means" unless they got serious. "What got them off dead center was the word that we would walk softly and carry a big stick," he summarized. Nixon was willing to try the same in Vietnam.[75] As he told listeners in a radio interview, Hanoi must negotiate or face military reprisal. The president "should make very clear to the enemy that we are not going to tolerate this war going on and on." "If the enemy . . . does not go along with a program of live-and-let-live, then we have to have the option to move with more military power."[76]

Such escalation seemed untenable in late 1968. During the campaign, the candidate muted his hawkish rhetoric. He touted de-Americanization and peace with honor. His ambiguous promises worked wonders on the campaign trail but were of little value on the battlefield.

Preparing to enter the White House, Nixon faced the limits of American power. Hanoi remained unyielding. Saigon was growing stronger, but it was far from able to take over the war. The home front was collapsing, and Johnson had imposed limitations on the conduct of the war—namely the bombing halt and troop ceiling.

Making matters worse, Nixon, like his predecessors, had no concrete plan (secret or otherwise) for how to solve that conflict's dilemmas. Rather, he had a bundle of inclinations: local self-defense, US troop reductions, coercion, and great power diplomacy. De-Americanization, escalation, and linkage formed the basis of a three-pronged international strategy, but he had few ideas about the exact policies or their timing. As a candidate, Nixon had ruminated to journalist Theodore White, "It was important that we get out, but that we not be defeated. How do you liquidate that war with honor?"[77] It was the question that would consume his administration.

2

Only the Strong Survive

Nixon and Kissinger's Escalation of the War

January–March 1969

"We are caught in war, wanting peace," Richard Nixon declared in his January 20, 1969, inaugural address. "We are torn by division, wanting unity," he added. He cautioned enemies not to be tempted by America's discord. He vowed to pursue a compassionate, understanding, and healing peace, "not victory over any other people." He sought to show his determination while giving Americans "more than empty hope" that peace in Vietnam was attainable and forthcoming.[1] He believed he could succeed where others had failed.[2]

As the Nixon administration came together in January, it reflected few of these ideals. His advisers were as divided over Vietnam as the rest of the country. Secretary of State William Rogers and Secretary of Defense Melvin Laird fretted about the domestic situation and urged the president to de-escalate the war—the former through diplomatic compromise, the latter by progressive troop withdrawals. National Security Advisor Henry Kissinger insisted that credible threats and increased military pressure would compel Hanoi to settle. Making matters worse, the president lacked a coherent strategy and disliked confronting errant subordinates. In its first year, the administration went several directions at once.

The American home front was always at the forefront of their deliberations. "Time" was perhaps the most spoken word in the White House that year, its use connoting the image of an hourglass with the grains of popular support steadily running out. The administration acted on the assumption that ultimately the antiwar movement would succeed. It was a matter of when, not if.

Nixon faced an equally tough enemy in Hanoi. His inaugural promises of peace, by the nature of his goals and North Vietnamese persistence, would prove unattainable. Historian Lien-Hang Nguyen rightly contended, "Elected on the promise of extricating the United States from Vietnam, Nixon spent his first term waging war on all fronts in order to prolong the conflict in Vietnam in hopes of winning ultimate victory."[3] Winning meant preserving a noncommunist South Vietnam not for a decent interval, but in perpetuity. Victory was a predilection he shared with North Vietnamese leader Le Duan.[4] Each thought he could outlast the other.

Two paths lay before the Nixon administration: phased de-escalation or an expanded conflict. Caught "between the hammer of antiwar pressure and the anvil of Hanoi," the president trusted only the strong would survive.[5] Despite LBJ's tentative de-escalation, the domestic context, the counsel of more temperate advisers, and even his inaugural rhetoric, Nixon, goaded by Kissinger, went in a different direction. In early 1969, he chose to escalate the war for an elusive victory.

Building an Administration, Searching for a Strategy

The new president had a busy agenda ahead of his inauguration. Along with making appointments, he worked to centralize foreign policy decision-making in the White House and to develop a Vietnam strategy. Unencumbered by the Washington bureaucracy, he would act as his own secretary of state. His handpicked advisers would either help or stay out of his way.

For this reason, Nixon chose successful New York lawyer William P. Rogers to be his secretary of state. The two had worked together off and on since the 1940s. Their relationship developed into a close friendship in the 1950s when Rogers was Eisenhower's attorney general. Rogers had not participated in the campaign and expected no role in a Nixon administration. But as more forceful and experienced men declined the position, Nixon fell back on his friend, surmising that he would carry out his orders without advancing his own agenda. Rogers realized his status going in. "I was prepared to play a subordinate role," he recalled. "I recognized that he wanted to be his own foreign policy leader and did not want others to share that role. . . . I knew that Nixon would be the principal actor."[6] The secretary would become a consistent advocate of negotiations and a critic of escalation. Influential through 1969, he increasingly found himself outside the president's inner circle. Nixon would seldom allow him or the State Department to intervene in significant matters of foreign affairs. The Vietnam peace negotiations, the opening to China, and détente with the Soviet Union would all be the domain of the White House.[7]

Secretary of Defense Melvin Laird appreciated that a Cabinet position and a voice in the Oval Office did not correlate with real power. He was a brilliant political tactician who had campaigned with Nixon. He had not planned to leave Congress, and after the election he urged the president-elect to appoint Democratic senator Henry "Scoop" Jackson his secretary of defense. Only after Jackson refused did Nixon pressure Laird into taking the post. His acceptance came at a price: Laird demanded and won the ability to appoint Defense Department officials free from presidential oversight, giving him considerable authority.[8]

Dwight Eisenhower had warned Nixon that Laird was "the smartest of the lot, but he is too devious." Yet, both men acknowledged that the president needed this sort of cunning if he was to have any hope of running the Pentagon and getting congressional support for his policies. Even British observers spotted the representative's craftiness. "Laird has been seen as the real leader of the Republicans in the House," they noted. "There are many who believe [House minority leader] Gerald Ford to be subservient to Laird's influence." He was "a professional politician *par excellence*," "an extremely tough character," and was "said to be mistrusted by liberals (and some conservatives)." Laird did not fight losing battles. Rather, he deftly used his political influence and control of the Defense Department to pursue his aims even when they were at odds with the White House.[9]

Laird was of a type from a now bygone age. He was not an idealogue, though he could play one if the situation or crowd demanded it.[10] For him, politics was sport. He gave as good as he got and had fun while doing it. He accepted that compromise was an art—done correctly, you could give a little and take a lot. He was both playful and clever.

Prohibited by the White House from accompanying the president to meet the pope in 1970, Laird decided to ride in on the helicopter that would carry Nixon out of the Vatican. He arrived well-ahead of the presidential motorcade (some say by design, others by happenstance). Invited to speak with the pontiff while they waited, he did so. He relished retelling how, in shock at the offer, he had stuffed his lit cigar into his jacket pocket. Moments later he was vigorously swatting out smoke. The papal audience mistook

Laird's actions for applause and began clapping. Whether factual or embellished, it made for a good story. But his real triumph came when Nixon and Kissinger arrived. "They were shocked to see me sitting there next to the pope," Laird later laughed. Remembering his boss's frustration, a former Kissinger aide explained, "Henry was convinced that when Mel was told they didn't want the defense secretary with the pope, that Mel did this helicopter exercise purely and simply so he could get Henry." He seemed to wake up every morning with new ways to torment and outwit Kissinger.[11]

Before he became Laird's main rival for influence over Nixon's Vietnam strategy, Kissinger was an ambitious Harvard professor and an adviser to New York governor Nelson Rockefeller. He was an unforeseen pick for national security advisor. He had helped broker the Vietnam plank at the GOP convention and had aided the Nixon campaign by providing inside information about the Johnson administration, the Paris talks, and the bombing halt.[12] He was angling for a position, but most observers expected he would at best receive a minor post at the State Department. Future Kissinger staffer Roger Morris recalled his desperate position: "For his decade of hard work and opportunities, there had been an embarrassing failure in Washington, two campaigns with a losing candidate, a diminishing academic base, accompanied by the usual acid faculty politics and the personal trauma of divorce. The record had an accumulating sense of the also-ran, the marginal, the unrealized." Yet, he had caught the president-elect's attention.[13]

Nixon had followed Kissinger's writing and career since the 1950s and found much to like. The two men shared a similar outlook on international relations. Both favored realism's emphases on the balance of power, the efficacy of force, and great power diplomacy. They shared a penchant for coercive diplomacy, and they believed US credibility mattered. Lacking a base of power in Washington, he would also owe his post to Nixon's patronage, leaving him beholden. Although initially ambivalent, Nixon chose Kissinger perhaps because of another shared belief: their mutual hatred of bureaucracy.[14]

Both men had long held that Washington's bureaucratic inertia and narrow-mindedness hindered what Kissinger described as "consequential diplomacy." Nixon's transition team not only fretted over governmental torpor but also feared that most of the foreign policy establishment was incurably liberal and would oppose the president's policies. As one memo put it, "Mr. Nixon's candidacy not only was unsupported by nearly 90% of the personnel of the Department of State—it was opposed, at least passively." Even

LBJ warned the president-elect that State was full of leakers and "needed considerable cleaning out." Given such a hostile environment, Nixon and Kissinger decided to disarm the bureaucrats. He offered Kissinger the national security advisor position on November 27, and the pair began a "quiet coup" to usurp power from the State and Defense Departments.[15]

In Manhattan's Hotel Pierre, they planned this shakeup and their strategy to end the Vietnam War. Privy to some of these discussions, Alexander Haig remembered the setting well. "The Pierre is a grand hotel of the old luxurious style that was already well past its best days in 1968. The small room in which Kissinger received me was crowded with reproductions of French furniture, overheated, underlighted, and more than a little shabby." Within these rooms they "promptly conceived and began what would become a seizure of power unprecedented in modern American foreign policy," wrote Roger Morris.[16]

The coup was not simply a cynical power grab: Nixon wanted to reinvigorate the National Security Council (NSC). He and Kissinger felt that John Kennedy's ad hoc task forces and academic seminar-style meetings as well as Johnson's informal Tuesday lunches were poor ways of conducting foreign affairs. A revitalized NSC would sharpen its analysis, improve the flow of information to the White House, and allow for larger, more effective NSC meetings. These administrative reforms would also enhance presidential authority at the expense of the departmental bureaucracies. Kissinger's proposed changes would increase the national security advisor's power by allowing him to set the agenda, approve other agencies' papers, and order national security studies. In theory, this restructuring would enable the White House to mold foreign policy debates or overwhelm unfriendly bureaucrats with needless research directives.[17]

This revised structure challenged Laird's and Rogers's authority. The secretary of defense recognized the danger straight away and conveyed his disapproval to Kissinger. He warned that the changes would isolate the president and the rest of the Cabinet from other sources of information and would give Kissinger's position too much power. He predicted that if a strong national security advisor closed the NSC channel, the Cabinet would have to go directly to the president. Rogers underestimated the threat and assented to the proposed changes. "It doesn't make any difference," he reasoned. "I have a relationship with the President."[18] Events would prove him wrong as Nixon attempted to carry out foreign policy independent of both men.[19]

The two secretaries had significant clout, though. Rogers had the weight of the State Department behind him as well as the relative freedom to make public pronouncements that twisted Nixon's arm. Laird retained control over the Pentagon and used an imaginative combination of leaks and political connections to lobby public opinion to his causes. Both men also had the president's ear in 1969, influencing him at key moments.[20] Kissinger and Nixon's consolidation of power took time and effort, but their goal was clear. With the bureaucrats and Cabinet distracted by domestic problems and the rest of the world, Nixon told Kissinger, "You and I will end the war."[21]

During the interregnum, they spent much of their time at the Hotel Pierre devising how they would wage and with luck end the Vietnam War. At the 1968 Republican Convention, they had accepted de-Americanization, but with Nixon elected they chose to survey all their options. They assumed some withdrawal of American troops, but they had not resolved how many and under what circumstances this reduction would occur. Even the term withdrawal could mean almost anything. An October 31 working paper argued that the next president could abandon South Vietnam, invade the North, continue the present strategy, or turn the war into "a long term *police/self-help operation*," which would only require 200,000 US troops. This last option "would be the best way to 'de-Americanize' the war," its authors concluded. "It *could* be the way out—an end to the war as we have known it." Kissinger and Nixon preferred to settle the war quickly through diplomatic negotiations backed by the threat of dramatic force. Nixon instructed Kissinger to investigate escalation. He was particularly keen to expand the war into Cambodia, where significant Vietnamese communist sanctuaries and supply lines existed. "I think a very definite change of policy toward Cambodia should be one of the first orders of business when we get in," he wrote.[22]

Kissinger's preinaugural statements made clear he stood by America's commitment to South Vietnam. His January 1969 *Foreign Affairs* article, "The Viet Nam Negotiations," urged a new, "less impatient strategy" that emphasized pacification, sought reduced US casualties, encouraged South Vietnamese political reforms, and strengthened ARVN forces so that American soldiers could return home. But the core US negotiating position—the phased mutual withdrawal of North Vietnamese and US troops—remained unchanged. President Johnson had staked his entire war and his legacy on this proposition only to come up short in 1968. Kissinger thought he could do better. Diplomats on both sides would bargain toward this end because allied forces would remain unbeatable. "Since [Hanoi] cannot force our withdrawal, it must negotiate about it," he wrote. As for the bigger picture, America would have to persevere in South Vietnam because its global credibility was on the line. "However fashionable it is to ridicule the terms 'credibility' and 'prestige,' they are not empty phrases," he argued. "Other nations can gear their actions to ours only if they can count on our steadfastness." In the context of rising American isolationism, defeat would add "unreliability to the accusation of bad judgment." A testament to Kissinger's ability to mask his hawkish views while addressing a broad audience, readers interpreted his article as proof that the new national security advisor agreed with them. The reality was that he never relinquished his fondness for a just peace attained through savage diplomacy.[23]

Behind closed doors, Kissinger revealed that more than American credibility was on the line and that the administration might take dramatic steps to prevent South Vietnam's fall. On December 19, he informed Singapore's prime minister, Lee Kuan Yew, that Nixon "cannot afford to accept a clear U.S. defeat. Four years from now the U.S. public will have forgotten the agonies of the war, but will remember that we lost in Vietnam and that it was the Nixon Administration that had agreed to the surrender." The president could never afford this political and historical albatross. Renewed bombing and continuing the war was preferable to abandoning the Republic of Vietnam.[24]

The following day, Kissinger told British officials the same thing: the Nixon White House would not countenance defeat in Vietnam and would instead choose a dramatic escalation of the war. He made clear that he already considered himself "Nixon's principal foreign policy adviser." He predicted there would be at least a year of difficult talks since Hanoi assumed America would abandon South Vietnam. He affirmed that the United States could never take this course. "I don't mean that we should go to nuclear war," he declared, but "some quite tough measures might have to be taken to persuade them of [American resolve]." Punishing military force might be necessary to make the North Vietnamese settle on American terms.[25]

Still weighing alternatives, Kissinger commissioned the RAND Corporation think tank to explore various strategies. The primary author, Daniel Ellsberg, tried to impress his doubts upon him. "I don't believe there is a win option in Vietnam," he humbly submitted. Kissinger disagreed, insisting there must be a way of ending the war with America's honor and the Republic of Vietnam intact. Following this conversation, Ellsberg added what Kissinger wanted: "military escalation aimed at negotiated victory." The resulting paper identified seven options, ranging from Kissinger's "negotiated victory" to the "unilateral withdrawal of all U.S. forces within one to two years" with or without a settlement. Most of these had adherents within the government, the exception being precipitate withdrawal, which Kissinger changed to a "substantial reduction in US. presence while seeking a compromise settlement"—a prospect he still found unappealing. As he traced and retraced the alternatives, he kept coming back to coercive diplomacy.[26]

In mid-January, Kissinger offered the president elect several options. He could maintain the current effort while retaining the option to escalate the war or avoid escalation and begin reducing the American presence in South Vietnam. Advocates of the former, he noted, predicted that escalation might lead to outright North Vietnamese military defeat and perhaps even the collapse of the communist regime. American persistence and escalation promised "speedy war termination" as Hanoi began sincere negotiations to avoid destruction and defeat. Kissinger's options for escalation included resumed interdiction campaigns over North Vietnam, air and ground operations in Cambodia and Laos, the unrestricted bombing of North Vietnam, limited incursions into North Vietnam and Laos, and perhaps even a full-scale invasion of North Vietnam. "Actual escalation could lead to substantial domestic controversy unless it brought a quick settlement," he conceded. "The domestic controversy, in addition to its adverse internal consequences (which could be quite serious) might encourage Hanoi to hold out without concessions, expecting the US to be forced ultimately to withdraw."[27]

De-escalation would be less risky and might induce ARVN improvements even as it demonstrated America's desire to negotiate an honorable settlement. This strategy would "improve the domestic political situation in the US." Troop reductions would prolong American staying power.[28]

Kissinger also suggested a third option: *threatening* major escalation. To work, he argued, the threatened violence would have to go well beyond a resumption of Johnson's bombing campaigns. This "ultimatum" might deter a North Vietnamese offensive, could increase Soviet, Chinese, and North Vietnamese desire for a settlement, and could prepare the way for actual escalation should the gambit fail. It was a risky move: should Nixon be "caught bluffing," American credibility (and possibly allied morale) would suffer. Hence, the national security advisor reasoned that they would almost certainly have to act on their threats even if they proved inconsequential militarily. Kissinger's memo offered a blueprint for Nixon's war in 1969.[29]

Nixon liked what he read. He had revealed his own "Madman Theory" to his aide H. R. Haldeman during the campaign. He would threaten to bring untold destruction upon North Vietnam if they did not compromise. With Hanoi aware of Nixon's reputation as an inveterate anticommunist, the bluff would work. "Ho Chi Minh himself will be in Paris in two days begging for peace," he boasted.[30] With Kissinger at his side, the duo represented a "mad pair."

His other close adviser, Laird, counseled moderation. No one understood the domestic context better than Laird. Like Nixon and Kissinger, he remained committed to preserving the Republic of Vietnam. But he believed the United States must begin bringing troops home to stop the unraveling of American society and ease pressures to end America's commitment to South Vietnam. "That primary goal was dictated by the American public, not by anybody else," Laird recalled. Popular support had plummeted. Congress increasingly threatened not only the war's funding but the whole defense program, potentially crippling weapons development and other Cold War commitments. And the fear of violent and politically damaging protests hung in the background. Laird believed that "public opinion" was a ticking "time bomb." In early 1968, he had fused the twin pillars of Vietnamization: the buildup of South Vietnam and the systematic, unilateral withdrawal of US forces from Southeast Asia. He now had to make this concept a reality. During the transition, he turned to his predecessor.[31]

Laird visited Clark Clifford often in the weeks preceding Nixon's inauguration, primarily to determine which staff to retain. His initial emphasis on personnel rather than Vietnam frustrated Clifford, but his purpose was to find those Pentagon officials who could put meat on the bones of his de-Americanization idea. After nearly a month of meetings, Clifford grumbled, "He has said *nothing* [on Vietnam]; nor does he now show any inclination to talk." When Vietnam finally came up, Clifford later wrote, he "was particularly pleased to discover that [Laird] saw as his first major task finding a way out of the Vietnam morass." In private meetings, Clifford and Assistant Secretary of Defense Paul Warnke pressed him to withdraw American forces regardless of what occurred at the Paris negotiations. Laird kept his cards close to his chest, refusing to give any indication of future policies. He had found his man, though. He requested that Warnke stay on at the Department of Defense.[32]

Laird needed him to help draw up the program. Warnke believed America's entrance into the war had been a mistake and that it was impossible to win with the number of troops the United States could reasonably commit. His reasoning had influenced Robert McNamara's and then Clifford's change of heart on Vietnam. In 1968, he had developed a plan to withdraw 50,000 US troops. He remarked to Clifford in early January that his staying on was "an opportunity to warp their little minds while they're still young," but Laird needed no convincing. He was already Nixon's strongest advocate for de-Americanization. He would use Warnke to develop it. Warnke's preliminary planning became the basis for Vietnamization.[33]

Nixon too recognized the domestic constraints on escalation. He believed that armed conflict alone could not end the war and that escalation might jeopardize his goal of establishing better relations with the Soviet Union and the People's Republic of China. Perhaps most importantly, he doubted he could hold the country together long enough to win the war militarily. In a preinaugural meeting, he told the new American head of the Paris peace talks, Henry Cabot Lodge Jr., to inform the South Vietnamese that while they could count on Nixon's strong support, "they should understand that American public opinion was in a highly critical condition." The public simply would not sustain the American casualties needed for a military victory. Laird agreed, and in meetings with the president-elect he consistently focused on de-Americanization.[34]

No one could offer with any certainty a plan that would save South Vietnam and quiet the US home front. "As I studied the option papers before my inauguration," Nixon recalled, "I realized that I had no good choices. But presidents are not elected to make easy decisions."[35]

Nixon declined to settle on a strategy before his inauguration. For fifteen years, he had told presidents how to conduct the wars in Indochina. Once elected, he had trouble deciding whether to renew hostilities against the Democratic Republic and strike the elusive, decisive blow or de-Americanize the war with the hope of preserving both domestic tranquility and South Vietnam. He found himself caught between escalation and withdrawal with no happy medium and with Laird and Kissinger tugging him in opposite directions. All the while, the domestic context became an ever-present third adviser, always shaping Nixon's thinking on Vietnam. Kissinger and Laird gave him options; the polls, press, and Congress gave demands.

No Time Left for You

While Jerry Butler's "Only the Strong Survive" climbed the *Billboard* charts in early 1969, The Guess Who sang "No time left for you." If the former fit Nixon and Kissinger's determination, the latter could describe their reading of the domestic mood. From the outset, the White House closely monitored public opinion. Nixon recognized that although only a small number of radicals advocated an immediate, unilateral withdrawal, the erosion of domestic support limited his options. "What we needed most was time," he remembered after leaving office. "Because my predecessors had exhausted the patience of the American people with the Vietnam War, I was acutely aware that I was living on borrowed time."[36] In early 1969, the administration concluded that support for the war would continue to decline, steadily eroding American credibility in the Paris negotiations while making escalation less and less welcome.[37]

Noisy demonstrations at Nixon's inauguration underscored this conclusion. As counterinaugural protesters threw rocks and debris at his motorcade, the president must have sensed that time was not on his side. In the face of the jeers, signs, and waving NLF flags, he was characteristically defiant. He ordered the limousine's sunroof opened and stood "so the people could see" him. Outer resolve masked inner doubts about popular patience for an endless war.[38]

In actuality, domestic support for the war was holding steady. In early 1969, Gallup found that 52 percent of Americans believed US intervention had been a mistake, *down* six points from October 1968. Moreover, hindsight did not translate into a desire to cut and run. Less than one-fifth of those polled wanted an immediate end to the war regardless of the consequences. The majority wanted the president to find some way to end the war honorably: 32 percent backed escalation, 26 percent favored gradual de-Americanization, and 19 percent would have the war continue as it was. Fifty-seven percent wanted monthly US troop reductions, but a solid majority opposed any policy that would bring about South Vietnam's fall. These numbers made clear that any president who embraced a strategy of precipitate withdrawal and an end to the Republic would face a political reckoning.[39]

Polling conducted by the Republican Party (and shared with Nixon) found the same. Thirty-seven percent backed escalation to achieve military victory, 51 percent favored a two-year withdrawal timetable while both sides pursued a negotiated peace, and 30 percent favored any settlement that would end the war quickly. Tellingly, 66 percent okayed six months of increased military pressure that included bombing and blockading North Vietnam (but with no additional US forces) while seeking a compromise settlement that included supervised, free elections in South Vietnam. Kissinger's concept of "military escalation aimed at negotiated victory" had popular appeal even if the White House doubted that it did.[40]

The Nixon administration's fear of a faltering home front was thus a matter of perception rather than reality. Based on the deterioration of support that had followed the 1968 Tet Offensive, officials projected that the downward trend would continue. This perception gave rise to the institutional belief that policymakers were running out of time and some change in strategy was necessary.[41]

The 91st Congress underlined this conclusion. Nixon was the first president since Zachary Taylor in 1849 to enter his first term with the opposition controlling both houses of Congress. He understood he was "26 votes short in the House" and "9 votes short in the Senate." His "legislative prospects" were grim.[42]

Beyond partisanship, there was also an institutional and ideological rebellion against Cold War foreign policy. The fracturing Cold War consensus on defense, alliances, and the containment policy along with an increasing number of antiwar votes in Congress made support contingent. As reporter Mary McGrory observed, the "great tide of anti-military, anti-war sentiment that has swept through the country" was apparent in Congress and threatened defense appropriations. A growing number of congressional leaders also wanted to scrutinize executive defense commitments to other countries and reduce costly deployments. Foreign policy was not a strictly partisan issue. Fellow Republicans, especially those in the Senate, were not reliable supporters of Nixon's policies. Meanwhile, some of his strongest support came from staunchly anticommunist southern Democrats.[43] In 1969, Senate doves lacked cohesion and numbers, but the administration saw Congress as a real and growing challenge to its control of foreign policy. Hence, that body acted as a brake on Nixon's war even if it did not intend to do so.[44]

Congressional and popular attitudes sparked revived debates about what Nixon and others identified as a "new spirit of isolationism in the United States." Growing numbers of Americans considered their nation overstretched. Leading voices in Congress like Senator Fulbright lambasted the "heedless interventionism of Vietnam" and demanded America begin shedding its commitments abroad.[45] Consequently, US actions in Vietnam became a bellwether for its global credibility. Should the president give in to the "isolationists," South Vietnam would fall and America's credibility with its allies and enemies would evaporate. A fear of rising isolationism further encouraged the White House to seek a quick and honorable end to the Vietnam War.[46]

Nixon thus concluded that the clock was winding down, a trend he counterintuitively thought justified escalation in 1969. He assumed that an increasing number of Americans opposed escalation. Although polling indicated public reservations about Johnson's bombing halt, Nixon believed it "had been enormously popular" and had nearly cost him the election. Bombing North Vietnam might exacerbate social tensions, provoke antiwar dissent, and catalyze the public's metamorphosis into doves. He explained to Senator Barry Goldwater that spring that "he didn't think the American public would stand for an all-out military assault on North Vietnam. He said he was in a no-win situation." But he held that only escalation could end the conflict in 1969. That being the case, Kissinger argued that Nixon should act while the public was quiescent.[47]

Nixon and Kissinger assumed the White House could never pacify the doves and that public and congressional support would continue to erode. Kissinger warned the president that although things were calm at present, "there is little question that domestic controversy will begin to mount, certainly within a few months." Meaningful talks would take time, "and time is not on our side." He recognized that troop reductions on the order of 75,000 men "would buy us a considerable amount of time at home," but any withdrawal announcement needed to come *after* Nixon had impressed the communists with his resolve. Otherwise, Hanoi would interpret the reduction as proof of America's fading will. Ending the president's customary political honeymoon early to take decisive military action made more sense to Kissinger. He explained to Nixon's chief of staff, H. R. Haldeman: "What will determine the President's position in public opinion will be whether the war is wound up 15 months from now. If it isn't, having received a favorable editorial now will do him no good; if it is, having been clobbered by the NY Times this week won't harm him." Nixon agreed, telling the Cabinet in January that "he was very much aware of the domestic issues but that he would rather take the heat now and achieve a sound settlement subsequently." The United States had to achieve peace with honor before the home front collapsed, even if that meant taking military measures that would accelerate this deterioration.[48]

Nixon's de-Americanization scheme fit into this larger strategy. For over a decade, he had been adamant about the need to build up indigenous forces while avoiding US troop commitments. He had campaigned and in part won the election on his de-Americanization strategy, but as Vietnam confronted him in early 1969, withdrawing soldiers was a matter of priorities. The president understood what NSC staffer John Holdridge noted in a January briefing paper: America's military presence in South Vietnam was "the principal bargaining element on the Allied side."[49] An early reduction, while good politics, diminished US leverage whereas ramping up the war might improve the allied position militarily and diplomatically while offering a chance to compel North Vietnamese capitulation.

Administration doves disagreed. They believed escalation would do little to improve the situation in Vietnam and would only exacerbate America's internal tensions. De-escalation was the safe and necessary course. There were three paths toward de-escalation: negotiations, reducing the tempo of US ground operations in South Vietnam, and de-Americanization. Rogers hoped that early concessions, including recognition of the NLF in Paris, would start productive talks with Hanoi. Nixon understood the political value of continuing public talks, but apart from North Vietnam's surrender, he believed they were unlikely to secure the Republic of Vietnam. Stale negotiations could sustain public support for only so long. Lodge begged Nixon on February 12 to adopt the second course by directing the generals to find ways of reducing American casualties in Vietnam to prolong public support and thereby improve the US negotiating position. Nixon ignored such advice.[50]

Progressively removing American soldiers was a third way of de-escalating the conflict. Politicians, journalists, and policymakers had discussed de-Americanization for nearly a year, but no one had turned this talk into policy. The political necessity was clear; the execution uncertain. As Lodge's predecessor, W. Averell Harriman, reminded Washington officials, "It was essential to reduce American casualties and get some of our troops coming home in order to retain the support of the American people."[51] Looking for a faster, more honorable way out of Vietnam than any of these alternatives allowed, Nixon inadvertently chose a longer war.

Starting Nixon's Vietnam War

The president's second National Security Council meeting (January 25, 1969) underscored that unilateral withdrawal existed as a coda to tougher measures and hard bargaining. CIA director Richard Helms's briefing reflected the budding optimism that followed the Tet Offensive. He "concluded that under the present ground rules, assuming the withdrawal of our troops, South Vietnam would be able to go it alone in approximately one year." Representing the Joint Chiefs, the next briefer offered a similarly optimistic view. These reports confirmed the president's belief he could end the war that year.[52] Thereafter, he confidently insisted that it would take just "six months of strong military action" to soften Hanoi's negotiating position. He requested contingency plans for resuming the bombing of North Vietnam. "We do have the internal problem in the U.S.," he conceded, "and it will be very difficult without some change."[53]

After listening to Nixon's concerns, Rogers opined, "I think we can expect more from the American people, especially if we could at some point reduce our commitment by perhaps 50,000." Although Nixon wanted six months of hard fighting, he concurred that such a gesture might buy some time and public support. Undersecretary of State Elliot Richardson wondered why the president could not pursue negotiations and a robust military offensive while removing a small number of US troops in three or four months. After a short discussion, the president agreed. He proposed they continue to pacify the South Vietnamese countryside, strengthen the South Vietnamese regime, and negotiate with the North. Then, in a few months, "bring home a few troops unilaterally as a separate and distinct action from the Paris negotiations, and as a ploy for more time domestically, while we continue to press at the negotiating table for a military settlement." Until then, American forces would "continue to punish the enemy."[54]

While working closely with the president on these punitive measures, Kissinger sought to distract the bureaucrats and consolidate his institutional power. The January 25 NSC meeting had confirmed his instincts about bureaucratic paralysis. "'Why did Nixon hire these guys?' he asked, throwing up his hands in mock despair. 'Defense is opposed to the use of force; State is obsessed by compromise. They'll sabotage everything the President tells me he wants to do in foreign policy.'"[55] He believed that he and Nixon alone could develop an aggressive, statesman-like foreign policy.

His first opportunity to distract policymakers came when one author of the preinaugural RAND paper on Vietnam suggested that he "put a series of questions to the different agencies, make them answer separately, and compare the discrepancies." The exercise would provide detailed information on how the various government agencies viewed the war, and it would swamp the bureaucrats with busywork and internecine debates. "I'm tying up the bureaucracy for a year and buying time for the new president," he explained to an aide.[56] Kissinger thus issued National Security Study Memorandum (NSSM) 1 on January 21 as a diversionary tactic. Addressed to the CIA director and the secretaries of state and defense, it had pages of detailed questions. In the meantime, he would seek to negotiate a settlement favorable to the United States and South Vietnam.[57]

To this end, Kissinger began taking over Secretary Rogers's role as chief diplomat. In late January, he met privately with South Vietnamese ambassador Bui Diem to discuss the Paris talks and American intentions. He contrasted Nixon's approach to foreign policy deliberations with his predecessor's. Kissinger believed Lyndon Johnson had lost control of his team in 1968: Clifford denounced the Republic, Rusk praised it, and all the while Harriman sold Saigon out in Paris. The South Vietnamese reasonably did not know who to believe. The independence of LBJ's advisers, he concluded, had produced the "atmosphere of suspicions" that defined allied relations in late 1968. He affirmed that he alone would be speaking for the president and that he would meet frequently with Bui Diem to establish an "atmosphere of confidence." Should the ambassador hear something different from the press, Pentagon, or State Department, he could safely ignore it.[58]

News of their meeting alarmed State officials. In a private note, Assistant Secretary of State William Bundy warned the secretary that unless he stopped these contacts, Kissinger would jeopardize his "personal and institutional position."[59] Foreign ambassadors could "whipsaw" the United States by surveying both the State Department and the White House to determine where best to apply pressure. More likely, the White House could use Kissinger's independence to provide a different "slant" on diplomatic matters, subverting State's purview and perhaps cutting them out of important bilateral talks. Despite Bundy's alarm, Rogers did nothing. Kissinger aggrandized his power and, with Nixon, planned the very escalation of the war many State Department officials found misguided.[60]

The administration continued LBJ's late 1968 escalation of the ground war in South Vietnam. Operations like Speedy Express in the Mekong Delta and Dewey Canyon in the northern part of South Vietnam sought to destroy the enemy despite significant American and, in the case of Speedy Express, civilian casualties. Meanwhile, the Accelerated Pacification Campaign (November 1968 through January 1969) sought to exploit enemy setbacks to expand government control in the countryside. As allied soldiers and firepower swept through South Vietnam, the communists had to retreat or break their forces down into smaller units to survive. The White House, along with the US military and Saigon, suddenly had good reason to believe that such actions would further cripple the enemy's infrastructure and overall strength in South Vietnam. The Republic's control of the countryside, they believed, would increase allied leverage in the negotiations and help it survive America's exit.[61]

But, with the talks stalled in Paris, escalation elsewhere appeared necessary. On January 30, Kissinger met with Laird and the chairman of the Joint Chiefs of Staff (JCS), General Earle Wheeler, to discuss contingency plans for increasing the military pressure on the Democratic Republic. Recognizing the political danger of resuming the air war over the North, he "asked what could be done in South Vietnam which could convey to the North that there is a new firm hand at the helm." Wheeler recommended pursuing enemy units into Cambodia. He suggested that since attacking North Vietnam was politically off limits, the administration should strike enemy forces and their sanctuaries and logistical centers in Cambodia. Laird disagreed, cautioning that such action "would represent a difficult political problem." Nixon and Kissinger shunned his advice.[62]

As Wheeler had recommended, they prepared to bomb Cambodia. They hoped a large enemy offensive or communist rocket attacks on Saigon would occur to justify the bombing publicly. Alternatively, they considered keeping the escalation secret and, if caught, would blame the raids over neutral Cambodia on navigational error. On February 19, Nixon ordered the military to finalize its plans for the campaign. Three days later, North Vietnam launched a mini-Tet offensive, which the president saw as a "deliberate test" of his mettle as a leader.[63] With the military and Kissinger urging him to attack, he all but authorized an immediate air campaign.[64]

Not for the last time, Laird warned the president of the possible domestic consequences of escalation. He expressed his willingness to execute his orders but cautioned that the public would oppose it and that Nixon's critics "would then create, or attempt to create, difficulty for you and for all of us through contacts in the Congress and in the press." The Washington establishment was too aware of the Cambodian option to believe it an accident. As a former hawk, Laird appreciated the tactical benefits of hitting communist sanctuaries and supply lines in Cambodia, but he counseled Nixon to wait for North Vietnamese provocations that justified retaliation. With a trip to Europe approaching, Nixon postponed the operation.[65]

On returning to Washington, the president and Kissinger reviewed contingency plans. The Joint Chiefs provided options for actual or feigned attacks against North Vietnam and the supply lines in Laos and Cambodia. As Kissinger's military aide, Alexander Haig, noted on March 2, they exceeded what they sought. The Joint Chiefs went so far as to include the possible use of nuclear weapons and an invasion of North Vietnam. To break North Vietnamese will, they also suggested "deception operations" to "create fear in the Hanoi leadership that the United States is preparing to undertake new highly damaging military actions." Upon reviewing these alternatives, Kissinger agreed with Laird that they were too risky domestically and internationally at that time. The military had the right idea, though. Subtle moves implying a credible threat of escalation might cow Hanoi without inciting a media or public backlash. Plans to expand the war in Cambodia gained traction despite pleas from administration doves for moderation.[66]

Rogers marshaled his department's influence to stay the president's hand. He warned that escalation would "shorten the period of full public support for the whole war effort" and "throw large and significant segments of public and congressional opinion into a critical and impatient posture." Patience would stabilize domestic support and perhaps even help the administration build a case for future action. The secretary also hoped for a breakthrough in Paris. Without presidential authorization, he told Soviet ambassador Anatoly Dobrynin on March 8 that the United States was willing to discuss political and military issues simultaneously and that the Saigon regime and the NLF could engage in private talks. Nixon had agreed to neither point. Kissinger fumed that Rogers had ruined the opportunity for the administration to "take [a] hard line" with the communists and that Nixon should boot Rogers up to the Supreme Court. The president disregarded Rogers's concerns and removed the secretary of state from the planning.[67]

Unlike Rogers, Nixon and Kissinger believed the war had turned in America's favor and they should press the advantage. The national security advisor declared on March 8 that the US military effort was one of the "few bargaining weapons" they had, and any act of de-escalation would benefit the communists. "Thus, de-escalation would amount to a self-imposed defusing of our most important asset and the simultaneous enhancement of [their] most important asset—terrorism. We would, in effect, be tying the hands of our forces in Vietnam." Reduced fighting would also increase domestic pressure to bring the apparently superfluous troops home. He assured the presi-

Only the Strong Survive   49

dent that he was working on a "game plan." "There is not going to be any de-escalation," Nixon concurred. "We are just going to keep giving word to Wheeler to knock hell out of them." The general gladly obliged, submitting plans in mid-March to mine Haiphong harbor as part of a larger, sustained air campaign against North Vietnam. Nixon thought it too soon to strike the North, but he concluded that it was time to attack enemy sanctuaries and logistics in Cambodia.[68]

The president's expansion of the war into Cambodia was no rash decision.[69] He and Kissinger had weighed the risks, especially at home, alongside their larger Cold War aims. What became known as Operation Menu would punish the North Vietnamese for the ongoing mini-Tet offensive, prod them to negotiate, signal the Soviets that the White House was serious about ending the war, and improve the situation in South Vietnam (in that order).

Covertly hitting communist forces and depots in Cambodia would demonstrate what awaited the North Vietnamese if they dithered in Paris. As military historian Gregory Daddis has noted, Cambodia was Nixon and Kissinger's "first foray into coercive diplomacy." If Hanoi continued its southern offensive and intransigence in Paris, Nixon told Kissinger, "We'll crack the North and crack it good."[70]

An element of feigned madness figured into these calculations. "When you have a weak poker hand, you shouldn't be too cautious," Kissinger argued. "We shouldn't set [sic] here and do nothing." "The more reasonable we sound, the worst off we are," he added. "We should have the option open that we might go back to the Dulles position [of nuclear brinkmanship]." Wild threats of North Vietnam's destruction made credible by a dramatic show of force in Cambodia would surely compel Hanoi's capitulation and convince the Soviets of Nixon's determination.[71]

Operation Menu also reflected Nixon's considerations of the broader Cold War context. Presidential and national credibility would affect how the war ended. And how it ended, in turn, would affect personal and national credibility. Beyond a general desire to see the Republic of Vietnam survive, Nixon believed that failure in Vietnam would catalyze America's latent isolationism and confirm allied and communist doubts about its resolve. With Kissinger and Laird, the president maintained that without strength—of which America's stand in Vietnam was the prime manifestation—the communist great powers would not seek improved relations with the United States. Ending the Vietnam War honorably was thus critical to achieving

Nixon's larger foreign policy goals in an era of domestic constraints. The administration would pursue strength alongside strategic retrenchment, partnership with greater allied responsibility, and negotiations to ease Cold War tensions among the great powers.[72]

Having opened a back channel with the Soviets in February, Nixon and Kissinger hoped to induce their cooperation in ending the war.[73] The president thought that without Sino-Soviet aid and diplomatic support the North Vietnamese would cease their conquest of South Vietnam.[74] Moscow did want a more stable world and better relations with the United States, especially after fighting with China had erupted along the Ussuri River in March 1969. The widening Sino-Soviet split in turn made it more important for both parties to seek rapprochement with America. Nixon and Kissinger hoped that internal communist tensions might make it possible for them to link Vietnam to global issues. They saw rapprochement with China and détente with the Soviet Union as a means of containing communism worldwide through diplomacy rather than military confrontation. America could make concessions on issues like nuclear superiority, anti-ballistic missile defense, or diplomatic relations with China if the communists would reciprocate by helping end the war.[75]

Détente was the carrot, and playing the mad president was the stick.[76] Again cutting Rogers out of the loop, Kissinger warned Dobrynin in late February that Nixon would "have to respond very strongly" to a North Vietnamese offensive in the South. Now that Hanoi had justified American escalation, perhaps Operation Menu would convince Moscow and Hanoi that the president would do whatever it took to preserve South Vietnam and end the war. Although unsure how the Soviets could coerce the North Vietnamese, Kissinger wrote, "We must worry the Soviets about the possibility that we are losing our patience and may get out of control." Establishing a pattern that would endure throughout 1969, he and Nixon conveyed threats of radical escalation to the Kremlin, vainly hoping they would choose détente over their allies in Vietnam.[77]

Finally, they believed that bombing Cambodia would improve the military situation in South Vietnam and consolidate the gains of 1968. Since the early 1960s, Cambodia had served as an enemy staging and supply area as well as a sanctuary for retreating communist forces. The Ho Chi Minh Trail ran through it, as did supply lines running from the port of Sihanoukville. Cambodia, along with Laos, represented a key conduit of men and matériel.[78]

Hence, the US military had urged Washington to expand the war into these countries.[79] Nixon had already increased the bombing in Laos to some 13,000 sorties every month, but the military demanded more.[80] Playing upon the public's (and some policymakers') desire to de-Americanize the war, the generals sold the expanded bombing as a way to improve the military situation and enable US troop withdrawals. As General Andrew Goodpaster told MACV officials on March 1, hitting the Cambodian enclaves would reduce enemy capabilities, thus giving the White House "all kinds of elbow room" to take American troops out or adopt other politically popular tactics. Escalation could be a prerequisite to Vietnamization. With the enemy's 1969 military offensive and renewed communist shelling of South Vietnamese cities underway, Nixon approved the bombing.[81]

On March 15, Nixon authorized the Breakfast Plan—named for "the breakfast group" of officials who met in February to consider the situation in Cambodia. The State Department and Rogers were "to be notified only after the point of no return." The clandestine bombing of Cambodia would continue off and on through May 1970.[82]

Although Kissinger had strongly supported this action for nearly a decade, he approached the final decision with temerity, fearing this violence would tarnish his reputation if it became public. Secrecy and deception were paramount to protect himself and the White House from the anticipated antiwar backlash. He was instrumental in the fabrication of phony logbooks and fake reports designed to sustain the lie that the aircraft were hitting targets along the Vietnamese-Cambodian border or had simply gone off course. He also had top officials wiretapped so that he could plug any leaks.[83] One observer recalled that until the bombing began, "He was still wringing his hands and seeking moral support to be sure that we could do it and do it without having it in the newspapers."[84]

The thrill of the moment temporarily eclipsed these concerns. Upon reading the first military reports, Kissinger contemptuously wrote Rogers, "Either Abrams knew what he was talking about or this was the storage area for firecrackers for the Chinese New Year!" He had room to boast; he had supplanted the secretary of state, as Nixon chose his militant course over Rogers's moderation. Days later, when Hanoi agreed to private bilateral talks, he felt further vindicated. His strategy of "military escalation aimed at negotiated victory" appeared to be working. Little wonder then that Nixon tasked Kissinger and not Rogers with leading the secret talks in Paris. Rogers had proven too weak to survive the national security advisor's tenacious pursuit of power. Kissinger was closer than ever to the president.[85]

On Kissinger's advice, Nixon had expanded and escalated the Vietnam War despite the domestic risks. He and Kissinger hoped to force an end to the conflict before public support gave out, and they had taken the plunge together. With bombs raining down on Cambodia, the two men began planning their next move: threatening the destruction of North Vietnam with a concerted and sustained air and naval campaign if Hanoi refused to stop its aggression against South Vietnam. As the "mad pair" schemed and escalated the war, Melvin Laird quietly and methodically prepared to set America on a different course out of Vietnam.

3

My Way

Laird and Vietnamization

March–June 1969

Secretary of Defense Melvin Laird sought an exit from Vietnam not beholden to the Paris talks or escalation. He was no dove. Like Nixon and Kissinger, he had spent the better part of the decade pushing a tough line on Indochina. Though he had come to accept that the American war could not continue at its present level without destroying the United States, he was not ready to abandon South Vietnam. He pursued a policy of Vietnamization to achieve the same ends as Nixon and Kissinger, but his strategy would prolong the war to enable South Vietnamese self-defense in the absence of a peace settlement.

As Laird defined it, Vietnamization was "the effective assumption by the RVNAF of a larger share of combat operations from American forces" so that the latter "can be in fact withdrawn in substantial numbers."[1] Though he rarely divulged it, he envisioned a total US withdrawal from Vietnam—there would be no residual force as there had been in postwar Europe and South Korea. Theoretically, as the RVNAF grew in quality and quantity, allied manpower and effectiveness would stay the same, keeping the heat on communist forces. Meanwhile, the reductions would prolong public backing for the war and prevent a domestic crisis. With the military pessimistic and Kissinger and Nixon pursuing an entirely different strategy, he would do it, as Frank Sinatra crooned that spring, "My way."

Selling Vietnamization in Saigon and Washington

Laird refused to allow other matters to distract him from reducing US troops in Vietnam. His experience on the House Defense Appropriations Subcommittee and his consultations with Robert McNamara, Clark Clifford, Paul Warnke, and other current and former defense officials in the preinaugural period enabled him to assemble a crack team of policymakers. He also had the benefit of focusing almost exclusively on Vietnam. He tailored his daily schedule accordingly. Laird and his "8:15 group" began the morning by looking at public affairs and legislative issues in order, as he put it, to keep Defense "on message." He kept continuous contact with Congress, the media, and the military to maintain the trust and support necessary for his policies. At 9:00 a.m., he met with his handpicked Vietnam Task Force, which included his military adviser, Robert Pursley, and various other Defense and CIA officials. They focused almost exclusively on Vietnamization and ensured that the program received top priority.[2]

Johnson and Clifford had left no plan for de-Americanizing the war, yet Laird adapted a Johnson-era scenario for mutual withdrawal to suit his purpose. He took the T-Day plan for redeploying troops after a negotiated settlement and made it the basis of de-Americanization planning. "By removing the 'T' from the plan (standing for 'Termination') we had a start for our plan," Laird recalled. In other words, he took a proposal predicated on the negotiated, mutual withdrawal of US and North Vietnamese forces and *adapted it for a total, unilateral American withdrawal.* In his view, the Republic of Vietnam would have to contend with both the North Vietnamese Army (NVA) and indigenous NLF forces. With the T-Day plan as his model, he and his Vietnam Task Force immediately started the Defense Department working on a de-Americanization strategy.[3]

By March, they had developed the contours of Vietnamization, but to sell his plan to the president and make it work, Laird first needed to confer with the US military command in Vietnam and South Vietnamese leaders on what reductions were possible. Lasting from March 5 to 12, his first trip to Vietnam as secretary of defense was an important milestone in his push for Vietnamization. He assessed the situation in the South and secured President Thieu's and General Abrams's approval for his ideas.

For Thieu, it was an easy sell. The situation in South Vietnam had never looked better; the government was consolidating its control of the countryside and ARVN forces were growing in strength and numbers.[4] He believed the Republic could handle the insurgency alone and only needed US aid in deterring and expelling the North Vietnamese regulars. He was also preparing reforms to win over villagers. Given this progress, he wanted to postpone any concessions or settlement. Yet an appreciation of American impatience permeated Saigon. As Thieu admitted, he was "no 'super hawk'"—he would have to prepare the nation to survive some political and diplomatic accommodation of the NLF. Comparing South Vietnamese and American attitudes, journalist Kevin Buckley noted, "The two clocks of war weariness are running at drastically different speeds." Time was expiring in America, while South Vietnamese leaders hoped for a longer war as the situation there steadily improved.[5]

They feared an American abandonment. Thieu's staff compiled a daily file of US and international press clippings, which he diligently read. He often confided to officials that "his greatest concern is American opinion about Viet-Nam." He worried Nixon's honeymoon with the public and Congress would be short-lived. Though communists had continued to bombard Saigon with rockets and mortars after the October bombing halt, Thieu opposed resuming the bombing of North Vietnam, fearing such action would incite American dissent and jeopardize public support for the war.[6] The Paris negotiations might placate US opinion and buy his regime time, but nothing would be quite as effective as troop reductions. GVN diplomats and officials agreed: US public and congressional opinion demanded a Vietnamized war.[7]

Even as American policymakers refused to let the South Vietnamese in on the formulation of Nixon's Vietnam strategy, Thieu continued to speculate publicly that Washington could begin bringing its troops home.[8] In late January, South Vietnamese officials began developing a public information operation to explain and justify the withdrawal as a "replacement" of US forces by Vietnamese. This replacement would be discussed between the two governments, should increase American political and economic support for South Vietnam, and must be separate from the Paris talks. They calculated that since "we are becoming stronger, America will support us more." In February, Thieu implemented this "New Opportunities" campaign to rally his people and explain why American domestic pressures necessitated withdrawals but not abandonment. Prime Minister Tran Van Huong followed the president's lead, declaring that 1969 "will be a year in which we must be more self-supporting and self-sufficient than ever before. Whether the war drags on or peace is restored we shall assume more responsibilities." He suggested that America could withdraw around 10,000 soldiers per month. Privately, Thieu and his advisers created de-Americanization plans in anticipation of (and perhaps to influence) Washington's decision-making. Thieu's optimism proved infectious. Many South Vietnamese felt that they were "ready, at long last" to shoulder the burden, expedite the American exit, and "march forward proudly as rulers of our own destiny."[9]

Given Thieu's long-standing support for troop reductions, obtaining his consent was a formality rather than a diplomatic breakthrough. In a private conversation on March 8, Laird told him the US public would give the administration roughly six to twelve months to figure out how to end the war. Thieu acknowledged that "South Viet-Nam has given American administrations and the American people many problems." He added that he and the South Vietnamese were prepared for a reduction of 50,000 to 70,000 troops by the end of the year.[10]

American military leaders in Vietnam were less sanguine. One report noted that pacification was making steady progress but that the post-Tet gains were vulnerable to another enemy offensive. MACV appreciated "the realities of the American political situation," concluding that "time then, is running out." Commanders wanted to use their men and resources, especially airpower, to the utmost to cripple the enemy before time ran out. In February, Laird tipped his hand when he denied MACV new funding for facilities, instead instructing them to focus on essential RVNAF modernization requirements. Reticent as MACV was about Vietnamization, it guessed Laird's intentions before he arrived in Saigon.[11]

While preparing to brief him, Abrams's intelligence officer, Major General Phillip Davidson, remarked that secretaries of defense always had a hidden agenda when they visited Vietnam. McNamara had come to question Westmoreland's use of troops. Clifford wanted to know how the US military was improving the South Vietnamese army. Speculating on Laird's motive, Davidson remarked, "My guess is that the hidden theme this time, and there's no word of it on the agenda, is, 'When can you start withdrawing troops? . . . How can you cut down the *cost* of the war in either manpower, matériel, or cut down the psychological and political costs?'" Lamenting outside pressure to de-escalate, Davidson and others asserted that MACV's strategy to win the war should be, "Let's kick the hell out of [the enemy]." "Now that means that you're going to get men killed and hurt. The *furtherest* [*sic*] thought from our mind is, 'How can you reduce casualties?'" Made the day before Laird's March 6 briefing, these comments indicated the military's deep concern about de-escalation.[12]

Proving Davidson correct, Laird stressed the fragility of the situation at home and the need to begin de-escalation before American patience ran out. "Just as it was [the military leadership's] duty to provide for me the picture of what was happening in Southeast Asia, it was my duty to provide for them the realities of the situation in the United States," he recounted to Nixon after the trip.[13] He warned Abrams and others that the public was giving the president a brief grace period. Domestic factors thus limited how long they had to strengthen South Vietnam, and "we've got to make the best *possible* use of the time that we *do* have." He and the MACV commanders must develop a plan that showed the people they were committed to protecting US troops from undue risk while preserving self-determination in South Vietnam. According to Laird (and as predicted by Davidson), the plan would also have to "reduce the United States contribution, not only in the form of men, but in casualties and matériel and in dollars." Assuming that Nixon had only three or four months to lay out an acceptable policy, he suggested that Abrams begin planning for a withdrawal of 44,000 troops within the next three to nine months.[14]

Certain that Abrams's cooperation was vital to the program's success, Laird worked hard to obtain it. He realized he was asking the impossible. Abrams "had been engaged in a limited war—using limited means, with a limited objective—against an enemy whose objectives were not limited," Laird remembered. "Now he would have to continue fighting this war and, at the same time, guide the withdrawal of our men and train the South Vietnamese army."[15] Although ARVN forces were improving, the general believed that without US troops and military aid, South Vietnam would not survive a coordinated attack from the NLF and the PAVN. Should negotiations for a mutual withdrawal fail, he insisted the United States predicate any unilateral withdrawal on pacification of the countryside, improvement of the South Vietnamese military, and a diminished North Vietnamese threat. Provided sufficient time and resources, he believed that Vietnamization could work and he began drawing up withdrawal plans. Demonstrating his support, Abrams on March 22 suggested a 20,000–25,000-man reduction during the summer and another by year's end. Laird had gained a powerful ally. He returned home to persuade Nixon to accept Vietnamization.[16]

Back in Washington, Laird finished the plan with the aid of Warnke and Pursley and forwarded it to the president on March 13.[17] He bemoaned the slow progress of ARVN modernization and recommended that the United States step up efforts to arm the South Vietnamese. He made clear that his sole purpose for modernizing ARVN was to allow Washington to begin "replacing American forces in South Vietnam with better trained, better led, and better armed South Vietnamese military and para-military personnel." He acknowledged the Johnson-era condition that the United States could not reduce its troops without a similar withdrawal of North Vietnamese troops, but he frankly informed the president that America's national interests and global commitments did not permit it to "indulge in this assumption." He assumed rather that no peace deal would be forthcoming, Hanoi would not give up its designs on the South, US policymakers could not escalate the war, and true self-determination required the "capability for sustained self-defense and self-reliance."[18]

The secretary of defense argued that the removal of 50,000–70,000 American troops by the year's end would not endanger allied forces in Vietnam.[19] Instead, it would maintain American support for the war and encourage Vietnamese responsibility and political reforms. Nixon continued to weigh his options.[20]

An interagency dispute soon erupted over the state of the RVNAF and whether the United States could reduce troops without diminishing the overall combat capability of allied forces. American officials agreed that even a modernized and expanded South Vietnamese army could not handle both NLF and PAVN forces without extensive military assistance. JCS Chairman Wheeler doubted that the South Vietnamese could defeat the indigenous guerrillas, much less a renewed North Vietnamese offensive, until after the second phase of the ARVN improvement program finished in 1972. Although estimations of allied capabilities would change during 1969, domestic needs rather than military assessments motivated US reductions.[21]

Congress reminded Nixon that spring that de-Americanization remained politically imperative. The legislators gave the new administration its customary honeymoon, but it showed signs of an early ending. An open letter from the Senate Foreign Relations Committee to the president offered a stark choice: submit his foreign policy for "consent" or face congressional "dissent." In February, Senator Fulbright, the committee's chair, announced the creation of an Ad Hoc Subcommittee on US Security Agreements and Commitments Abroad to examine the nation's treaties, executive agreements, overseas deployments, and foreign aid programs. Although Vietnam was excluded, the group sought to limit new executive agreements and expose old ones, particularly those that risked US intervention. That same month, Fulbright reintroduced a resolution to constrain the president's power to make new commitments without congressional assent.[22] As Nixon and other policymakers saw it, these investigations and resolutions brought unwanted public scrutiny to America's global commitments, disheartened allies, and emboldened enemies.[23]

In March, congressional opposition to the administration's proposed anti-ballistic missile (ABM) program confirmed White House worries. Nixon saw the ABM system as necessary for nuclear deterrence—if successful, it could shoot down intercontinental ballistic missiles—and a vital bargaining chip with the Soviets. As an increasing number of senators lined up against the program, the administration expected a close vote. By mid-March, the Senate seemed to be challenging his foreign policy in every area save Vietnam, and that too was changing.[24]

Senate doves initially believed that Nixon was pursuing peace in Vietnam and so attacked defense appropriations and the ABM proposal instead, but in March they concluded he was moving too slowly. No one demanded the immediate abandonment of South Vietnam. Even Fulbright conceded that it was "premature to start bringing large numbers of troops home now."[25] But they brought increased pressure to alter course. As journalists Rowland Evans and Robert Novak reported, "The very fact that Fulbright, Sen. George McGovern of South Dakota and other doves are beginning to stir again, after an unusual period of quiet, is pushing the Administration harder in the direction of Laird's plan."[26]

Laird bore the brunt of these attacks on Capitol Hill. "You've got to do something radical to change this war or we're going down the drain," Fulbright berated him on March 21. "Soon it will be Nixon's war, and then there will be little chance to bring it to an end." The senator appealed to Laird's political sense: "De-escalating and settling the war would not only be a great service to the American people, but I am sure would also be good politics." To do otherwise would invite domestic catastrophe, as the people would lose faith in the government. Nixon could either reap political gains by de-escalating and ending the war or provoke devastating dissent by continuing an unwinnable conflict.[27]

At a subsequent briefing with Rogers, Senate doves remained adamant. "We do not want to hamper your negotiations now," declared Claiborne Pell (D-RI). "But time is running out, and we again may have to take a role as we believe we did with the last administration and push you harder if within a very few months these things have not been resolved." When Rogers protested that the Nixon administration was doing the best it could, he reiterated, "Time runs out nevertheless."[28]

As a former congressman, Laird understood the congressional realities. "The Congress is a *reflection* of our country," he averred. "Public opinion is reflected in the Congress faster than any other place." He took Fulbright's words as further evidence that Americans "were fed up with Vietnam" and that Congress would terminate the war's funding unless the administration began reducing the number of troops in Vietnam. Laird could cite the ABM debate and testy hearings as proof that Congress would not tolerate escalation or delay in de-Americanizing the war.[29]

Nixon faced this congressional opposition firsthand when he met privately with Fulbright on March 27. The senator warned him against escalation and the "siren song" of victory. He argued that Nixon had been elected to end the war and that preserving the Republic of Vietnam was not vital to American national security or to containing communist China. He blamed the lack of progress in Paris on American and South Vietnamese diplomats, and he urged the president to let the Vietnamese "fight it out" should talks fail. South Vietnam's fall would damage neither American interests nor the president's reputation. Kissinger considered Fulbright one of the "unpacifiable doves" identified by their "escalating concessions," but Nixon could not ignore them. The following day, he decided to plan troop reductions.[30]

Much of the March 28 NSC meeting focused on de-Americanization. Although bureaucratic disagreements over the war remained, most participants assumed some level of de-escalation and at least a token withdrawal of US soldiers. "We must move in a deliberate way, not to show panic," Nixon cautioned. "We cannot be stampeded by the likes of Fulbright." If the administration appeared to give into the doves, the pressure to end the war would only increase and the United States' negotiating position would be weakened.[31]

Nixon needed "some symbol" that the situation warranted US troop withdrawals, and at this moment the word "Vietnamization" entered American parlance. In the 1968 election, he had made US reductions contingent on the buildup of ARVN forces, but at a March 14 press conference he had added progress on pacification and a reduction of the enemy threat to the mix. Rogers pointed out that control of the countryside was "a poor explanation" for troop withdrawal. Nixon had already ruled out conditioning unilateral withdrawal on the negotiations' progress lest he bind reductions to North Vietnamese actions. The discussion then went back to ARVN improvements as an appropriate measure to justify unilateral withdrawal. Betraying his frustration with the current state of de-Americanization and US public opinion, Nixon declared: "We need a plan. If we had no elections, it would be fine. . . . The reality is that we are working against a time clock. We are talking 6 to 8 months. We are going to play a strong public game but we must plan this. We must get a sense of urgency in the training of the South Vietnamese." Laird immediately suggested that instead of using the term de-Americanization, they develop "a term Vietnamizing to put the emphasis on the right issues."[32] Vietnamization sounded less like retreat and more like a goal-oriented program to reduce the American presence while protecting South Vietnam from communist aggression.[33]

Timetables for steady reductions were still missing as the administration focused on a negotiated settlement that provided for mutual withdrawal. Nixon and Kissinger believed they would have a deal by the end of the year, and so they resisted de-escalation. When the president asked how long the Paris talks would last, the veteran diplomat Philip Habib responded, "Providing the North sees no flagging in our determination . . . a settlement should probably occur this year."[34] A public timetable for reductions would send the wrong message to Hanoi. After the March 28 meeting, Nixon decided that there would "be no de-escalation except as an outgrowth of mutual troop withdrawal."[35]

The White House had turned a corner, though. An unspoken outcome of the meeting was the decision to make a token withdrawal of US troops as early as July, assuming no drastic changes in the military situation in Vietnam. The official historians of the Joint Chiefs of Staff later noted this decisive shift: "Now, for the first time since its involvement in the Vietnam war, the United States was moving toward a reduction of its effort."[36] The administration would continue to study negotiations and Vietnamization in the interim while preparing two presidential speeches to announce these developments and bolster domestic support. Beyond that first reduction, it would be up to Laird to make troop withdrawals the heart of America's exit strategy from Vietnam.[37]

Former policymaker William Bundy accurately identified March 1969 as the "month of decision."[38] Laird's trip to Vietnam, growing dissent in Congress, and that month's policy meetings forced several important decisions. Nixon acted on his campaign rhetoric by deciding an improved ARVN would be an appropriate yardstick to justify the unilateral withdrawal of US troops. The United States would also remove troops sometime that summer. The president hoped to assuage public opinion and buy time to implement his diplomatic and military offensives. He also commissioned studies on Vietnamization and mutual withdrawal. Like his predecessor, Nixon hoped for a mutual withdrawal of North Vietnamese and American soldiers, but he authorized high-level planning for Vietnamization. He also decided to launch an intense bombing campaign in Cambodia.

As Washington reporters understood, Kissinger and Laird were pulling Nixon's Vietnam strategy in different directions.[39] Coercive diplomacy could not coexist with unilateral reductions. That spring, the battle over strategy escalated, but so too did campus unrest and congressional calls for a new strategy in Vietnam. Time was running out.

Wild Threats and Loose Lips

Despite progress on Vietnamization, Nixon delayed any decision or public announcement. The president and his staff kept the deliberations secret and instead considered ways to escalate the war. He denied to journalists that he was planning any troop withdrawals. He hoped the bigger the surprise, the bigger the public relations windfall.

Certain there was no time for such public relations shell games, Laird leaked his Vietnamization strategy to reporters. As journalist Douglass Cater famously quipped, "The primary cause for the almost constant revelation of behind-the-scenes episodes of government is the power struggle that goes on within the government itself or among the governments doing business in Washington."[40] By publicizing Vietnamization, Laird hoped to ensure its survival and give it respectability and the appearance of legitimacy even before Nixon approved it. If the public accepted this strategy, it would be much harder for the White House to delay or stop troop withdrawals. His leaks also gave Congress and the media notice that reductions were forthcoming, prolonging the administration's political honeymoon.[41]

Nixon and Kissinger were not pleased. Though Laird remained anonymous (even accusing Kissinger of the leaks), the national security advisor blamed him, telling Rogers that "by the time we do anything [on reductions] it will be a disappointment." Nixon followed with a harsh memo to his Cabinet putting a moratorium on public talk of reductions. "When we make our troop withdrawal statement," he wrote, "I think the President should be in a position to make the announcement without having the entire impact of it eroded by leaks and dope stories prior to that time." He feared these leaks made it appear that he had "lost control of his team," with everyone "going off in different directions." Of course, Laird and Kissinger were going in different directions.[42]

Laird ran further afoul of the president and national security advisor as well as top military officials when he unilaterally reduced the number of Operation Arc Light B-52 sorties in South Vietnam and announced his decision to the media on April 1. Kissinger argued that it was inconsistent with and contrary to Nixon's wishes and that it threatened to undermine their coercive diplomacy. "The only thing we are trying to avoid is the impression of de-escalation," he berated the secretary. And yet Laird had reduced air operations that kept military pressure on the enemy. Moscow, Hanoi, and the American news media would interpret this move as evidence of war-weariness and an eagerness to settle.[43] He also upset the military, who saw Arc Light as critical to the ground war and Vietnamization. Abrams argued that the sorties provided the "equivalent punching power" of several divisions. Ignoring the White House and the military's concerns, Laird understood that Congress was increasing its scrutiny of defense expenditures. Without some voluntary decreases, it might enact intolerable cuts. Reducing costly air operations would save millions while ameliorating these tensions.[44]

Though frustrated at Laird, Kissinger remained undaunted. His communications with Johnson administration officials confirmed that the 1968 bombing halt was not sacred. Walt Rostow "made it clear" that Johnson had "purposely left his March 31 speech vague" so that his successor could resume the bombing of North Vietnam. Indeed, Rostow felt the resumption was justified since the enemy was massing men and matériel in the DMZ, shelling South Vietnamese cities, and taking advantage of the halt to improve logistics and sustain the mini-Tet offensive. Aware of Johnson's attitudes, Kissinger could ease Nixon's fear of a partisan attack from his predecessor should they end the bombing halt.[45]

Kissinger outlined his coercive diplomacy in an April 3 memo. He reasoned that Nixon could either continue the stale Paris talks or take "extraordinary procedures" to induce a settlement. "I have concluded that our best course would be a bold move of trying to settle everything at once," he wrote. "It is the only way to end the war quickly and the best way to conclude it honorably." Building on prior plans, the White House would involve the Soviets by promising détente and strategic arms limitation talks (SALT) in exchange for help in ending the war. It would also make clear that Nixon would "not be the first American President to lose a war, and he is not prepared to give in to public pressures which would have that practical consequence." He would make one last attempt to compromise with Hanoi, giving them two months to respond; thereafter, he would take "other measures" to end the war. Kissinger cautioned Nixon that the Washington bureaucracy would oppose and perhaps even try to sabotage this policy. He further advised that if the president chose this alternative and threatened Hanoi, failure to act would destroy his credibility.[46]

Nixon agreed. Buoyed by "some real faith in Kissinger's plan," he reaffirmed to the Cabinet that the war would be over in a few months. He ordered Kissinger to plan more bombing in Cambodia but not inform the Pentagon until later, lest the civilians there undermine this effort. He also authorized Kissinger to deliver a threat to Dobrynin.[47]

Kissinger told the Soviet ambassador on April 14 that Nixon was making one more push to end the war diplomatically, but added that if the talks failed to produce results by late August, he would take decisive measures to end the war. "In dealing with the President, it was well to remember that he always did more than he threatened and that he never threatened idly," he emphasized. Kissinger let Dobrynin read Nixon's talking points, which reiterated that he would not be the first president to lose a war and that Soviet-American relations were at a "crossroads"—settling the war would improve them, whereas its continuation would jeopardize détente. Dobrynin justifiably countered that the Soviets had little influence over Hanoi, but concluded that "this has been a very important conversation."[48]

As Nixon and Kissinger moved their chess pieces for the final, masterful stroke, rogue North Korean pilots intruded. Thirty-one servicemen died when on April 15 North Korean fighters shot down an American EC-121 surveillance plane over international waters. Nixon and Kissinger interpreted the attack as a test of presidential will and sought immediate retaliation. "Every time [the] US fails to react, it encourages some pipsqueak to do something," the president reasoned. He would respond even if he had "to overrule everybody in the State Department." He ordered ongoing surveillance flights and the immediate deployment of a US Navy carrier to the region. For Laird, the situation at home appeared too fragile to tolerate new hostilities on the Korean Peninsula. Again, he acted independently, ignoring a presidential order and limiting provocative US air, naval, and surveillance operations near North Korea.[49]

Determined to demonstrate their resolve somewhere, Nixon and Kissinger shifted back to Cambodia. They hoped that another bombing campaign—codenamed Operation Lunch—would send the same message to communists worldwide as hitting a North Korean target and would establish Nixon's credibility as a dangerous adversary. "If we strike back, even though it's risky, they will say, 'This guy is becoming irrational—we'd better settle with him,'" Kissinger argued. "But if we back down, they'll say, 'This guy is the same as his predecessor, and if we wait he'll come to the same end.'" Assaulting Cambodia a second time, rather than attacking North Korea or North Vietnam, became the next step in Nixon and Kissinger's Vietnam strategy. Although the clandestine expansion of American bombing into Cambodia received scant domestic attention, unrest and congressional dissent continued to grow that spring, quickening the administration's moves toward Vietnamization.[50]

For all the attention paid to 1968—the year that "rocked the world"— 1969 saw more violent protests in the United States. The clashes between police and activists at the 1968 Democratic Convention had cost the peace movement popular support. Antiwar activity waned in early 1969. Still, demonstrations marred Nixon's inauguration, and Easter Sunday witnessed protests nationwide. Dissent grew more radical and violent. The reform group Students for a Democratic Society (SDS) faced increasing factionalism in early 1969 as the militants usurped power and pressed the organization to abandon nonviolence. One of those pushing SDS in this direction, Bill Ayers declared, "Kill all the rich people. Break up their cars and apartments. Bring the revolution home, kill your parents, that's where it's really at."[51]

In fact, the university was where the revolution was "really at." Arrests for campus violence doubled in 1969, and approximately 300 universities witnessed major protests that spring, with one quarter having buildings forcibly occupied by students. Occupations at the University of Wisconsin and Harvard precipitated violent interventions by the National Guard and local police, respectively. The most prominent incident was at Cornell University in upstate New York, where armed African Americans seized Willard Straight

Hall on April 18. Though the occupation ended peacefully, journalists as far away as London reported that America was "on the brink of racial revolution."[52] Looking back, sociologist Tom Wells summarized these events, "Political violence was escalating. There were at least eighty-four bombings, attempted bombings, and acts of arson on campuses in the first half of 1969, twice as many as the previous fall. America's high schools were the scenes of twenty-seven bombings and attempted bombings. . . . Talk of armed revolution was as common as hot dogs at a baseball game." Most of this turmoil was unrelated to Vietnam, but the unrest increased fears that a dramatic, public escalation of the war in Indochina would worsen the disorder.[53]

The administration approached this unrest with caution. Officials worried the protests and occupations would weaken American credibility with Hanoi, encourage popular antiwar sentiment, and expose Nixon to political attacks for having failed on law and order. One analyst noted that students around the world were adopting the style of "provocation, confrontation, [and] violence," and predicted that the radicals' influence would increase regardless of what governments and universities did. Popular fears of social dissolution could increase the numbers of those seeking an immediate end to the war. "A lot of people took the students seriously—a lot more seriously than they should have been taken," recalled Nixon's speechwriter Ray Price. "This itself was a kind of snowballing political problem for us." Roger Morris explained, "We saw the seriousness of the early antiwar movement not so much in an analysis of whether it was a minority or a majority—it was always a minority. We saw that as affecting overall public opinion, we saw that as affecting the Congress, and as furthering the defection of the press. . . . This might be a bunch of wild-eyed kids or little old ladies in tennis shoes walking down Pennsylvania Avenue . . . but it had an insidious effect in public opinion and in the Congress." Another staffer argued that groups like SDS were urging "student radicals to shave off [their] long hair, don the 'Establishment Uniform' of a coat and tie, and obtain summer or extended employment with workers in industry or government for the purpose of proselyting them."[54]

Indeed, the White House saw these campus protestors as revolutionary terrorists bent on destroying society. "This is the way civilizations begin to die," Nixon told an audience in late March. "None of us has the right to suppose it cannot happen here." The White House exaggerated the impact of student unrest and activism, but the fear that the antiwar movement would become mainstream heightened the sense that time was working against American objectives in Vietnam.[55]

Nixon was not afraid to use this unrest to his political advantage. He sought to marshal the quiet Americans by appealing to the anger, antagonism, and fear produced by the campus disorders. A spring Harris poll found that "52 percent [of Americans] now opposed *peaceful* demonstrations by students."[56] "Decency rallies" occurred nationwide as Nixon's "silent Americans" protested the protestors. Anti-antiwar sentiment and law and order politics swirled together, catalyzing the backlash to postwar liberalism, especially among working-class whites. The president turned the politics of polarization to his benefit even as it further fractured national unity.[57]

Laird too saw the political advantages, but he hoped to calm a dangerous domestic situation. Vietnamization could eliminate the war as a controversial issue. He also proposed a draft lottery to relieve youth hostility. Given antiwar attitudes and the uncertainty created by the draft system, many young men viewed the draft as a death sentence. At the University of Pennsylvania's spring commencement, graduates handed out fliers that read: "The somber male graduate in the assemblage before you is angry and afraid, for he is contemplating death for the first time. Many of those wearing cap and gowns today will die—or worse—kill in Viet-Nam." Aware of this mood, Laird believed conscription was "the most combustible element in the campus tinderbox." With universities erupting in violence nationwide, his long-term vision was an all-volunteer force, which would remove the draft issue entirely. He readied a draft reform plan as an expedient so that Nixon could announce it in mid-May. The proposed system based conscription on birth dates chosen by lottery. This reform would make one's odds of being drafted clear, and thus would free most young people from needless angst. The US Army's chief of staff, General William Westmoreland, understood what the secretary was doing. "That was Mel Laird's baby," he remembered. "He was trying to defuse the younger generation."[58]

Shoring Up the Numbers

As April ended, progress on Vietnamization quickened. The White House had made only a tentative decision to withdraw some troops as early as July. Laird's staff had to confirm this decision and finalize planning for the first reduction. Although Deputy Secretary of Defense David Packard instructed Pentagon officials that henceforth "Vietnamizing the war should have the highest priority," early estimates had reviews of the draft program taking place in August.[59] The domestic context catalyzed this planning. "Political realities may force a decision on troop withdrawal sooner than anticipated," noted a May 9 update. The president needed a range of alternatives before Congress and the public turned against the war. Even Kissinger recognized the need to reveal a troop reduction before speculation robbed the announcement of its public impact. In May, the White House, the Republic of Vietnam, and the Pentagon came together to determine the size and timing of the first reduction and thus shore up public support for the war and Nixon's handling of it.[60]

Events also prompted Nixon to deliver his first nationally televised address on Vietnam. He and Kissinger had been working on the speech for about a month when the NLF garnered global attention by announcing a ten-point peace proposal that demanded a unilateral withdrawal of all US forces, an interim coalition government, and the eventual reunification of Vietnam. Although their proposal represented a "hardening" of the communist negotiating position, this apparent peace overture encouraged more Americans to demand that Nixon explain how he intended to end the war.[61]

Intrigue within the administration provided another compelling reason for Nixon to speak. Rogers was eager to announce his own peace plan, and the president feared that the State Department would leak it. The secretary was willing to accept many of the NLF's bargaining points if they would lead to a settlement.[62] Nixon thought such compromise would undermine his goal of preserving the Republic of Vietnam. Hence, his speech sought to alleviate domestic and international concerns while preventing members of his Cabinet from making their own declarations.[63]

The May 14 address focused on the Paris peace negotiations and avoided almost any hint that the administration would shortly remove some soldiers. As part of his efforts to guarantee that the first withdrawal announcement surprised the public and his critics, early drafts were pessimistic about any reduction. After seeing one such draft, Laird urged the president to include some reference to their efforts to bring troops home apart from success in Paris. Should the president announce a reduction so soon after this speech on negotiations and mutual withdrawal, the enemy would interpret it as evidence of America's weak bargaining position. Nixon modified the speech.[64]

The president informed the American people "that progress in the training program has been excellent and that, apart from any developments that may occur in the negotiations in Paris, the time is approaching when the South Vietnamese forces will be able to take over some of the fighting fronts now being manned by Americans." This indirect reference was Vietnamization's only mention in this first major address on Vietnam.[65]

The speech reflected Nixon's belief that his administration would soon end the conflict through a combination of military pressure and negotiations, making a program of unilateral disengagement unnecessary. He rejected precipitate withdrawal as a disguised sellout. He maintained that abandoning South Vietnam would "risk a massacre" of innocent Vietnamese, forfeit America's credibility, and encourage communist hardliners worldwide. An honorable end to the war was critical, he believed, to moving "from an era of confrontation to an era of negotiation." He stood by mutual withdrawal and South Vietnamese self-determination. North Vietnamese military forces must leave not only the South but also Laos and Cambodia. He signaled to communist leaders that "if the needless suffering continues" in Vietnam, he would reconsider his military and diplomatic options. Wrapping up the address, he vowed: "Our fighting men are not going to be worn down; our mediators are not going to be talked down; and our allies are not going to be let down." Despite the administration's conviction that the speech represented the most comprehensive American peace plan to date, historian Robert Dallek correctly noted that "hindsight demonstrates how unimportant the speech was."[66]

The speech failed to spur progress in Paris or assuage domestic critics. Eight House Democrats countered by proposing a cease-fire with the simultaneous withdrawal of 100,000 US troops. Making matters worse, Abrams's aggressive ground operations sparked domestic blowback. Congressional doves took the bloody and inconsequential May 13–20 battle for "Hamburger Hill" as proof that Nixon, like his predecessors, was wedded to military victory. Having scores of Americans sacrificed for a South Vietnamese hill, which the military promptly abandoned, inflamed this sentiment. Fulbright staffer Lee Williams urged Congress to seize the moment with a television program to "force the American people to face the fact that these are their sons bleeding and dying in Vietnam." Perhaps by showing mangled and crippled soldiers in army hospitals, Congress could bring more pressure against the White House to end the war. *Life* magazine indeed brought the war home in a compelling June issue that featured the pictures of 241 American soldiers killed in one week of fighting. Meanwhile, Senator Edward Kennedy's (D-MA) vocal criticism of administration policy added partisan politics into the equation, as the administration feared a Kennedy challenge in 1972. And the president's May 14 speech did not boost public support for his peace efforts. According to a Gallup poll, nearly 60 percent of Americans believed it was time to begin monthly reductions of US forces in Vietnam.[67]

Nixon could no longer put off withdrawals. He decided to reveal Vietnamization alongside Thieu in early June. But there was still no unanimity on the size or timing of the first withdrawal.

In Vietnam, Abrams realized that accelerated ARVN improvement would not yet justify US reductions. "That would be just a case of the United States kidding itself, and [pounding the table] *by god* you mustn't kid yourself!" he growled. That said, the general believed the military situation was the best it had been since PAVN regulars began pouring into the South in late 1964. Given this strong position, he thought that the president could withdraw two divisions (roughly 40,000 combat troops) within the next six months.[68]

Thieu agreed, letting Washington as well as the Saigon press corps know that he would accept a 50,000-man reduction. "We are determined and we will make untiring efforts to gradually take over full responsibility in the present fight with only an effective material assistance from allied nations," he told the people in April. Later that same month, he added, "We need weapons and money from the supporting Allies because we are a poor country, but in bones and blood we are ready to replace the Allies here to fight to the last drop of blood despite losses." Government officials intimated to the press that they were anticipating 50,000 soldiers would leave in July, 150,000 by the end of 1969, and 200,000 by the 1970 midterm elections.[69]

South Vietnamese military and political confidence were critical to these expectations, but so too were grave concerns about the US home front. In his private conversations with Ambassador Bui Diem, Kissinger downplayed the impact of domestic factors on Nixon's foreign policy. The diplomat was unconvinced. He warned Thieu that withdrawals were certain and that the Pentagon was driving this planning. From Saigon, Australian journalist Denis Warner remarked, "They fear, along with many Americans here, that anti-war feelings may develop avalanche proportions and that the Nixon administration within six months may be forced into concessions to public opinion that seem inconceivable now." Senator Tran Van Don judged that American politics was "unstable," and he debated a goodwill mission to the United States to explain the Republic's progress. Thieu similarly told a Canadian official that he was losing faith in "the ability of the Nixon administration to hold its own line at home." Having consulted with the White House on the May 14 speech, he wanted a public meeting with his counterpart to help win over the American public and announce an initial reduction. As Thieu and his supporters saw it, the problem was in America, not South Vietnam.[70]

In Washington, the administration feuded over troop numbers and the larger Vietnamization timetable. Although Laird wanted an initial redeployment of 50,000 troops, he worked with the Pentagon to arrive at a number. These negotiations reduced it to 35,000. Kissinger and the Joint Chiefs considered this number still too high. Kissinger worried that a large reduction would hurt their bargaining position. Despite Abrams's support for the larger redeployment, the JCS feared that the loss of even 35,000 soldiers would slow progress in the ground war. Conversely, Laird believed that without a sizable withdrawal congressional and domestic opinion would quickly turn against the war. All parties finally agreed on an initial reduction of about 25,000 military personnel.[71]

By May 21, Nixon had decided to make the announcement in a meeting with Thieu at Midway Island. The American president worried that continued speculation about an impending withdrawal was eroding its political value. He saw the trip as an opportunity to shore up support for the Republic while using the troop reduction to undercut those groups within America calling for the immediate withdrawal of US forces. Even the date and site of this declaration—the small Pacific island of Midway—reflected this domestic context, as Nixon sought to avoid giving a university address possibly fraught with protestors and feared that inviting Thieu stateside would unleash widespread riots.[72]

The decision to reduce American forces did not sadden or upset Thieu, as is often claimed; he had been urging this strategy upon US policymakers for over a year.[73] He agreed that withdrawals were necessary to stave off a complete collapse on the US home front and believed that his political and military strength made them possible. As he traveled to Midway, he declared his nation's readiness to replace American troops now and in the years to come. "We are determined to take over the responsibility. We are ready to do that. And we are able to do that."[74]

If the South Vietnamese were ready to assume any burden, Nixon feared that Americans were ready to abandon their global responsibilities. Addressing the Air Force Academy's commencement before he left for Midway, he condemned those "new isolationists" who blamed America for the world's ills and sought to curtail its international commitments. He was strident. "You are entering the military service of your country when the Nation's potential adversaries abroad have never been stronger and when your critics at home have never been more numerous," he asserted. "It is open season on the Armed Forces." Nixon was reacting to a perceived wave of antimilitarism while trying to shore up conservative support before Midway's de-escalation. He also aimed to confuse the news media, hopefully delaying the publication of any leaked information on withdrawals and so increase Vietnamization's value as a political surprise. Instead, he made more enemies.[75]

One of the supposed "neo-isolationists," Senator Fulbright noted his disappointment at the president's tone.[76] "It looks to me like he is going all the way back to [the militant anticommunism of] Whittaker Chambers and Joe McCarthy and I confess I see very little hope for much change." He ended his moratorium on public criticism of the war and the administration after the Air Force speech. Nixon had traded congressional patience for a temporary boost. Presiding over an increasingly divided nation, he hoped for a big public relations win at Midway.[77]

Nixon and Thieu met at Midway on June 8 to discuss America's internal problems and demonstrate allied unity.[78] Nixon told Thieu that "the U.S. domestic situation is a weapon in the war." He remained steadfast: there would be no sellout in Paris, nor pressure for a coalition government. He told Thieu he was trying to enlist Soviet help in ending the war and insisted that Johnson's limited war strategy had been wrong. Thieu understood his counterpart's plight and vowed that South Vietnam would facilitate the withdrawal of American forces. He only desired increased military and economic aid, which the American president promised to deliver over the next eight years. Having secured Thieu's approval in person, Nixon announced the first redeployment of US troops.[79]

The presidents explained the decision to the assembled press. The withdrawals would begin almost immediately. The two nations would consider additional reductions "at regular intervals thereafter" based on RVNAF improvement, the Paris talks, and enemy activity. The drawdown would stop if they endangered allied forces or the Republic's survival. In his remarks, Thieu noted that he and his country had been preparing for these withdrawals for the last twelve months. Whereas Nixon had used the setting to recall the decisive World War II battle of Midway, Thieu emphasized the Pacific

Ocean—a body of water named for peace and "pious hope." He opined that sailors of old "knew that they had to rely on their strength, determination, and perseverance when they run into stormy weather. But after the tempest and typhoon, the sun always rises over the inland straits of the blue waters. Therefore, we are always confident of a bright and beautiful tomorrow." Nixon and Thieu could anticipate a better tomorrow even as US soldiers returned home.[80]

Americans reacted favorably to the news that the Nixon administration would remove 25,000 US troops by August 31, 1969. Support for his handling of the war jumped from the mid-40s to 52 percent. Sixty-two percent opposed the immediate withdrawal of US troops (29 percent favored), instead backing monthly reductions. "President Nixon has undoubtedly bought more time for his strategy with the American people," a *New York Times* reporter wrote, although he added that the numbers were "so modest and the time period for the first withdrawal so short that [the president] must . . . face the issue of more withdrawals very soon." The announcement bought Nixon time; how much remained uncertain.[81]

Still, Laird's persistence had paid off. He had challenged or ignored presidential requests for escalation that spring while convincing Nixon to accept Vietnamization and authorize the first reduction of troops. He had done it his way.

4

Going Up the Country

*Vietnamization, Duck Hook, and the
Nixon Doctrine in the Global Context*

June–August 1969

President Richard Nixon's troop withdrawal announcement on Midway Island surprised few international observers. All recognized that US domestic pressures dictated unilateral withdrawals, and, given South Vietnamese military and political progress, they seemed warranted. Saigon hoped the reductions would satisfy the American people and Congress, while Hanoi counted on US domestic politics to override a prudent withdrawal program. The two Vietnams had the most to gain and lose from Vietnamization. Both took the Midway announcement in stride as they pressed on toward their goals.

Despite early allied concerns, the administration seemed to be handling its critics well, especially given the growing internal lobby for international retrenchment. This threat remained in the future that summer as Nixon chose the most conservative of reductions, maintained a strong military posture in Indochina, and fortified his political position in the United States. Many foreign observers believed that the American president might be able to save the Republic of Vietnam through the "long haul" Vietnamization strategy. At a July stop on Guam, he further indicated that he would apply Vietnamization to the world. What came to be called the Nixon Doctrine—relying on regional partners to carry the burden of their own defense—sought to balance America's needs with its global obligations. Nixon held domestic forces in check, but the storm clouds of congressional and public opinion remained on the horizon.

With antiwar forces gathering strength, the president worried that his support would not last. Certain that the nation's credibility (as well as his own) was at stake in Vietnam, he decided that summer to make a push for a quick settlement. "What is on the line is more than South Vietnam," he reasoned. "It's a question of what happens to the balance of Asia and to the rest of the world." A US defeat might embolden its enemies, frighten its friends, and turn Americans inward. The administration must talk and act tough. And it must win in Vietnam. Laird's Vietnamization provided no guarantee that Nixon could sustain public and congressional support long enough to turn the Republic into a nation capable of self-defense. If his time was running out at home, so was his patience with Hanoi. Thus, Nixon backed Kissinger's scheme to deliver an ultimatum to the Democratic Republic: agree to settle or face an American blitz.[1]

The president recalled that during this period he and Kissinger developed an "elaborate orchestration of diplomatic, military, and publicity pressures" to force the North Vietnamese to negotiate.[2] With Vietnamization, he attempted to rally support at home. He also traveled abroad to reassure allies that troop reductions and changes in US grand strategy did not mean abandoning South Vietnam or other global responsibilities. To friends, he hinted that as his patience wore thin escalation remained a serious option. To enemies, he left little doubt that he had issued an ultimatum. If the world spent the summer reacting to Vietnamization, Nixon quietly moved toward a more aggressive strategy.

The "Race against Time": Vietnamization in Vietnam

The summer of '69 was popularly remembered as the apotheosis of 1960s music. Young men and women were humming what became Woodstock's unofficial anthem, Canned Heat's "Going Up the Country," as they traveled to rural upstate New York that August. *Time* hailed the open-air music festival there as "history's largest happening"—more than 400,000 attended—and potentially a watershed moment in "the baffling history of mankind." "In its energy, its lyrics, its advocacy of frustrated joys, rock is one long symphony of protest," its writers observed. They interpreted the concerts and mass gathering as another indictment of square culture and, by proxy, the war in Vietnam. "This was only the beginning," warned singer Jimi Hendrix. The festival's music, lyrics, drug use, and photographs reinforced the sense that the old order was crumbling.[3]

All the while, officials were going up and down the Vietnamese countryside evaluating Vietnamization. But even there, American youth culture and counterculture were omnipresent as policymakers considered Nixon's emerging strategy. Was it one of disguised defeat, patient victory, or something else?

Unexpectedly, Saigon accepted the Midway announcement with pride. Nixon had neither demanded President Nguyen Van Thieu's resignation nor announced a significant reduction in America's fighting force. Popular and editorial opinion had dreaded a sellout or American pressure to form a coalition government with the communists. Thieu's stand against the Paris negotiations proved that he was no US puppet, but the populace continued to fear that the Americans would cut off aid, precipitously withdraw, or overthrow the Thieu government to achieve some semblance of peace so that they could leave. "The Americans are too anxious to get peace," Prime Minister Tran Van Huong declared on May 20. "They always talk about peace," which encouraged the enemy and coalition talk. The NLF's contemporaneous formation of the Provisional Revolutionary Government heightened these concerns. Politicians and journalists urged Thieu to resist American demands for additional concessions.[4]

So pervasive were Vietnamese fears that relief, rather than shock, characterized their reaction to the first troop withdrawals. Thieu had well-prepared the populace for this eventuality. Foreign opinion and South Vietnamese newspapers noted that the reductions "came as no surprise in Saigon." If anything, the 25,000-man withdrawal was less than expected, and South Vietnam assumed that America would increase its military and economic aid in exchange. Most interpreted Vietnamization as proof of South Vietnam's military and political strength as well as its readiness to assume the burden of its defense.[5] Though the South Vietnamese recognized Vietnamization's real aim was to placate American opinion, most believed Nixon could withdraw even more troops so long as military and economic aid continued. The United States had been fighting a "rich man's war," so it seemed reasonable that the RVNAF could take over with US financial support and still save America considerable money. Some Saigonese thus identified Vietnamization as the "U.S. Dollar and Vietnamese Blood Sharing Plan," but the majority saw it as an opportunity to "do things the Vietnamese way" by avoiding the overuse of firepower. That the 9th Infantry Division was the first to leave pleased many because of its reputation for inflicting heavy civilian casualties.[6] The

National Assembly similarly approved the Midway meeting. "It will help President Nixon appease the opposition in the United States" while encouraging South Vietnamese responsibility "because it will show that the U.S. commitment here is not unlimited," stated the secretary general of the lower house, Tran Ngoc Chau.[7]

Thieu's political standing rose sharply after Midway. He appeared to be a determined nationalist who had stood up to American impatience by opposing a coalition government with the NLF. To reassure the hawks, he took a tough line in a June 9 press conference. He distinguished between the "replacement" of American forces by Vietnamese and that "defeatist term . . . 'withdrawal.'" He argued that American "withdrawals" should come only as the product of a settlement that removed North Vietnamese forces. He condemned those who advocated a coalition government. Saigon residents and South Vietnamese politicians largely applauded this harsh rejection. As foreign analysts noted, the people might not universally love Thieu, but he could defeat the communists in an election. Vietnamization had not hurt his legitimacy or his leadership. Nevertheless, he recognized he must consolidate his popularity in South Vietnam and stave off the erosion of international support. His summer projects had both audiences in mind.[8]

Thieu pledged qualitative and quantitative RVNAF improvements to enable further allied reductions. As the ARVN expanded and replaced US ground troops, better and more numerous territorial forces—the Regional Forces (RF), Popular Forces (PF), and local Popular Self-Defense Forces (PSDF)—would handle insurgents in secure areas. Johnson-era modernization programs had begun to pay off in 1969 with the RF and PF finally having the small arms and firepower necessary to match the NLF. In terms of his larger Vietnamization strategy, Thieu claimed these gains meant "local communities will care for themselves against local threats," leaving ARVN regulars to fight the PAVN. He understood that militias could choose personal safety over confronting the enemy—or worse, enable NLF infiltration, allowing insurgents to use the system to gain income, arms, and protection.[9]

To win loyalty in the countryside, Thieu pursued what historian Andrew Gawthorpe has called "the civil side of Vietnamization": better village administration to promote democracy and connect the peasants to Saigon. The head of American pacification efforts, William Colby, recalled that the South Vietnamese president took US suggestions for rural reform and adapted them to "the real world of Vietnam." That spring, Thieu backed new village elections while outlining plans to give villagers greater autonomy. Better governed, more democratic communities would be freed of the tyranny of despotic centralized rule—whether communist or Diemist—and would thank the Second Republic for protection and freedom. Republic officials also worked on reforms that would give farmers their own parcel of land. The government hoped that by raising standards of living and eliminating the attraction of communism, it would better its position in Paris, promote economic development, and build a base of rural loyalty.[10]

Confident in his popularity and his government's legitimacy but pessimistic about American patience, Thieu moved toward recognizing the NLF as a political entity. He had previously considered any talk of communist political participation traitorous, but he also believed that "the time will come when we will be strong enough to take bacteria into the system." That time had come. Throughout 1969, he expressed genuine openness toward the NLF, initially offering to meet them privately. In the spring, South Vietnamese officials considered extending negotiations and political participation to the NLF. On April 7, Thieu announced a six-point peace proposal that would give amnesty to those members who renounced violence and communism.[11] He expected rejection, but he hoped such a gesture would draw off some insurgents and benefit the RVN's image abroad.[12]

As Thieu prepared for another major public speech on the NLF, dialogue with US policymakers confirmed the international importance of such a move. Rogers and other State Department officials told Bui Diem that American opinion considered Thieu's government undemocratic and corrupt. Ignoring the recent history of the Second Republic, they urged the ambassador to press Thieu to hold free elections, promote "liberalization," and build a "broad-based government." Such foreign criticism was unfair, but both Bui Diem and Thieu understood that Midway provided only a temporary reprieve. By July, US congressional and public opinion was again becoming "very impatient" on Vietnam. The "time problem" had returned. American officials doubted Thieu's concessions on NLF participation would spark a response from Hanoi or the NLF, but the United States was the critical theater.[13]

On July 11, Thieu announced his willingness to accept a settlement with internationally supervised, free elections, open to NLF participation. Such elections would follow the mutual withdrawal of American and North Vietnamese forces. The NLF needed only to renounce violence and promise to abide by the results.[14] His government would accept the outcome. He noted that if the communists held 80 percent of the population, as they claimed, then they should accept.[15]

South Vietnamese opinion was mixed on the offer. Many in the National Assembly praised it as another demonstration of allied goodwill that would highlight communist intransigence. Most recognized the move for what it was: an attempt to buy the Republic more time with international opinion. Representative Tran Quy Phong believed that the communists would ignore the offer and that the allies should "give nothing for nothing." "The gift will help Nixon appease public opinion at home where he faces growing impatience over when the Vietnam war can be brought to an end," he opined. Thieu defended the move as "an assault weapon" against communist propaganda abroad, but for the moment he had run out of ammo.[16]

South Vietnamese hawks fretted about Thieu's offers. Many in the military already thought that the allies had given away too much. Having stopped the bombing of North Vietnam, initiated US troop withdrawals, and proposed NLF amnesty, the acceptance of a coalition government seemed near. The National Assembly's hardliners and Vice President Ky made clear that America and South Vietnam had made "too many concessions." They condemned Thieu's entreaties as a unilateral, executive move toward conciliation and a violation of the Republic's constitution, which forbade communist political participation. For the hawks, the episode became yet another example of America and South Vietnam making concession after concession only to have Hanoi repay their goodwill with violence. Although US troop reductions could continue, South Vietnam must prosecute the war.[17]

In a notable July 26 speech before civil and military officials, Thieu assessed the foreign and domestic situations while outlining his aims. He expressed confidence that the DRV faced manpower shortages, that the balance of forces favored South Vietnam, and that 99.9 percent of the South Vietnamese population would not vote for the NLF. Defeated in Vietnam, he argued, "The communists have shifted the war from Vietnam to the field of world and U.S. opinion." There, Hanoi and the NLF were winning victories that could offset the Republic's gains. "We will never triumph if we do not nurture a world opinion which is favorable to us and condemns the communists," he added. His decision to talk with the NLF sought "to win world public opinion to our side and the U.S. side so that the American people will support their President."[18]

Thieu saw that only "two roads are left." Nixon could "decide to use strong pressure to force the communists to enter into serious peace talks and end the war." Or, if American politics made this path untenable, "the free world must help us to do this task, help us achieve self-reliance," knowing that the war could continue another three to five years. In short, the allies could go all out to end the war quickly or the United States could provide the financial and military assistance the Republic needed to soldier on alone. Thieu thought either course could work, though he acknowledged that America had often been parsimonious in its assistance and that the South Vietnamese economy depended on foreign aid. "We lack means, weapons, and money and not patriotism and the will to make sacrifices." He trusted that US and South Vietnamese concessions along with American troop reductions would turn the propaganda war in their favor. "Faced with this ever-mounting dissatisfaction and impatience among the American people, no U.S. President—however influential he may be—can maintain the policy of supporting us" at the present level of commitment. By removing American soldiers, "pressure upon the U.S. administration [will be] alleviated."[19]

South Vietnamese optimism hinged on the US domestic forces that had motivated Vietnamization. "If the pace of our troop reductions takes place at a pace faster than the Vietnamese are confident that they can take over," Ambassador Ellsworth Bunker argued, "it could destroy their self-confidence and all that we have built up here step by painful step."[20] If America's uncertain domestic situation dictated hasty withdrawals, South Vietnam could crumble.

North Vietnamese leaders recognized this truth and so carefully followed American politics and unrest. According to Henry Cabot Lodge Jr., they believed that Nixon was "on the toboggan" of US public opinion. British diplomat Gordon Philo cabled from Hanoi that the Nixon administration seemed to be under heavy domestic pressure for peace, a view he gained not from communist propaganda "but the reporting of non-communist news media and even the American press itself." Philo doubted the US situation was as weak as reports suggested. "The crux of the matter," he added, "is that from the point of view of Hanoi's intentions the facts of American opinion count for less than what Hanoi *believes* the facts to be." To the North Vietnamese, Vietnamization confirmed American weakness since Nixon had given in to popular pressures.[21]

North Vietnamese and NLF policymakers and soldiers alike fixed upon the American home front as their beacon of hope. Official press organs argued that Vietnamization "was a trick aimed at coping with the [antiwar] movement," "a propaganda act aimed at easing public pressures and dodging" foreign demands for America's exit. NLF member Hai Cầu warned his comrades that Nixon's escalation of the war was like that of "a wild beast in its death throes." The insurgents must persist because US withdrawals demonstrated that the president was caught in an "inextricable dilemma": he could not simultaneously intensify the war to end it quickly and remove soldiers to ease dissent. Ho Chi Minh similarly encouraged his people to take heart in America's travails, not fall for the Vietnamization "trick," and press on "till complete withdrawal of U.S. troops and till total collapse of the puppet army and administration."[22]

Privately, North Vietnamese leaders believed a Vietnamized war offered risks and potential benefits. They assumed that Midway marked the start of a total, unconditional US troop withdrawal. The American war would end, replaced by "indigenization." A proud RVNAF could hurt communist propaganda, while Thieu's continued mobilization could hamper military progress and NLF recruitment. A prolonged civil war would also deepen North-South divisions, making eventual reunification and national healing more difficult.[23]

The Democratic Republic of Vietnam also faced domestic problems. Rising desertion and sagging morale worried the communist leadership. Although the US bombing halt and expectations of peace had buoyed popular sentiment, the people suffered, according to CIA intelligence, "an emotional letdown" as the talks proved stillborn. As the CIA acknowledged, the actual impact of any war-weariness was negligible. Le Duan and the Politburo cracked down on the black market and suspected reactionaries. Waning enthusiasm in no way hindered their ability to continue fighting.[24]

More worrisome were North Vietnam's international difficulties. China had interpreted Hanoi's decision to pursue negotiations with the United States as an ideological shift toward the Soviet Union, which had favored a diplomatic solution to the conflict. In the context of a widening Sino-Soviet split, Beijing would not tolerate this development. It reduced assistance, stopped the flow of Soviet military and economic aid to North Vietnam through its territory, and pulled its antiaircraft personnel out by March 1969. Hanoi also feared that Nixon might successfully link an end to the war with Soviet-American détente, possibly jeopardizing its relationship with its last great power patron.[25]

In the South, pacification took a toll on communist efforts. It became difficult to enlist new members, and their access to local food supplies diminished. In the Mekong Delta, a reliable sanctuary for the NLF, the number of recruits fell from 16,000 in 1968 to about 100 in 1969. Defections there more than doubled the 1968 figures.[26] Increasingly, Hanoi would have to replace killed or injured NLF soldiers with troops from the NVA. Historian Pierre Asselin aptly observed, "Thus, as the war effort on one side was de-Americanized and South-Vietnamized, on the other it became de-South-Vietnamized and North-Vietnamized." Hanoi still believed it would win.[27]

Although Politburo moderates wanted to reduce hostilities and return to protracted warfare, Le Duan clung to his "talking while fighting" strategy.[28] He recognized that a weakened military position had reduced North Vietnam's leverage in Paris. Hanoi thus sent more soldiers south to replace 1968's losses while strengthening its logistics infrastructure and air defense in anticipation of resumed American bombing. He also launched two southern offensives in the first half of 1969. Refusing to abandon the goal of reunifying Vietnam under communist control, he bought time to regroup and regain the initiative so that he could dictate the terms in Paris.[29]

As for talking, Hanoi created the Provisional Revolutionary Government of South Vietnam (PRG) on June 6 to coincide with the Midway meeting. Though it adopted the veneer of legitimacy and claimed to represent the southern people, the PRG was in fact a North Vietnamese diplomatic tool controlled in Paris by Le Duan's faithful friend Le Duc Tho and the northern negotiator Xuan Thuy. As the British appreciated at the time, the PRG's formation was a "tactical manoeuvre" lacking "any of the real attributes of Government." Nevertheless, the PRG gave the NLF political and diplomatic leverage against the Thieu regime. Its spokespersons, like the smart and photogenic Madame Binh (Nguyen Thi Binh), did global tours, successfully garnering international attention and support. The PRG would serve as a rallying point for Thieu's detractors inside and outside of South Vietnam.[30]

Faced with punishing military pressure in the South, Le Duan altered his strategy in July by suspending his goal of decisive military victory. As set forth in COSVN Resolution 9, communist forces would continue their strategic offensive but prepare for a prolonged war. Hanoi remembered the French "yellowing" strategy in the First Indochina War, and so anticipated Nixon's Vietnamization and acknowledged its domestic purpose. Tactically, Resolution 9 emphasized inflicting casualties on Americans to weaken US resolve, thereby increasing public pressure for sizable and frequent withdrawals that would undermine allied military and pacification efforts. As Kissinger noted, the directive also ordered local operatives "to play on popular fears of the consequences of the withdrawal" to increase the number of South Vietnamese converts. More importantly, Resolution 9 lowered the overall tempo of communist operations, preserving and rebuilding NLF numbers and strength. Vietnamization could endanger North Vietnam's conquest of the South, but by husbanding its resources, encouraging further US reductions, and emphasizing the necessity of America's unilateral departure to Vietnamese and world opinion, Hanoi hoped to cripple the program at the start.[31]

Communist leaders thus increasingly spoke of their own "race against time." Given their military and political setbacks in South Vietnam, momentum seemed to be with the enemy. COSVN officials urged their soldiers to revive their "revolutionary fervor." "If the United States is reluctant to withdraw its troops, if the Puppet forces are in a stronger position after the Americans' withdrawal or if the NFLSVN plays only a minor role in the coalition government," one memo warned, "*it is definitely certain that we do not win.*" A difficult, long war lay ahead against a stubborn enemy. North Vietnam accordingly changed the General Offensive and General Uprising into "a process aimed at repelling the enemy step by step and gaining partial victories one at a time" rather than a singular, decisive blow. PAVN regulars and the remaining NLF guerrillas received the same message: "We secure victory not through a one-blow offensive, not through a phase of attack, not even through a series of attacks culminating in a final kill. Victory will come to us, not suddenly, but in a complicated and torturous way."[32]

Overall, Vietnamese communist forces had suffered greatly since the 1968 Tet Offensive, and the new US president had given them no reprieve. Yet, America's internal travails cheered them. Thinking back to 1969, one veteran recalled, "We knew that even though we faced tremendous difficulties, so did they. They had terrible problems, especially at home. We don't think their government could stand it in the long run. That gave me heart."[33]

Going for Broke

Richard Nixon and Henry Kissinger also questioned whether their government and people could stand the war in the long run. The announcement of troop withdrawals at Midway Island seemed to indicate that Laird had won the battle over Vietnam strategy. More US soldiers would come home as the South Vietnamese grew stronger. By instituting a policy of gradual, unilateral de-escalation, the administration appeared to understand the domestic mood without giving in to it completely. Nixon bought time to achieve US goals in South Vietnam.

This strategy did not please everyone. Until late spring 1969, Kissinger assumed that Nixon would follow his blueprint for ending the war. The president had authorized the military to apply maximum pressure against the enemy. In March and April, he had expanded the bombing in Laos and Cambodia. Meanwhile, he had Kissinger inform the Soviets that unless Hanoi began negotiating in earnest, the administration would have to take other measures—a veiled reference to escalation—to end the war. At almost every step, Nixon had followed the national security advisor's plan, but Laird's Vietnamization strategy challenged Kissinger's designs. Kissinger worried that Nixon would adopt some combination of Vietnamization, escalation, and negotiations. For him, regular withdrawals and negotiations were incompatible. That summer, he sought to undermine Vietnamization while convincing Nixon to go for broke.

Even before Midway, Kissinger saw Laird as a dangerous rival. On April 1, without any presidential authorization, the secretary of defense had announced that the United States was reducing the number of B-52 sorties in South Vietnam. When two weeks later a North Korean jet shot down an EC-121 surveillance plane, Laird had again acted on his own, ignoring a presidential order that risked new hostilities in Korea and more dissent at home. He didn't write a memo. He didn't ask for permission. He simply stopped surveillance flights worldwide and stalled the deployment of an aircraft carrier to the region, all undercutting Kissinger's intended image of a mad, vengeful president. Not for the last time, Kissinger fumed, "How can he do this? He has a direct order from the President."[34]

Laird could ignore the White House because of his influence in Congress, his mastery of bureaucratic politics, and his focus on what mattered to national security and Nixon's reelection. The president could not risk Laird's resignation; he needed the secretary to manage congressional relations. Nixon's dislike of confrontation also gave Laird the leeway to outmaneuver the military and Kissinger.[35] Finally, he valued the secretary's political judgement. He and Laird knew that ending the American conflict in Vietnam was essential to Nixon's political standing and broader foreign policy aims. As

Laird reminded Kissinger in a call during the EC-121 crisis, "What we're trying to do is get the war in Vietnam over with."[36] Kissinger understood the sentiment, but he believed Laird's caution and Vietnamization policy undermined that goal.

Kissinger's aides confirmed his belief that Laird's Vietnamization was flawed. The White House had predicated it on the continued expansion of ARVN forces, but NSC staff member Dean Moor questioned this assumption. He noted South Vietnam's chronic manpower shortages and warned that "at present rates of loss both through casualties and desertions, Saigon will not be able to do the job with the available personnel." He added that South Vietnam's growing inflation and budget deficits also threatened to cripple Vietnamization. With Morton Halperin, Moor also cast doubt on Saigon's control of the countryside and the progress of pacification.[37]

An article in the *St. Louis Post-Dispatch* raised similar concerns and concluded that the Republic's odds of political survival were "poor and worsening." Nixon deemed the author a "violent leftist" and dismissed his claims as "completely incorrect." Kissinger responded that Thieu had failed to build grassroots appeal and cited a US survey of South Vietnamese public opinion that revealed only 20 percent thought the RVNAF could replace all American forces within two years. The Tet Offensive and subsequent events had demonstrated the Republic's resiliency, but in the absence of a settlement that removed the NVA, it would face severe challenges.[38]

Time also seemed against Vietnamization. In a June 26 conversation with Kissinger, Bui Diem noted South Vietnam's increased optimism after Midway but cautioned that "international and U.S. public opinion might not allow enough time for the GVN to succeed in doing all it would have to do." Kissinger responded that Nixon had said he "could not be the first president to lose a war" and that the president needed alternatives. The ambassador explained Thieu's "Long Haul, Low Cost" strategy of Vietnamization abetted by American aid, not soldiers. Both understood that US opinion would decisively influence congressional budget debates.[39]

In Paris, the young diplomat and assistant to Lodge, Richard Holbrooke, also agreed that time was short and North Vietnam's will was strong. He told his friend and Kissinger staffer Anthony Lake that Hanoi had "substantially hardened their negotiating position in the last two months." The North Vietnamese seemed willing to pay any price for reunification and were preparing to continue fighting into the 1970s while adopting a diplomatic strategy intent on undermining Washington-Saigon relations. Holbrooke argued that Vietnamization might buy "time with the American public" but it could not end the war on acceptable terms. Americans should propose a cease-fire and then continue to compromise with Hanoi until they reached a deal.[40]

Nixon seemed to confirm the rapid Vietnamization of the war when he publicly responded to former Secretary of Defense Clark Clifford's *Foreign Affairs* article on Vietnam. Clifford had traced the evolution of his views on the war from fervent hawk to cautious dove, but he also offered a proposal to end the conflict.[41] America should gradually disengage its troops, help modernize the South Vietnamese army, and continue to provide air support. After Midway, this prescription seemed identical to the president's stated policy, but Clifford went further by calling for the withdrawal of 100,000 troops by year's end, with the remainder to be out by the end of 1970. Unlike Laird's flexible program, he proposed that the United States remove its troops "in accordance with a definite schedule and with a specific end point." Nixon's Vietnamization program was opaque, he claimed, and it withdrew troops too slowly.[42]

The president responded in a June 19 news conference. He criticized the former secretary of defense for failing to initiate troop withdrawals during his tenure. "As far as how many will be withdrawn by the end of this year, or the end of next year," he declared, "I would hope that we could beat Mr. Clifford's timetable, just as I think we have done a little better than he did when he was in charge of our national defense." Nixon's assertion that he hoped to exceed Clifford's plan rested on his belief that he would end the war in his first year in office.[43]

Kissinger feared that the president's statements jeopardized that outcome. He considered unilateral troop withdrawals a bad policy, and Nixon's new promise to have more than 100,000 troops out by the end of the year only intensified his anxiety. Chief of Staff H. R. Haldeman noted that the press conference "shook [Kissinger] pretty badly." Haldeman correctly discerned that Nixon's statements sought to "hit back at Clifford," but he could not assuage Kissinger's concern that the president had committed a major diplomatic blunder. "Our insistence on mutual withdrawal was by then drained of virtually any plausibility," Kissinger later wrote. "Our commitment to unilateral withdrawal had come to be seen, at home, abroad, and particularly in Vietnam, as irreversible."[44] Contrary to this retrospective analysis, the president's remarks only briefly depressed him. Instead, he stepped up his efforts to halt Vietnamization and bring powerful military pressure against North Vietnam to force a negotiated settlement.[45]

In late June and July, Kissinger pressed the case that Vietnamization would not work and that Nixon should give peace one last chance before acting on threats to punish Hanoi. "I do not believe the Vietnamese armed forces will be able to achieve the necessary combat effectiveness within the timeframe visualized under the Vietnamization game plan," he wrote. "This underlines the need for reciprocal withdrawals by the NVA." Steady unilateral withdrawals precluded this type of settlement, and negotiations could take longer than public opinion would allow. "Withdrawal, at some point becomes irreversible even if Hanoi steps up upon its efforts." In turn, accelerated withdrawals undermined South Vietnamese confidence in the Thieu government while bolstering Hanoi's belief that it could wait out the United States. Vietnamization would become a thinly disguised policy of unilateral withdrawal that would ultimately abandon the Republic of Vietnam to communism, weakening US foreign policy abroad. "If it turns out that judgment [on withdrawals] is wrong, then the whole replacement program will have consequences other than those that we intend," Kissinger explained to the press.[46] South Vietnam would fall, taking American credibility with it. He reminded the president that he would bear responsibility for any settlement well after the ink had dried. "I believe that the point is approaching where we may be forced to choose between Vietnamization and political negotiations," Kissinger concluded.[47]

The national security advisor did not propose allied concessions in Paris; he was preparing Nixon to implement decisive military escalation designed to compel a negotiated settlement. Haldeman recorded that with Rogers and Laird "constantly pushing for faster and faster withdrawal," Kissinger "wants to push for some escalation, enough to get us a reasonable bargain for a settlement within six months." To this end, Kissinger collaborated with the military to work on secret contingency plans—thus attempting to keep Laird in the dark—while urging Nixon to delay more troop withdrawals.[48]

Duck Hook became Kissinger's belligerent alternative to Vietnamization. Picking up where he left off in April, Kissinger suggested that summer that the administration offer the most generous terms possible to North Vietnam and set a deadline for acceptance. If Hanoi still refused to bargain, the United States would give it "incentive to negotiate a compromise settlement through a series of blows." The administration would halt troop withdrawals and execute Duck Hook to break the diplomatic deadlock. Although it originated as a plan to mine Haiphong, Kissinger and military planners combined it with other proposals so that it grew into a ferocious air and naval offensive designed to decimate North Vietnam. The United States would relent when Hanoi agreed to its terms.[49]

As the summer progressed, Nixon moved in this direction. When Kissinger met Dobrynin on June 11, the ambassador confirmed that the Soviets had relayed his April message to Hanoi.[50] He asked if Nixon wanted Moscow to forward "an ultimatum." Kissinger reiterated that the president would end the war "one way or another" and would not allow Hanoi to erode public support. Nixon read incoming intelligence with a view toward Kissinger's planning. When the CIA reported "war-weariness" among the North Vietnamese people, he requested Kissinger's insight, wondering how their "anticipated action" would affect enemy morale. He also had Kissinger and General Wheeler ascertain the feasibility of such escalation. And he ordered that this planning be kept strictly "in our circle," thus excluding the secretary of defense. By early July, Kissinger had convinced Nixon to "go for broke." Hanoi would enter the talks in earnest or face an all-out American assault.[51]

At a July 7 NSC Executive Committee meeting aboard the presidential yacht *Sequoia*, Laird and Rogers pulled the president in the opposite direction.[52] Basing their judgment on the lower-than-expected allied casualty rates, US officials surmised that enemy forces had reduced the level of violence in South Vietnam, raising several questions. Recalling their confusion, Kissinger later wrote, "Did [the lull] result from Hanoi's exhaustion, from a new negotiating strategy, or from an attempt by Hanoi to achieve de-escalation by tacit understandings?" Laird and Rogers (along with Attorney General John Mitchell and Deputy CIA Director Robert Cushman) argued that the lull in the ground war justified faster US troop withdrawals. Regardless of North Vietnam's intentions, they believed the administration had to reciprocate or face public criticism for not responding to the enemy's ostensible desire to ease tensions. Kissinger and Wheeler disagreed: only maximum military pressure would produce an honorable peace. As was his nature when faced with dueling advisers, Nixon avoided making any decision that night. On Laird's suggestion, he authorized a review of the mission statement for American troops in Vietnam. It was an opening the secretary of defense could exploit. Citing the *Sequoia* meeting, he would change the mission from defeating and forcing the withdrawal of communist soldiers to supporting Vietnamization.[53]

Although Abrams had begun moving in this direction in 1968, the decision marked another victory for those forces favoring disengagement.[54] The mission statement was more a formality than a guide, but for Laird it confirmed that the administration was de-escalating the war. He explained on the *Sequoia* that the mission was no longer one of "maximum pressure" on the enemy but "maximum assistance" to the South Vietnamese. He would use the statement as leverage against both military hawks and congressional doves. In a telephone conversation with Kissinger the next day, he expressed his pleasure with the meeting's outcome. Hinting at things to come, Kissinger responded, "For Laird's *own* use, the President has not excluded the possibility that he could take the option to the right in order to wind up the war quickly." Kissinger left the *Sequoia* determined to develop an alternative based on military escalation, not disengagement.[55]

Going "the Last Mile for Peace"

Nixon and Kissinger had already conveyed an informal ultimatum to Hanoi via the Soviets. On July 15, the president, on Kissinger's advice, sent a personal letter imploring Ho Chi Minh to settle, as "delay" would only "increase the dangers and multiply the suffering."[56] They delivered the ultimatum repeatedly as they traveled abroad in late July and early August, giving friend and foe alike advanced warning of their intentions.

Historians typically remember Nixon's July 23–August 3 trip for his celebratory meeting with the Apollo XI astronauts after their momentous return from the moon, his Guam speech, and his stop in communist Romania. All were significant, but the president set out to do more than celebrate the moon landing, informally discuss America's commitments, and deliver a threat to Hanoi via Romanian intermediaries. He visited Saigon—the first such trip by a sitting president—to discuss strategy with Thieu. He also stopped in Thailand, India, and Pakistan to explain the Nixon Doctrine and US regional commitments. And he ended the trip in England discussing geopolitics, politics, and Vietnam with Prime Minister Harold Wilson. It was a wide-ranging and important itinerary that reflected Nixon's emerging problems at home, changing geopolitical realties, and his scheme to end the war quickly.

That summer, Congress challenged the administration on foreign policy. In June, senators overwhelmingly passed a nonbinding resolution stating that the president should consult the Senate before making new foreign commitments.

It thus excluded Vietnam, but the White House and US allies worried that it portended things to come. Already, the Senate Foreign Relations Committee was demanding that the administration reveal and explain its defense arrangements with Thailand and other nations lest a Gulf of Tonkin-like incident create another Vietnam. The Senate Foreign Relations Committee conducted its own international tours and investigations and promised hearings in the fall to review existing commitments.[57]

The day before his departure, Nixon spoke privately with senior officials and congressional leaders in the context of the debate over the surtax on individuals and corporations and the fiscal problems caused by Cold War and domestic spending. Participants noted the dollar's continued weakness, even though budget cuts and the surtax sustained its parity with gold. Those present identified foreign concerns over US debt and spending. At home, they observed an "inflationary psychology" that had Americans buying up things in anticipation of inflation and an end to the gold standard. Chairman of the House Ways and Means Committee Hale Boggs (D-LA) argued that the public did not understand the gravity of the situation: without tax and budget reform, America "faces a panic, a real panic. God knows what happens after that. I think we would have the most devastating depression under the most difficult set of social circumstances that have ever prevailed in our country. The disorientation in the cities, the conflict between the young and the old, the programs needed to rebuild our cities; all these would go down the drains. Our country would just be in one hell of a fix." Nixon agreed. He voiced support for "unpopular" but necessary financial legislation, and then explained the importance of his forthcoming trip.[58]

Nixon began by summarizing his understanding of the global situation. "As we look around the world today, we can of course find trouble every place we go." "I think all of us as we look at the world tend to have our whole view of the world somewhat obscured by the central problem of Vietnam." With Congress, he would seek "an honorable end to the war." But "beyond Vietnam and after Vietnam," the United States needed "preventive diplomacy" to avoid another such conflict. Nixon understood that a segment of popular and congressional opinion felt that "once we get out of Vietnam, then let's be sure we stay out of Asia as much as we can. . . . Leave Asia to the Asians." The president insisted that, as a Pacific power, the United States could not adopt such a position.[59]

Instead, it should adjust its grand strategy to new circumstances— financial and military overstretch, internal discord, anticipated Soviet strategic nuclear parity, and the rise of China. The United States would continue to provide a nuclear shield to its allies, but its friends must assume responsibility for the defense of their nations and their respective regions. South Korea, Thailand, Taiwan, India, and Japan were all models of what Asia could become with American support. The United States also needed to show interest in Eastern Europe, hence the Romanian visit. Nixon believed that "looking at the long road of history," Eastern Europeans would naturally gravitate toward the West rather than Russia. In doing so, there was "some hope for change" and gradual reform. "Looking down the long road," he concluded, American interests lay in furthering Asian economic development, having allies assume the burdens of national and collective defense, and opening "dialogue with Communist China." Détente with the Soviet Union was not worthwhile if it isolated China. Nixon ended by reaffirming that his trip would reassure America's friends about its resolve while explaining the limits of its power. In short, he sought to develop the structures of peace—détente and the Nixon Doctrine.[60]

The president departed on July 23 to share in the jubilation of the lunar landing and the Apollo XI astronauts' return, but his informal remarks in Guam two days later created an international stir. There he set forth his "perspective" on foreign policy. Noting allied fears of a US retreat from Asia, he emphasized that America was not getting out, only changing its methods. It would keep its treaty commitments, but Asians would have to shoulder the responsibility for their internal security. They alone would have to deal with insurgencies. "Where we must draw the line is in becoming involved heavily with our own personnel, doing the job for them, rather than helping them do the job for themselves," he reiterated. Henceforth America would pursue "a policy not of intervention but one which certainly rules out withdrawal." The United States would stay in Asia but it would avoid commitments that could produce another Vietnam.[61]

Historian Jeffrey Kimball rightly contends that Nixon's statement hardly represented a doctrine, but his extemporaneous remarks did reflect the core principles that guided his Vietnam and global strategies.[62] Alexander Haig recalled that the speech "sprang fully formed, unrehearsed and spontaneous, from the brow of Nixon. Nobody in the government had any advance warning that he was going to say what he said, and at first not even Kissinger was sure exactly what he meant."[63]

Throughout his career, Nixon had developed the principles he rehearsed in Guam. He harkened back to his first trip to Indochina in 1953 as well as his understanding of President Eisenhower's strategy for defending the Third World from communist aggression. America would build up noncommunist forces and let them do the fighting and dying while it provided financial aid and perhaps air and naval support. Nixon believed that deploying US troops to combat insurgencies was a recipe for political problems at home and allied dependency abroad.

During the 1968 campaign he had revived this old strategy as a "new diplomacy." "Economically, diplomatically, militarily, the time has come to insist that others must assume the responsibilities which are rightly theirs," he declared. "The other nations of the world must begin, and quickly, to pick up a greater share of the burden of common defense." Working on a major foreign policy radio address, "To Keep the Peace," speechwriter Ray Price noted, "It's time we made sure that in the future we help others fight their war, if necessary, but we don't do the fighting for them." In the finished speech, Nixon observed that Asian strength meant they could defend themselves without US troops. Only if this resistance failed would America intervene. He added that even European allies would have to contribute more to their collective defense. US partners would have to assume the burdens America could no longer afford, politically or financially. In short, he argued that recognizing the limits of American power and having self-sufficient allies were paramount to "ensuring that we have no more Viet Nams."[64]

Thus far, his Vietnam strategy had conformed to these tenets. He built up the South Vietnamese and began withdrawing the politically costly US soldiers while punishing the enemy with American airpower in Cambodia and Laos. The United States was not abandoning Vietnam any more than it was abandoning Asia. But domestic pressures dictated a change in strategic emphasis.

Nixon then stopped in Saigon on July 30 to demonstrate allied unity, highlight the capital's safety, and discuss with Thieu his plan to resume bombing North Vietnam. The South Vietnamese president explained that he was satisfied with the war's direction. Given time, his country would expand pacification, build popular support, broaden the government, and eradicate the Vietcong insurgents. As he understood it, Nixon could choose escalation "to speed up the war" or continue Vietnamization. Thieu decisively favored the latter, advocating a "long haul, low cost" policy that would strengthen South Vietnam while allowing gradual American disengagement. "You help us so we can take over more and more," he reasoned. He understood that the upcoming 1970 congressional elections weighed on the American president and that while a devastating air campaign against Hanoi might shorten the conflict, it could also destroy US domestic support. Thieu doubted the communists would ever give up their dreams of conquering the South, and he believed they had adopted a "fight-talk-fight" strategy so that they could endure a protracted war. Vietnamization would give the Republic the resources to do the same.[65]

Nixon thought escalation was the safer path. He had wearied of waiting for the other side to compromise. He knew American patience had limits. US troop reductions bought some time, and he also wanted withdrawal planning kept secret to leave the enemy guessing and prevent the doves from demanding more. Both leaders agreed that they had conceded as much as they could in Paris and that it was now Hanoi's turn. "We can't have you nibbled away," Nixon declared. "That is something that we are not willing to permit." He then impressed upon his host that the White House would set a three-month timetable for Hanoi to begin sincere talks. Should they delay, he would take steps "to force Hanoi to negotiate seriously." LBJ had failed to bring "the full might of USA air and sea power" against North Vietnam. Nixon again vowed that he "had no intention of going down in history as the first American president to have accepted defeat in a major war."[66]

Speaking publicly at Independence Palace, Nixon reiterated the war's geostrategic importance and affirmed that the allies had made their last concession. "I wish first to point out that what happens in Vietnam, the kind of peace that we are able to achieve in Vietnam, will have an enormous impact on the future of peace and freedom in all of Asia." Given the stakes for "all the people of the Asian area and, of course, the people of the world," he added, "We have gone as far as we can or should go in opening the door to peace, and now it is time for the other side to respond." Hanoi would be accountable for whatever suffering befell the North Vietnamese people because of its obduracy.[67]

Nixon's presence boosted South Vietnamese trust in the president even as the Guam speech reinforced their understanding that they would soon bear responsibility for their country's fate. Thieu's aides marveled at Nixon's confidence and private pledges, ending their doubts about his commitment to the Republic. That he and his wife had traveled to Saigon despite the threat of communist mortar and rocket attacks and that he apparently left most of the security arrangements up to the South Vietnamese deeply impressed his listeners. "If there were any doubts left in anyone's mind about the sincerity of the American commitment to Vietnam," commented the *Vietnam Guardian,* "those doubts were certainly dispelled." The paper recognized the Nixon Doctrine speech as equally important. "Just in case we had not got the message earlier, President Nixon has spelled out the situation for us in unmistakable terms: we're going to be on our own in the future," its editors noted. Other Asian nations reached similar conclusions.[68]

In Thailand, Nixon again affirmed America's commitments. Bordering Indochina, that nation was fighting communist forces in South Vietnam and Laos while dealing with its own insurgents. As historian Richard Ruth has noted, the Thai government, media, and public saw this "military action [as] necessary to maintain Thailand's stability and independence in the face of external aggression directed from Beijing and Hanoi." Given increasing congressional scrutiny, Thai officials assumed that Nixon would have to reduce US forces stationed there, and at the beginning of 1969 they were among those most concerned about an American withdrawal from Vietnam. Nixon's visit and rhetoric buoyed their faith in US resolve. He confirmed that America would honor its commitments while asking Asians to "shoulder the responsibility" for regional peace. He appealed to their national pride, arguing that "if domination by the aggressor can destroy the freedom of a nation, too much dependence on a protector can eventually erode its dignity." Nonetheless, he swore that America would defend Thailand from threats "abroad or within." His statesmanlike personal diplomacy yielded diplomatic dividends. An anonymous Ministry of Foreign Affairs official remarked in apparent praise, "He is not like a politician. He could be a lawyer or a university professor." Nixon's visit had calmed their fears.[69]

From Asia, the president traveled to Europe to reinforce his threats to North Vietnam while securing allied support for escalation. His Romanian stop demonstrated the tour's aim to move Eastern Europe toward the West and secure its help to end the Vietnam War. On August 2 and 3, he met with Nicolae Ceausescu, trusting that the communist leader would convey his determination to Hanoi. In their August 3 conversation, Nixon reviewed American peace overtures and North Vietnamese intransigence. "I never make idle threats," he averred. "I do say that we can't indefinitely continue to have 200 deaths per week with no progress in Paris." Should there be no movement by November 1—the anniversary of LBJ's bombing halt—he would adopt more violent means to end the war. As with the Soviets, he held

President Richard Nixon and National Security Advisor Henry Kissinger, February 1972. The pair had a similar outlook on geopolitics and diplomacy as well as a distaste for the Washington bureaucracy. White House Photographic Office (hereafter WHPO), #8391-08, RNPLM.

Nixon and Secretary of Defense Melvin Laird, January 1969. Nixon valued the Wisconsin Republican's political instincts enough to put up with his independence. Laird told me he always had Nixon's best interests in mind when he defied presidential orders or wishes. Photograph courtesy of the Office of the Secretary of Defense Historical Office. Special thanks to Ryan Carpenter for his help in acquiring the OSD images.

Kissinger and Laird—the "dueling Machiavellis." Photograph courtesy of the Office of the Secretary of Defense Historical Office. Credit goes to Laird biographer Dale Van Atta for the apt characterization of the pair as "dueling Machiavellis."

Nguyen Van Thieu versus the world, Honolulu, July 19, 1968. In Hawaii for a conference with Lyndon Johnson, the Republic's president faced wavering American resolve and indefatigable communist enemies. Photograph by Yoichi Okamoto, WHPO A6588-2A, LBJPL.

General Secretary Le Duan toasting China's Chairman Mao Zedong in August 1964. Having displaced Ho Chi Minh as de facto leader of the Democratic Republic, Le Duan committed his nation to forcibly unifying Vietnam under communist rule. No sacrifice would be too great, no war too long. Special thanks to Pierre Asselin for sharing this image.

Nixon discusses the Vietnam War, and presumably American troop reductions, with General Creighton Abrams, Chairman of the JCS General Earle Wheeler, and Laird on May 12, 1969. WHPO #1036-11A, RNPLM.

Nixon and Thieu announcing the first withdrawal of US forces. Midway Island, June 8, 1969. WHPO #1269-20, RNPLM.

The cover from the summer 1969 Duck Hook contingency plan. NSC 98:1, RNPLM.

Headed to Vietnam aboard Air Force One, Nixon discusses the war with Ellsworth Bunker, General Abrams, Marshall Green, and Kissinger. WHPO #1630-3a, RNPLM. Special thanks to Ryan Pettigrew for his help in acquiring this and other images from Nixon's July trip.

Bunker, Nixon, Thieu, Nguyen Phu Duc, and Kissinger at the Presidential Palace, Saigon, July 30, 1969. There, Thieu laid out his "long haul, low cost" strategy, whereas Nixon favored escalation and resumed bombing of North Vietnam. WHPO #1630-18, RNPLM.

Nixon and Thieu, Saigon, July 30, 1969. The alliance between the Republic and the United States had scarcely been closer than it was that summer. WHPO #1630-28a/29a, RNPLM.

Nixon also met with US troops serving in Vietnam. July 30, 1969. WHPO #1631-3a, RNPLM.

George Romney, Barbara Walters, and Nixon alongside stacks of congratulatory telegrams after the November 3, 1969, Silent Majority address. WHPO #2325-14a, RNPLM.

Nixon beaming at an October 31, 1970, political rally in Tennessee. Even after the Cambodian incursion, the president retained the silent majority's support, though he had lost critical ground in Congress. WHPO #4973-10, RNPLM.

Recently trained South Vietnamese forces preparing to return to their villages, circa 1970. Photograph by the US Information Agency. RG 306 #306-MVP-14(6), NA.

A member of the US 5th Infantry Division looks over the A Shau Valley in 1969. Vietnamization would prove a long and uncertain journey home for American servicemen. RG 111 11-SC-652473, NA.

out linkage as a carrot, arguing that peace in Vietnam would improve US relations with Romania, the Soviet Union, and China. "It will be a breakthrough to finding peace all over the world," he declared. After politely listening to Ceausescu's advice that a settlement would be forthcoming if America would only drop the Thieu regime, he repeated his warning. "We cannot and will not just pull out. Second, we cannot and will not continue indefinitely to talk in Paris with no progress and while the fighting continues in Vietnam." He would not accept an unelected coalition government and would resort to force if necessary to end the war on acceptable terms.[70]

That same day, Nixon stopped at the Royal Air Force station in Mildenhall, England, to meet with Prime Minister Harold Wilson. This understudied detour proved significant in two respects. First, Nixon hinted at the possibility of renewed bombing of North Vietnam and solicited British support. Second, the conversation at Mildenhall confirmed the quiet evolution of British policy on the war, as Wilson voiced his approval of American aims in Vietnam. In 1964 and 1965, he had disputed Johnson's claim that US credibility was on the line there.[71] He now argued that this was the case, and that the regional and global consequences of a precipitate American withdrawal that led to South Vietnam's collapse would be disastrous.

Whitehall had been developing this argument throughout 1969, and British officials impressed upon the prime minister the need to support the United States. They considered America's defense of South Vietnam vital to regional security. Asian nations needed to strengthen themselves politically and militarily with Western aid, recognizing that British and American intervention was unlikely. The Foreign and Commonwealth Office (FCO) noted that these regimes were far stronger than they had been, but they still wanted US and UK soldiers nearby, waiting in the wings to deter communist attacks.[72]

Events in Paris and Vietnam also influenced the prime minister. President Johnson had acted on his advice in adopting the bombing halt and opening the peace talks. Hanoi was taking advantage of both, and Wilson continued to insist that mutual withdrawal should be the basis of any settlement.[73] Meanwhile, British officials praised the Second Republic, Thieu's progress, and Vietnamization. They did not interpret Midway or the Guam speech as the beginning of an American sellout. They saw Vietnamization as Nixon's attempt to "buy time" at home while pursuing the military and diplomatic measures necessary to achieve a settlement. As the British ambassador to South Vietnam noted, there was a "long haul ahead," but the prospects were "good provided the Americans withdraw with patience and understanding."[74]

The US home front disturbed Wilson. He and other officials feared that "neo-isolationism" was on the rise and that defeat in Vietnam would encourage what they believed was an isolationist lobby in Congress.[75] Rather than seeing the Senate's national commitments resolution as part of a natural restoration of congressional prerogatives, Britons worried that American postwar internationalism was waning. Defeat in Vietnam would make things worse.[76]

Together, the 1968 bombing halt and negotiations, Hanoi's subsequent intransigence, Vietnamization, tentative British optimism on South Vietnam's survival, and fears of American neoisolationism prompted Wilson's conversion to something of a hawk. Nixon's formula for peace with honor matched what he had been advocating. The prime minister further believed a precipitous US withdrawal would undermine America's credibility while harming British interests in Asia. His support would grow stronger as Vietnamization progressed. The Mildenhall meeting provided a snapshot of this transformation. It also acted as an allied echo chamber, with Wilson's and Nixon's views reinforcing one another.

Although Kissinger briefed Wilson on the Nixon Doctrine, the president kept the meeting's focus on Vietnam. He informed the prime minister that "he was not hopeful about the prospects for the Paris talks, but that he had gone the last mile for peace." He argued anything other than peace with honor "would destroy the faith of Asian countries in America's sincerity and determination." Wilson "fully accepted this argument" and reasoned that "a withdrawal on such terms would cause consternation beyond the predictable countries," affecting the foreign policies of even nonaligned countries like India. The domino theory remained alive and well. Nixon added that defeat in Vietnam would start "a possibly uncontrollable move into isolationism, with consequences going beyond Asia," perhaps leading to an American retreat from Europe as well. Wilson expressed concern over US isolationism and its potential to cause the United States to reduce its military contribution to the North Atlantic Treaty Organization (NATO). Avoiding defeat in Vietnam while continuing prudent troop withdrawals seemed the safest course. He gave Nixon his support. It is not clear that he understood the implications of the American's tough talk, but Nixon concluded he would "back us all the way" if the situation changed after November 1. The president returned home confident his global tour had been a success. He left Kissinger in Europe to impress upon the North Vietnamese that he was deadly serious about his ultimatum.[77]

On August 4, Kissinger had his first secret meeting with North Vietnamese negotiators. The White House had sought private high-level talks for months, and the opening of this diplomatic front suggested that Nixon's resolve might be paying off. The president hoped that by avoiding the propagandistic public negotiations and cutting out the State Department and South Vietnamese, they could hammer out a deal. At this Paris meeting, Kissinger emphasized US concessions and a willingness to negotiate, but he made the threat clear: "If by November 1, no major progress has been made toward a solution, we will be compelled—with great reluctance—to take measures of the greatest consequences." North Vietnamese negotiator Xuan Thuy reaffirmed his country's willingness to continue fighting. His delegation remained steadfast in its demands for the prompt, unilateral withdrawal of all American forces from South Vietnam and the creation of a provisional government without Thieu. Unbeknownst to the Americans, Hanoi had opened this secret channel mainly "to delude American policymakers into thinking it wanted a diplomatic settlement" and thus preclude Nixon's escalation of the war, particularly a resumption of the bombing.[78] Nonetheless, Kissinger had delivered Nixon's ultimatum.[79]

Overall, Nixon's world tour announced a new era in US foreign relations even as the president sought the same ends—containment of communism and the preservation of US interests worldwide. His administration desired détente, but it would try to maintain existing commitments and seek an honorable end to the war. Everything hinged on a successful outcome in Indochina. Nixon had gone "the last mile for peace." Hanoi would have to act or suffer renewed bombing.

Drawing the Battle Lines

Upon returning home, President Nixon faced rising dissent. Midway provided only a temporary boost in popular support for the war. Due perhaps to Vietnamization, most Americans again backed Nixon's handling of the war, but according to Gallup 40 percent also considered Vietnam the nation's most important problem. Among those who thought about what to do next in Vietnam, only 10 percent favored escalation while 12 percent advocated an immediate withdrawal. To combat his perceived enemies in the media and build a base of domestic support for more militant measures, Nixon launched a "Presidential Offensive" that summer. He sought to create a "pro-Vietnam Committee" of prominent citizens who supported his policies and could serve as a visible counter to the antiwar protestors.[80] By August, his public relations offensive had made little progress on the home front.[81]

Military preparations for escalation had continued, though. "Plans for escalating the war were always lying on the shelf," recalled Kissinger aide Anthony Lake. Using old ideas, the military formulated what became Kissinger's "option to the right." Johnson had solicited JCS contingency plans like what Kissinger wanted, but he never acted on them because he feared such naked aggression would provoke Chinese or Soviet intervention. In the spring of 1969, Chief of Naval Operations Admiral Thomas Moorer secretly authorized his staff to revamp one such proposal for air and naval attacks against North Vietnam. Unlike earlier bombing campaigns, this option called for rapid, dramatic escalation, with air raids decimating North Vietnam's war-making capability and with naval forces imposing a blockade. Moorer's proposal, called Pruning Knife, satisfied the military component of Kissinger's strategy, and it became part of Duck Hook, which grew to include all of Pruning Knife's punitive measures but on a grander scale. Moorer claimed that the world would interpret Duck Hook "as a show of determination, whereas a year ago it might have been regarded as recklessness." Of course, Nixon and Kissinger's strategy was as much about demonstrating resolve as it was about inflicting military damage.[82]

Kissinger's staff integrated Duck Hook into Nixon's broader international scheme. Should Hanoi continue to prove intransigent at the bargaining table, an August 5 memo proposed the administration quietly halt troop withdrawals and present the ultimatum to North Vietnamese negotiators. If these measures failed to elicit a favorable response, the United States would use military escalation to "induce the other side to negotiate or erase their impression that time is on their side." Nixon had been pondering this strategy for most of the year; Kissinger now had a formal alternative to Vietnamization.[83]

As the two men moved toward an expanded conflict, they made a concerted effort to keep Laird and Rogers out of the secret negotiations and Duck Hook planning, lest either sabotage their plans through press leaks or bureaucratic resistance. When Kissinger met the North Vietnamese delegation, Secretary of State Rogers frantically told an aide, "I don't understand what's happening in Paris. Something's going on and I don't know about it."[84]

Laird experienced no such panic. Although Nixon and Kissinger "agreed not to tell Laird about the meeting in Paris," he knew of their machinations. Moorer, who was instrumental in Duck Hook's planning, reported his conversations with Kissinger, Nixon, and Haig to Laird. Laird also used his many contacts, particularly in the Army Signal Corps, to monitor White House deliberations, conversations, and trips. Knowing about the secret Paris talks and having some awareness of Duck Hook, he needled Kissinger about congressional interest in these contingency plans. For the moment, he let the president and Kissinger play their game of grand strategy and world intrigue. Meanwhile, he planned the second troop reduction and continued to use his position to de-escalate the American ground war.[85]

At the July 7 *Sequoia* meeting, Nixon had opted to review the mission statement and possibly change it to reflect a Vietnamization strategy, but a policy of American de-escalation and allied assistance rather than military pressure contradicted his aggressive stance with Hanoi. The president soon had second thoughts and attempted to countermand the order before the new mission statement went into effect on August 15. In typical Laird fashion, the secretary of defense sent a memo to Nixon, who was then relaxing in San Clemente. Unless he heard otherwise from the president, he would adopt the new mission statement. Attending to other matters, staff at the "Western White House" overlooked this seemingly trivial note. Receiving no response, Laird issued the formal order and officially announced the change just a few days later. He stated that Vietnamization was the Defense Department's "top priority" and that US forces were moving toward a supportive role in South Vietnam. He and the military also determined the size of the second withdrawal.[86]

As before, the numbers game began in Vietnam. After reviewing the Vietnamization criteria and the situation on the ground that summer, Abrams and his advisers proposed a redeployment of another 25,000 soldiers. Thieu was comfortable with this number, and all agreed that a gradual "cut-and-try" approach to withdrawals was the safest course. Militarily, there was growing optimism that if they maintained the present policies the enemy's destruction was "inevitable." Yet, Abrams and other MACV officials questioned whether modest reductions could pacify the home front. He fumed,

The situation in the United States, I mean—all these fine words of yours [about increasing the time between withdrawals] just doesn't make a *dent* in it. If we can manage somehow to keep this thing moving along, and putting out a few sops to the pressures that exist *there*—keep the *goddamn* thing from falling *apart*—then we will have done a *magnificent* job. The *pressures* are *fantastic!* And what you've got is a small group of about six advisors, pitted against *thousands.* Don't underestimate the thousands. That has to do with elections, and it has to do with a lot of things.

Vietnamization would buy time to continue the war, but US opinion and politics could decide South Vietnam's fate.[87]

Laird too appreciated domestic circumstances as he planned individual reductions as well as Vietnamization's longer timetable. That summer, he quarreled with Wheeler on what would happen to redeployed US forces. The general believed that geostrategic requirements and American credibility dictated their staying on active duty as part of the Pacific reserve. The secretary urged that they return stateside, some of them for deactivation, due to "the psychological benefits likely to be derived from the return of troops."[88]

He understood that public pressure would eventually require all US troops to leave Vietnam; there would be no large residual force as after the Korean armistice. Draft Vietnamization papers as late as August 8 assumed a residual American strength of over 250,000 soldiers. Although he backed the flexible "cut and try" approach to withdrawals, Laird ordered the JCS to prepare and equip the RVNAF to handle both PAVN and NLF forces. As for the second reduction, Laird acceded to Abrams's 25,000 proposal and urged Kissinger and Nixon to make the announcement before August 27. Delay would run into the Labor Day holiday and dilute its public impact. From origin to implementation, Laird's Vietnamization had the domestic audience in mind.[89]

Nixon chose to postpone the second troop announcement until sometime in September. The ostensible reason was Hanoi's intensification of the ground war that August. Thereafter, even Laird favored keeping the current troop ceiling because of heavy American casualties.[90] *New York Times* journalist Neil Sheehan saw through Nixon's rhetoric and identified his real reason for delaying Vietnamization. On August 24, Sheehan speculated that "the president hoped by a display of toughness on his own part to nudge the

North Vietnamese and the Vietcong into concessions at Paris."[91] "We have to impress Hanoi with our staying power or they won't negotiate seriously," confirmed an anonymous high-ranking administration official.[92] The delay completed the second phase of Kissinger's strategy. By postponing troop withdrawals, Nixon signaled his willingness to halt Vietnamization and escalate the war if North Vietnam did not make significant concessions by the November 1 deadline. The clock was ticking.

5

Come Together

The Decision against Duck Hook and for Vietnamization

September–November 1969

The debate over Vietnamization and Duck Hook came to a head during the fall. Before taking office, Richard Nixon had championed US airpower and local self-defense. Once elected, he faced difficult choices. He had made a token troop withdrawal and had promised more, though on a timetable apparently only he knew. He had intensified the war in South Vietnam, Cambodia, and Laos. He had threatened Hanoi with further escalation and set a November 1 deadline for serious talks. He had authorized contingency plans for renewed bombing of North Vietnam and delayed further troop withdrawals. He had bound his credibility as a decisive statesman (or mad president) to the threat. He had this one opportunity to get it right and "go for broke" in Vietnam.[1] Henry Kissinger later falsely claimed that he and Nixon "never examined [escalation] more than halfheartedly."[2] In truth, by September 1, everything was in place except for the final attack plan and presidential approval.

Escalation still hinged on the American domestic context. In late August, Haldeman reviewed Kissinger's plan and warned there would "be a tough period ahead if we go to it."[3] Congress increasingly scrutinized the Vietnam War, and antiwar forces prepared for an October 15 nationwide moratorium to show that the vocal minority of antiwarriors was actually a majority. "We want to make it clear that the 2 percent that people talk about on the campuses are really 70 percent—that they're not just 'crazy radicals' but your 'sons and daughters,'" the former head of Youth for McCarthy, Sam Brown, declared on June 30. As Nixon and Kissinger threatened Hanoi, the Vietnam Moratorium Committee imposed on the administration an ultimatum of its own by announcing this event three months in advance "to give the President some time to act." Congress and the protestors promised the White House no respite.[4]

Melvin Laird responded to these domestic pressures with Vietnamization. Congressional antipathy and antiwar protests lent credence to his arguments against Kissinger's escalation. The secretary of defense reasoned that Duck Hook could unleash violent unrest, congressional inquiries, and perhaps decisive cuts to war appropriations, while Vietnamization might sustain public support and provide the best chance of victory in South Vietnam. At a crossroads, Nixon confronted the most difficult decision of his first year in office: choosing a long, Vietnamized war or renewing the bombing of North Vietnam to compel a quick settlement.

September: Laird versus Kissinger

As the summer ended, Laird recognized that his strategy faced growing criticism from Nixon, Kissinger, and the military. In August, the president had postponed a second troop reduction to prove to Hanoi that American withdrawals were not inexorable and that he was serious about the November 1 ultimatum. After Labor Day, Laird urged him to make the second withdrawal announcement. Stalling the second reduction, he believed, had hurt Vietnamization's "momentum" and given the military an opportunity to whittle the numbers down. General Abrams had originally backed a reduction of 25,000 soldiers, but the Joint Chiefs soon argued that further redeployments "would involve significant risks" and that the United States should remove no more than 50,000 troops in 1969. Laird countered that, regardless of the diplomatic or military merits, delaying or canceling the second reduction was dangerous domestically because it gave "people the impression that we don't have a program." Without steady cuts, Americans would pressure the administration to terminate the war.[5]

In a September 4 memo, Laird recommended accelerating withdrawals. He warned the president against taking solace in the antiwar movement's recent quiescence; respite from criticism was likely "an illusory phenomenon." "The actual and potential antipathy for the war is, in my judgment, significant and increasing," he wrote. "We need demonstrable progress, and the prospect for continued progress, in Vietnamization to elicit continuing domestic support across a broad front. We need a positive and understandable program, even if its dimensions are not fully defined and are subject to change, which will appeal to the U.S. people." He agreed with the Joint Chiefs that a faster rate of Vietnamization risked the pacification and military gains, but he warned that slower reductions hurt them at home. "The necessity for support by the U.S. people is the overriding factor involved," he argued. With Chairman Wheeler's assent, he proposed the adoption of a twenty-four-month schedule to remove half of the American personnel in South Vietnam, leaving a residual force of around 267,500 until North Vietnam agreed to a mutual withdrawal.[6]

This tentative twenty-four-month reduction timetable was itself a major accomplishment. In June, Laird had concurred with the military that even a forty-two-month timetable to remove half of US personnel would interrupt pacification and that a faster withdrawal "could result in serious setbacks to the pacification program, a significant decline in allied military capability, and the possibility of a GVN collapse."[7] The dynamics on the ground had not changed his stance, but rather Wheeler's willingness to accept an accelerated schedule. Laird exploited every opportunity to push for faster and larger reductions.

Indeed, he entered the Pentagon with the desire to redeploy all American forces from Vietnam quickly and completely. "I want this [withdrawal program] to [leave] *zero* [US troops] on the ground," he told aides in early 1969. Since the military and the White House opposed such drastic reductions, he often proposed policies different from those he was developing. In the September 4 memo, he had supported a large residual force because he only offered what he believed he could sell to the JCS and President Nixon. At the same time, he left the timetables flexible so that he could accelerate withdrawals as domestic pressures mounted or as the hawks became more malleable. Buoyed by a recent trip to South Vietnam, Wheeler accepted the twenty-four-month schedule in late August. Laird pounced on this opportunity to speed up Vietnamization, and thus skillfully avoided a row with the military while advancing his agenda.[8]

In his September 4 memo, Laird also formally proposed a radical reorientation in Vietnamization policy. Antecedents of his program assumed the mutual withdrawal of US and North Vietnamese forces, leaving South Vietnam to grapple with only the insurgency. Few military experts believed that the Republic could fight off the PAVN main forces and NLF local units without significant US aid and military support. In August, President Nguyen Van Thieu considered 300,000 American troops a safe figure until North Vietnamese forces left Laos and South Vietnam.[9] MACV's views varied with the changing situation, but in September they agreed that Vietnamization could prepare South Vietnam to handle the insurgents but not the NVA. Abrams became increasingly concerned about the pace of Vietnamization.[10] "Somewhere in here you've got to prepare for *defeat, or* accept that you can't go any *further* [on withdrawals]," he growled. Laird disagreed and ordered the JCS to prepare and equip the South Vietnamese to handle both regular and guerrilla forces. He believed that the insurgency was a diminishing threat while ARVN forces were growing stronger. This planning was consistent with his desire to develop an exit strategy not predicated on the negotiated withdrawal of North Vietnamese soldiers. For Laird, Vietnamization constituted the most practical way of ending the US ground war before domestic pressures compelled a pullout. The United States could train and equip the South Vietnamese army to withstand its enemies, but it could not perpetually send its sons to fight alongside them.[11]

Kissinger, meanwhile, continued to favor decisive escalation. "We've been very forthcoming; we've attempted to make concessions which have been unrequited and I refuse to believe that a little fourth-rate power like North Vietnam does not have a breaking point," he asserted in a pep talk with aides. "It shall be the assignment of this group," he continued, "to examine the option of a savage, decisive blow against North Vietnam. . . . You are to sit down and map out what would be a savage blow." This "savage blow" would unleash enough firepower to force Hanoi's capitulation in a matter of days or weeks. Unspoken, though understood by all, was that anything longer than two weeks would precipitate a backlash at home that would encourage the North Vietnamese to continue waiting out the Americans. With his staff refining Duck Hook, Kissinger attacked Vietnamization from every possible angle.[12]

In his memos and conversations with Nixon, Kissinger reviewed the long history of excessive optimism about South Vietnam and warned that policymakers were deluding themselves about strengthening ARVN forces.[13] The South Vietnamese could not fill the gaps left by redeployed American soldiers, especially if US sentiment necessitated a faster withdrawal schedule.

Vietnamization would encourage Hanoi to "wait us out" rather than "make real concessions in Paris." Most important, he doubted that reductions would assuage the public. Moderates had now turned against the war, and any popular gains derived from withdrawals could easily evaporate, especially in the wake of the upcoming October demonstrations. "Withdrawal of U.S. troops will become like salted peanuts to the American public: The more U.S. troops come home, the more will be demanded," he wrote. "This could eventually result, in effect, in demands for unilateral withdrawal—perhaps within a year." Vietnamization would be a long process and the people would not afford them "this much time"; if anything, withdrawals sped up the clock. The president must seek other means to get an honorable settlement.[14]

Kissinger outlined possible options: keep the current strategy, focus on the talks, accelerate Vietnamization, or pursue military escalation while halting Vietnamization to coerce a negotiated settlement. He delineated the problems with the first three options, stressing again that, "*The fundamental problem is time.*" Negotiations assumed that North Vietnam would accept free elections and that the Republic would willingly cede some territory to the NLF to get a settlement; neither assumption was realistic.[15] He further emphasized that "accelerated Vietnamization would be a road to swift disaster," possibly undermining the Thieu government and giving the appearance that America was abandoning South Vietnam. He did not list the negatives associated with military escalation since he and his staff were ironing out its wrinkles. Reflecting on Kissinger's advice, Nixon began consulting other policymakers.[16]

At a September 12 meeting, the National Security Council took up the postponed second troop reduction and discussed other options in Vietnam. The president's explicit instruction to cut Laird and other Cabinet members out of his and Kissinger's planning meant that very few were aware of Duck Hook or Kissinger's recent memos.[17] Nixon used the meeting as a sounding board for the various alternatives.

The negotiations' prospects were grim. The North Vietnamese "have adopted a strategy of waiting us out," diplomat Philip Habib told the president. Hanoi's demands for an unconditional withdrawal of US forces and a coalition government in Saigon were incompatible with American objectives. North Vietnamese diplomats reacted to allied concessions with further intransigence. According to Rogers, the Democratic Republic reaped a public relations and propaganda bonanza by keeping the negotiations open, and the charade continued with little hope of real diplomatic progress.[18]

With the Paris talks at a standstill, Nixon surveyed the NSC's thoughts on military escalation "with all targets open," including the North Vietnamese levee system, the destruction of which would flood fields and villages. Generals Abrams and Wheeler openly questioned the effectiveness of such escalation. Kissinger was incredulous. "There is nothing that can hurt them?" he asked. "They can carry on," Abrams replied, to which Wheeler added, "There would be no fatal blow through seeking a no-holds-barred solution in a couple of weeks." Both men observed that Hanoi had used the bombing halt to harden its infrastructure against attack and that it had sufficient stockpiles to carry on the war in the South. Only a sustained air assault— something they knew the White House was unwilling to consider—could do any real damage. With two of America's top generals dismissing a two-week blitz, the council moved to other issues.[19]

Vietnamization was the final topic of discussion. With the public and Congress wondering if the administration had an exit strategy, Laird thought it imperative that the White House publicly outline its Vietnamization program. The administration did not need to give firm figures and timetables, but it must be proactive. "We have some time but we can't wait until the home front erupts," he warned. Nixon agreed that the withdrawals bought time, but he doubted they could pacify the doves. "There are three wars—on the battlefield, the Saigon political war, and U.S. politics," he noted. The allies were winning the first two and there was a "lull" in criticism on the third. Rogers chimed in that most Americans favored Nixon's policies, but he also backed Laird's assertion that they needed to convince the public that they were moving ahead with Vietnamization. He worried that any hint Nixon was pursuing military victory would destroy domestic support. "We need a plan to end the war, not only to withdraw troops," a disappointed Kissinger exclaimed, but this meeting was not the forum to elaborate his secret plan. The administration decided to continue its flexible approach to Vietnamization.[20]

The president announced on September 16 that the United States would withdraw 35,000 more troops by the year's end, but this statement did not preclude Duck Hook. The inability to halt Vietnamization demoralized Kissinger. Resignations on his staff that same month, many over his "whirlwind style of operation," weakened his ability to push his agenda in the White House.[21] Yet, Nixon's announcement served as another justification for bombing North Vietnam. In addition to US troop reductions, he enumerated his efforts to end the war peacefully. The United States would settle so long as there were mutual troop withdrawals and South Vietnam had the right to self-determination. "The time has come to end this war," he concluded. "Let history record that at this critical moment, both sides turned their faces toward peace rather than toward conflict and war." With the November 1 ultimatum on the horizon, Nixon and Kissinger wanted it known that they had made every effort for peace. If carrots failed to entice the North Vietnamese, they would brandish the stick.[22]

Nixon and Kissinger continued their planning unabated. In private, they agreed that "the long route cannot possibly work." "The doves and the public are making it impossible to happen," the president reasoned. Escalation appeared the surer path to an honorable settlement.[23]

On September 25, Wheeler forwarded Kissinger an updated draft of Operation Pruning Knife. According to its author, Admiral Thomas Moorer, the plan emphasized "the use of surprise and concentration of effort to achieve maximum practicable psychological and military impact." The emphasis was decidedly on the former, though, as he noted only a "sustained campaign" could inflict meaningful damage. Despite its concentrated attacks on North Vietnamese logistics, air defenses, and infrastructure, Duck Hook was simply too short.[24]

Late that month, NSC staffers Tony Lake and Roger Morris set forth their study of Duck Hook. They bemoaned the lack of analysis surrounding the plan: no one had adequately thought about Hanoi's possible reactions, much less what the United States hoped to achieve. Starting with Kissinger's assumption that only extraordinary violence would bring Hanoi to the negotiating table, they argued that the operation "must be brutal and sustainable" to succeed. North Vietnam had endured much, and its leadership would trust they could survive the bombing until US domestic pressure forced another halt. The pair avoided explaining what "brutal" or "sustainable" meant—no one knew what it would take to make the indefatigable North Vietnamese quit. They warned that the White House could face the choice of caving once again to antiwar critics and the enemy's resolute will or resorting to tactical nuclear weapons. Given the domestic and foreign risks involved, Lake and Morris urged the president to decide in advance how far he would go.[25]

Finally letting the secretary of defense in on the planning, Kissinger instructed Laird on September 30 to begin making "fresh" contingency plans. Nixon needed them "fairly quickly" because "the President has a foreign policy reason for wanting to do this." With the November 1 deadline set and military options beginning to pour in, Nixon ordered his staff to "stir up the hawks" in Congress and the media to support his leadership.[26]

The hawks had been relatively silent for most of Nixon's term. They had long favored something like Duck Hook, but they afforded the president the freedom to find an honorable path out of Vietnam. Given the mood at home, even a conservative like speechwriter Pat Buchanan feared that recruiting outspoken politicians to demand renewed bombing would inflame domestic sentiment. The press and the public believed the bombing halt and the troop withdrawals were irreversible. Should the White House change either, he warned, "all hell will break loose on the left." Congressional liaison Bryce Harlow was more optimistic, noting that a number of House Republicans were still all out for "total victory in Vietnam" and would support escalation.[27]

On September 30, Nixon disclosed to congressional Republicans that he was seriously considering military escalation. Knowing that they would leak, he intended the meeting to send a message to Hanoi and gain conservative backing for Duck Hook. He had overestimated their fervor. The president's talk "scared the hell out of me," an anonymous attendee recalled. Even among Republican hawks, such escalation had become politically inconceivable. Their constituents' attitudes had changed in the wake of Vietnamization from "let's win or get out" to "if we are going to get out, let's get out," reported the *New York Times*. At most, these declawed hawks would defend the president's aims and existing policies. After the White House meeting, only Senators John Tower and Barry Goldwater supported bombing North Vietnam if Hanoi did not soon demonstrate a willingness to negotiate.[28]

Nixon and Kissinger were undeterred. The latter was awash in memos and revisions related to Duck Hook. He expected that the president would act if the ultimatum passed without a favorable response from Hanoi. The national security advisor appeared poised to shatter both North Vietnamese resolve and Vietnamization. As he explained to Haldeman on October 2, "There's a lot to be said for winning."[29]

Early October: Choosing the "Long Road"

In October, the entire country seemed determined to influence Nixon's Vietnam strategy. Violent protests wracked Chicago. Congress debated legislation to end the war. And millions of Americans prepared to take October 15 off work and school to make a dignified stand against the war. Laird responded with Vietnamization. Kissinger sought another way out of Vietnam.

His October 2 memo on contingency operations was the ultimate expression of his strategy to end the war. Its length—some eighty pages—testified to how much time and attention he gave the plan. Of course, Duck Hook was a variant of what he had been pushing throughout the war: Hanoi would have a final opportunity to settle, but if it refused it would face the unrestrained fury of America's military might. Kissinger was not as crass as those hawks who shrieked, "Bomb them back to the stone age," but his aim and methods were little different.[30] Echoing Morris and Lake, he noted that if Nixon chose to proceed, he must do so with "a firm resolve to do whatever is necessary to achieve success." "*The action must be brutal.*" The president would have to convince North Vietnamese leaders that it was not a last, desperate gamble but a deliberate, relentless move that ignored the domestic political consequences.[31]

Disregarding the generals' concerns over the plan's brevity, the national security advisor concentrated it "into intense phases of short duration" so that it would last somewhere between four and eight days. While he deferred addressing the use of nuclear weapons, virtually everything else remained on the table. US air and sea forces would devastate the country's military and economic infrastructure while quarantining it with mines and a naval blockade. Rail lines, power stations, airports, factories, storage depots, naval vessels, and even the levees that protected North Vietnam's rice paddies and villages from devastating floods were potential targets. But the real bullseye was North Vietnamese society and will, with the hit list prioritized on the presumed "shock value" of their loss even as political buildings were off limits. "Considerable NVN civilian casualties" were a given. Isolated, hungry, and facing a myriad of hardships, the North Vietnamese people and leadership would bow to American wishes. In the interim, Nixon must not relent until they agreed to an internationally supervised mutual withdrawal from the South.[32]

Kissinger acknowledged Duck Hook's potential geopolitical ramifications and the likelihood that Soviet assets would be damaged or destroyed during the operation. American escalation could jeopardize détente and SALT—sacrifices he was willing to make. It also risked an expanded Cold War conflict. "We must be prepared to spill Soviet blood and to inflict damage to Soviet ships," he charged. Should they intervene and attack US air or naval forces, he argued, the latter should fire back and, in the case of air attacks, pursue their enemies. A third world war seemed doubtful, but Kissinger countenanced a global, reciprocal response to any Soviet interference.[33]

Above all, he saw Duck Hook as the means of ending the Vietnam War and preserving US credibility. Its benefits exceeded any diplomatic or domestic repercussions. Besides diminished North Vietnamese morale, he offered little evidence that Hanoi would buckle under the strain. As one staffer put it, Duck Hook was a "*fairyland* in terms of the projections." But it was Kissinger's fantasy and his alternative to Vietnamization.[34]

The moment of decision approaching, Laird went on the offensive. Although Kissinger's plan was similar to the air and naval attacks he had called for in the early 1960s, Laird believed that public sentiment would no longer tolerate massive escalation. The opportunity for that strategy had passed with the large-scale commitment of US troops in 1965 and the subsequent decline of popular support for the war. Vietnamization could both de-escalate the war and preserve South Vietnam so long as Kissinger did not delude the president into taking drastic military action.

As for Kissinger's attempts to hide his machinations from the secretary of defense, Laird's biographer Dale Van Atta correctly argued, "Any expectation that they could keep him in the dark was folly." His contacts monitored White House communications, and he had access to the deciphered cables from Hanoi's diplomats in Paris.[35] From his relationships with Wheeler, Moorer, and other top military leaders, he knew about Kissinger and Nixon's schemes well in advance of September 30. A master of the art of political intrigue, he let Kissinger play his hand before responding.[36]

In anticipation of November 1, Nixon ordered Laird "to start selling" the administration's Vietnam policy to the public, making clear that "we've gone as far as we should" and that Americans should stand with their president. Laird sold Vietnamization instead. Speaking to union members, he extolled its virtues. It was "something new" and "a major change not only in emphasis but also in objectives." No longer was the United States tied to a negotiated mutual withdrawal. Vietnamization would end the American war even if the talks failed since it developed the South Vietnamese military, economy, and security so that they could stand alone. Laird drew on the history of collective bargaining, reminding his audience that the United States needed to negotiate with persistence, perseverance, and from strength. Vietnamization provided the stamina to make peace possible. He appealed for labor's support. "I cannot promise a miraculous end to the war," he admitted. "But I can say to you that we are on the path that has the best chance of minimizing U.S. casualties while resolving the war in the shortest possible time without abandoning our basic objective."[37]

On October 8, Laird sent Nixon a memo attacking the JCS-Kissinger proposal. He began by noting that though hostilities on the ground had lessened, dissent had risen. He doubted the American public, economy, allies, or South Vietnamese society could sustain a significant escalation of the war. Such action would provoke demonstrations at home. "The plan would involve the U.S. in expanded costs and risks with no clear resultant military or political benefits," he cautioned. He supplemented his critique with a CIA analysis warning such an operation would little benefit the ground war and would exacerbate international tensions. Sticking with Vietnamization was the only feasible option.[38]

Kissinger and his staff dismissed Laird's evaluation of Duck Hook as a "smorgasbord of speculations, assertions and evidence." They disparaged him for ignoring the plan's psychological features and for failing to compare escalation with the disadvantages of maintaining the current strategy. Kissinger also criticized a JCS plan that lacked the *short, sharp military blows of increasing severity* necessary to compel Hanoi's capitulation. He could improve Duck Hook, but Vietnamization seemed hopelessly bound to internal pressures.[39]

Of course, Laird's strongest argument was always that domestic circumstances dictated troop reductions and precluded escalation, and events that fall seemed to confirm his wisdom. Congressional doves attacked Vietnam as an immoral, misguided, and endless war. Whether young student radicals or suburban housewives, more and more Americans agreed. Violent dissent and campus unrest were worrisome enough to White House officials, but the erosion of support among moderates in and out of Congress was truly alarming. Escalation would pour gasoline on a dangerously explosive fire.

Many historians have emphasized the October 15 Moratorium's role in killing Duck Hook, but Congress was even more critical to the president's decision.[40] As one contemporary noted, Congress was in an "anti-military mood." That summer, Nixon narrowly won the fight over continuing the ABM program with Vice President Spiro Agnew's tie-breaking vote in the Senate. Doves thought the battle "a small victory" that had demonstrated their ability to work together against military programs and the war.[41] Defense appropriations faced growing scrutiny. Laird was already pinching pennies at the Pentagon. He had cut NATO spending and reduced B-52 sorties in South Vietnam to relieve some of the budgetary pressures. "I am getting money short over here you know," he bemoaned to Kissinger in a September telephone call. "I am going to be very money hungry." Duck Hook would be too costly—financially and politically.[42]

As for Vietnam, Congress was increasingly dissatisfied with Nixon's efforts to end the war.[43] Doves like Fulbright refused to be "bought off" by Vietnamization. Frank Church (D-ID) and Mark Hatfield (R-OR) argued that it "would not be to get us out, but keep us in." The American war might continue another eight to ten years unless Congress acted. Members of Congress introduced eleven antiwar resolutions early that fall. One such proposal even tied troop reductions in Vietnam to America's total military manpower so that the authorized level of US forces would fall on a one-to-one basis with those leaving South Vietnam. Most resolutions simply called for a faster end to the conflict. Republican senator Jacob Javits of New York offered legislation to repeal the Gulf of Tonkin Resolution and withdraw all US combat forces by the end of 1970. The war had to end, he insisted, to restore "domestic tranquility and national unity." "With the mood of the nation once again outpacing the actions of the Congress, the time has come to move beyond mere exhortations. The Congress must face up to its responsibilities and capabilities for bringing an end to the war." His colleague Charles Goodell (R-NY) similarly proposed an amendment that would suspend war funding on December 1, 1970. Although Laird complained that senators should "start voting and stop talking" about the war, this chatter worried the administration. Doves lacked the numbers to reduce Vietnam appropriations, but Laird and Nixon feared that Congress might soon begin doing its own cutting.[44]

Attacking the war from the center and rallying doves in and out of Congress, Fulbright demanded that Nixon drop the Thieu regime for the sake of peace at home and abroad. He opposed Vietnamization. "When we say withdrawal, we are talking about the liquidation of this war," he explained. "Withdrawal is simply one of the means to that end." Conversely, Vietnamization perpetuated Thieu's rule and prolonged the conflict. The senator charged that the president's troop reductions amounted to "a nice opiate" intended to calm domestic dissent and buy Thieu and Nixon more time. This sense of time was a delusional side effect. He feared that "every day that this war goes on the *sickness* of American society worsens." He promised to hold televised hearings on the war as well as provide Senate counsel "to help [the] President in finding a way out of the Vietnam morass." Such "help" worried the White House. The symbol of the moderate antiwarrior, Fulbright applauded civil protest while ridiculing Nixon's efforts to snuff out dissent. "Rather than a moratorium on criticism, which kills no one, we who criticize continuation of the war seek, instead, a moratorium on killing," he told the Senate.[45]

The White House had anxiously watched the antiwar movement all year, and the upcoming Moratorium heightened fears that escalation would provoke severe unrest at home. In August and September, administration officials predicted unprecedented protests and polarization that fall. Early October demonstrations surrounding the Chicago trial of those allegedly responsible for the violence at the 1968 Democratic National Convention validated this concern. The trial of the Chicago Eight (later Seven) was a who's who of 1960s activism: Abbie Hoffman, Bobby Seale, Tom Hayden, Jerry Rubin, David Dellinger, and three others. The whole thing made for a captivating public spectacle inside the courtroom.[46] Outside, the bombing of a police statue as well as vandalism and wanton destruction marked these "Days of Rage." The small number of radicals present prompted one participant to comment, "This is an awful small group to start a revolution." Yet, as the activist-turned-scholar Tom Wells later contended, the "Days of Rage contributed to the growing sense of domestic crisis in America and fed both public and official perceptions that the war was risking social cohesion at home." Already officials believed campus unrest was "quickly reaching the proportions of a national epidemic"; now violence was expanding to the streets. Escalation in Vietnam would escalate the crisis at home.[47]

On October 13, NSC staffer William Watts warned Kissinger that Duck Hook was a military pipedream that would have serious domestic consequences. "The Nation could be thrown into internal physical turmoil," he wrote. "Widespread mobilization of the National Guard could become inevitable. . . . The Administration would probably be faced with handling domestic dissension as brutally as it administered the November plan." The fall disturbances were only a small indication of what the nation would face if Nixon inflicted savage blows on North Vietnam. The White House also understood that the protests encouraged congressional doves to propose antiwar legislation. In sum, congressional dissent and social unrest gave Laird's domestic arguments against escalation the ring of authenticity.[48]

Developments outside the United States also affected the president. After the summer offensive, the ground war entered another lull. American deaths in battle dropped from around 250 per week in mid-August to a two-year low of ninety-five in late September.[49] The lower number of casualties gave the appearance that the communists were de-escalating the war. Some observers, like Rogers, hoped the lull was a sign that the war would fade away by tacit, mutual withdrawal, but Nixon and Kissinger interpreted it as a political move to discourage them from acting on their ultimatum. Should the United States suddenly launch an intense air and naval campaign against North Vietnam, the administration would look like the aggressor, provoking dissent.[50]

Meanwhile, MACV had a renewed sense that it could see the light at the end of the tunnel. The allies were expanding their control of the countryside, and the RVNAF continued to grow in strength and confidence. Abrams believed the enemy was on the defensive and that the "cut-and-try" approach to withdrawals was working. His and General Wheeler's positive assessments added weight to Laird's argument that a sound Vietnamization program could succeed.[51]

Finally, Ho Chi Minh's death in September led to speculations about new leadership in Hanoi. Thanks to the enterprising research of Lien-Hang Nguyen and Pierre Asselin, historians now know that Le Duan, not Ho Chi Minh, was running North Vietnam during the American war years. Le Duan's rule and his determination had not changed in the slightest in 1969. But US policymakers misunderstood who had been ruling the DRV.[52] For them, Ho's passing could translate into a fresh start at the bargaining table. All indications were that Hanoi was hardening its diplomatic position, but again, Nixon would appear to have squandered an opportunity for peace if he attacked.[53]

Ho's death, Laird's and the military's doubts about Duck Hook's effectiveness, their faith in Vietnamization, and the domestic context caused the president to waver. He had been all for "going for broke" that summer, but in October, he increasingly felt that Vietnamization was the only option that could preserve his presidential standing, tranquility at home, and South Vietnam. Haldeman recorded on October 9 that Nixon "still is pondering the course. Does *not* yet rule out K's plan as a possibility, but *does* now feel [Vietnamization] is a possibility when he did not think so a month ago." Increasingly, he spoke of escalation as a response to some future North Vietnamese offensive rather than fulfillment of the November 1 ultimatum. Around October 11, Nixon postponed Duck Hook.[54]

This decision was clear in his October 11 meeting with Laird, Kissinger, and the Joint Chiefs. He originally called the gathering to improve the military's contingency planning, but he used it to confirm his emerging Vietnam strategy. Kissinger admitted that Hanoi had reduced the fighting in South Vietnam "to put us into a position where we cannot act" on the ultimatum. He implored Nixon to go through with Duck Hook anyway to cripple the North Vietnamese economy and will to fight. Instead, the president focused on time and domestic sentiment. "In Vietnam the real question is how long can we hold public opinion," he stated. Although he claimed that he would not allow congressional and popular pressure to sway him, his deliberations centered on these factors. Duck Hook offered to solve the problem of eroding public support through force and a quick end to the war. But when domestic and international developments made escalation appear too risky, Laird provided an alternative that could maintain domestic support and secure American aims in Vietnam.[55]

As the meeting continued, Nixon chose Vietnamization. Having just returned from South Vietnam, Wheeler expressed optimism about the war and the RVNAF.[56] Nixon agreed "that if we hold the line politically Vietnamization will work, provided we have time to do it deliberately." He trusted that Americans would support a sound program of withdrawal and that he could maintain public support for the remaining US combat units for about a year. The student radicals alienated most Americans, he noted, but Congress presented a difficult "purse problem." Vietnamization would be a perilous "long road," requiring time, money, and public patience. "If the Congress cuts appropriations then we are finished," he said. "Now this is a problem, Mel. Do you think we can hold that long?" Laird responded that they could get money now, and then in eighteen months US forces would not be engaged in ground operations, removing American casualties as a political issue. Vietnamization "will work if we stick to it."[57]

Conversely, Laird and Wheeler criticized Duck Hook. Both men warned that it would take longer than two weeks of bombing to break Hanoi's will; Laird speculated "at least a year." Given the predicted backlash, it would be better to stick with Vietnamization. When Wheeler affirmed that Duck Hook was too short to accomplish military objectives, Nixon countered that he had missed the point. The purpose of the two-week campaign was to achieve the maximum psychological effect in North Vietnam while minimizing civilian casualties and destroying North Vietnam's ability to wage war. Nixon and Kissinger hoped this shock and awe campaign would break the stalemate in Paris. The president emphatically instructed Laird, "*We must keep the Air and Navy forces available*" should Hanoi remain intransigent after the November 1 deadline passed.[58]

Yet, Nixon quickly returned to Vietnamization. He summarized his strategy. He would not abandon South Vietnam, but he would seek to end America's Vietnam War by gradually removing US combat troops while building up the RVNAF. "If there is a chance that Vietnamization will work we must take this chance," he concluded at the meeting. But he would retain the "option to do more." Contingency plans would await a suitable provocation. The administration would put Vietnamization first and use a scheduled November 3 speech—initially intended to announce the beginning of Duck Hook—to build domestic support.[59]

Why did Nixon abandon Duck Hook? He and Kissinger had told so many allies and enemies about his ultimatum that he knew he would forfeit his credibility. When Hanoi called his bluff on November 1, it would be clear he had backed down. He could (and would) continue making threats, but he would be foolish to think that foes would believe him. Fear of Duck Hook's domestic cost moved the president away from Kissinger's plan. Congressional and antiwar dissent were inescapable in October. Moreover, he likely understood that no two-week air and naval campaign would compel the North Vietnamese to quit. It would thus involve the greatest of risks with a limited chance of success. He first wavered. Then, timely as ever, Laird (with the Joint Chief's backing) offered similar ends with different means: Nixon would not surrender to Hanoi or the protesters but would patiently prepare the Republic of Vietnam to stand on its own. Vietnamization appealed to his philosophy of allied responsibility and his self-image of being the resolute statesman who was unafraid to take a perilous "long road." He shelved Duck Hook.

Knowing he had lost, Kissinger grew despondent. To improve his influence with the president, he interjected himself into the Oval Office. Haldeman recorded that after October 11 Kissinger became a nuisance to the president, who then wanted to cut him out even more. Nixon at times reconsidered his plan of extreme threats. But Duck Hook and an end to unilateral US withdrawals were no longer under consideration. For the remainder of the month, Nixon appeared to take the hard line even as he accepted Vietnamization.[60]

Late October: Taking a Stand

Ruling out escalation created problems for the White House. With the ultimatum still in effect, Nixon and Kissinger sought some action to convince the communists of their sincerity. It was a long shot predicated on Nixon's credibility as a mad president, but they hoped it might yet achieve a settlement that year. The president also needed support for the "long road," especially after millions of Americans registered their discontent during the Moratorium.

That event magnified domestic sentiment as a foreign policy consideration and increased Nixon's reservations about escalating the war. Antiwar leaders scheduled it for Wednesday, October 15, and they envisioned it as a national mass protest that would appeal to moderates. Historian Melvin Small summarized their vision: "On that day, people would participate in a moratorium from work or school for anywhere from a few minutes to several hours to register their opposition to the continuation of the war at rallies, marches, vigils, prayer sessions, or by leafleting and participating in whatever activities local moratorium committees organized." Around 2 million people participated. "So many of these folks—far from being professional liberals or agitators or youths simply trying to avoid the draft—were pure, straight middle-class adults who had simply decided, in their own pure, straight middle-class way, that it was time for the U.S. to get the hell out of the war in Viet Nam," noted a Chicago journalist. Their orderly protests were a stark contrast to the violent demonstrations that had defined the antiwar movement for many Americans. The intimate, local gatherings of earnest students, mothers, workers, former soldiers, and politicians were sobering. One housewife found it cathartic. "When I went to that meeting this morning, I believe that I was emotionally committed. Now it is more than that. I've enlisted," she confessed. *Time* magazine's post-Moratorium cover asked the question on everyone's mind: "What if we just pull out?"[61]

The Moratorium's coverage and subsequent polling, as well as the participation of family members, reinforced policymakers' conviction that the American public would not tolerate escalation of the war. With good reason, *Life* magazine hailed the Moratorium as "the largest expression of public dissent ever seen in this country." The decorum and large turnout made it a focal point of media attention. "No other antiwar activity either before or after the October 15 Moratorium was treated so generously and favorably by the networks," Small concluded. Gallup found that afterward 55 percent of Americans considered themselves doves. Adding weight to Kissinger's "salted peanuts" argument, 45 percent said they wanted faster troop reductions, and 56 percent backed Senator Goodell's proposal for all US forces to be out by the end of 1970. For many officials, this sentiment came home. Laird, Watts, Lake, and others had children or spouses who participated in the day's protest.[62] "Nixon cannot escape the effects of the antiwar movement," *Time* aptly observed.[63]

The president felt he had to do something to show that he would not be cowed by the protests. He grounded strategic aircraft to feign preparation for a nuclear offensive before ordering aggressive military exercises that simulated such an attack against the Soviet Union. Laird believed an already scheduled maneuver was sufficient, but Nixon demanded he go through with both exercises.[64] Nixon later wrote that by lending credence to the idea that public opinion limited his options, the Moratorium "had probably destroyed the credibility of my ultimatum to Hanoi." He hoped this threatening posture would rebuild that credibility while underscoring his unpredictability.[65]

With the nuclear alert in the background, he played the madman role to the hilt. When Kissinger met Dobrynin, Nixon instructed him to shake his head and say, "I am sorry, Mr. Ambassador, but he is out of control. . . . You don't know this man—he's been through more than the rest of us together. He's made up his mind and unless there's some movement" there will be dire consequences. The president also ordered Laird to hit the DMZ and Cambodia with air strikes so that the North Vietnamese "know we are getting trigger happy." He vainly hoped these bold actions would intimidate Hanoi and its Soviet patrons, but his strategy remained Vietnamization.[66]

On October 17, Sir Robert Thompson encouraged Nixon to stick with Vietnamization. His opinion mattered because his counterinsurgency ideas were credited with helping the British defeat a communist revolt in Malaya. His early 1969 book, *No Exit from Vietnam,* had argued that the situation in Vietnam was "almost to the brink of defeat" when Nixon had assumed office. In that book and his meetings with the president, he urged the White House to adopt a "long haul low cost strategy" instead of resuming attacks on North Vietnam. Nixon and Kissinger nonetheless sought his views on the "option to the right." Their dilemma was "a problem of time": Vietnamization would work "given sufficient time," Kissinger noted, "but if we're being squeezed, a bold strike might help." Though Thompson believed "the future of Western civilization was at stake" in Vietnam, he told the Americans that "he would rule escalation out." It would turn US and world opinion against the administration and would not help South Vietnam stand on its own. Even a bold, surgical strike like Duck Hook carried far greater risks than possible benefits. He assured the president that Vietnamization could produce allied victory in two years. Nixon asked him to travel to South Vietnam to ascertain whether such optimism was warranted and whether they were pursuing Vietnamization properly. Above all, Thompson's enthusiasm provided the strategy a significant endorsement.[67]

Kissinger's doubts remained. When the Vietnam Special Studies Group (VSSG) convened on October 20, the participants noted the need for better analysis of Vietnamization.[68] With "big decisions coming up," Kissinger argued, the White House needed it soon to "settle debates," and his staff contributed to this process. On October 21, Morris and Lake questioned whether any option could save the Republic of Vietnam. They believed that public opposition to the war "will grow quickly, and that 'Vietnamization' will not significantly slow it down. We believe that the dangers of our course to domestic cohesion will begin to outweigh *any* foreign policy interest in Southeast Asia." "In the long run," they concluded, "'Vietnamization' will become unilateral withdrawal." Kissinger shared their criticism of Vietnamization with the president while also attacking the assumptions underlying the program. He also disagreed that the South Vietnamese could replace redeployed US troops and that Vietnamization would mitigate public opposition to the war. He doubted the US government's ability to maintain unity at home for the long haul.[69]

A decisive military campaign against North Vietnam remained the most attractive option to Kissinger. With the president's authorization, he drew up plans for three-, seven-, and fourteen-day air strikes, but he now predicated their implementation on escalation by the enemy, not diplomatic intransigence. The ultimatum would expire not with an assault on North Vietnam but with a speech designed to unite the home front.[70]

Nixon's November 3 "silent majority" speech followed his shift from escalation to Vietnamization. It derived from a hawkish national address originally intended to rally Americans behind Duck Hook; Kissinger had even attached a militant draft to the plan. According to the September 27 draft, the president was to deliver the speech after the United States had taken "swift, concentrated, and punishing" military action against North Vietnam.

He would remind the American people of his peace overtures while blaming Hanoi for "prolonging this tragic war." He would then announce that he had made the "inescapable" and "irreversible" decision to bomb North Vietnam. "Further intransigence by [North Vietnamese] leaders would only compound their agony," he would warn. Like his oft-stated promise not to be the first American president to lose a war, he would declare, "I was not elected to preside over the senseless attrition of American lives by a deluded foe." A later version made clear that Vietnamization was only a demonstration of good faith and not a definitive program. As Nixon moved away from escalation, so too did the speech's emphasis.[71]

With Duck Hook no longer under consideration, the message shifted toward perseverance and domestic solidarity. The renumbered "first" draft reaffirmed America's commitment to South Vietnam and kept much of the preceding content but acknowledged the lull in fighting and explained Nixon's decision not to escalate the war.[72] If anything, this version merely affixed a different ending to the original Duck Hook draft. With the Moratorium, subsequent revisions focused on dissent and presidential leadership. "The public debate should be judged not by how loudly voices are raised, but how clearly and courageously the real issue is faced," the October 15 draft added. Americans would have to persevere in Vietnam and end the conflict honorably; giving into "a vocal minority in the streets" would only undermine the nation's "future as a free society" as well as its credibility abroad. In light of the Moratorium's sizable participation, newer versions adopted a softer tone while still pleading for unity. Nixon would conclude the speech by promising, "And we will *have* that peace, my fellow citizens, if we seek it together—unified and determined—for Hanoi will then know it has no choice but a negotiated peace." Domestic unity would be the address's major theme, but with escalation on hold, the speech lacked a reason why the public should support Nixon's war.[73]

Presidential advisers divided over the speech's new direction. Kissinger continued to push for "a very hard line" similar to the September draft but with references to the bombing campaign removed. The speech would proclaim that the communists and public opinion would not bully US policymakers into eschewing military force or abandoning South Vietnam. Initially, Nixon had left Laird and Rogers out of the drafting process, but after canceling Duck Hook he solicited their advice. Although he claimed to do so "only for cosmetic purposes," their input proved critical. Rogers wanted the address to emphasize a "sober and compassionate" government that understood domestic needs as well as the suffering the war caused. Nixon should stress the opportunity for peace at Paris and encourage the North Vietnamese to respond in good faith. Until they did so, he should continue with Vietnamization but leave a small residual force until Hanoi agreed to mutual withdrawal. Still others sought to highlight Nixon's efforts to de-escalate and peacefully end the war apart from the Paris talks, perhaps even adding a date for the last US withdrawal.[74]

Laird insisted that Vietnamization should be the speech's theme. Despite Nixon's initial reservations about his help, he proved decisive. He reasoned that a viable Vietnam strategy must not expand or escalate the war, alienate allies, undermine other commitments, or destroy South Vietnamese society. Instead, it should continue the war at a tolerable cost and maintain domestic support. Only Vietnamization "meets these criteria," he told the president. "It is still my firm view that your policy of Vietnamization should occupy the main portion of your remarks and the thrust should be: 'We have a program; and we are moving.'" Showcasing its merits, Nixon would try to convince the public that "Vietnamization is a positive program to transfer to the South Vietnamese responsibility for *all* aspects of their own affairs." Laird's draft tied Vietnamization to the broader Nixon Doctrine. It was both "an end and a beginning: an end to the American involvement in Asian combat and the beginning of our new policy for peace in Asia." By building up the South Vietnamese military while withdrawing troops, it would end America's war without sacrificing US objectives in Southeast Asia. In short, it was a vital part of Nixon's policy to defend Asia with American arms and financial aid rather than with its soldiers. Nixon later claimed that Laird had contributed little to the speech. "I wrote the whole damned speech," he growled to Kissinger. That was untrue.[75]

Best remembered for its appeal to the "great silent majority" of Americans who were not protesting the war, the November 3 address firmly established Vietnamization as the administration's strategy. Nixon hailed it as "a plan which will bring the war to an end regardless of what happens on the negotiating front." Contrasting it with those that would have the United States immediately withdraw from Vietnam, he reiterated, "[Vietnamization] will withdraw all of our forces from Vietnam on a schedule in accordance with our program, as the South Vietnamese become strong enough to defend their own freedom. I have chosen this second course. It is not the easy way.

It is the right way." He made clear that he would "not hesitate to take strong and effective measures to deal with" any attempt by the enemy to take advantage of American withdrawals by launching a new offensive. Nonetheless, he emphasized the administration's peace overtures and its adoption of Vietnamization as its strategy of choice. The address also marked a fundamental change in postwar foreign policy. On Laird's suggestion, Nixon declared that Vietnamization would end one war while the Nixon Doctrine would work "to prevent future Vietnams." America would keep its commitments, though at a reduced cost. The absence of militant rhetoric and the positive references to Vietnamization symbolized Laird's victory over Kissinger.[76]

Laird's faith in Vietnamization, Duck Hook's obvious shortcomings, and events that fall had caused Nixon to abandon Duck Hook. "I began to think more in terms of stepping up Vietnamization while continuing the fighting at its present level rather than of trying to increase it," he later wrote.[77] Instead of acting on his ultimatum, the president chose to pursue a long, Vietnamized war. On November 3, he asked a "silent majority" of Americans to come together and join him on "the long road." It had been a hard decision and it was a turning point in the Vietnam War. Barring a diplomatic breakthrough, Vietnamization would remain administration policy. Laird had scored a decisive victory that would determine America's role in Vietnam for the next three years.

6

Give Me Just a Little More Time

The New Optimists

November 1969–March 1970

Late 1969 and early 1970 was a period of cautious optimism in America's Vietnam War. Informed opinion generally agreed that the political, social, and military challenges were manageable. Vietnamization had stanched dwindling US support for the war and proven a popular choice for its continuation. In Indochina, it appeared to offer a successful strategy that would eventually allow the Republic to stand on its own. American officials and other observers indeed grew so buoyant by early 1970 that one journalist dubbed them "the new optimists."[1] These positive reports were snapshots of a fluid situation. Vietnamization might provide the basis for an allied victory, but the war was far from over.

The "Great Silent Majority": Vietnamization as a Political Panacea

Richard Nixon had long appealed to a silent majority of Americans, but as he prepared his November 3 address, he doubted he could rally the people. He knew he was no Jack Kennedy. "Let me make this one point, some public men are destined to be loved, and other public men are destined to be disliked," he told CBS interviewer Mike Wallace during the 1968 campaign. "As far as the charisma and all the PR tricks and everything else that's supposed to make you look like a matinee idol, forget it. If that's what they want in a president, I'm not the man."[2] Lacking personal magnetism and knowing that the public and the news media expected him to announce some diplomatic breakthrough, Nixon approached November 3 with dread.

His aides had doubts too. "Problem is there won't be [a breakthrough], and the letdown will be tremendous," Haldeman recorded. It is "obvious [journalists] are intentionally building him up for the biggest possible fall. Even the stock market is soaring on peace hopes." The chief of staff prepared for damage control and predicted "a massive adverse reaction" that might continue into the scheduled November antiwar protests "with horrible results." Moments before Nixon began to speak, Kissinger told journalists, "Probably nothing that we have done since we came into office has been done with as much seriousness, I may say with as much anguish, as this speech." As the president sat before the cameras, he resolutely defended South Vietnam, but he doubted that his fellow citizens shared his concern for this faraway land.[3]

He did not expect the "great silent majority" to rush to his defense after the speech.[4] Had he believed this group really existed, he would have gone through with Duck Hook. Instead, he solemnly braced himself for disappointment. He had failed to deliver "peace with honor." Vietnamization promised only a longer war.

Yet Nixon, his speech, and his policies proved surprisingly popular. Vietnamization was paying political dividends even before the November 3 speech. Opinion surveys revealed that 80 percent of Americans were "fed up and tired of the war," yet most opposed any decision to "cut and run." *Time* reported that "half of the general public would be willing to back Nixon in one last attempt to escalate and win." A solid majority desired peace with honor and supported the president's rate of US troop reductions and his aim of ensuring South Vietnam's right of self-determination. And the political stakes were enormous: 67 percent "said that they would oppose him if the Communists took over the South Vietnamese government." Despite their war-weariness, Americans remained "unwilling to quit" in Vietnam.[5]

The silent majority address fortified this consensus. Rising dissent, as seen in the October Moratorium, led many Americans to think that their neighbors and coworkers must be turning against the war, creating something of a bandwagon effect. When Gallup asked that October, most responded with what they thought was the acceptable answer: they said they were doves.[6] But the president's speech reflected what most were feeling: frustration at the antiwar movement and the stalemate in Vietnam. Little wonder that Merle Haggard's country ballad against the antiwar and counterculture movements, "Okie from Muskogee," rapidly climbed the *Billboard* charts that fall.[7] Nixon's acknowledgment of a patriotic "silent majority" encouraged them to express their hostility toward dissent. The speech's emphasis on Vietnamization also promised a way out of Vietnam.

Immediately after the address, the supposed silent majority told pollsters as much. Seventy-three percent of Americans considered themselves part of the silent majority. Around eight in ten supported the president's plan for ending the war. An equal number accepted Vietnamization, and 39 percent said they would back it for as long as it took to develop South Vietnamese defense.[8] Among those who heard the address, only 6 percent remained dissatisfied with Nixon's handling of the war. In general, the percentage of those unhappy with his Vietnam policies dropped from 32 to 25 percent. The October 15 Moratorium may have been a law abiding, orderly protest, but 72 percent agreed with Nixon that it was "harmful to the attainment of peace." Even after the initial fervor had dissipated in December, a sizable majority of Americans still backed Nixon's handling of the war as well as the timing and pace of troop reductions. Photographed surrounded by stacks of congratulatory telegrams, Nixon was uncharacteristically euphoric. "The President feels that he is in pretty good shape on Vietnam," Kissinger told Laird. "He thinks he has the doves for once."[9]

Nixon sought to consolidate this "solid base of public support." He instructed administration officials and congressional Republicans to increase the momentum by praising Vietnamization's progress and deriding critics. He unleashed Vice President Spiro Agnew on both the media and protestors. Nixon and Haldeman believed that, despite his crudeness and vitriol, he said "what people think." Agnew had so cowed the television networks that they refrained from covering the mid-November demonstrations live. GOP leaders saturated media outlets, though, defending Nixon's policies. With the White House's blessing, young billionaire Ross Perot bought up hours of commercial time and sponsored a television program to highlight the plight of American prisoners of war (POWs) and encourage individuals to support the president.[10] Responding to Kissinger's entreaties, even Democrats like former Vice President Hubert Humphrey and former Secretary of State Dean Acheson publicly applauded the president's policies. Impatient with those who unfairly criticized Nixon, Acheson contended in a November 4 interview that "the plan he laid out last night is the best plan anyone has ever thought of yet as to how to deal with this problem." Vietnamization and Nixon's moderation won over the masses and the moderates.[11]

With the second Moratorium scheduled for November 15, the White House sought to enlist the silent majority in nationwide counterdemonstrations. Veterans Day (November 11) became the occasion for "a special Week of Honor and Dedication" for soldiers' sacrifices in the quest for peace. With celebrity comedian Bob Hope acting as chair, "national unity week" sought to foster patriotic sentiment and endorse Nixon's war policies. White House aide Bryce Harlow believed that by flying or carrying the American flag, countless citizens could show national unity and thus counter the Moratorium's divisiveness. "In all likelihood," he argued, "the display of flags would be so widespread that it would more than counterbalance all other forms of demonstration, including the March in Washington." Veterans Day observances became symbols of pro-Nixon sentiment, and a "Freedom Rally" at the Capitol drew 15,000 participants. Overall, Nixon's address and the subsequent public opinion offensive galvanized grassroots support for the long road ahead.[12]

The antiwar movement responded with its own dramatic show of force. The November 13 "March against Death" in Washington had 45,000 participants. The Moratorium two days later drew nearly half a million demonstrators to the Capitol. These events marked a turning point.[13]

Thereafter, the key group behind the Moratoriums, the New Mobilization Committee to End the War in Vietnam, began to disintegrate as radical militants tried to turn the movement away from large demonstrations and toward acts of civil disobedience. This radicalization drove the antiwar movement to the political fringes. As a result, the planned December Moratorium attracted few protestors. Even the mid-November revelation of the brutal March 1968 massacre of Vietnamese civilians by American soldiers at My Lai failed to provoke an antiwar crisis within the United States. In December, the administration implemented a lottery system that made the draft more transparent and equitable, thus removing it as a major issue. With the antiwar movement sputtering, Nixon had one more reason to celebrate.[14]

The president's congressional critics were similarly on the defensive after November 3. The House of Representatives overwhelmingly passed—333 to 55—a resolution commending his efforts to end the war. His silent majority address dejected those antiwar senators who had hoped he was going to announce further de-escalation or a cease-fire. The doves lacked cohesion, a consensus on an alternative, and the will to challenge the president. Senate doves needed majority leader Mike Mansfield (D-MT) to join their antiwar cause, but Vietnamization and the silent majority address left him reticent to do so. Instead, he privately promised to help Nixon in Congress. When the Senate Foreign Relations Committee resumed in early 1970 its hearings on the war, observers noted that they seemed devoid of acrimony or passion.[15]

Nixon's efforts to occupy the middle ground led congressional doves to begin disassociating themselves from the Moratorium protestors even before the movement's radical turn. In part, this development stemmed from the surge of public support for the president. Fulbright's mail ran 2-to-1 in favor of Nixon immediately after the speech and about 1-to-1 thereafter, with a continued slight preference for him. "The President has mesmerized the country for the present," the Arkansas senator wrote Arthur Schlesinger Jr.[16] The Democratic National Committee similarly observed that Nixon had "accurately gauged the sentiments and attitudes of the American people." His resolve and the Vietnamization strategy were popular. Its research revealed that despite winning the closest of presidential elections in 1968, Nixon had gained the support of most Americans.[17]

His popularity derived from his policies. The silent majority speech seemed to be more than empty rhetoric. Americans saw his earnestness, his behind-the-scenes efforts to end the war, and especially his commitment to bring the troops home with honor. Altogether, the troop withdrawals, draft reform, and reduced US casualties alleviated domestic pressure. And Vietnamization held out the promise of victory in Vietnam. Should that strategy fail militarily, Americans were reassured that with the South Vietnamese assuming the burden of the war, their kin would not be dying in Indochina. To sustain this momentum, Nixon on December 15 announced a third troop reduction; another 50,000 men would return home by April 15, 1970. By year's end, pundits and policymakers agreed that the president had built an impressive base of political support. For the moment at least, the countdown against the war had stopped. "For the first time in my experience with Vietnam, I now was certain that time was working on our side," Kissinger informed Dobrynin in late December.[18]

American opinion remained a critical factor. Reduced casualties and troop withdrawals eased public pressures, but they could also threaten military progress in South Vietnam. As Kissinger had warned, reductions were a sort of political elixir that created the temptation to use them both to quiet dissent and buttress the president's standing. "We were under immense domestic pressure to give an appearance of a kind of steady diminution of the American role," White House adviser Ray Price recalled. "And we had to keep bringing troops out at a pace which would sustain that appearance. The appearance became as important as the fact in the U.S." Although 1969's withdrawals had been prudent, political necessity might override a sound schedule. Moreover, Nixon conceded in a January 1970 press conference that the "policy of Vietnamization is irreversible." He recognized that he could not stop troop reductions.[19]

Congressional opinion also remained fluid. Congress had only briefly suspended its criticism. In mid-December, the Senate began using the power of the purse to curtail America's commitments in Indochina. The resulting Cooper-Church amendment restricted military aid to Laos and Thailand while forbidding the use of American ground forces in those countries. As a former congressman, Laird understood that Congress would soon target Vietnam appropriations. He warned the military, South Vietnamese, and the White House that though diminishing public support was no longer a problem, congressional budgetary constraints could restrict US operations in Vietnam. What he called the "budget realities" threatened Vietnamization and became his overriding concern.[20]

Nevertheless, Nixon ended the year on a high note. His November 3 speech had marked a critical moment in America's Vietnam War. He had made clear that his administration was staying in South Vietnam, and the response to his address demonstrated that a majority of Americans was similarly committed to ending the war with honor. Vietnamization gave them hope that Nixon could end the American fighting while preserving the Republic of Vietnam. "In essence, the president had succeeded in neutralizing the opposition and galvanizing a national majority behind his policy of slow, deliberate withdrawal," historian Andrew Johns concluded. "Even Nixon's critics had to admit that he had scored a significant public relations victory with the address."[21] By year's end, support for the war as well as the president's standing had risen. His approval rating went from 56 percent before the speech to 67 percent thereafter.[22] For the first time since Tet 1968, the home front appeared to be holding. Vietnamization had proven a political panacea.

"We Are on the Winning Trend": Vietnamization as a Successful Strategy

Then and now, journalists and scholars have known that Vietnamization was good politics and that its American origins lay in domestic factors.[23] Its basis as a military strategy has been less well understood. Indeed, numerous historians have depicted the silent majority address as indicative of Nixon's decision to accept a decent interval between an American exit and South Vietnam's inevitable collapse—"a sort of slow-motion defeat," as one author put it.[24] Likewise, historian Robert Dallek has characterized it as "a combination of hope and illusion—the hope that Vietnamization would actually work and the illusion that after eight years of advising and training Saigon's forces to fight the insurgency, they could finally stand on their own."[25] From the vantage point of the Republic's fall in 1975, perhaps this judgment seems sound.

In late 1969, this outcome was far from certain and even judged unlikely by many. The South Vietnamese thought they could stand on their own. Hanoi feared they might pull it off. The Americans were the most skeptical. Painfully aware that overly optimistic intelligence had misled them before, allied officials worldwide were, if anything, more critical than in years past. And yet in 1969, policymakers evaluated Vietnamization with "guarded optimism." To be sure, there was an abundance of hope and a fair amount of self-delusion, but a prudent Vietnamization program seemed to have the makings of a successful strategy that could build a base of domestic and foreign support and promote continued military progress on the ground. It seemed a psychological, political, and military winner. Surveying these positive reports, Nixon concluded that he had made the right decision—the only interval that existed was the one between November 3 and the allies' ultimate success. Or, as Thieu himself confidently declared: "We are on the winning trend."[26]

Of course, the same US domestic context that had convinced Nixon to embrace Vietnamization affected Saigon. At a high-level September meeting at the presidential palace, Thieu and other officials agreed that Americans were "tired" and that the Republic would have to press on toward economic and military "self-sufficiency." The October Moratorium reinforced their fears that the antiwar movement was gaining influence on Congress, the press, and public opinion. The Republic sought to counter this sentiment and communist propaganda even as it acknowledged that it might be too late to change international opinion. "I have thought a lot about this problem and I come to the following conclusion," Bui Diem complained from Washington. *"No matter what I do here through speeches and appearances on Television, it will have very little effect."* Vietnamization seemed the only option that could sustain American support while affording the Republic a chance of survival.[27]

Nixon's silent majority address and the popular response eased fears of abrupt abandonment, thereby encouraging the South Vietnamese to make Vietnamization work. Most were satisfied that Nixon had made no further concessions even though he established that all US combat forces would eventually leave. The *Vietnam Guardian* summarized the feeling in Saigon that "our trust in our American allies has been resuscitated and bolstered." More than Nixon's words, the speech's warm reception in America heartened the South Vietnamese. Officials concluded that the address and Vietnamization had calmed US tensions. They understood that congressional and antiwar dissent could quickly revive while inflation and racial unrest could influence White House thinking on Vietnam. But, there was new hope that the American public could endure the long and difficult road Vietnamization offered.[28]

The South Vietnamese embraced Nixon's second and third troop withdrawal announcements with optimism and determination. "Vietnamisation is now accepted by the majority as a fact of life," reported the British embassy in Saigon. As reflected in local editorials, the Vietnamese understood that the "decisions were being taken solely with an eye to domestic U.S. developments." Yet, the redeployments were much smaller than expected, and most believed the RVNAF could take up the slack. The press acknowledged that while withdrawals had been cautious thus far, Vietnamization "is also irreversible." "Easy days are not ahead," the *Vietnam Guardian*'s editors concluded. "The war has 'reached a turning point.' It is our war now. . . . We have to rise up to the situation and we believe we're ready to do so."[29]

Vietnamization also seemed to bolster South Vietnamese nationalism, with the people "wholeheartedly behind" it. Caught up in this fervor, the National Assembly passed by a large majority a statement in favor of Vietnamizing the whole country politically and militarily to minimize American influence and strengthen South Vietnamese governance and defense. Laird noted in February 1970, while on his second trip to Vietnam as secretary of defense, that the South Vietnamese leadership "discussed Vietnamization with enthusiasm and pride." With the military, political, and security situation improving, they saw it as an opportunity to strengthen their nation to continue the war independently of their great power patron.[30]

As 1969 ended and a new decade began, many Vietnamese looked to a brighter tomorrow. "The future holds out the promise of being much more attractive," the *Vietnam Guardian* hoped. "Too often we have been fooled—and fooled ourselves—by shimmering lights that flicker and die at the end of a tunnel . . . but at least we now have a rational basis for optimism." Yet, the South Vietnamese recognized that leaders in Washington and Hanoi could upset their progress. They had difficulty understanding the Moratoriums and congressional dissent given the great strides their country had made in 1969. They had faith President Nixon and his silent majority would remain firm for a while longer, but their doubts lingered, especially as Hanoi's intentions were unclear. "We hope that [the North Vietnamese] realize by now that there will be no winners in this war. We are already all losers," one editorial somberly remarked. Nevertheless, the South Vietnamese had weathered the Tet Offensive, the Paris talks, and Vietnamization. As commenter Nguyen Ngoc Linh put it, "Even if our American allies were to desert us, it is not so certain that the world will see or hear the last of the South Vietnamese."[31]

President Thieu deserved much of the credit for this confidence. Throughout 1968 and 1969, he had successfully sold US withdrawals as a positive rather than a menacing policy forced upon a client state. By leading South Vietnamese opinion, he ensured that Vietnamization did not become a synonym for American abandonment.[32] He understood that the reductions reflected US needs and that sooner or later his country must stand on its own. His public statements proclaimed that the Republic would fight on with or without the United States. As for future withdrawals, he informed Americans and the public that he could tolerate a 150,000-man reduction in 1970 if the United States provided the essential arms, aid, and equipment.[33]

He was sanguine as 1969 ended. "The President spoke with great self-confidence, zest and restrained optimism," British ambassador J. O. Moreton reported of a December 26 meeting. Thieu anticipated a two-year timetable to complete the American withdrawal, with logistical and economic support continuing thereafter. "A long drawn out struggle" lay ahead, but he was "convinced the communists were losing the war both militarily and politically." Given sufficient time and aid, he would make Vietnamization work.[34]

Thieu's confidence rested on post-Tet battlefield and pacification gains. Vietnamization hinged on the expansion and modernization of South Vietnamese military forces. In 1969, the ARVN had increased by approximately 35,000 men; overall, the RVNAF grew from nearly 820,000 personnel to around 970,000. The president hoped to increase the latter by another 148,000 in 1970.[35] Polls of the RVNAF indicated the new strategy had not hurt their morale and that they did not interpret it as a "sellout."[36] "You support us and we will fight the battle," one officer affirmed. "But we need your good will. We can do the job if you will turn over the responsibility gradually, but, it will be bad if you pull out too quickly." Given the enemy's widespread adoption of the AK-47 before the Tet Offensive, distribution of the American M16 to ARVN forces in 1968 and Regional and Popular Forces in 1969 leveled the playing field. Vietnamese journalist Van Ngan reported that the new M16s had increased the Regional and Popular Forces' military capabilities and morale; their old World War II-era M1 Garand rifles "were sometimes larger than the man carrying them." The desertion rate had fallen, and soldiers were no longer fleeing from pitched battles. Others were not as confident. The general mobilization swamped the system with less desirable recruits, pay remained low, and the training and military leadership poor. But in early 1970, the RVNAF appeared to be doing as well as expected under Vietnamization.[37]

Pacification also seemed to be progressing.[38] Thieu believed it was critical to every aspect of the war: political legitimacy, military security, economic growth, and diplomatic leverage in Paris. In September, he privately reiterated to government officials the importance of building democracy and improving people's lives in the countryside. Security and reforms like "Land to the Tiller"—then stalled in the National Assembly—were critical to this vision. Allied control of the countryside slowly expanded, with a January 1970 report showing 93 percent of the hamlets being relatively secure. Although such metrics remained unreliable, there was a general sense that life was improving as travel became safer, refugees returned home, and agricultural production increased.[39]

In March 1970, the Land to the Tiller legislation passed. In the Mekong Delta alone, some 70 percent of farmers paid rent, and the communists had long exploited tenancy as an issue. Even though the NLF had enacted land reforms and redistribution in areas they controlled, their "taxes" amounted to another form of rent. Thieu wanted to offer villagers something better than exploitation by either landlords or communists. Looking to fulfill the 1967 constitution's promise to make "the people property owners," Vietnamese officials had been working on a land reform program for some time, even studying communist approaches. The proposed redistribution—some 60 percent of the cultivated land in South Vietnam—met resistance in the National Assembly, where wealthy landowners wielded considerable influence. Ultimately, the program would redistribute more than 2.5 million acres to some 900,000 families as it sought to break up large estates, end tenancy, increase the amount of cultivated land, raise farm incomes, and deny the communists part of their economic appeal. As its architect Cao Van Than remembered, Thieu and his officials did not want to make just more farmers, but also better and more affluent ones. Looking to the future, South Vietnamese and American policymakers trusted that the Republic could build on this progress and so eliminate the insurgency, foster a national noncommunist political community, and pursue economic growth and self-sufficiency.[40]

Indeed, MACV and US officials were more optimistic about the situation in Vietnam than about matters back home, especially given Laird's "budget realities." General Creighton Abrams lived with the ever-present fear that domestic pressure would tie the president's hand and force faster withdrawals, but he believed Nixon had done as well as any president could. He thought US forces were understrength, but looking at South Vietnam provided grounds for optimism.[41] William Colby, who replaced Robert Komer as head of US pacification efforts in Vietnam, told Senator Jacob Javits that "if you add up your balance on both sides, I think you come to a conclusion that a successful outcome is possible, but not inevitable." Intelligence revealed an enemy hurting in South Vietnam. Pacification and other programs had upset communist recruitment, and thanks to Thieu's efforts, over 3 million South Vietnamese had volunteered for the People's Self Defense Force. ARVN soldiers were coping well with American withdrawals, but they needed to prove themselves in battle to gain confidence. Even the Senate Foreign Relations Committee's December fact-finding mission to South Vietnam concluded that though Vietnamization would be a long, difficult, and uncertain road, it could work.[42]

To be sure, this guarded optimism rested on constantly changing circumstances. Abrams frequently warned that this present success could deceive Americans and Vietnamese alike. Pacification was slowing, the NLF rebuilding, and the RVNAF were performing less well than they should. The

Give Me Just a Little More Time 135

ARVN did not seem to want "to carry the fight to the enemy." "Three-fourths of the PSDF [Thieu was counting on to defend the countryside] couldn't find their way to the outhouse," the general coarsely lamented. And as relative tranquility descended upon Saigon, old political divisions and score-settling returned, stalling critical reforms. In a moment of candor, Abrams conceded to the New Zealand ambassador that "technically Vietnamization was going according to plan but there were many problems and dangers." He feared that the "Vietnamese had done just enough to make some Americans pleased" but "not out of conviction." The training, morale, and dedication to the Republic might simply prove skin deep, in which case, Vietnamization, with its American gifts of "boats and helicopters and the M16s and the artillery, is for *nothing*." Elsewhere, he noted that the North Vietnamese justly feared that "if that [Vietnamization] gambit works out, they've *really* got a problem." The America home front would not matter "if the South Vietnamese have turned into a bunch of tigers."[43]

That was precisely the gamble: whether or not they could fix these deficiencies and turn the South Vietnamese into dedicated anticommunist "tigers" before the last GI left or congressional support dissipated. In a January 1970 MACV briefing, US military adviser John Paul Vann aptly characterized the situation: "Our chances of getting out of this alive are about 50–50, or 49–51. Now I agree if we're doing better all the time maybe our chances are 60–40, but there's so many things can go *wrong*."[44] Despite these concerns, tales of progress in Vietnam made their way to Washington, reinforcing Nixon's belief that he had chosen the correct path.

As he had promised the president in October, Sir Robert Thompson personally surveyed South Vietnam. Reporting back to the White House, he expressed faith in Vietnamization. He assured the president that the South Vietnamese people had decided that the NLF was unlikely to win and that this confidence in the government along with the pacification program had forced the guerrillas out of the villages. He further projected that in two years allied forces would eradicate the Vietcong, leaving only the PAVN, which the ARVN could handle with the support of no more than 50,000 residual US troops. Thus far, withdrawals had been appropriate in size and timing and had encouraged South Vietnamese nationalism. Despite his positive message, he warned, "We had not won the war, and the situation was still fragile."[45]

Numerous US policymakers shared Thompson's cautious optimism, though skepticism remained high. "Most judges, including many in the

Administration, were being too pessimistic about the situation on the ground," Undersecretary of State Elliot Richardson remarked in November. The Australian embassy in Washington reported that "the Americans are no longer talking of stalemate and the inability of either side to 'win,'" though "officials remained reluctant to push good news" lest they invite a backlash from the press or doves. Although generally reserved, Laird testified to the House Appropriations Subcommittee that Vietnamization "could lead the way to a military victory in the sense of the South Vietnamese being able to defend their country, even against North Vietnam." The State Department found that the ratio of ARVN volunteers to conscripts ran about 3 to 1. They also estimated that only 3 to 4 percent of the population was under direct NLF control, although they stressed that the main point was not statistical accuracy but the sharp decline of NLF strength and influence. In Vietnam, American officials noted similar pacification gains even as they found at least one village where presumed GVN control masked the reality of communist domination—local forces would avoid or cooperate with the NLF while claiming the area was secure.[46] The CIA conceded ongoing South Vietnamese leadership and manpower problems but still judged that there had been impressive progress by all measures. "Vietnam is stronger militarily and politically today than ever before," the agency concluded. "The Tet 1968 landmark was very much a watershed for the Vietnamese and a cautious political cohesion and military competence has been achieved and at an accelerating rate." As one American official put it, "On the ground the situation had never looked better from our point of view and this state of affairs was likely to continue."[47]

Things indeed looked promising in early 1970. The NLF was still reeling from the disastrous 1968 offensives, and the NVA had pulled back. At the same time, the Republic had survived its political and military trials. South Vietnamese control spread, and the RVNAF grew in numbers and confidence. People naturally imagine and act on apparent trends, all the more so when the stakes are so high (and the alternatives so distasteful). Embarking on Vietnamization required a certain amount of wishful, or perhaps hopeful, thinking. And while the allied gains were real, they remained, as so many remarked, "fragile." Counting arms and men were easy. As Kissinger noted, it was far more difficult, if not impossible, to evaluate potentially decisive qualitative considerations like loyalty, motivation, and leadership. And as other officials warned, two of the most important factors—communist determination and American patience—were beyond their control.[48]

Hence, not everyone joined the ranks of the "new optimists," and the Vietnam Special Studies Group became an internal forum for the critical analysis Kissinger and others felt was lacking. Its research revealed that while allied forces had twice the number of soldiers as the enemy, as well as superior firepower and mobility, they had yet to achieve a decisive military advantage, raising real concerns about what would happen once American troops returned home. Indeed, the VSSG attributed much of the military progress since Tet to US operations and tactical mistakes by the enemy rather than an improved RVNAF. It also expressed concerns about pacification, noting that "the net situation country-wide could continue to develop in the GVN's favor" but US reductions would hurt local control in the short-term. In the absence of a settlement and the removal of North Vietnamese regulars, Hanoi would retain the military initiative and ability to disrupt pacification.[49]

On behalf of the VSSG, Kissinger aide Lawrence Lynn surveyed the situation on the ground in early 1970. The optimists put countryside control at 90 percent, but Lynn estimated that only 50 to 60 percent of the country-side was secure. Despite post-Tet gains, the population remained "more apathetic" toward than loyal to the Republic and "pacification momentum is faltering." The enemy also proved increasingly adept at countering allied efforts, especially after US advisers handed responsibility to the South Vietnamese. Without American forces and support, pacification would fail. "The odds are at best about even the GVN will survive and that GVN control in the countryside will be maintained or improved during the period of American troop withdrawals," he concluded. "It is far more likely that the GVN will lose control than it is that they will significantly increase it. . . . There is no sign that the enemy has given up."[50]

Kissinger agreed and he remained Vietnamization's chief critic. He warned the president that winter that official reports were too optimistic and that reality could soon catch up with the withdrawals. North Vietnam remained strong militarily, there was no clear evidence of RVNAF improvement, and MACV and Washington bureaucrats felt pressured to make positive reports. Realistic appraisals were critical because, as he told Australian diplomats, "We can't fool Hanoi."[51] Even if ARVN forces were filling the gap left by departing Americans, the North Vietnamese could send more regulars south to upset the military balance. He admitted that Saigon had greatly increased its control over the countryside after 1968, but he reminded Nixon that "the war in Vietnam is not over." His prescription for stalled negotiations remained the same: slower withdrawals and punishing North Vietnamese intransigence with renewed bombing. He also worried that the White House lacked oversight of Laird's Pentagon, expressing concern that the secretary of defense might unilaterally reduce American support for South Vietnam to meet budget needs elsewhere. In an era of renewed optimism, Kissinger, Lynn, and the VSSG pinpointed some of Vietnamization's underlying deficiencies. Events would bear them out.[52]

Laird pushed on with accelerated withdrawal timetables. In late 1969 and early 1970, he initiated plans to reduce the US military presence to as few as 190,000 soldiers by September 1971, and then to a small advisory role by September 1973. Rumors circulated in Washington that he "didn't care what the President announced, he was going to continue withdrawing troops." He sought to reassure Kissinger that "he takes his orders and follows them," but he insisted that Nixon had "no overall plan" on troop withdrawals. He would provide the direction the White House needed.[53]

Following Laird's template and the new optimists' reports, Nixon remained "cautiously optimistic" that South Vietnam "would be able to measure up to any new threat which North Vietnam could mount against them and to survive it." Citing Thompson and other sources, the president boasted of South Vietnamese progress when he announced the third reduction. There would be hiccups and periodic doubts, he allowed, but this uncertainty was part of the process. "Looking to the future," he continued, "I believe that we can see that the Vietnam war will come to a conclusion regardless of what happens at the bargaining table. It will come to a conclusion as a result of the plan that we have instituted on which we are embarked for replacing American troops with Vietnamese forces."[54] As he explained to the British prime minister, North Vietnam's "position in South Vietnam was progressively disintegrating" and "they no longer had the capacity" to launch another Tet-like offensive. He had rallied the silent majority to Vietnamization, and the North Vietnamese "could not now hope to turn the division of American public opinion to their own advantage." Responding to Kissinger's concerns about the ARVN, he declared, "They *must* take responsibility if they are *ever* to gain confidence. We have to take risks on that score." Vietnamization was as sound a military strategy as they could put together given their political constraints.[55]

And besides, Nixon retained the option of escalating or expanding the war. Although he had canceled Duck Hook, he continued to consider airpower as a potentially decisive reserve force. Why should he quickly withdraw US forces or take a bad deal in Paris when a solid majority of Americans backed Vietnamization, the allies were making progress in Vietnam, and he had untested military options at his disposal?

Hence, in late 1969, Vietnamization was not a means to effect a "decent interval" between an American departure and South Vietnam's fall. Rather, Nixon hoped it would provide the means to secure South Vietnam with local forces backed by US airpower if necessary. He believed it would work, as did his South Vietnamese counterpart. Together, Thieu and Nixon joined "the new optimists." Meanwhile, the North Vietnamese faced difficult conditions in early 1970, though they too looked forward to ultimate success.

"Difficulties will increase": North Vietnamese and NLF Assessments of Nixon's War

North Vietnamese and NLF leaders had a complicated relationship with Vietnamization. They identified it as the "keystone" of Nixon's strategy to end the American conflict: "The enemy's hope [is] in the Vietnamization [of the war] and his illusion in his plan of Vietnamization of the war," observed a top PAVN general. They saw it as a scheme to "appease and deceive" American and international opinion through gradual reductions. Based on their failure to disrupt Vietnamization and pacification in 1969, they also realized that it was not a camouflaged retreat. As one communist official noted, Nixon's Vietnamization "proved that he is cunning and stubborn. He has a long-range plan to counter our class struggle movement." It would take grim determination in the face of increasing hardships to outlast America and South Vietnam.[56]

Le Duan believed they could do it. The North Vietnamese leadership privately admitted that their offensives along with US and South Vietnamese policies had crippled the southern insurgency. Recruitment fell precipitously. Reviewing the military and political setbacks, the January 1970 18th Plenum acknowledged "this situation has affected the growth of our armed forces and our ability to retain the initiative on the battlefield." The view was even grimmer for cadres on the ground. "We lived like hunted animals," Truong Nhu Tang, an NLF leader, recalled. "Weariness and tension were the companions of every waking moment, creating stresses that were to take an increasing toll on our equanimity as the American bombers closed in on our bases and sanctuaries in late 1969." The communists realized that they had entered a new phase in the conflict. Nixon's war would be "difficult, decisive, and complicated."[57]

Hanoi faced other challenges. As tensions flared between the Soviet Union and the People's Republic of China in 1969, the Democratic Republic found itself juggling its great power patrons. Upset that Hanoi had ignored its advice and pursued talks in Paris, China reduced its aid while also removing most of its troops from North Vietnam. Moscow appreciated that the North Vietnamese were "exhausted" and continued its assistance while easing diplomatic pressure on Hanoi to settle in Paris.[58] Johnson's and Nixon's increased use of airpower in Laos as well as the latter's expansion of the war into Cambodia caused additional military and logistical difficulties. And while Ho Chi Minh's September 1969 death did not change the leadership, it did rob the regime of its inspirational figurehead, its most famous international celebrity, and its most effective mediator between the Soviets and Chinese. Ho's death dampened communist spirits throughout Indochina.[59]

Given the barrage of bad news and physical hardships, the morale of North Vietnamese and NLF forces suffered in 1969 and early 1970. Communist documents and discussions as well as Hai Nguyen's scholarship show that these soldiers were not supermen and women.[60] In the wake of Ho's demise, one directive recorded, "Those who are natives of NVN assigned to combat duties in SVN are afraid that the Revolution will be prolonged. They balk at hardships, fear to make sacrifices, and are now anxious to return to their native villages and families." Another noted that many of the cadre were no longer "confident in our success," especially as the NLF failed to disrupt pacification and the recruitment of ARVN soldiers. "100 percent of our personnel were afraid of a protracted war and did not believe that [decisive victory] would materialize," a third reported. As worrisome was the rate of defection to the South Vietnamese government, especially those departures leaders deemed "acts of mass desertion." The GVN's Chieu Hoi (Open Arms) program received over 45,000 defectors in 1969 alone—double the 1968 number. Throughout South Vietnam, communist forces were short on food, supplies, recruits, reinforcements, and especially confidence—something Vietnamization's nascent success made worse. "Morale was at rock bottom," a captured NLF officer complained. "Should [the] ARVN have a chance to develop, the VC would have no chance for victory."[61]

Officials sought to correct "erroneous views" like the "fear of a protracted war" as well as a tendency to retreat to Cambodia rather than stand and fight. They attempted to do so through "reorientation courses" and tracts. "We have to visualize the enemy and ourselves as two athletes who are running a race in a stadium and are approaching the finish line," one such effort exhorted. "One (we) is supported and encouraged by the spectators, and the other (the enemy) does not receive any support. If we make an additional effort in the last moment, we will gain the victory."[62]

In a test of wills, Vietnamization was both a danger and a ray of hope. Hanoi correctly saw it as Nixon's way of maintaining public support by using "Vietnamese to fight Vietnamese" so that he could "indefinitely prolong the war." North Vietnamese leaders were getting what they had demanded in Paris—unconditional American withdrawal—yet after the silent majority address, they feared that Nixon had beaten back his domestic challenges. Internal pressure had led to the bombing halt, negotiations, and Vietnamization. With public opinion now under control, he could continue the war. Analyst Brian Jenkins concluded that the North Vietnamese "do not fear the success of Vietnamization in South Vietnam as much as they fear the success of Vietnamization in disarming American domestic opposition to the war. Real success in Vietnamization may accelerate the withdrawal on the basis of South Vietnam's capability to continue on its own, but it also may decelerate withdrawals on the basis of decreased American participation in combat, hence fewer American casualties, hence decreased domestic pressure to pull out." The North Vietnamese and NLF appreciated that a protracted war increased the likelihood that the president would renew the bombing of North Vietnam or expand the war into Laos and Cambodia. A Vietnamized war offered as many risks as benefits.[63]

The promise of a stronger South Vietnamese military also denied the North Vietnamese the advantage of time, creating no small dilemma. Should they try to embarrass ARVN forces too soon, Nixon could slow or stop withdrawals and use airpower to punish them. The longer they postponed the offensive, the stronger the South Vietnamese might become. Eventually, the Saigon regime could prove practically invincible. It was a frustrating gamble either way. "The longer [North Vietnam] delays," Kissinger explained, "the worse it finds itself militarily in the South—always the key element in Hanoi's calculations. Meanwhile, by stalling on the negotiations, Hanoi permits the U.S. to carry out Vietnamization at its own pace." In March 1970, the Politburo decided to escalate the southern war to mar Vietnamization while launching a diplomatic offensive to boost North Vietnamese morale and play on US politics. It recorded that they had to intensify the war on all fronts "to doom [Vietnamization] to failure ... and to create a new change in the war situation so as to win gradual victories and eventually to win a decisive victory."[64]

Vietnamization was not an insurmountable challenge. Hanoi would continue the war regardless of the physical and human costs. "As we approach the final victory," General Vo Nguyen Giap acknowledged, "difficulties will increase."[65] Hanoi would continue the war regardless of the physical and human costs. At COSVN's mobile headquarters, leaders affirmed that while they had failed to defeat the enemy, "We should make unremitting efforts to preserve our offensive position so as to impede the US from implementing the 'Vietnamization plan.' We should also make the enemy realize that if he remains stubborn, he will be destroyed."[66] In Paris, Le Duc Tho displayed this same tenacity. He informed Kissinger, "If you prolong the war, we have to continue to fight. If you intensify the war in South Vietnam, if you even resume bombing North Vietnam, we are prepared. We are determined to continue the fight until we win victory. If our generation cannot win, then our sons and nephews will continue. We will sacrifice everything, but we will not again have slavery. This is our iron will. We have been fighting for 25 years, the French and you. You wanted to quench our spirit with bombs and shells. But they cannot force us to submit."[67] Le Duan, Le Duc Tho, and innumerable cadres had devoted their lives to the communist cause and reunification. They remained willing to pay any price. Although Vietnamization seemed to be succeeding, Hanoi made clear that the war was far from over.

If new optimism typified the mood in Washington and Saigon, then renewed determination rather than new pessimism characterized Hanoi. Both sides saw the other as stubborn and foolish for refusing to quit. Perhaps the optimism in early 1970 was more than a mirage, but the prospect of a peaceful oasis was far in the distance. Meanwhile, troubles in Cambodia and Laos loomed like sandstorms, threatening to disorient the allies as they began their trek on the long road of Vietnamization.

7

It's Too Late

Vietnamization's Frailties

April 1970–December 1971

Richard Nixon and Nguyen Van Thieu were riding high as spring 1970 arrived in America and Vietnam. Vietnamization had strengthened Nixon's political position and calmed domestic tensions. It appeared to be a sound strategy for ending American fighting while establishing a firm basis for South Vietnamese survival. But a long and dangerous road lay ahead.

Events quickly revealed Vietnamization's frailties. Nixon's and Thieu's actions gravely undermined the program in 1970 and 1971. The new optimism had become hubris. Each president sought short-term solutions to the complex problems created by US troop withdrawals and North Vietnamese obduracy. In doing so, they alienated the constituencies they needed to sustain support over the long haul. Nixon's decision to invade Cambodia revived antiwar dissent, particularly in Congress. Thieu increasingly defied the National Assembly as he grappled with Vietnamization's economic consequences. The improved RVNAF fought well in Cambodia but suffered a telling defeat in Laos. Military, economic, and political problems grew more challenging in Saigon and Washington, with the White House becoming increasingly desperate to find some other path out of Vietnam. Hanoi simply carried on.

Cambodia: An Error of "Epic Proportions"

In early 1970, Nixon thought he had the doves and the war under control. Relying on reports that the military situation was approaching a tipping point, he and Kissinger took every opportunity to push the enemy further back, though the president would not halt US troop reductions.[1] With Thieu's backing, he announced on April 20 that the United States would remove another 150,000 soldiers by the following spring. He believed he had the time, flexibility, and resources to prosecute the war as he saw fit. He misread the calm at home.

Always one of his weaknesses, Nixon had personalized the debate on the war. He and his national security advisor vilified moderates rather than seeking understanding, much less consensus. "There is a much deeper [antiwar] conspiracy than any of us realize," Nixon alleged. "These opponents are out to get the Presidency and you," Kissinger echoed. "You can't placate the doves." All the while, popular acclaim for the silent majority address blinded them to congressional realities.[2]

Southern Democrats, who backed Nixon's stand in Vietnam and his conservative domestic policies, gave him the votes he needed to continue the war. This emerging alliance raised Nixon's hopes that he could produce "a new alignment" in American politics.[3] His refusal to surrender in Vietnam abetted the rise of the conservative movement in the new decade. But in 1970, the Senate remained a domain of liberal politics.[4]

Congressional doves initially lacked the numbers to affect administration policies, but Vietnamization was a "long haul" strategy that needed billions a year in aid and a strong US alliance to work. It required a durable partnership between the White House and Congress, something Nixon had failed to establish in 1969 and early 1970. Instead, he and Kissinger became confident that they could manage the war without Congress. They were wrong. Senate doves lacked cohesion or an alternative to Vietnamization, but they increasingly had the votes to challenge the appropriations South Vietnam depended on. Laird warned the White House that they could not afford to "take on everybody on the Vietnam war" or "polarize people." "If we keep up this way we're going to affect what we're trying to do in Vietnam." A successful end to America's war in Vietnam required moderation and consensus politics.[5]

Contrary to popular belief, handing over responsibility to Vietnamese forces was almost as expensive for US taxpayers as Lyndon Johnson's Americanized war.[6] Laird was already slashing the defense budget and reducing tactical air operations to appease the doves and direct scarce funds toward Vietnamization. Despite Saigon's pleas for increased military and economic assistance, the secretary of defense had to fund RVNAF military improvement plans within a shrinking budget and meet America's global obligations. He asked Congress for little (certainly less than Thieu wanted). "There is no practical chance that supplemental funds could be obtained," he explained to Kissinger. "The very act of making a supplemental request would, in fact, open the door for Congressional actions which could prove inimical to our interests in Southeast Asia." Even at the apex of Nixon's standing in December 1969, the Senate pushed through an amendment restricting the use of defense appropriations and American ground troops in Laos and Thailand. Harsh presidential rhetoric or escalation would make these "budget realities" all the more difficult. Ignoring this advice, Nixon trusted his silent majority to back him if he chose to escalate the war to protect Vietnamization and attack enemy forces and logistics outside of South Vietnam.[7]

As Nixon understood when he had expanded the bombing into Cambodia, Indochina was one strategic theater. In their study of French colonization, Pierre Brocheux and Daniel Hémery noted that even then Cambodia was "a 'sanctuary' for the Vietnamese guerrillas of the south, and the key to the Mekong basin." Hence, France incorporated Cambodia into its growing Southeast Asian empire. Laos had similar importance. The fateful 1953 French decision to reoccupy the remote northwest outpost at Dien Bien Phu derived from the need to defend Laos from Vietnamese anticolonial forces. After the demise of the French empire, American leaders wrestled with the intertwined nature of Indochina. Despite the 1962 international agreement to respect Laotian neutrality, neither side would concede the area. US diplomats continued to insist that the NVA withdraw not just from South Vietnam but also from Laos and Cambodia.[8]

What became the 1970 American-South Vietnamese incursion into Cambodia was not unlike Dien Bien Phu: strategically correct from a military perspective but tactically mismanaged and politically disastrous. The presence of Vietnamese communist sanctuaries and logistical routes in Cambodia had been a military challenge throughout the American war. Men and matériel flowed down from the Ho Chi Minh Trail as well as east from the Cambodian port of Sihanoukville. As a result of COSVN Resolution 9, communist forces had pulled back from South Vietnam and expanded and improved their border sanctuaries in Laos and Cambodia while awaiting American troop withdrawals. Pacification had expanded markedly in the South while large swaths of territory in Laos and Cambodia fell under Hanoi's control. In early 1970, the South Vietnamese estimated that the communists occupied half of Cambodia and had 40,000 combat troops there.[9] Worryingly, North Vietnam appeared to be building up its forces in Laos and Cambodia in preparation for another large-scale offensive against South Vietnam.[10]

Practicing what scholar Raymond Leos called "opportunistic neutralism," Cambodia's Prince Norodom Sihanouk acquiesced in this presence and clung to his country's neutrality. But, as Vietnamese numbers grew and America seemed poised to leave the region, he tilted toward the United States. He received Nixon's intermediaries, largely ignored the Operation Menu bombing, and publicly decried Vietnamese communist activity in his country. By the end of 1969, the United States had restored relations with Sihanouk's government. Nixon's diplomacy had bought the allies relative freedom in Cambodia. Still, Sihanouk faced severe internal challenges. The Vietnamese presence and a contemporary economic crisis set in motion events that led to Prime Minister Lon Nol's March 18, 1970, coup.[11]

Nixon abandoned Sihanouk and recognized the new, staunchly anticommunist regime. General Lon Nol's desire to expel Vietnamese communists opened another front in the war, but the White House feared that the battle-hardened enemy forces would topple the fragile Cambodian government. In mid-April, the PAVN began pushing toward the capital, Phnom Penh. Lon Nol frantically appealed for US assistance.[12]

The military and Kissinger pressed Nixon to act. In March and April, General Creighton Abrams had expressed concerns about the pace of US troop withdrawals and the budget realities that reduced the strategic airpower he had been substituting for diminished American manpower. Vietnamization was moving too quickly. MACV argued that an allied invasion of Cambodia could destroy communist sanctuaries and supply lines, inflict heavy enemy casualties, diminish the threat in South Vietnam, and boost "South Vietnamese morale and confidence which would enhance Vietnamization." Thieu agreed, and the Republic had already begun minor operations within Cambodian territory.[13] Eager to restore his standing with the president after Duck Hook fell through, Kissinger also backed the incursion. The collapse of the Lon Nol regime would hurt South Vietnamese morale, he claimed, but an allied incursion into Cambodia would demonstrate America's commitment to the region and could compel Hanoi to compromise at the secret talks. The president weighed these factors alongside his popularity at home.[14]

Nixon reasoned that the United States must respond, and in late April he decided to send US forces into Cambodia. The move would "show that we stand with Lon Nol," "help him survive," disrupt communist logistics, shield Vietnamization, demonstrate his resolve to Hanoi, and perhaps "shorten the war." Only American boots on the ground could prove his and the nation's commitment to the Cambodians and Vietnamese. Since he would take "flak" from the doves for even a South Vietnamese-only incursion, "we might as well do it right," he figured. Laird opposed a large-scale incursion, arguing there would be no decisive military gain but almost certainly devastating domestic fallout. Nixon brushed off "the probable adverse reaction in some Congressional circles and some segments of the public." On his and Thieu's orders, 5,000 South Vietnamese and 10,000 American soldiers entered Cambodia on April 29–30. Several days later, he launched "protective reaction" air strikes across the DMZ into North Vietnam, ending the November 1968 bombing halt.[15]

Nixon made the decision personal. Writing to Kissinger, he castigated the "lily-livered Ambassadors from our so-called friends in the world" who had refused to defend America's aims and actions in Vietnam. "We are going to find out who our friends are now," he swore, "because if we decide to stand up here [in Cambodia] some of the rest of them had better come along fast." The president's April 30 televised speech explained the controversial operation's purpose, but it was no more conciliatory. Speechwriter William Safire, who played only a minimal role in crafting this address, recalled that it "gave it to the people 'with the bark on,' as Nixon liked to say—patriotic, angry, stick-with-me-or else, alternatively pious and strident." After reasonably laying out the military basis for the incursion, Nixon dropped his measured tone in favor of raw forthrightness. "If, when the chips are down, the world's most powerful nation, the United States of America, acts like a pitiful, helpless giant, the forces of totalitarianism and anarchy will threaten free nations and free institutions throughout the world," he declared.[16]

The president was equally gruff with Congress: "Those Senators think they can push me around, but I'll show them who's tough." He informed so few people beforehand that even key congressional allies were upset. He defended this secrecy and his actions, arguing that it "was a particularly *personal Presidential* decision. This was the kind of decision I had to make myself." Having made it, he would reap what he had sown.[17]

Laird's warnings proved prescient. The *Boston Globe* aptly called the incursion an error of "epic proportions." Expansion of the war ruined Nixon's image of careful moderation. It incited "easily the most massive and shattering protest in the history of American higher education." After the Ohio National Guard fired on students at Kent State, killing four, approximately 450 colleges and universities had to suspend classes, some ending their terms early rather than risk ongoing protests and closures. The demonstrations went beyond college campuses. More than 100,000 people marched in the nation's capital to protest the war.[18]

As the Vietnam War again returned home as a daily fixture on America's streets and news broadcasts, policymakers struggled to assess and explain the incursion's military value. Abrams likened its presumed success to a "basketful of fog." Since Nixon had already paid a steep political cost by crossing into Cambodia, the general wished to chase communist forces even deeper to effect a rout, though he understood the war would still be won or lost by the South Vietnamese in South Vietnam. Overall, the enemy had recovered by that summer. That said, the destruction of the border sanctuaries and disruption of enemy logistics did buy the allies time in South Vietnam and perhaps forestalled a major offensive. Moreover, the ARVN performed well, easing fears in South Vietnam that Vietnamization would not work. The operations exposed their continued dependence on American logistics and firepower, but the optimists countered that these deficiencies would be addressed in due time. Indeed, a sense of success and the ARVN's ability to continue operations in Cambodia influenced Nixon and Thieu's move into Laos the following year. Long after the conflict ended, the American president still boasted that the Cambodian incursion had been "the most successful military operation of the Vietnam War."[19]

However militarily effective it might have been, it made a partnership with Congress virtually impossible. Preceding Nixon's decision, Senators John Sherman Cooper (R-KY) and Frank Church (D-ID) tried to deter such escalation by proposing an amendment to prohibit the presence of US ground troops in Cambodia. Nixon's actions transformed a theoretical restriction into a bill to remove American forces from Cambodia by June 30 and halt aerial missions and RVNAF support there as well. The president instructed aides to attack the legislation and "hit 'em in the gut." Yet, facing a major defeat in Congress, he curtailed US operations in Cambodia. Although it would not pass in the House until December 1970 (and the House version

It's Too Late   149

allowed American air strikes to continue), the Cooper-Church amendment revived congressional debate on the war and demonstrated that body's willingness to limit the executive's options.[20]

The Cambodian incursion's greatest toll for Nixon was the loss of moderates like Senate majority leader Mike Mansfield. The senator had been empathetic about Nixon's having inherited a difficult war and had privately pledged to help the president in Congress. He had been willing to let Nixon lead and deferred to him on the timing and composition of troop withdrawals. "Cambodia tore it," he told journalists. Thereafter, he allied with others to build a Senate consensus against the war. He would endorse the Gulf of Tonkin Resolution's repeal and put forward an amendment to remove all US forces after Hanoi returned American POWs. The president badly needed foreign aid to develop the Nixon Doctrine and Vietnamization. Mansfield worked to reduce or deny such requests. The House better reflected the silent majority and softened much of the Senate's legislation. Even so, the needed Vietnamization aid and war appropriations grew harder to get.[21]

In June, Secretary of the Army Stanley Resor reported to MACV officials, "Mr. Laird has a very real world problem—he can't *get* any more money. In fact, he's going to get a billion dollars less than he asked for. . . . Up to now it's been, whatever was needed out here we somehow got the money from Congress and you got it. But the climate in Congress is *so different* now."[22] Nixon, Laird, and Thieu had predicated Vietnamization on congressional goodwill and largesse. The president forfeited that in Cambodia.

The White House confronted a growing crisis. The row with Congress and the Cooper-Church amendment represented a political challenge to its Vietnam policies. Some top aides, including Kissinger, interpreted Senate actions as a dangerous, "constitutional revolution" to restrict presidential authority on foreign affairs. At the same time, he and the VSSG found American strategy in Vietnam deeply flawed. New evidence before the group indicated that even after Vietnamization had begun US forces remained largely responsible for the military and security gains in South Vietnam. Despite this progress, the NLF infrastructure had survived and could contend for most of the rural population, leaving skeptics to wonder how the RVNAF would cope once the last GI departed. Kissinger also predicted that without greatly increased foreign aid, which Congress was unlikely to approve, the Republic would face a severe economic and political crisis as US troop withdrawals continued. Again, he urged the president to slow the reductions, continue

South Vietnamese operations in Cambodia, and maintain the current level of US air operations against the enemy. "We should withdraw enough forces to calm public opinion but we should do so slowly enough to give Hanoi an incentive to negotiate and to avoid risks to our forces," he wrote.[23]

Laird disagreed, warning that budget, fiscal, manpower, and political realities dictated steady US troop reductions not just in Vietnam but worldwide. Ultimately, US policy followed Laird's timetables. After Cambodia, Nixon accepted the need to "get out" via "troop withdrawal" even as he still sought "a lasting peace."[24] Thieu too accepted the quickened pace of American withdrawals, acknowledging that there would be no residual US military force.[25] In May 1970, Laird proposed that the United States have 260,000 soldiers in South Vietnam at the end of Fiscal Year (FY) 1971 (i.e., June 30, 1971), 152,000 at the end of FY 1972, and 43,000 at the end of FY 1973. As it happened, there were 239,200 at the end of FY 1971, 47,000 at the end of FY 1972, and less than 250 at the end of FY 1973, though the last figure reflected the post-settlement drawdown. That there were 100,000 fewer troops than anticipated in the 1972 election year was a significant feat. Despite JCS and White House reticence, Laird would achieve the goal he had set in early 1969—effectively no American forces remained in Vietnam as Nixon's first term ended.[26]

The Cambodian incursion and its fallout reasserted the primacy of domestic considerations in the conduct of Nixon's Vietnam War. "The Cambodian operation narrowed his already thin margin for error," historian George Herring noted.[27] It also demonstrated the widening schism within American society. In a dramatic shift from November 3, Fulbright's mail flow reached an unprecedented high after the president's April 30 address, with 93 percent of the correspondents opposing Nixon's actions.[28] Renewed antiwar protests followed the incursion, but so did prowar demonstrations. The May "hard hat" riots in New York City saw construction workers assaulting antiwar protestors. Events there culminated in a patriotic parade with some 150,000 participants. Nationwide, public opinion rebounded in the president's favor, with 61 percent of Americans in August 1970 deciding he had been right on Cambodia. Another summer poll revealed that 82 percent of Americans disapproved of college protests. Congress and the protesters indicated the limits of presidential action, but "backlash politics" fueled polarization. The public desired neither defeat nor an endless war in Vietnam. It would accept escalation if that would prevent both.[29]

It's Too Late   151

Table 1. Total US Military Personnel in South Vietnam, 1968–1973

Date	Total
June 30, 1968	534,700
December 31, 1968	536,100
June 30, 1969	538,700
December 31, 1969	475,200
June 30, 1970	414,900
December 31, 1970	334,600
June 30, 1971	239,200
December 31, 1971	156,800
June 30, 1972	47,000
December 31, 1972	24,200
June 30, 1973	Less than 250

Source: Herring, *America's Longest War*, 182.
Note: Laird essentially achieved his goal of removing all US troops by the end of Nixon's first term.

Vietnamization plus aggressive bombing remained popular among the "silent majority," but US troop withdrawals also made it easy for Americans to forget why they had intervened in Vietnam. Vietnamization shifted conservative attention from demanding military victory to defending Nixon and countering antiwar forces. Prowar appeals to American patriotism and emphasis on the return of the POWs bought Nixon public support and time to continue the war. Such appeals further separated the war from national security concerns, making the conflict seem peripheral to American life and interests as the troops returned home. As an editorial in the *Vietnam Guardian* observed, "The false euphoria surrounding the American attempts at de-escalation in Vietnam has become an absolutely dangerous condition. Many of us, as well as our allies, have been lulled into the belief that all it takes for peace in Vietnam is the removal of U.S. and other allied troops. Of course the next logical step is for us to forget all about the war."[30] With Congress turning against the US commitment to South Vietnam and Americans forgetting about it, the Republic of Vietnam had good reason to worry after the halcyon days of 1969.[31]

The Economic Consequences of a Vietnamized War

Nixon was not the only leader afflicted with the mistaken notion that he could spurn his legislature. President Nguyen Van Thieu's overconfidence led him to adopt policies that alienated him from the National Assembly. His concessions on the bombing halt and NLF participation in post-settlement elections had already upset militant anticommunist solons. South Vietnam's difficult economic situation produced renewed political unrest in Saigon that further undermined the unity necessary for the Second Republic's survival.

The economy and Thieu's proposed austerity taxes had been a top government concern throughout 1969. South Vietnamese finance ministers recognized that the country's trade and budget deficits would create serious economic imbalances and inflation. In war-ravaged Vietnam, consumption far exceeded production. The loss of American soldiers' spending exacerbated these economic problems. The Republic had enough trouble financing its share of the defense burden before the allied withdrawals began. The South Vietnamese looked to South Korea and Taiwan for inspiration and hoped they too could pull off an economic miracle.[32]

Thieu understood that real Vietnamization required economic independence. "The economy is the key problem," he argued. "Though dealing with self-reliance and self-strengthening in our struggle, we do not have a self-sufficient economy." Privately, he exhorted finance and other top officials to do the impossible: reduce budget deficits, curb inflation, promote economic growth, and expand the RVNAF. The Republic weighed devaluing the piaster, enforcing tax collection, raising taxes on luxury goods and some commodities, and striking nonessentials from the budget. Addressing the people on the need for austerity taxes, the president reminded them, "Allied troops are not inexhaustible nor is allied money. Our allies cannot aid us forever even if they want to. Should they want to aid us forever, they could not keep their aid at a high level forever. A dictum said: 'One usually helps people in temporary need and never helps people in permanent poverty.' Therefore, our allies will continue to provide aid, but only for those who are laborious and accept sacrifices and not for those who are lazy and dodge their responsibility." Yet, even discussing essential economic measures prompted dissent.[33]

The incorruptible Prime Minister Tran Van Huong was an early political casualty. In July 1969, ninety-two members of the National Assembly's lower house signed a letter of no confidence, citing the proposed taxes and reforms.

While the solons decided not to remove the prime minister, Huong's harsh response soured relations between the politicians and his office. Needed legislation stalled. A month later, National Assembly anger and a row between Thieu and Huong over the number of civilians in the Cabinet led to the latter's departure. Thieu hoped that his replacement, the able interior minister and deputy prime minister General Tran Thien Khiem, would appease Assembly hardliners, improve his political position, and break the logjam on economic reforms.[34]

That fall, the Ministry of Economy proposed taxes on imported goods, luxuries, and gasoline to prevent inflation. Khiem's new economic minister, the young Western-trained technocrat Pham Kim Ngoc, insisted that the Republic must adopt these measures or face economic ruin. A "Vietnamization of the economy" must occur alongside military improvements if it was to survive. "Austerity," he declared, would be the order of the day. When the National Assembly again delayed, the ministry cited a 1961 law to implement the austerity taxes without legislative approval. Thieu accepted them, though he worried about the backlash.[35]

Indeed, the austerity taxes and import licensing restrictions ignited a flurry of protests. The National Assembly balked, and the lower house staged an antitax walkout. Many deputies called the move "unconstitutional." One incredulously labeled its consequences "more disastrous" than the 1968 Tet Offensive. The ensuing legislative revolt and protests made for a difficult political situation. Needed reforms and sacrifices were opposed, weakened, or ignored. Speculation and hoarding rose. So too did the cost of living. The taxes upset thousands of South Vietnamese who aspired to own refrigerators, televisions, and motorcycles or who faced rising prices on food and transportation due to the fuel tax.[36]

Making matters worse, Thieu had grown sensitive to calls for accommodation with the NLF before a settlement. Hoping to intimidate his critics, he made an example of Tran Ngoc Chau—a moderate National Assembly member who, like many Vietnamese, had family serving with the communists. Respected by the Americans for his work on pacification and by Vietnamese politicians for his integrity, Chau's calls for conciliation with the enemy upset Thieu. Even though they had once been friends, he needlessly worried that the legislator could become a lightning rod for those favoring a coalition government. Even if their numbers were small in the Assembly, he feared they could hurt support for the Republic in the United States and encourage Hanoi to persist. Chau's failure to report his conversations with his communist brother, which violated security laws, became the pretext for his prosecution. When the Assembly protected its colleague, Thieu denigrated once-loyal nationalists as "political sorcerers." Among them, Senator Tran Van Don defended Chau and worked at creating a "People's Bloc" within the Assembly to challenge Thieu's unilateralism.[37]

Support for the government fell daily in early 1970. Insiders worried that the president's "authoritarianism and reliance on Catholic support would push many of the uncommitted over to the Viet Cong." When police dragged Chau out of the National Assembly building that February, Thieu confirmed the fears of many. One of Chau's attorney's, Tran Van Tuyen, stressed that his client's trial "was a test case of Vietnamese democracy, and democracy lost." Things were not quite so bleak. Still, the "great spirit of unity" had ended.[38]

The need for economic reform continued. Inflation and the budget deficit kept rising. Government employees and soldiers felt the crisis in their pocketbooks: their real purchasing power was half what it had been in 1967.[39] The Assembly acted as a relief valve for this frustration, with solons venting their anger at taxes and inflation. Thieu also faced rising political dissent from students, Buddhists, and other groups while the Republic's Supreme Court invalidated the austerity taxes, creation of a military court, and convictions of dissidents. Vietnamization complicated matters.[40]

Its effect on the Republic's economic growth was a growing concern in 1970. Nguyen Duc Cuong, the Cabinet minister for economic development, recalled, "Vietnamization created a significant and growing strain on the financial and human resources of the country. Deficit financing, already the norm during the years of Americanization of the war, grew larger each year, and began to create a dual problem: inflationary pressure due to declining US foreign aid coupled with depressed economic activity due to the loss of income." American troop withdrawals reduced GI in-country spending, hurting Vietnamese businesses and tax revenue. At the same time, an increasing share of the national budget had to go to expanding South Vietnam's military and security forces. In short, Vietnamization dried up the flow of US dollars into Vietnam at the precise moment they were most needed.[41]

Government officials had an acute understanding of America's "budgetary constraints." On his second tour of Vietnam in February, Laird explained the political and budgetary situation to MACV and Thieu. Bui Diem's dispatches from America confirmed the same. Still, Thieu and South Vietnamese officials protested that they were not getting the assistance Nixon had promised at Midway. Congressional fallout from the Cambodian incursion made this worse. In late May 1970, the embassy in Washington warned that Congress and concerns about America's own economy would reduce foreign assistance. Even urgent requests for rice and supplemental aid for ARVN soldiers proved difficult. South Vietnamese and American political problems compounded an already difficult strategic environment.[42]

South Vietnamese policymakers weighed these matters as they sought to promote self-sufficiency and survival. Their requests for additional US military, financial, or food aid became measures of "last resort" to be taken only after the Republic had "tried its best" to be self-sufficient. Officials recognized their dependence on foreign aid despite "the independent spirit of our government." "Vietnamization requires a continued transfer of U.S. resources to complement, and in many instances, to offset the local resources used in the war effort," the Ministry of Economy concluded. "Without such financial aid, it is impossible for Vietnam, a small and poor economy, to accommodate a major war." Other officials argued that a substantial increase in American aid was necessary to "realize the Vietnamization program." Budget deficits, inflation, and an addiction to imports and foreign aid posed difficult choices: accept runaway inflation as a wartime necessity, pursue significantly higher taxes, raise interest rates to as high as 24 percent, devalue the piaster, or secure more foreign aid. If Nixon sped up withdrawals, it would exacerbate South Vietnam's economic problems. The Republic also needed to free up resources to expand rural production. Officials recognized that Americanization had disrupted Vietnamese life and culture, creating a "fake abundancy" that blinded citizens to the harsh economic realities that would set in as Vietnamization began.[43]

Overall, South Vietnamese policymakers saw a stark choice between fixing the economy, stabilizing politics, or reducing military activity. Vietnamization and decreased foreign aid would lower standards of living, increase inflation, and create "political disruption detrimental to the war effort." Alternatively, the Republic could redirect resources from the war toward the domestic economy, but this reallocation would slow Vietnamization. State economists were clear: "There will not be any magical policies." If the pace of Vietnamization quickened and the government failed to act, or

South Vietnamese citizens refused to sacrifice their standards of living, the Republic would face dark days.[44]

Learning from the 1969 austerity backlash, Thieu worked with the National Assembly on a "Program Law" that would give ministers the latitude necessary to implement necessary reforms. He and his team of technocrats could take the blame for making hard decisions while affording the legislature some degree of oversight. Still, it was a Vietnamese election year, and senators held up the legislation with its potential for tax increases until after the polls had closed that fall. With the law passed, Pham Kim Ngoc gained the freedom to modify the exchange rate, raise taxes, and tackle the black market. Pioneering measures like a value-added tax and a floating exchange rate followed. Rice production, real wages, tax revenues, and other economic measures improved. The Republic also attracted long-term foreign commercial investments and loans.[45] Though tamed, the budget deficit, speculation, inflation, and other structural problems remained fearsome.[46]

Pham Kim Ngoc was still pleased by what they had accomplished in 1970 and 1971. "Vietnamization would not be decided by how the war was fought," he exhorted his fellow citizens. "It will be judged by how the war is sustained militarily, socially, and economically."[47]

By those measures, Thieu had achieved a fair amount of success, though he also made serious blunders. The need for stringent economic and political reforms was real, but he too often responded with contempt rather than conciliation. Like Nixon, he chose the political right over the center. Also like Nixon, he increasingly kept decision-making within a tight, inner circle. After seeing the situation in Saigon firsthand in late 1969, Bui Diem worried that Thieu was becoming a "prisoner of the Palace" and "institutionalizing his natural shyness into official austerity." Thieu aspired to the economic programs and grassroots authoritarianism of Chiang Kai-shek and Park Chung Hee, ignoring the complexities of Vietnamese politics that made such mass loyalty impossible. He jailed dissenters, ignored the National Assembly, and overruled the courts and other government bodies when they opposed him. Even longtime friends were not immune, as former allies like Tran Ngoc Chau found themselves incarcerated. Thieu chaffed at criticism. "They cannot do better than me," he asserted.[48] Perhaps not, but as he aggrandized his power and cracked down on dissent, he became more the dictator American doves had long held him to be.[49]

Lam Son 719: Vietnamization at the Start of the Big War

South Vietnamese military performance in Cambodia, Thieu's tentative rapprochement with the legislature, and Ngoc's economic reforms provided enough glimmers of success in 1970 to sustain optimism in the presidential palace and the White House. There was no turning back from Vietnamization, but to Thieu and Nixon, American troop reductions had bought South Vietnam time and US aid. The RVNAF advanced in numbers, equipment, and fighting prowess. Pacification appeared to be proceeding well.

North Vietnamese leaders had experienced real setbacks in 1968 and 1969. Rather than quit, they redoubled their efforts. Relative calm in South Vietnam did not mean Le Duan had abandoned reunification; he had simply redirected his forces to shore up his position in the larger Indochina theater while awaiting America's exit.

In 1969 and 1970, Hanoi focused on Laos. Nixon's increased bombing and American support for noncommunist Laotian and Thai troops had repulsed communist forces there in 1969. North Vietnam and the Pathet Lao—the Laotian communist military and political organization—tenaciously held on and introduced Soviet-supplied tanks, heavy weapons, and advanced logistical support to the battlefield. In early 1970, they launched a counteroffensive that pushed US allies further back. Communist soldiers slowly consolidated these gains. Meanwhile, DRV losses and setbacks in Cambodia, particularly the closure of the Sihanoukville Trail, raised the stakes in Laos. "If Hanoi wanted to win, it *had* to keep the [Ho Chi Minh] trail open," military historian John Shaw wrote. Disrupting supply lines in Laos would choke off the flow of men and matériel southward. North Vietnam also saw the war there as a test of Vietnamization. "The US setback in Laos constituted a writing on the wall for the 'Vietnamization' of the war in South Viet Nam," the *Vietnam Courier* argued in early 1970. "'Puppet troops + US fire-power and air force': such a formula was intensively applied in Laos," and it had failed.[50]

Instead, the Nixon administration saw the deteriorating military situation in Laos as an opportunity to prove Vietnamization's strength. The president believed that the Cambodian incursion had demonstrated that ARVN forces could take the fight to the enemy. The communist decision to retreat rather than make a stand in Cambodia further encouraged allied aggressiveness. MACV and the JCS had long pushed for expanding the ground war into the Laotian panhandle. They saw it as a way of cutting off the enemy's logistics, inflicting high rates of attrition, and buying the Republic time and breathing space along its northwestern frontier.[51]

The American military drawdown and congressional dissent left a closing window on such a cross-border offensive. Both political parties were restive about Vietnam, and unfortunately for Nixon, Republicans had lost seats in the House in the 1970 midterm elections. Congress had already prohibited the use of funds for the deployment of US soldiers in Laos or Thailand. Congressional approval of the Cooper-Church amendment in December 1970 prevented US ground troops from entering Cambodia and highlighted that body's opposition to escalation. In early 1971, the South Vietnamese could proceed with US air support, including the essential American-piloted transport helicopters and gunships. The advisers so critical to coordinating maneuvers and communicating with US fire and air support would have to remain behind.[52]

Despite these tactical limits and the political risk, the White House committed itself to what became Lam Son 719. Perhaps recalling that the silent majority had swung around to accepting the Cambodian incursion as a good idea, Nixon gambled that he could absorb another political blow for escalating the war and then satisfy public opinion with the "salted peanuts" of troop withdrawals. The same day Congress passed the Cooper-Church amendment, he approved the operation. "Right now there's a chance to win this goddamn war," he growled. Ideally, the operation would validate Vietnamization, demonstrate his resolve, disrupt an impending communist offensive, and ensure Thieu's reelection later that year. Indeed, he hoped it could "break the back of the enemy." An offensive into southern Laos also offered the prospect of seizing enemy stockpiles and cutting off the Ho Chi Minh Trail before it branched out into Cambodia and South Vietnam. In Washington and Saigon, the town of Tchepone came to symbolize this fabled strategic crossroads—forty to sixty trucks passed through it every night, and it was only forty kilometers from the South Vietnamese border. Thieu and his military advisers heartily approved the American plan. After the Americans' Operation Dewey Canyon II had reopened the nearby base at Khe Sanh as a staging area, South Vietnamese forces entered Laos on February 8, 1971.[53]

Things soon went awry. Laotian weather and geography as well as a relentless and stronger than expected enemy would have tested the ablest commander. Leading the offensive, Lieutenant General Hoan Xuan Lam was at best an average officer—tennis and politics were his fortes. Route 9, the main artery into Laos, was a mess. Flanked by a river on one side and forested mountains on the other, the dirt road was largely impassable. South Vietnamese bulldozers and engineers feverishly worked to enable the ARVN advance. At the same time, elite South Vietnamese forces, inserted by US helicopters, established fire bases to protect the column. Thieu's caution further stalled the offensive. With poor visibility hampering air support, he ordered Lam to halt halfway to Tchepone. The ARVN had only ten miles to go, but considering that Lam Son 719 was supposed to last into April, perhaps the Vietnamese president thought that a slow-and-steady approach would enable success. He instead conceded the initiative to the enemy.[54]

Hanoi saw holding Laos as critical to its ultimate victory and believed that Lam Son 719 would be a "strategically decisive battle." Mirroring Nixon, Le Duan and his advisers concluded that defeating the invading ARVN would prove Vietnamization was a hollow strategy, would hurt Nixon and Thieu politically, and would move the United States to withdraw its forces faster or settle in Paris. The communists decided to effect a rout. There would be no tactical retreat as there had been in Cambodia. In late 1970, they were already moving men and matériel into the Laotian panhandle, something American officials knew from intelligence reports.[55] Making matters worse, North Vietnam had extensive knowledge of the allies' plans from the media and embedded spies.[56] Ten thousand South Vietnamese soldiers marched into a trap. Thieu's delay allowed some 60,000 PAVN troops to surround his army on three sides. These troops were better equipped and fighting on familiar territory. The PAVN had Soviet tanks and advanced antiaircraft guns. Thieu had not expected his adversaries to have either these numbers or these arms.[57]

On February 20, the South Vietnamese fire bases began to fall. The Rangers fought bravely, often to the death, in pitched battles against superior enemy forces. The lack of US advisers on the ground and the language barrier between Vietnamese troops and American air and tactical support hastened the collapse. Those who could escape certain death or capture did so via US helicopters. Photographs of South Vietnamese soldiers desperately clinging to the helicopters' skids provided another of the war's indelible images— lacking the moment's context but powerfully reinforcing ingrained views of the conflict and America's ally. Still, Nixon demanded that Thieu press on.[58]

Counting casualties and facing the prospect of a humiliating defeat (in a Vietnamese election year), Thieu ignored the US president's entreaties. He ordered his forces to utilize American air mobility to leap over the enemy, seize Tchepone long enough to "take a piss," and then retreat. Often surrounded, those South Vietnamese troops who made it out alive did so only with the help of near round-the-clock US air sorties.[59] They left behind thousands of dead, wounded, or missing. "We ran like wounded dogs," one South Vietnamese soldier confessed. The last of Thieu's forces were out of Laos by the end of March.[60]

Publicly, the White House and presidential palace touted Lam Son 719 as a victory. "Vietnamization has succeeded," Nixon bragged in a major television address on April 7. He affirmed that Lam Son 719 enabled even faster US troop reductions. Pointing to the raid on Tchepone, Thieu similarly depicted the operation as a resounding success.[61]

The reality was impossible to hide. A "complete fucking disaster," said one US adviser close to the action. Half of the Republic's forces in Laos were killed or wounded. PAVN losses were significantly greater, but that was a small consolation. Lam Son 719 also revealed two major deficiencies of Vietnamization: without their American advisers, South Vietnamese forces proved unable to accomplish essential tasks such as coordinating artillery and air support; they also wilted under fire. Vietnamization had given them better military equipment, but it was unable to inspire decisive battlefield leadership or instill tactical skills and knowledge. When General Abrams admitted to the press that the operation was a failure, Kissinger privately and bitterly complained, "I don't know what possessed Abrams to tell the truth." The truth hurt, but not as much as it hurt the administration's faith in Abrams and Thieu. Nixon and Kissinger concluded that both men had badly mismanaged the operation and that Thieu lacked the guts to see it through.[62]

For those inclined toward optimism, including Nixon and Thieu, Lam Son 719 was but a momentary setback for Vietnamization. Even with US air support, the ARVN had faced overwhelming enemy forces in a hostile environment. Judged against this military imbalance, South Vietnamese soldiers did well. The offensives in Cambodia and Laos as well as the destruction of enemy stockpiles also delayed the expected PAVN offensive, buying the Republic more time. Thieu addressed deficiencies in military leadership while MACV began providing better arms, including newer tanks, to the RVNAF so that they could match the improved communist forces.[63]

The operation's domestic toll was immense. In America, it sparked renewed congressional and antiwar dissent. Historian Robert Brigham rightly noted, "What Kissinger never fully appreciated, and what Laird had tried to impress upon him repeatedly, was that in a democracy military actions always have political consequences. He had hoped to slow the clock for Saigon by attacking Laos, but public pressure to the war actually intensified as a result of the invasion. . . . Each new military escalation brought a sharp public rebuke, and Kissinger never quite learned how to manage this reality." Even Nixon's loyal Republicans complained they were "sick of Laos, sick of Vietnam, and disenchanted with the president's exit plan." "You don't see any hawks around here," Senate minority leader Hugh Scott explained to Laird at an informal GOP dinner. "The hawks are all ex-hawks."[64]

In Vietnam, Lam Son 719 significantly influenced subsequent events. The relative freedom of the press in Saigon meant that the public followed the operation. In early February, opinion had excitedly rallied around the advancing forces. There was even talk of marching to Hanoi. Shock and then sadness followed as the tide turned against the ARVN. Playing politics, Vice President Nguyen Cao Ky and others blamed Thieu. Lam Son 719 showed that his government was a "sinking boat with a deceptively good coat of paint," Ky charged. The popular reaction was one of mourning. Given the Vietnamese belief that, far from home, the unburied dead would wander for eternity, many were stunned that they had left so many dead and wounded behind. Sobbing masses, hoping to find their loved ones among the living, met the battered returning forces at Khe Sanh. ARVN morale fell. Despite US air support (and a substantial number of American combat forces still in South Vietnam acting as a reserve force), Vietnamization had failed to inflict lasting damage on the enemy. Overall, Lam Son 719 dealt a devastating psychological blow to the nationalists. The cause seemed hopeless.[65]

Hanoi was jubilant. The North Vietnamese interpreted Lam Son 719 as proof of South Vietnamese weakness: Laos really had shown that "Puppet troops + US fire-power and air force" was a recipe for failure. By April, communist forces had regrouped and restored their logistics in Laos. In Moscow that month, Le Duan touted "the victory on Highway 9." He and like-minded Soviet officials convinced the general secretary, Leonid Brezhnev, to increase military aid to North Vietnam. The PAVN would soon have heavy artillery, T-54 tanks, and advanced antiaircraft missiles. The North Vietnamese also persuaded China to increase its supply of arms. The former brazenly built major roads through the DMZ, rightfully judging that nearby American artillery would not fire on them.[66] Based on their battlefield success and perceptions of a demoralized enemy, Hanoi thus prepared for a decisive general offensive in 1972.[67]

Pacification and Politics in South Vietnam

The National Liberation Front had not been idle in South Vietnam. An influx of North Vietnamese regulars offset NLF losses in 1968–1970, but the CIA believed guerrilla numbers were stable and that they were getting enough food to survive. In hotbeds like Long An, American officials discerned that the communist infrastructure was solid and even able to run schools and hold public meetings in the daytime. Moreover, the insurgency underwent a revival. Pacification progress peaked in 1971.[68] American province senior advisers reported that the NLF had significant power, influence, and numbers. The country was "pockmarked with areas where both advisers and their counterparts are suffering from a euphoria which the VC could negate overnight," one US official observed. What scholar Martin Clemis identified as the "communist antistate" survived and spread fear, terrorism, and total revolution within its sphere of influence.[69]

Conversely, the Republic continued to inspire little motivation or anticommunist nationalism in the countryside. Its officials promoted the "Principle of Community Spirit" to bind local politics, needs, and resources to the state. Reports and Thieu's frequent tours of the countryside gave him no small amount of confidence.[70] Like Nixon, he saw himself as a man of the people, and much like his counterpart's appeals to the silent majority, these rural rallies made him feel like a populist leader.[71] But the results, as measured by village tax revenue or voluntary service, were scant. Personal and familial security trumped national sacrifice. This phenomenon was as true of soldiers as it was government officials, especially as terrorism claimed the lives of more than 16,000 civilians from 1969 through 1971. Another 32,867 were wounded, and 13,410 were either abducted or forced into joining the insurgency. Subsequently, the regional, popular, and police forces and administrators who were supposed to replace the ARVN regulars (who were supposed to replace the Americans) never developed. Fear rather than love or patriotism often defined loyalty. "The terror of Vietnam is being in the middle," wrote journalist Ian Wright.[72]

Trying to quickly clear and hold the entire country, Thieu failed to eradicate the communist infrastructure, secure the borders, or generate the selfless devotion necessary to sustain the Republic. Millions of civilians were caught in the middle. With the Americans departing and the ARVN overstretched, he confronted intractable problems.

The 1971 presidential election further undermined the Republic's popular support. The political fiasco began as an effort by Thieu and the National Assembly to limit the number of candidates and avoid a repeat of the 1967 election wherein eleven slates denied any ticket a majority. The legislation required a candidate to have so many Assembly or Council signatures that very few could gather enough support, given the fragmented nature of South Vietnamese politics. Liberal and moderate groups felt excluded, while military rivals like Duong Van ("Big") Minh, who had the necessary signatures, doubted they could defeat the president. Meanwhile, Thieu sought a decisive win to confirm his popularity.[73]

Fallout from Lam Son 719 and Vietnamization's economic woes gave his opponents an opening. Using sophisticated polling and computer analysis, Thieu's aides predicted he would win between 55 and 70 percent of the vote in a two-person contest with Minh. With Ky and Minh gaining support among those most affected by the war and inflation, a three-way race could be fatal. Thieu feared that Ky would split the conservative vote and ultimately give Minh the victory. He desperately wanted to vanquish Minh once and for all as a political rival. A free and fair two-party contest would do this, but he could not risk defeat. He worked to block Ky from having the signatures to run even as his aides warned that the gambit might cause Minh to drop out of the race in protest.[74]

Ellsworth Bunker and others pleaded with Thieu to soften the legislation and enable a free, fair, and open election. A one-man election would be "disastrous" for South Vietnamese nationalism and support in Congress. The New Zealand ambassador implored Thieu to change his mind. The president responded that "international opinion . . . could be looked after later." As for domestic opinion, he argued, "Only Vietnamese could really understand what Vietnamese felt and think." "Hatred of Ky and the corruption of power seem to have blinded his vision and distorted his judgment," the diplomat wrote afterward. "In these circumstances, as the Samoans say a man can put out his eye with his own finger."[75]

The election played out as predicted. Big Minh lacked the cash and popular support to mount an effective campaign; the Buddhists he had counted on judged Thieu the stronger leader. Aware of the president's efforts to influence, bribe, or intimidate National Assembly members and election officials, he knew that Thieu was leaving nothing to chance. Pessimistic about their chances, neither Minh nor Ky cared to stomach defeat at the ballot box. Their (and Thieu's) vanity got in the way of nationalist unity and what should have been a cathartic political process. When Minh dropped out of the race and Ky refused to run, the election became a farce. Officially, Thieu won 94 percent of the vote. Truthfully, the election did irreparable harm to the Republic's legitimacy.[76]

Just as Lam Son 719 represented a military "turning point," the presidential election, according to historian Sean Fear, was "a point of no return for South Vietnam." Thieu's mishandling of it was part of a pattern: frustrated by factional politics and a critical press, he took illiberal actions to do what he thought was necessary to stabilize the Republic. After 1971, even the loyal opposition had good reason to wonder if the Republic was worth dying for; others questioned whether the president was capable of saving it. Enthusiasm for Thieu and the Republic waned. He had blinded himself to foreign and domestic realities.[77]

The cost was grave in America. The election came amid US congressional debates over presidential war powers authority and the cost of an endless war. Thousands of antiwar protestors swarmed the capital in May, leading to the largest mass arrest in US history. Weeks later, the *New York Times* published the Pentagon Papers—an internal Defense Department review of Truman-, Eisenhower-, Kennedy-, and Johnson-era Vietnam policies that demonstrated conclusively that presidents had lied to the people. Southern hawks kept the doves at bay in Congress, but they had their own concerns. The chairman of the Senate Armed Services Committee, John Stennis (D-MS), feared that the CIA and White House were usurping congressional oversight to wage an undeclared war in Laos. The Pentagon Papers reinforced his belief that executive agencies were not forthright with the legislature. He lobbied fellow senators to take up war powers legislation and restore constitutional balance. Nixon's continued refusal to share intelligence, military planning, and other information inflamed the situation. Meanwhile, Thieu's one-person election catalyzed congressional budget cuts just as Bunker, Bui Diem, and others had predicted. The Senate defeated a $565 million aid bill for South Vietnam.[78]

Still, Nixon concluded that he must stand with his counterpart. Thanks to both men's intransigence, budgetary concerns became ever more stark "budgetary realities." Without this money, Vietnamization's odds narrowed. All the while, upheavals in the international environment also hurt the Republic's cause.

Diplomacy and Détente

Vietnamization framed America's exit from Vietnam, though Nixon and Kissinger continued to seek a negotiated settlement that would enable South Vietnam's survival. The crisis that followed the Cambodian incursion made clear that military victory was no longer possible and that Hanoi was unlikely to accept mutual withdrawal. Lam Son 719 aroused nagging doubts that the ARVN might never measure up to the PAVN. The sham election further undermined the Republic's legitimacy. The Nixon administration needed an honorable peace that accommodated the increasingly isolationist mood at home and larger Cold War interests abroad while providing a reasonable chance of the Republic's survival.[79]

Given his doubts about Vietnamization, Kissinger believed the United States needed an agreement in Paris to protect American credibility and give South Vietnam more time to develop. He understood that any acceptable peace deal would have to give both North and South Vietnam a chance to secure their aims thereafter—hence, the need for equilibrium.[80] He explained to the president, "Rather than run the risk of South Vietnam crumbling around our remaining forces, a peace settlement would end the war with an act of policy and leave the future of South Vietnam to the historical process." "We could heal the wounds in this country as our men left peace behind on the battlefield and a healthy interval for South Vietnam's fate to unfold," he added. "In short, Vietnamization may be our ultimate recourse; it cannot be our preferred choice."[81]

Nixon too understood that a settlement was necessary. He distrusted the communists. Their goal was "to keep talking and to screw you behind your back while they are doing it," he insisted to aides. But he needed an agreement to justify continued aid to South Vietnam and the use of American airpower to deter or thwart any North Vietnamese violation. Without a settlement, both actions would be difficult to defend before the public and Congress after the last GI departed. Historian Johannes Kadura well described their diplomatic strategy: a "Plan A" or "equilibrium strategy" to uphold South Vietnam, and a "Plan B" or "insurance strategy" to protect America's global credibility in case the former failed. Periods of presidential optimism reinforced Nixon's faith that the Republic could survive.[82] "Whoever thought that we would be in this position with Vietnamization working, and the Vietnamese capable of defending themselves?" he bragged in late September 1971. Yet, doubts that Saigon could make it without an agreement pushed the White House toward Hanoi.[83]

Ever since Lyndon Johnson had offered peace talks, mutual withdrawal had been the basis of any possible agreement; after Cambodia, Nixon bowed to military and diplomatic realities. In September 1970, Nixon dropped the stipulation requiring the mutual withdrawal of North Vietnamese and US forces.[84] The administration retreated further after Lam Son 719, offering a cease-fire-in-place but with American troops leaving. In October 1971, the national security advisor offered up Thieu's resignation to the DRV delegation as part of a deal that would lead to a new election with NLF participation. As the president's personal envoy, Kissinger was eager to keep the talks open. And he remained perpetually hopeful that alternating bouts of compromise and escalation would produce a breakthrough. He instead "bargained away many of America's first principles one by one," Brigham noted. Anticipating a successful general offensive in 1972, Hanoi rejected such terms.[85]

At the same time, Nixon decided he could no longer predicate détente on a Soviet-backed diplomatic breakthrough in the Paris talks. He and Kissinger believed that strength and progress in Vietnam were essential to convincing communists worldwide to improve relations rather than take advantage of American weakness. In 1969 and 1970, they dangled détente as a carrot to induce Soviet assistance on Vietnam, but by 1971, it was clear that this approach had failed. Better relations and limiting the proliferation of strategic arms were too important to postpone. Nevertheless, détente and "triangular diplomacy"—playing on the suspicions and jealousies of the Chinese and Soviets—might lead Hanoi's patrons to reduce military and economic assistance or even put pressure on the North Vietnamese to settle. In July 1971, the president revealed that his administration's secret diplomacy had restarted Sino-American relations for the first time since Mao's People's Republic was born in 1949. Raising the stakes and his prestige, he promised a personal visit to Beijing in 1972. A breakthrough with the Soviets soon followed.[86]

The Vietnamese realized that a changing geopolitical landscape created risks as well as opportunities. Saigon hoped that US rapprochement with China and détente with the Soviet Union could put pressure on Hanoi to settle. But reduced great power tensions could make defending South Vietnam less important; why should American taxpayers spend billions fulfilling Vietnamization when waging and winning a global Cold War no longer mattered? Thieu understood that much depended on Nixon's intentions. In Hanoi, leaders feared a "big-power sellout." Nevertheless, Le Duan would not stop his efforts to reunite Vietnam. In late 1971, all sides prepared for another military offensive in the context of an American election year.[87]

Still, events in 1970 and 1971 had damaged the allied relationship and South Vietnamese morale. South Vietnam and the United States had been partners for nearly two decades, but like the 1971 Carole King hit about two lovers who had lost the attraction, it became increasingly clear to a growing number of Americans and Vietnamese that it was "too late, though we really did try to make it." As Nixon put it, "We cannot go along with this sort of dreary business of hanging on for another four years. It's been too long." America's war in Vietnam would end one way or another.[88]

8

Alone Again, Naturally

The Collapse of the Second Republic

1972–April 1975

For Americans, Vietnamization had been what President Richard Nixon called in January 1972 "the long voyage home."[1] It had taken three years, but the number of US troops in Vietnam had dropped from nearly 550,000 men in 1969 to around 150,000 in early 1972. There would be less than 25,000 when that year ended.[2]

But for South Vietnam's anticommunist nationalists, Vietnamization left them, like the protagonist of Gilbert O'Sullivan's 1972 song, "alone again, naturally." Beyond the steady allied troop reductions, they faced a massive enemy offensive in 1972 and watched helplessly as Washington and Hanoi engaged in terrifying bilateral diplomacy that could seal their fate by forcing them into a coalition with their sworn enemies, or worse. They cheered Nixon's political victory, although the congressional elections gave them reason to worry. Vietnamization enabled the Second Republic to endure 1972's trials. But the final American troop withdrawals, US domestic politics, and the 1973 Paris Peace Accords on Vietnam left South Vietnam facing an uncertain and lonely future. Events soon demonstrated how imperfect Vietnamization had been.

1972: Vietnamization's Three Tests

Nineteen seventy-two was a year of triumphs for Nixon. There was the "trifecta": the dramatic presidential trips to Beijing and Moscow and the breakthrough that produced the Paris Peace Accords.[3] There was also his landslide

Alone Again, Naturally   169

reelection. But it was also a year in which Vietnamization faced challenges in three different arenas: military, political, and diplomatic. Its performance suggested and shaped what was to come.

On March 30, communist forces launched an artillery barrage across the DMZ, heralding the start of yet another election-year offensive. The *Nguyen Hue* (named after the Vietnamese leader who defeated an eighteenth-century Chinese invasion) or Easter Offensive (in the West) sought to destroy ARVN forces and achieve total victory within ten to fifteen months. "The time had come to lay all cards on the table [and] sweep away the Saigon forces and regime," Le Duan declared. The party secretary assumed at a minimum that the invasion would leave his forces in control of the northern third of South Vietnam, disrupt détente and rapprochement, and hurt Nixon in the presidential election. Local forces had borne much of the burden of the 1968 offensives, but this was a conventional assault with regular PAVN forces, tanks, and heavy field artillery. Thousands of communist soldiers poured into the South from North Vietnam, Laos, and Cambodia. Ultimately, Le Duan would commit all but a handful of his infantry divisions. As more and more territory fell, he appeared on the cusp of achieving the decisive victory he had long sought.[4]

Again Le Duan misjudged situations in and out of Vietnam. Nixon defied what Hanoi believed to be his political restraints. "We are not going to let this country be defeated by this little shit-ass country," the president bellowed. Publicly, he praised South Vietnam's military performance, and he announced that another 20,000 American troops would be returning home. Privately, he feared the worst: Vietnamization was a hollow strategy and the Republic would collapse at the worst possible moment—right before the November election. The president steadily rolled back the 1968 bombing halt restrictions before finally mining Haiphong and unleashing an intense bombing campaign—Operation Linebacker—against North Vietnam. The RVNAF, backed by massive US air and firepower, eventually halted the communist advance. American politics worked against Le Duan in the short-term, as the silent majority backed the president's dramatic use of airpower.[5] China and the Soviet Union similarly disappointed Hanoi by declining to condemn the United States or halt détente. The Soviets continued planning for Nixon's summit in Moscow and refused to help remove the mines. On the ground, communist forces had more than 100,000 casualties. North Vietnamese morale slumped. Le Duan once again failed to achieve total victory, but the offensive was not a complete loss.[6]

Table 2. Richard Nixon's Troop Withdrawal Announcements, 1969–1972

Date	Total to Be Removed
June 8, 1969	25,000
September 16, 1969	35,000
December 15, 1969	50,000
April 20, 1970	150,000
April 7, 1971	100,000
November 12, 1971	45,000
January 13, 1972	70,000
April 26, 1972	20,000
June 28, 1972	10,000
August 29, 1972	12,000

Note: The "salted peanuts" of US troop withdrawal announcements quickened in the 1972 election year. On November 30, 1972, the White House declared that there would be no more public announcements. There were then only about 27,000 US servicemen left in Vietnam.

South Vietnam suffered enormously during and after the invasion. The fighting killed tens of thousands more civilians and created another wave of refugees. Perhaps as many as 1 million people fled their homes. Places like the provincial city An Loc, which the PAVN surrounded and ravaged for weeks, were devastated. One witness found it "completely smashed, broken into pieces, reduced to rubble." Nick Ut's Pulitzer Prize-winning photograph of a napalm-scorched girl in Tay Ninh captured "the terror of war" in 1972. The offensive also set back pacification and economic progress in South Vietnam. It left pockets of communist control throughout the northern part of the country. Politically, Thieu used the offensive to enlarge his power and crack down on dissidents, the press, and his critics. "The measured optimism of 1967 now contended with anxiety and despair," scholars Tuong Vu and Sean Fear wrote of the mood in this period. The Republic had weathered yet another storm, but there would be no break in the clouds.[7]

The RVNAF's mixed performance contributed to this gloom. The Easter Offensive had been a test of Vietnamization, and as CBS's Bob Simon observed, "So far the results are not encouraging." During the offensive's darker moments, Nixon and Kissinger even speculated about the possibility of outright military defeat. As General Abrams acknowledged, the South Vietnamese had relied on unprecedented US firepower to halt the enemy advance. They would need significantly better armor and weapons to destroy the heavy PAVN tanks in the future.[8] Once again, South Vietnamese military leadership had proven grossly deficient. Vietnamization's architect was frustrated. "You can't win the damn thing just with air power," Laird barked at Kissinger in early May. "You gotta win this damn thing on the ground." Using his well-developed political antennae, the secretary of defense knew that the American war—on the ground and in the skies—was ending and that the South Vietnamese had a long way to go.[9]

Much had changed since Tet 1968. After that offensive, President Lyndon Johnson had expanded the US troop commitment before deciding to level it off. During the 1972 spring offensive, American troop reductions continued. When asked if the onslaught of well-armed communist forces threatened Vietnamization, Laird firmly responded that his program would equip the South Vietnamese to handle this new threat and "completely terminate American involvement in Indochina."[10] He was close to achieving the latter. There were less than 50,000 US military personnel in South Vietnam by the time the fighting subsided that summer.[11]

And as Laird had promised, Vietnamization proved a political winner for Nixon. The Canadian embassy in Washington expressed its astonishment at this feat: "It would have been beyond belief in 1968 that [the] Vietnam War could still be raging four years later without being [a] millstone around neck of admin seeking re-election."[12] Yet, it wasn't. The president gave the American people what they wanted: the return of their brothers, sons, husbands, and fathers and the prospect of ultimate success or at least peace with honor in Vietnam. For that, they repaid him at the ballot box. He won in a landslide, receiving nearly 61 percent of the votes and carrying forty-nine states. "Vietnam elected Nixon twice," Laird recalled. He "won the 1968 and 1972 elections because of the War."[13] The secretary, of course, attributed these victories to the Republican de-Americanization pledge and the subsequent Vietnamization program.

US troop withdrawals worked political wonders for Nixon, but they left the Republic exposed and vulnerable. The American ground war was over: less than 25,000 US military personnel remained in South Vietnam by the end of 1972. Just as Laird had intended in January 1969, Vietnamization had reduced America's combat role to zero in less than four years. This fundamental change in the war *preceded* any peace agreement. Hanoi had attained its goal of expelling US soldiers.

Nevertheless, four years of Nixon's war had not been kind to North Vietnam. Rather than the progressive de-escalation it had hoped for in late 1968, it had suffered renewed and expanded American bombing as well as allied incursions into Cambodia and Laos even as US forces slowly returned home. For a time, communist insurgents and main forces faced great difficulties. The *Nguyen Hue* offensive improved North Vietnam's position in the South, but the Republic had survived. Meanwhile, Nixon's retaliation had devastated North Vietnam economically and psychologically.

In June 1972, the Politburo switched from a "strategy of war" to a "strategy of peace." It was a dramatic and unexpected shift. Scarcely a month before, Le Duc Tho had been gloating in Paris. "The man was as defiant as if he had won the war after all," Kissinger observed. The offensive's staggering military and economic losses coupled with détente's "choking warfare"—Nixon had persuaded China and the Soviet Union to put limited pressure on Hanoi—had a decisive effect. Hanoi needed time to rebuild and regroup. Le Duan softened his negotiating position and dropped the demand for Thieu's removal. At that moment, Kissinger offered an attractive compromise: a four-month standstill cease-fire followed by an American exit and the return of American POWs. "We believe that peace is at hand," the national security advisor prematurely boasted to the press in late October.[14]

That fall, the Democratic Republic and the United States nearly reached an agreement. The talks broke down over whether the 17th parallel dividing North and South Vietnam constituted a political or provisional boundary. The North Vietnamese understood that accepting the former could justify South Vietnam's existence as well as another US intervention. At the same time, Thieu's displeasure with the draft accords made the White House reluctant to offer Hanoi additional concessions.[15]

Frustrated with both the North and the South, Nixon launched on December 18 what became known as the Christmas 1972 bombing campaign. Its planners sought to minimize civilian casualties while leaving the Vietnamese with little doubt about American will and firepower. "I want the people of Hanoi to hear the bombs," ordered JCS chairman Admiral Thomas Moorer. Linebacker II decimated North Vietnam's infrastructure and economy as wave after wave of B-52s pummeled that nation from the air. One survivor likened it to "living through a typhoon with trees crashing down and lightning transforming night into day." "Even Le Duan and his regime had a breaking point, and they had reached it," Pierre Asselin concluded.[16]

Despite Nixon's assurances and Linebacker II, Thieu justifiably suspected a bad deal. As in 1968, he believed that by continuing the war the allies could thwart the communists' ambitions. A settlement now would leave PAVN soldiers in the South and possibly force a coalition government on the nationalists. He pushed for greater enemy concessions and played for time to shore up his domestic position and prosecute the war. He doubted that Vietnamization had, by then, empowered the Republic to survive a disingenuous peace.[17]

American political realities were closing in on the Second Republic, though. Nixon's landslide notwithstanding, Vietnamization and the silent majority had not carried down-ballot Republicans to victory: the Democrats kept both houses of Congress and gained two seats in the Senate. As the president and other US officials explained, Thieu must agree to the terms or expect Congress to cut off aid. Given the composition and mood of the incoming 93rd Congress, this was no idle threat. There was also the possibility of a bilateral deal between Hanoi and Washington. Having no more leverage than in 1968 and thereby admitting that his efforts to Vietnamize the peace had failed, Thieu accepted reality. With Nixon's written promises of aid and airpower (powerfully reinforced by the Christmas bombing), Thieu assented to what he considered a bad deal.[18]

Linebacker II brought all sides back to the diplomatic table, resulting in the Paris Peace Accords of January 1973. The United States would end its military role, accept PAVN's presence in South Vietnam where it existed on the cease-fire date, pay "reparations" in the form of postwar reconstruction aid, and affirm South Vietnam's right to self-determination. The Democratic Republic would return US POWs, accept Thieu, and negotiate with a transitional South Vietnamese government. After the bombing, the North Vietnamese delegation further conceded the language on the 17th parallel, agreed to a limited US military presence in South Vietnam, and relaxed its demand for the release of political prisoners there.[19]

"Essentially, these terms reestablished the *status quo ante bellum,* the state of affairs that had existed before the war's Americanization in 1965," Asselin rightly noted. "Vietnam was going right back to where it had been nine years earlier."[20] Johnson had rescued Saigon from the brink of disaster. Nixon had bought the regime four more years. Events would determine whether South

Vietnam had used the time wisely. What followed then was not just a test of Vietnamization but the sum of American and Vietnamese actions from 1965 through 1972.

Le Duan, Nguyen Van Thieu, and Richard Nixon knew the war would go on. Each hoped he could achieve his aims after the accords went into effect. The settlement gave North Vietnam a much-needed break from the fighting and got the Americans out of the war. Once it had caught its breath, Hanoi trusted it could prove how hollow Vietnamization had been. Nixon and Kissinger believed the agreement would justify continued US assistance to South Vietnam and intervention with airpower should North Vietnam violate it, though they hoped that deterrence and great power diplomacy would make such violence unnecessary. Perhaps they could buy the Republic additional time to mature. Thieu sensed that his country's odds of surviving were narrowing, but he refused to quit. In January 1973, Vietnamization was still a work in progress, and he outlined a spate of reforms to strengthen the Republic. But South Vietnam needed ongoing military and economic aid. This funding required congressional cooperation.[21]

Thieu and Nixon both expected Congress to keep writing the checks, although neither had spent the previous years developing the requisite good-will. Thieu blindly trusted Nixon to get what he needed. He also reasoned that since Americans had so generously helped postwar Europe, "Why not Vietnam?"[22] The 1971 presidential election and the 1972 crackdown hurt him in the US Capitol. He did little to curry its favor thereafter.[23]

Nor did Nixon. Rather than work with legislators, he often treated them as enemies. His secrecy and escalation of the war had hardened congressional opposition. Predictably, Linebacker II had galvanized Senate doves. A poll of seventy-three senators taken on December 21, 1972, revealed that only nineteen favored the bombing and forty-five advocated legislation to end America's involvement in South Vietnam. They were in no hurry to push such legislation after Nixon's landslide, but Vietnamization required a durable relationship with Congress. In the afterglow of his 1972 landslide and the January 1973 Paris Peace Accords, the president saw "a massive problem developing within the Congress." He predicted that it would be difficult to get the appropriations necessary to sustain South Vietnam and uphold the peace agreement. He believed that "what is really involved here is the possible success or failure of our entire foreign policy." He ordered his top aides to try to rebuild support in Congress. They had little success.[24]

The 1973 Paris Peace Accords made it easy for Americans and others to turn a blind eye to South Vietnam's plight. After the US POWs and soldiers had returned home, it was no longer America's war. Senator George McGovern's 1972 prediction was right: "When the corpses changed colors, American interest diminished."[25] Vietnamization had made the Republic strong enough to weather 1972's military and diplomatic travails and had helped to reelect Nixon. Thereafter it would be a Vietnamese war. Even then, blowback from Vietnam continued to influence US politics.

1973–1975, Denouement

In 1971, journalist David Halberstam argued that authoritarianism in South Vietnam had made its way to America. The war had "politicized" every aspect of life, he noted. "There is a new arrogance to this country, a lack of willingness to compromise, to temper personal prejudice," he penned. Vietnam had exposed America's internal divisions and "magnified all faults," producing "what will surely be an age of disillusion here at home." Instead of exporting democracy abroad, Halberstam believed, "We are all being Vietnamized, all a little differently, none of us the same." America's institutions seemed less democratic and more corrupt, particularly the White House.[26]

The June 1972 Watergate break-in was the culmination of the Nixon administration's attempts to use wiretaps, surveillance, and burglary to deal with dissent and win reelection. Watergate and the war ran together. Journalists broke the story during the 1972 campaign, but it was not until 1973 that the ongoing reporting and government investigations transfixed the public. Catalyzed by the emerging scandal, Congress restricted and curtailed the already limited support given to America's Southeast Asian allies. Even without Watergate, Congress and the public would have been reticent to resume the bombing of North Vietnam and risk new POWs. The redeployment of US soldiers was unthinkable. Watergate considerably reduced the president's power and options further still.

Desperate to hold onto office, Nixon consented to new restrictions on the use of force, including a de facto prohibition on US military activities in Indochina. What began as a spring 1973 effort by Congress to stop the American bombing of Cambodia became in the wake of Watergate an explicit prohibition on the use of military appropriations for US operations anywhere in Indochina. Nixon vetoed the original legislation. But with the

Watergate scandal unfolding and Senate majority leader Mike Mansfield determined to keep attaching it to other bills "again, again and again until the will of the people prevails," the president realized that summer that he did not have the political capital to sustain an endless fight with Congress over Vietnam. He gave in. As passed, the prohibition was only on money earmarked for fiscal years 1973 and 1974, but it set a powerful precedent. "That finishes us," Kissinger lamented. The American airpower Nixon and Thieu had counted on to deter or punish Hanoi was no longer available. One South Vietnamese general recalled the Vietnamization formula this way: "Saigon's Infantry + American Fire Power > NL[F] + NVA." "Because one critical variable was missing in this strategic equation," he concluded, "we inexorably ended up losing the war."[27] Thanks to Watergate and the subsequent congressional restrictions, Vietnamization had lost its mean left hook.[28]

Military and economic assistance to South Vietnam went next, tying Vietnamization's other arm and exposing it to a sharp body blow. Between 1968 and 1973, Nixon delivered most of what he had promised Thieu: annual economic aid fell by $100 million, but military aid increased from $1.2 billion to $3.3 billion. As the Paris Peace Accords went into effect and the Watergate revelations shocked the nation, the money dried up. America's own monetary and economic woes little helped, as rising inflation and the 1973 oil embargo powerfully reminded the country of its limits. The strategy also lost its foremost advocate in Washington. Laird, who thought no individual should serve as defense secretary for more than four years, resigned in January 1973.[29]

On the front line of battles with Congress, Deputy Secretary of Defense William Clements captured the administration's growing desperation along with its determination to shift the blame to Capitol Hill. He frequently complained to Kissinger that the Pentagon wanted additional aid for South Vietnam, but despite urgent needs, he understood that an amendment for more money "just won't walk" in Congress. "There isn't a snowball's chance in hell of getting an amendment."[30] "We ought to put the responsibility where it belongs—on Congress," he concluded.[31] Following Laird's example of asking for little or even proposing cuts to appease legislators, in late 1973 Clements recommended slashing military and other aid to South Vietnam. Congress approved, and the money and supplies crucial to Vietnamization vanished. Despite the Pentagon's role in mismanaging and reducing aid to the Republic, Congress became the scapegoat. In January 1974, Kissinger echoed the need to "put the responsibility (for continued peace in Indochina) on their back." To which Clements added, "And early. Henry, we're almost out of soap. We're running out of money, and damn fast."[32]

The rise of human rights concerns in Congress sparked even more opposition to aid for South Vietnam. Revelations regarding the Saigon regime's "tiger cages" for torturing political prisoners reinforced perceptions of its cruel and undemocratic nature. The news media had exposed the tiger cages years before, but they reemerged as a human rights concern in 1973, becoming one more issue to condemn the Republic. "The growing pains of a young democracy had played out in the press and on U.S. television: the repression, the corruption, the Tiger Cages, and the heroin smuggling, to name but a few," summarized historian George Veith. Growing numbers of representatives and senators sought to wash their hands of the Second Republic. In 1974, Congress decreased the administration's requests for economic and military aid to Indochina by one-third. Even then, it appropriated less than it had authorized.[33]

These cuts came as heavy fighting returned to the Vietnamese countryside. Thieu had placed little faith in the accords. Minor communist attacks and infiltration validated his hunch that the enemy would not abide by the cease-fire. He counterattacked in January and February 1973. With the pendulum momentarily swinging in Saigon's favor, Hanoi responded by sending significantly more men and matériel into the South. As so often happened throughout the war, both sides embraced violence to achieve their ends. With the Politburo's tacit blessing, communist forces in the South went on the attack that spring. By late 1973, the accords were in tatters, and the balance of forces increasingly favored the communists. America's internal travails encouraged Le Duan to take ever more aggressive actions.[34]

In contrast, each congressional reduction hindered Thieu's ability to carry out operations or replace essential resources and equipment. "You can roughly equate cuts in support to loss of real estate," the head of US defense assistance in South Vietnam acidly observed. Cut off too much, and America should just "write off [South Vietnam] as a bad investment and a broken promise." The RVNAF was rapidly burning through fuel, ammunition, and military hardware to hold onto what territory it had. By late 1974, the aid cuts meant that, barring a miracle, they would lack the means to keep fighting sometime in mid-1975. "The RVNAF *will not be able to defend* against the Communists, who are better equipped and better supplied since the Paris

Agreement," warned Thieu's top general. South Vietnam's soldiers and civilians read the writing on the wall.[35]

Congressional restrictions on American military involvement and reductions in aid represented only part of the problem as the South Vietnamese faltered while the North Vietnamese remained determined to unify Vietnam by force. Economically, South Vietnam faced rising unemployment and inflation as US aid diminished, the 1973 oil shock drove up oil and gas prices, military needs rose, and a large balance-of-payments deficit compounded fiscal and budget problems. The Republic made noble (and often successful) efforts to spur production and increase tax revenues.[36] Thieu offered to accept a fixed date to end US assistance if Congress would give his country enough aid—$4 billion dollars over eight years—to "achieve 'Economic Vietnamization.'" America had little appetite or even the capacity for such largesse. The weakening value of the US dollar further eroded assistance. The foreign aid, time, and peace Thieu had banked on never materialized. "The smattering of official and private citizens whom I talked to express a sense of hopelessness," reported one American. Economic distress gravely strained South Vietnamese society and hurt Thieu's popularity.[37]

By mid-1973, the Second Republic constituted a political failure, and Thieu did little to repair this damage thereafter. His efforts to rally the nationalists and create a unified political front failed. He remained unwilling or unable to deal with the systemic corruption in South Vietnamese society and the military. To the extent it had existed, the collapse of South Vietnamese nationalism preceded military defeat.[38] Evidence that elites were bribing officials so that they or their sons would avoid the draft indicated that fewer and fewer of them felt the Republic was worth dying for. It also confirmed to the lower orders that the regime was hopelessly corrupt. By 1975, South Vietnam was splintering, with religious sects, ethnic minorities, villagers, and the wealthy all seeking their own safety and interests.[39]

Still, the Second Republic died not from an economic collapse or internal revolution but from military defeat—the one contingency Vietnamization was supposed to prevent. The South Vietnamese military was mismatched and overstretched. It maintained over 1 million people under arms, but only 290,000 of them were regular troops. The communists could field about the same number of conventional forces in the South and could choose the time and place of the engagement.[40] Conversely, Thieu vainly tried to hold onto the entire country even as economic constraints led him to contemplate reducing the size of his forces. He insisted that the military learn "to fight a poor man's war" and demanded they husband scarce ammo and fuel. "We are short everything, except wounded men," one military doctor lamented as the fighting escalated in 1974. Facing cuts in pay and struggling to feed their families, some soldiers began selling arms and other goods either on the black market or to the enemy. Despite post-1972 reforms, poor leadership continued to plague the army, and it never developed the support or logistics expertise necessary to replace the Americans. The RVNAF did well through early 1974, but the loss of American aid along with US logistical and military support slowly crippled its operations.[41]

Hanoi knew few such political, economic, or military challenges. The North Vietnamese had developed a well-oiled military machine capable of succeeding in almost every arena, from management, command and control, and logistics to tactics and grand strategy. The Soviet Union and China continued to pour aid and military supplies into North Vietnam.[42] Hanoi bided its time and regrouped before beginning to expand its presence in Laos and Cambodia. Le Duan launched another major offensive against South Vietnam in late 1974. Finding success and no American retaliation, North Vietnam accelerated its operations. The RVNAF wilted. The Republic quickly lost key provinces and, in a state of crisis, Nguyen Van Thieu resigned. On April 30, 1975, the Republic of Vietnam ceased to exist.[43]

Conclusion

South Vietnam's fall in 1975 made it easy to look back on the 1969–1972 period as a lost opportunity (for military victory or an early peace via US concessions) or the beginning of a national self-deception, with "peace with honor" as a mask for American retreat. Some historians argue that Richard Nixon intended to defend the Republic of Vietnam with US airpower after the 1973 accords but that his ability to sustain a "permanent war" in Indochina withered with the Watergate investigation. Others contend that the post-Tet period represented "a better war," which the United States lost by failing to press the military advantage, withdrawing too quickly, and cutting off the aid and airpower the Saigon regime needed to survive politically and militarily. A third group maintains that Nixon and Kissinger sought merely a "decent interval" between American withdrawal and South Vietnam's defeat. Finally, a fourth group—the post-revisionists—draw on newly declassified sources, international research, and the benefit of time.[1] These scholars seek to avoid the ideologically charged nature of prior debates and synthesize the evidence and arguments, often drawing on aspects of the other three. Where others see easy answers, the post-revisionists see complexity and contingency.

Of the four schools, the "decent interval" has dogged Nixon's policies the most. Assuming that he and Kissinger were fully aware of Hanoi's resolve and Saigon's alleged weakness, adherents of this thesis concluded that the two men prolonged the war simply to preserve their own credibility. Ken Hughes argued that "Nixon and Kissinger realized South Vietnam would fall without American troops. Leaving meant losing." "Vietnamization was not a strategy Nixon seriously pursued," Hughes wrote, "it was a fraud he perpetrated."[2]

Nixon had better intentions when he decided upon Vietnamization in 1969. Key advisers, particularly Secretary of Defense Melvin Laird, argued that he had chosen the best course given America's domestic context. The military echoed this judgment. The president also trusted that his "superpower diplomacy" with the Soviet Union and the People's Republic of China, as well as his recourse to airpower, would compel Hanoi to settle.[3] Ultimately, he judged that Vietnamization was the best and perhaps only way the United States could withdraw honorably and preserve the Republic.

The South Vietnamese affirmed their willingness and ability to assume the burden of their own defense. President Nguyen Van Thieu understood the American political and social context, embraced de-Americanization as a crucial means to maintain US support, and went in with eyes wide open. The strategy might have been a "minefield," as General Tran Van Don remembered, but the South Vietnamese were not "blindfolded," as he alleged.[4] There was a great deal of hope in Saigon that the Republic of Vietnam would survive the US withdrawal.

Overall, the new sources and perspectives contained in this book demonstrate the contingency and the significance of the decisions made by all sides from 1969 through 1971. Leaders in America, South Vietnam, and North Vietnam faced difficult choices. They looked for progress, found it, and pursued their aims despite the desperate odds and human costs. A longer war did not prove a better war. Rather, it catalyzed forces that remade both Vietnam and America.

"No Good Choices": Assessing Nixon's Decision to End America's War

In the midst of the May 1970 Cambodian crisis, Richard Nixon wandered about the Lincoln Memorial before dawn. The president had been replaying his choices. He believed he had done "the right thing" by sending American soldiers into neutral Cambodia. He had made the hard decision. But doubts lingered. He decided to engage the protestors and young adults hanging out there. He tried to convince them that he and they sought the same things: the good of their country and peace in Vietnam. The conversation turned to civil rights, the environment, and travel abroad. Slowly, the walls came down. The students opened up for a moment, but soon the enmity about the war returned. Nixon wanted dialogue and mutual understanding, but neither side convinced the other. He left the memorial with the weight of the world still pressing on his shoulders.[5]

By 1969, the Vietnam War had cost thousands of lives, ravaged Indochina, polarized US politics, and destroyed presidential credibility. Canada's Department of External Affairs reviewed the recent past: "The massive US intervention in Vietnam has cost more in American lives, money, national unity and international prestige than any US government would have knowingly accepted for the objectives attainable by military means in the Vietnam environment." Vietnam was a war of regrets and second-guesses, but both the Americans and the Vietnamese were unwilling to quit as Nixon took office.

It remained then a war of choice. Intractable dilemmas and anguished decisions were as present at the end of America's Vietnam War as at its beginning. Nixon chose to continue the war rather than face the hard reality of personal and national defeat.

In January 1969, his options were "few and awful," as Fredrik Logevall aptly put it.[6] "I had no good choices," Nixon himself remembered. Military escalation to achieve military victory was, he believed, incompatible with "political reality" and larger foreign policy goals like détente. Continuing the war at its present level risked domestic support. But he refused to give up. He declined to blame the Democrats for this mess and order an immediate exit from Vietnam. He also understood that a compromise settlement that left a coalition government in power would be a death sentence for noncommunist South Vietnam. "Neither my head nor my heart would permit me to sacrifice our South Vietnamese allies to the enemy," he recalled. He sought a better exit that did not concede the South to an "inevitable" conquest by North Vietnam.[7]

Moreover, the Second Republic's nascent strength seemed to make hasty withdrawal unnecessary. International observers believed the country had ceased to be that "sick patient" of the mid-1960s. On the outlook in 1964–1965, Logevall noted, "The chief consideration for all of the skeptics of U.S. policy, whether domestic or foreign, whether in Asia or elsewhere, was the utterly dismal politico-military situation in South Vietnam. The essential prerequisite for any successful struggle—a stable Saigon government enjoying reasonably broad-based support—was not merely absent but further away than ever from becoming reality."[8] But by 1969–1970, American and foreign officials convinced themselves that the South Vietnamese government was legitimate, popular, and growing militarily and politically stronger. Nixon saw no good reason to throw away these gains simply to achieve an easy American peace. He accepted and pursued Vietnamization in good conscience. The confidence that made Vietnamization possible also made abject abandonment an unreasonable choice.

Conclusion   183

President Nguyen Van Thieu agreed. He appealed for foreign patience and for sympathy based on this newfound strength, and he proposed US troop reductions as a way to prolong American goodwill and support. "In 1965, we [were] like a patient afflicted with a serious disease," he acknowledged. "The patient's condition was serious. And so South Vietnam called on the allies to come in and help treat our wounds. Now that we are on the road to recovery, we can gradually resume the duties they assumed during our illness, and permit them to go home." In early 1970, he pleaded, "If by internal political instability, if by the fact that our Vietnamese forces and our Vietnamese people cannot defeat the Communists, it is our responsibility and our fault. But we need your help. Help us honestly, correctly and adequately." Given the progress that followed 1967, many observers concluded that South Vietnam deserved this patience and assistance.[9]

Besides, the US public largely desired peace with honor. Many Americans still feared the blow to the nation's credibility that defeat might bring. A majority consistently told pollsters they opposed precipitate withdrawal—Vietnamization, yes; abandonment, no. Most Americans had voted either for Nixon or George Wallace in 1968. In 1969, surveys showed how little attitudes had shifted since the election. Even doves like J. William Fulbright did not advocate an immediate exit. Moderate Democrats like Hubert Humphrey endorsed Nixon's Vietnamization policy. Accordingly, the administration got most of the war appropriations it wanted from Congress.[10] Together, popular antipathy toward defeat and bipartisan support for South Vietnam meant that a decision to "cut and run" was not politically viable. And communist records confirm that there was no chance of a settlement that would remove northern forces and preserve noncommunist South Vietnam. Thus, any deal acceptable to Hanoi was unacceptable to Saigon and US opinion.

Nevertheless, the president's perception that public opinion was volatile and that a growing bloc of congressional doves would oppose any escalation narrowed his options. Concern over American war weariness came out in high-level meetings throughout 1969. Nixon thought that if his administration was going to take dramatic military action against North Vietnam, it would have to do so before antiwar sentiment swelled, something he believed would occur later that year. Events reinforced his fear that the domestic situation was fragile. Had he believed a strong base of public support existed, he might have postponed troop withdrawals and implemented Duck Hook.

Although Henry Kissinger frequently said he refused to let public opinion shape foreign affairs, he too recognized its impatience. He thought that the domestic context afforded only a brief window to employ coercive tactics against North Vietnam. He also wanted to stop Vietnamization before Americans became attached to the idea of regular, unilateral withdrawals. Every troop reduction eroded his bargaining power in Paris. He appreciated the strategic factors involved (though he misjudged North Vietnamese stamina), but his rival, Mel Laird, better understood domestic politics.

Laird held that the national mood necessitated Vietnamization, and without it the American people would insist on an end to the war regardless of the consequences. He took steps to protect and advance the program, deescalate the air and ground war, and limit the conflict's expansion. To do otherwise, he judged, risked increased dissent that would force worse choices and might imperil the country's larger Cold War interests.

Laird's arguments and faith in Vietnamization won out as events tipped the balance in his favor. After Nixon decided in October 1969 not to implement Duck Hook, Vietnamization became America's undisputed exit strategy from Vietnam. It avoided political disaster at home and offered the prospect of peace with honor over the long haul, although Laird often warned the president that it required a partnership with Congress and real reform in South Vietnam. Kissinger fought Laird and lost; the troop withdrawals would continue. He hoped for a breakthrough in the negotiations but resigned himself to the fact that Vietnamization was irreversible.

Judged by the optimism that accompanied Vietnamization in early 1970, the strategy appeared to be working at home and in South Vietnam. Nixon's public resolve, personal diplomacy, and prudent reductions made clear to the South Vietnamese that he was not abandoning them. His popularity indicated that he could handle foreign and domestic problems, but Vietnamization was a testament to domestic fragility.

The 1970 Cambodian incursion bore this out. Congressional and campus dissent exploded. Although the latter soon died back down, the former continued to grow. As witnessed at the Lincoln Memorial, Nixon defended his decision: the American cause in South Vietnam involved the good of the world. He sought only peace with honor. Yet, he understood that the US public and Congress would not accept an endless war. Cambodia reminded him that the silent majority had its limits. There would be no retreat from Vietnamization.

Conclusion 185

Cambodia represented a missed opportunity, though. Riding high in late 1969 and early 1970, the president could have spent his political capital on something other than an expansion of the war. Having embraced the strategy Laird and Thieu wanted, he should have worked with Congress to get the aid it needed. By agreeing to a gradual yet total US withdrawal, he might have gotten legislation that guaranteed assistance over a fixed period—Thieu's Midway proposal for four years of military aid, followed by four years of economic Vietnamization. Perhaps, he could have convinced legislators to pledge that American airpower would defend South Vietnam during this eight-year period. If Congress had been unwilling to fund in 1970 what they refused to pay in 1973–1975, the American war could have ended much sooner and at a much lower cost in US lives and treasure. Perhaps too America could have avoided the lasting toll the war's continuation exacted on its institutions.

Such a compromise would have forced Nixon to do three things he was loath to do. He would have had to ignore the concerns of other key advisers, namely Kissinger. He would have had to abandon the possibility of escalation and coercive diplomacy. And he would have had to work with Congress and embrace strategic transparency, thereby forfeiting the political theater of surprise withdrawal announcements.

But he enjoyed defying the doves and shocking the press with dramatic breakthroughs (as he did at Midway in 1969 and in opening relations with China in 1971). Counting on the silent majority to stand with him and throw the antiwar bums out of Congress, he chafed at cooperating with legislators on matters ranging from Vietnam to the ABM program, détente, and executive commitments to the nation's allies. He relished political confrontation. Laird warned the president that he could not "take on everybody," but all too frequently he did. Secretive, indecisive, and perennially hopeful that he could land a knockout blow on North Vietnam, Nixon continued fighting the war his way. Congress responded by tightening the purse strings.

"Victory" thus proved as elusive for Nixon as for his predecessors. On Capitol Hill, the president turned a potential ally into a foe. In Hanoi, he faced an implacable enemy. Nixon and Kissinger consistently underestimated their adversaries' breaking point. Conversely, they overestimated their own ability to use coercive diplomacy and America's vast military power to compel the Democratic Republic to quit. Nothing Nixon or Thieu could have done would have dissuaded Le Duan from seeking to unite Vietnam under communism. He was so determinedly confident that he would only accept abject American and South Vietnamese capitulation in 1968–1970. Allied perseverance and Nixon's use of brute force finally forced Le Duan to compromise, if only for a moment. The deal that Nixon accepted in 1973—however bad it may have been for South Vietnam—was simply not possible at the start of his presidency. But because American diplomacy failed to secure the mutual withdrawal of US and North Vietnamese forces, Vietnamization determined America's departure from Vietnam.[11]

The program prolonged America's military commitment, and its aid bought South Vietnam four more years of US support (seven if one counts 1973–1975), something that many observers had considered unlikely in 1968. It created lots of chances in 1969–1971 for Thieu and the RVNAF to get it right. The American president argued it was an act of going "the extra mile in standing by its friends."[12] He hoped that the Paris Peace Accords and continued aid would give South Vietnam a chance to survive.[13]

Nixon's stubborn optimism suggests that historians must weigh policymakers' hopes as they assess the Vietnam War. In both the French and American wars, every administration after Franklin Roosevelt appreciated that their chances of success in Indochina were slim. They gambled anyway. The United States bet on the French, Ngo Dinh Diem, American airpower, and Americanization. In 1968, Johnson staked his presidency and personal legacy (bound to some semblance of victory in Vietnam) on peace, and he lost. As Nixon—the inveterate poker player—weighed alternatives, he too concluded that a gamble on Vietnamization over the "long haul" was better than the certain political, personal, and diplomatic costs defeat would bring. And to be sure, he considered any early settlement that abandoned Thieu to be a defeat. There was always the hope that the Second Republic could reform, that the RVNAF would mature, or that the communists would tire of fighting a fratricidal war. Even when the odds worsened in 1972–1973, Nixon hoped that Hanoi's will would collapse first or that ARVN determination and skill would prove capable of defeating the PAVN. But dwindling domestic support and the finality of US troop withdrawals meant that this was the last bet. Crucially, Saigon willingly took this gamble.

Decent Chance: Vietnamization in Vietnam

President Nguyen Van Thieu faced his own hard choices, but he too concluded that the "long haul, low cost" strategy of Vietnamization was the best option. In 1968–1969, his American ally and patron suffered flagging resolve while the enemy refused to quit. Thieu and his officials understood they had only a limited amount of time—1972 on the short end and 1975 if they were lucky—to mobilize the population and make the necessary reforms. He championed US withdrawals to buy his regime more time and money.

Privately and publicly, Thieu was frank about the need to Vietnamize the war (and South Vietnam's economy, politics, and diplomacy) before the last US soldier departed and foreign aid slackened. America was giving them this "last chance" to get it right. Frequently, he affirmed Vietnamese responsibility. "If the U.S. people and U.S. government will give us adequate help, not only in the military field, but also in social and economic fields," he pledged, "we can say very solemnly and clearly that we are responsible for the fate of Vietnam." Economic Vietnamization abetted military mobilization. Every piaster counted, and Thieu's ministers ably managed the most trying of economic and financial conditions. South Vietnamese democracy and nationalism were also critical; he worked at building the legitimacy and popular support needed to win the anticipated political contest with the communists. Even when he faltered, he stuck with his attempt to save the Republic through Vietnamization.[14]

Despite allied military progress and some reforms, the Second Republic faced long odds. The nation remained riven by political, ethnic, and religious divisions. Much of the countryside was susceptible to insurgent activity, the indiscriminate use of firepower, and innumerable deprivations. The insecurity from uncertainty wore on the people daily. To the extent that Thieu promised to include rival nationalists or tackle corruption, these efforts were often window dressing aimed at an international audience. While American considerations were decisive on US strategy, the real war remained in Vietnam. There, Thieu chose the chimera of short-term, easy answers over personally risky reforms and sacrifices.

American troop withdrawals and cosmetic Vietnamese reforms pleased neither the US Congress nor the majority of South Vietnamese. Thieu needed a program of real Vietnamization: a vigorous anticorruption campaign, demonstrable democratic growth, open politics, and a pacification strategy capable of protecting most of the people all the time. Success required a durable South Vietnamese nationalism that might not have been possible. Instead, economic distress, corruption, political illegitimacy, and the threat of violent death reinforced family bonds and individual interests. Thieu's policies had done little to enable the Republic's survival. That his actions (and often inactions) failed to inspire the Vietnamese or antagonized the US Congress does not put the burden of responsibility on the United States. The South Vietnamese were agents of their own destiny, responsible for their own mistakes and errors of judgment.

For twenty years, the United States had given the Republic of Vietnam an opportunity for survival, and South Vietnam still proved incapable of defending itself against a relentless enemy.[15] Vietnamization was perhaps too little, too late.[16] Given Johnson's failure to begin such a program sooner, the narrowing domestic base of support for the war, and Nixon's own political missteps, it was the best the White House could provide. At the very least, Vietnamization lowered the political and diplomatic stakes and enabled US allies and the American public to turn their attention away from Vietnam.[17] All parties understood that Saigon would assume full responsibility for its fate and quickly.

"In the final analysis, it is their war," President Kennedy told Walter Cronkite on September 2, 1963. "They are the ones who have to win it or lose it. We can help them, we can give them equipment, we can send our men out there as advisers, but they have to win it, the people of Viet-Nam, against the Communists."[18] Truman, Eisenhower, Kennedy, Johnson, and Nixon had provided all of the above and then some. It was up to the South Vietnamese to win or lose the battle for hearts, minds, and territory. Beginning in 1969, the United States gave the Republic one last chance. As America's war ended, full responsibility returned to the Vietnamese.

In the final analysis, the United States proved it could end its participation in the war, but it could not unburden itself of the traumas that intervention created. When weighed against the human suffering and ecological devastation wrought in Indochina, America's toll in blood, treasure, and unity was comparatively light. Still, the United States lost too much. Surveying the war at home and abroad in 1967, Senator Fulbright warned, "The price of empire is America's soul and that price is too high."[19] The war's continuation compounded that cost. Instead of "buying time" for South Vietnam, America spent it at an enormous cost. Vietnam still darkens American politics and society, leaving us not unlike Nixon at the Lincoln Memorial, retracing the steps that led America in and out of Vietnam and imagining what might have been if leaders on all sides had made different choices.

Acknowledgments

This book represents years of research, writing, and revising. Many people guided, enriched, and encouraged this work. Its omissions and errors are, of course, my own.

For a book about endings, it is perhaps fitting to begin with those instrumental in its origins. Brooks Flippen was the first person to show me what it means to be a historian; it is an example I will strive to live up to. At Cornell University, I am thankful to whoever put Keith Taylor and Fredrik Logevall's course on the Vietnam War in Baker Lab (and that the class tolerated the chemistry student who joined it, appropriately enough, at the start of the Tet Offensive). Professor Logevall subsequently facilitated my migration from one discipline to another. Later, he offered suggestions on how to create a manageable, international history of Vietnamization. Chester Pach helped me find this topic and shepherded me through the project's early stages.

Numerous others assisted in big ways. Without the aid of the hard-working people at archives worldwide, this book would have lacked the necessary sources. Joseph Appelbaum and Tram Pham were essential translators. The talented and always cheerful Tram went above and beyond, helping me navigate the archives and Ho Chi Minh City. I am also grateful to Alex-Thai Vo for sharing his great work at the Vietnam War Oral History Project. Marvin Fletcher, Kevin Mattson, Ingo Trauschweizer, Paul Milazzo, Patrick Washburn, Dan Hummel, and Lubna Qureshi provided insightful comments on drafts of the manuscript. Luke Nichter and Pierre Asselin commented on portions of it while also offering kind words and sound advice. Tom Schwartz and Andy Johns were invaluable both as occasional sounding boards and as unflagging supporters. I am also grateful to the anonymous reviewers and my editor, Natalie O'Neal, whose suggestions made this a much better book.

I am also indebted to my lifelong learning students. For a generation of scholars born after the war, it is easy to forget that we are writing about real people and events. My students' memories, comments, and questions helped me think through the war and its lasting importance. Their enthusiastic support also kept me going.

George Herring, Jay Veith, and Sean Fear made sure I saw this project through to the end. Meeting George in person was one of life's unexpectedly wonderful moments. The attention he subsequently gave my manuscript was equally unexpected. His thorough comments made me a better writer, but his humility and care were profoundly touching. Fittingly, I met George and Jay on the same day. Jay too provided excellent comments and suggestions while urging me to persevere. I am grateful for the camaraderie we share via email and telephone. Then there is Sean. I would not have been able to research in Vietnam without him. More importantly, he has been a vital comfort and help at critical moments.

Most important of all have been the love, support, and encouragement of my family. Words cannot describe how much they mean to me, and so I will keep it short. James was born just as I began writing; John came as I started revising. I will treasure those years when they were a constant presence by my side (though naptimes were a blessing). My wife, Jaclyn, deserves my utmost praise and gratitude. More than anyone else, she stood by me and cheered my work on. She also endured many a research trip, patiently scanning thousands of documents. It felt like we carted off whole archives. She is a great research assistant, but more importantly, she is the perfect companion and wife. Throughout, the Byrds were a constant source of friendship.

My parents, Russell and Ann Prentice, were an immeasurable help and always willing to take the boys so that I could get more done. They, along with Jaclyn, James, and John, remind me that life is so much more than work. It is for my parents that I have dedicated this first book.

Notes

Abbreviations

APP	*American Presidency Project*
BDF	Bui Diem Files
CCP	Clark Clifford Papers
CDEC	Combined Document Exploitation Center
DEFE	Ministry of Defence
DPC	Douglas Pike Collection
ERR	Electronic Reading Room
FBIS	Foreign Broadcast Information Service
FCO	Foreign and Commonwealth Office
FRUS	Foreign Relations of the United States
GEP	George Elsey Papers
GFL	Gerald Ford Library
HAK	Henry A. Kissinger
HS	Hồ Sơ
IF	Institutional Files
JWFP	J. William Fulbright Papers
LAC	Library and Archives Canada
LBJPL	LBJ Presidential Library
LP	Laird Papers
MC	Miller Center
NAII	National Archives II
NAA	National Archives of Australia
NSF	National Security Files
NSSM	National Security Study Memorandum
PPS	Pre-Presidential Series
PSDF	Popular Self-Defense Forces
PTTVNCH	Phủ Thủ Tướng Việt-Nam Cộng hòa, 1954–1975
PTT	Phủ Tổng Thống Đệ nhị Cộng hòa, 1967–1975
RG	Record Group

RN	Richard Nixon
RNLBF	Richard Nixon Library Birthplace and Foundation
RNPLM	Richard Nixon Presidential Library and Museum
SMOF	Staff Member and Office Files
telecon	telephone conversation
TNA	The National Archives, Kew, England
VCA	Vietnam Center and Archive at Texas Tech University
VNAC2	Vietnam National Archives Center II
VNSF	Vietnam Special Files
VWOHP	Vietnam War Oral History Project
WHCA	White House Communications Agency Sound Recordings Collection
WHPO	White House Photograph Office
WHSF	White House Special Files

Introduction

1. See Ken Hughes, *Fatal Politics: The Nixon Tapes, the Vietnam War, and the Casualties of Reelection* (Charlottesville: Univ. of Virginia Press, 2015).

2. See Lewis Sorley, *A Better War: The Unexamined Victories and Final Tragedy of America's Last Years in Vietnam* (New York: Harcourt Brace, 1999).

3. See Mark Atwood Lawrence, *Assuming the Burden: Europe and the American Commitment to War in Vietnam* (Los Angeles: Univ. of California Press, 2005); Richard Filipink Jr., *Dwight Eisenhower and American Foreign Policy during the 1960s: An American Lion in Winter* (New York: Lexington Books, 2015); Marc Selverstone, "It's a Date: Kennedy and the Timetable for a Vietnam Troop Withdrawal," *Diplomatic History* 34, no. 3 (June 2010): 485–495.

4. Michael Beschloss, *Taking Charge: The Johnson White House Tapes, 1963–1964* (New York: Simon and Schuster, 1997), 372.

5. Quoted in Edwin Moïse, *The Myths of Tet: The Most Misunderstood Event of the Vietnam War* (Lawrence: Univ. Press of Kansas, 2017), 10.

6. Laird quoted in interview by John Noltner and edited by Teresa Scalzo, "The Statesman," *Carleton College Voice,* summer 2010, http://apps.carleton.edu/voice /?story_id=647708&issue_id=647703 (accessed June 3, 2022).

7. See, for instance, Robert Dallek, *Nixon and Kissinger: Partners in Power* (New York: Harper Collins, 2007).

8. Quoted in Jack Anderson and Michael Binstein, "Honor in the Heartland," *Indiana Gazette,* September 24, 1997.

9. While excellent books, Larry Berman's *No Peace, No Honor: Nixon, Kissinger, and Betrayal in Vietnam* (New York: Free Press, 2001) and Pierre Asselin's *A Bitter Peace: Washington, Hanoi, and the Making of the Paris Agreement* (Chapel Hill: Univ.

of North Carolina Press, 2002) are representative of the scholarly attention paid to the Paris talks.

10. For comparison, it took almost twenty years (and four presidents) for the United States to begin a total withdrawal from Afghanistan.

11. See, for instance, Jeffrey Kimball, *Nixon's Vietnam War* (Lawrence: Univ. Press of Kansas, 1998), 91; Robert Brigham, *Reckless: Henry Kissinger and the Tragedy of Vietnam* (New York: PublicAffairs, 2018), 26–27.

12. Thomas Schwartz's *Henry Kissinger and American Power: A Political Biography* (New York, Hill and Wang, 2020) is an excellent, recent corrective.

13. See Andrew Johns and Mitch Lerner, eds., *The Cold War at Home and Abroad: Domestic Politics and U.S. Foreign Policy since 1945* (Lexington: Univ. Press of Kentucky, 2018). On international views of the same, see David Prentice, "The Water's Edge from a Distant Shore: The Transnational Turn, Domestic Politics, and U.S. Foreign Relations," *Passport: The Newsletter of the Society for Historians of American Foreign Relations* 47, no. 1 (April 2016): 42–43.

14. Gregory Daddis, *Withdrawal: Reassessing America's Final Years in Vietnam* (New York: Oxford Univ. Press, 2017), 10–13.

15. For example, David Anderson misunderstands Thieu and overlooks his active role in developing Vietnamization. See David Anderson, *Vietnamization: Politics, Strategy, Legacy* (New York: Rowman and Littlefield, 2020).

16. Andrew Preston, *"Rethinking the Vietnam War:* Orthodoxy and Revisionism," *International Politics Review* 1 (2013): 37–48. See also Ed Miller and Tuong Vu, "The Vietnam War as a Vietnamese War: Agency and Society in the Study of the Second Indochina War," *Journal of Vietnamese Studies* 4, no. 3 (fall 2009): 1–16; Nu-Anh Tran, "The Neglect of the Republic of Vietnam in the American Historical Memory," in *The Republic of Vietnam, 1955–1975: Vietnamese Perspectives on Nation Building,* ed. Tuong Vu and Sean Fear (Ithaca, N.Y.: Cornell Univ. Press, 2019).

17. See, for instance, Edward Miller, *Misalliance: Ngo Dinh Diem, the United States, and the Fate of South Vietnam* (Cambridge, Mass.: Harvard Univ. Press, 2013).

18. Stephen Hosmer, Konrad Kellen, and Brian Jenkins, *The Fall of South Vietnam: Statements by Vietnamese Military and Civilian Leaders* (New York: Crane, Russak, 1980), 14–15; Nguyen Cao Ky, *Twenty Years and Twenty Days* (New York: Stein and Day, 1976), 125; Tran Van Don, *Our Endless War: Inside Vietnam* (San Rafael, Calif.: Presidio, 1978), 181, 183; Bui Diem, *In the Jaws of History* (Boston: Houghton Mifflin, 1987), 341.

19. George Herring, "The War that Never Seems to Go Away," in *The War that Never Ends: New Perspectives on the Vietnam War,* ed. David Anderson and John Ernst (Lexington: Univ. Press of Kentucky, 2007), 341–344.

20. David Schmitz, *Richard Nixon and the Vietnam War: The End of the American Century* (New York: Rowman and Littlefield, 2014), 109–110.

194 Notes to Pages 9–12

1. Good Times, Bad Times

1. See Lawrence, *Assuming the Burden;* Kathryn Statler, *Replacing France: The Origins of American Intervention in Vietnam* (Lexington: Univ. Press of Kentucky, 2007); Miller, *Misalliance*; Fredrik Logevall, *Choosing War: The Lost Chance for Peace and the Escalation of War in Vietnam* (Berkeley: Univ. of California Press, 1999).

2. Michael Beschloss, *Reaching for Glory: Lyndon Johnson's Secret White House Tapes, 1964–1965* (New York: Touchstone, 2002), 213 (emphasis in original).

3. On the NLF, its aims, and its fealty to Hanoi, see Pierre Asselin, *Vietnam's American War* (New York: Cambridge Univ. Press, 2018), 101–103, 107–109, 112–116.

4. Lloyd Gardner, *Pay Any Price: Lyndon Johnson and the Wars for Vietnam* (Chicago: Ivan R. Dee, 1995), 95–97; Francis Bator, "No Good Choices: LBJ and the Vietnam/Great Society Connection," *Diplomatic History* 32, no. 3 (June 2008): 313, 321–324. On Johnson's views of diplomacy and persuasion, see Doris Kearns Goodwin, *Lyndon Johnson and the American Dream* (New York: St. Martin's Press, 1991), 112, 126, 266; Mark Atwood Lawrence, *The End of Ambition: The United States and the Third World in the Vietnam War Era* (Princeton: Princeton Univ. Press, 2021), 82–86.

5. Intelligence Information Cable, CIA, December 11, 1968, #14, "Vietnam CIA Cables for December 1968," box 246, Country File—Vietnam, National Security Files (hereafter NSF), Lyndon B. Johnson Presidential Library, Austin, Texas (hereafter LBJPL).

6. Asselin, *Vietnam's American War,* 107–109, 112–116.

7. For US military personnel figures, see George Herring's *America's Longest War: The United States and Vietnam, 1950–1975,* 4th ed. (New York: McGraw Hill, 2002), 182. For the troop-contributing countries (South Korea, Thailand, Australia, Philippines, New Zealand), see Robert Blackburn, *Mercenaries and Lyndon Johnson's "More Flags": The Hiring of Korean, Filipino and Thai Soldiers in the Vietnam War* (Jefferson, N.C.: McFarland, 1994), 158.

8. Sean Fear, "The Ambiguous Legacy of Ngo Dinh Diem in South Vietnam's Second Republic (1967–1975)," *Journal of Vietnamese Studies* 11, no. 1 (2016): 15–27.

9. Kevin Buckley, "No One Can Be Sure What Thieu Is Thinking," *New York Times,* March 2, 1969; George Veith, *Drawn Swords in a Distant Land: South Vietnam's Shattered Dreams* (New York: Encounter Books, 2021), 13–22.

10. Buckley, "No One Can Be Sure What Thieu Is Thinking"; Lien-Hang Nguyen, *Hanoi's War: An International History of the War for Peace in Vietnam* (Chapel Hill: Univ. of North Carolina Press, 2012), 137–138; John Prados, "The Shape of the Table: Nguyen Van Thieu and Negotiations to End the Conflict," in *The Search for Peace in Vietnam, 1964–1968,* ed. Lloyd Gardner and Ted Gittinger (College Station: Texas A&M Univ. Press, 2004), 356; Diem, *Jaws of History,* 197–198,

205; Nguyen Tien Hung and Jerrold Schecter, *The Palace File* (New York: Harper and Row, 1986), 37–39; Hosmer, Kellen, and Jenkins, *The Fall of South Vietnam,* 63–66.

11. Tran Ngoc Chau, *Vietnam Labyrinth: Allies, Enemies, and Why the U.S. Lost the War* (Lubbock: Texas Tech Univ. Press, 2012), 287, 290–295, 299; Cao Van Vien, "Leadership," in *The Vietnam War: An Assessment by South Vietnam's Generals,* ed. Lewis Sorley (Lubbock: Texas Tech Univ. Press, 2010), 316; Hosmer, Kellen, and Jenkins, *The Fall of South Vietnam,* 63, 66.

12. See Veith, *Drawn Swords,* 234–238.

13. Thieu quoted in Thomas Ahern Jr., *Vietnam Declassified: The CIA and Counterinsurgency* (Lexington: Univ. Press of Kentucky, 2010), 281; Fear, "The Ambiguous Legacy of Ngo Dinh Diem," 27–30; Andrew Gawthorpe, *To Build as Well as Destroy: American Nation Building in South Vietnam* (Ithaca, N.Y.: Cornell Univ. Press, 2018), 103–110.

14. Memo, "A Christmas Message to Americans in Viet-Nam from Ambassador Bunker," December 25, 1968, #52a, "Bunker's Wkly. Rept. to the President 5/68–1/69 [B]," box 105, Country File—Vietnam, NSF, LBJPL.

15. On Johnson's failure to develop a coherent strategy during and after the Tet Offensive, see George Herring, *LBJ and Vietnam: A Different Kind of War* (Austin: Univ. of Texas Press, 1994), 161, 164.

16. Asselin, *Vietnam's American War,* 152–160.

17. Memo, CIA, "North Vietnam's Ability to Withstand Manpower Attrition," June 1968, #46a, "Miscellaneous CIA Material, Vol. 2 [5 of 6]," box 13, NSF-Institutional Files (hereafter IF), LBJPL. Allied casualty figures provided in Herring, *America's Longest War,* 267.

18. Memo, Robert Komer, April 24, 1967, *Foreign Relations of the United States* (*FRUS*), 1964–1968, 5:344–348; "Rostow Sees 'Light at the End of the Tunnel' in Vietnam War," September 12, 1967, item 2120903039, folder 3, box 9, Douglas Pike Collection (hereafter DPC): Unit 1—Assessment and Strategy, Vietnam Center and Archive at Texas Tech University (hereafter VCA).

19. Veith, *Drawn Swords,* 282.

20. David Prentice, "'Everything Depends on Us Alone': President Nguyen Van Thieu's Vietnamization Strategy," in *Republican Vietnam, 1963–1975: War, Society, Diaspora,* ed. Trinh Luu and Truong Vu (Honolulu: Univ. of Hawai'i Press, forthcoming).

21. Ibid.

22. Ibid.; Hoang Duc Nha, "Striving for a Lasting Peace: The Paris Accords and Aftermath," in *The Republic of Vietnam, 1955–1975: Vietnamese Perspectives,* 59–60; Nguyen Phu Duc, *The Viet-Nam Peace Negotiations, Saigon's Side of the Story* (Christiansburg, Va.: Dalley Book Service, 2005), 13, 20, 32–35.

23. Memo, Minister of Information Tôn-Thất-Thiện, "khai thác các vấn đề liên quan đến việc ngưng oanh tạc toàn diện Bắc Việt và hội nghị Balê mở rộng," November 9, 1968, Hồ Sơ (hereafter HS) 1228, Phủ Tổng thống Đệ nhị Cộng hòa,

196 Notes to Pages 16–18

1967–1975 (hereafter PTT), Vietnam National Archives Center II, Ho Chi Minh City, Vietnam (hereafter VNAC2); memo, Tran-Van-Phuoc, "Khai Thác Thắng Lơi Chính Trị Của Việt-Nam Cộng-Hòa," November 15, 1968, HS 829, PTT, VNAC2.

24. Diem, *Jaws of History,* 248; weekly roundups from Saigon, "Political Round-Up," November 12, 1968, and December 10, 1968, Foreign and Commonwealth Office (hereafter FCO) 15/1001, The National Archives, Kew, England (hereafter TNA).

25. Nguyen, *Hanoi's War,* 138–139; memo, Bui Diem (Washington) to Thieu and GVN, "Một Vài Nhận Xét Và Đề Nghị Đề Trình Tổng Thống Và Chính Phủ Việt-Nam Cộng Hòa," January 1969, HS 16671, Phủ Thủ Tướng Việt-Nam Cộng hòa, 1954–1975 (hereafter PTTVNCH), VNAC2; memo, Tran Chanh Thanh to Thieu and Prime Minister, "V/v tình-hình chính-trị tại Hoa-Kỳ trong 1 dl 1969," January 31, 1969, HS 16671, PTTVNCH, VNAC2; memo for the Prime Minister, "Tình hình chính-trị Hoa-Kỳ liên-quan tới Việt-Nam trong tháng 1–1969," February 7, 1969, HS 16671, PTTVNCH, VNAC2.

26. Thieu's delay essentially brought a four-power conference into being. Independently, Hanoi and the United States affirmed that the NLF would be able to attend and participate regardless of how many sides or flags there were. Moreover, the Johnson administration was so confident that Hanoi wanted peace that it had no plans to deal with what unfolded in Paris. As Saigon predicted, Johnson conceded US bombing, but rather than achieve peace, he inadvertently gave the NLF a global platform in Paris for its propaganda. See Gardner, *Pay Any Price,* 513–522.

27. Memo, Nguyen Van Huong (secretary to the President), "Tóm Tắt Buổi Họp-Đồng Tổng-Trưởng Ngày 5/11/1968," November 11, 1968, HS 39, PTT, VNAC2; memo, GVN, circa November 11, 1968, HS 1289, PTT, VNAC2; memo, Tran-Van-Phuoc, "Khai Thác Thắng Lơi Chính Trị Của Việt-Nam Cộng-Hòa," November 15, 1968, HS 829, PTT, VNAC.

28. Asselin, *Vietnam's American War,* 204–205; William Bundy, *A Tangled Web: The Making of Foreign Policy in the Nixon Administration* (New York: Hill and Wang, 1998), 50.

29. Memo, Tran-Van-Phuoc, "Khai Thác Thắng Lơi Chính Trị Của Việt-Nam Cộng-Hòa," November 15, 1968, HS 829, PTT, VNAC2 (emphasis in original); letter, Tran-Quoc-Buu to Thieu, January 23, 1969, HS 952, PTT, VNAC2; dispatches, Tait (Canadian Delegation, Saigon) to External Affairs, "Possible Visit to CDA of SVN Parliamentarians," August 22 and September 3, 1968, file 20-VIET S-9, vol. 11463, Record Group (hereafter RG) 25, Library and Archives Canada (hereafter LAC); memo, J. Fieldhouse, "Visit by South Vietnamese Parliamentarians, March 13, 1969—Meeting with Secretary of State for External Affairs," March 17, 1969, file 20-VIET S-9, vol. 11463, RG 25, LAC. See also Sean Fear, "Saigon Goes Global: South Vietnam's Quest for International Legitimacy in the Age of Détente," *Diplomatic History* 42, no. 3 (June 2018): 428–455.

Notes to Pages 18–20   197

30. *Vietnam Weekly,* folder "Vietnam Weekly," box 28, E-5414, RG 59, National Archives II, College Park, Maryland (hereafter NAII); weekly roundup from Saigon, J. W. D. Margetson, "Political Round-Up," January 7, 1969, FCO 15/1001, TNA.

31. Historian Martin Clemis defines pacification as "both a program and a *process*—a military, political, and socioeconomic method designed to systematically eliminate communist insurgency, establish government control over territory and population, and, ultimately, develop a national political community." See Martin Clemis, *The Control War: The Struggle for South Vietnam, 1968–1975* (Norman: Univ. of Oklahoma Press, 2018), 67–71.

32. Daddis, *Withdrawal,* 36–42; Diem, *Jaws of History,* 188.

33. Memo, January 18, 1969, folder "GVN Private Position 1969," box 26, E-5408, RG 59, NAII; Bunker quoted in Douglas Pike, ed., *The Bunker Papers: Reports to the President from Vietnam, 1967–1973,* vol. 3 (Berkeley: University of California, 1990), 674, 686; weekly roundup from Saigon, Roger Martin, "Political Round-Up," January 21, 1969, FCO 15/1001, TNA; dispatch, Canadian Delegation to ICSC (Saigon) to External Affairs, "USA Troop Withdrawals—SVN Position," January 22, 1969, file 20-22-VIETS-2-1, part 33, vol. 9402, RG 25, LAC.

34. Cable, Australian embassy (Saigon), "Viet-Nam: U.S. Contingency Military Planning," December 2, 1968, Item #8135165, Saigon-Vietnam-American/USA relations, A4531, National Archives of Australia, Canberra, Australia (hereafter NAA); telegram, GVN version of Abrams cable #3345 to Washington, January 1, 1969, HS 45, Hôi đồng An ninh phát triển (1969–1975), VNAC2; statement, Lieutenant Colonel Tran Van Lam (Director for Press Affairs of the Presidency), January 18, 1969, HS 602, PTT, VNAC2; weekly roundup from Saigon, Roger Martin, "Political Round-Up," January 21, 1969, FCO 15/1001, TNA; memo, Warnke to Clifford, January 25, 1969, #10, folder "Vietnam, Documents 9–10," box C31, Laird Papers (hereafter LP), Gerald Ford Library, Ann Arbor, Michigan (hereafter GFL).

35. Notes of Meeting, George Elsey, November 19, 1968 (#159) and January 6, 1969 (#206), folder "Van de Mark transcripts [2]," box 1, George Elsey Papers (hereafter GEP), LBJPL; audiotape conversations between LBJ and RN, October 7, 1968, conversation #13523, WH6810.03, available at the Presidential Recordings Program at the Miller Center, University of Virginia, Charlottesville, Virginia (hereafter MC).

36. Editorial, "New Versus Old," *Saigon Post,* January 1, 1969, 1; editorial, "Hopes and Expectations," *Vietnam Guardian,* January 1, 1969, 1; UPI, "S. Viets to Replace Some Allies—Thieu," circa January 3, 1969, item 2121304009, folder 4, box 13, DPC: Unit 1—Assessment and Strategy, VCA; minutes of Cabinet Meeting, December 4, 1968, "Cabinet Meeting 12/4/68 [3 of 5]," box 15, Cabinet Papers, LBJPL; "Pres. Thieu May Propose Reduction of U.S. Troops," *Saigon Post,* January 14, 1969, 1; "'To Alleviate U.S. Burden': President orders U.S. pullout," *Vietnam Guardian,* January 20, 1969, 1, 6.

198　Notes to Pages 21–23

37. Asselin, *Vietnam's American War,* 171; Foreign Broadcast Information Service (FBIS) Daily Report: Asia and Pacific, November 7 and 8, 1968, folder 3, box 4, DPC: Other Manuscripts—FBIS—Asia, VCA; "'De-Americanization' of the War of Aggression," *Vietnam Courier,* no. 199, January 13, 1969; FBIS Daily Report: Asia and Pacific, January 23, 1969, folder 8, box 4, DPC: Other Manuscripts—FBIS—Asia, VCA.

38. Johnson's secret conditions for the halt were recognition of the South Vietnamese government at the talks, respect for the DMZ, an end to the shelling and attacks on South Vietnamese cities, and a general understanding that North Vietnam would not "take advantage" of the halt. Privately, Johnson also asserted that there must be prompt (measured in days and weeks not months or years) diplomatic progress toward an honorable settlement, otherwise the bombing would resume. North Vietnamese diplomats had indicated that they understood but did not accept these conditions. The American government took understanding as synonymous with agreement and proceeded. Publicly, Hanoi touted the October 31 breakthrough as representing an unconditional halt and encouraged this popular understanding worldwide. Hanoi never accepted Johnson's "understandings." See Asselin, *A Bitter Peace,* 9–10.

39. Lewis Sorley, ed., *Vietnam Chronicles: The Abrams Tapes, 1968–1972* (Lubbock: Texas Tech Univ. Press, 2004), 133–134; Nguyen, *Hanoi's War,* 130–131; memo, Thomas Hughes to Rusk, January 8, 1969, #41, folder "Vietnam—3L(3), NVN Leadership Attitudes, 11/68–1/69 [1 of 2]," box 86, Country File—Vietnam, NSF, LBJPL.

40. In April 1968, Secretary of Defense Clark Clifford independently told the news media that the United States had capped its maximum troop commitment at about 550,000 personnel. President Johnson did not challenge or comment on the change. Learning from the bruising post-Tet debate over a troop increase, the military was not keen to ask for any more soldiers. On Clifford's unilateralism, see memo, Rostow to LBJ, April 29, 1968, #1g, folder "Meetings with the President, January–April, 1968 [1]," box 1, Walt Rostow Papers, NSF, LBJPL.

41. LBJ, *The Vantage Point: Perspectives of the Presidency, 1963–1969* (New York: Holt, Rinehart, and Winston, 1971), 529.

42. Audiotape of conversation between LBJ and Clifford, March 20, 1968, conversation #12826, WH6803.03, MC.

43. Dale Van Atta, *With Honor: Melvin Laird in War, Peace, and Politics* (Madison: Univ. of Wisconsin Press, 2008), 117–119.

44. Jeremi Suri, *Power and Protest: Global Revolution and the Rise of Détente* (Cambridge, Mass.: Harvard Univ. Press, 2003), 2, 164.

45. Quoted in Randall Woods, *LBJ: Architect of American Ambition* (New York: Free Press, 2006), 839.

46. Alan Brinkley, "1968 and the Unraveling of Liberal America," in *1968: The World Transformed,* ed. Carole Fink, Philipp Gassert, and Detlef Junker (Washington, D.C.: German Historical Institute, 1998), 227–228.

Notes to Pages 23–27   199

47. Bunker quoted in Howard Schaffer, *Ellsworth Bunker: Global Troubleshooter, Vietnam Hawk* (Chapel Hill: Univ. of North Carolina Press, 2003), 204.

48. RN, "A New Alignment for American Unity" (CBS Radio Network), May 16, 1968, in *Nixon Speaks Out: Major Speeches and Statements by Richard M. Nixon in the Presidential Campaign of 1968* (New York: Nixon-Agnew Campaign Committee, 1968), 20–24.

49. Quoted in Rob Kirkpatrick, *1969: The Year Everything Changed* (New York: Skyhorse Publishing, 2009), 9.

50. Harris polling quoted in Stephen Ambrose, *Nixon, Volume 2: The Triumph of a Politician, 1962–1972* (New York: Simon and Schuster, 1989), 199.

51. Ambassador E. Ritchie (Washington), "Vietnam and the Elections," September 27, 1968, file 20-22-VIETS-2-1, part 29, vol. 9401, RG 25, LAC.

52. Mark Kurlansky, *1968: The Year that Rocked the World* (New York: Ballantine, 2004), 105; George Herring, "Tet and American Hegemony," in *1968: The World Transformed,* ed. Carole Fink, Philipp Gassert, and Detlef Junker (Washington, D.C.: German Historical Institute, 1998), 48–49.

53. Memo, Lee Williams to Fulbright, March 8, 1968, folder "Memoranda 1968," box 13:7, Subseries 4 Office Memos, Series 95 Office Files, J. William Fulbright Papers, University of Arkansas, Fayetteville, Arkansas (hereafter JWFP).

54. See Chester Pach, "'We Need to Get a Better Story to the American People': LBJ, the Progress Campaign, and the Vietnam War on Television," in *Selling War in a Media Age: The Presidency and Public Opinion in the American Century,* ed. Kenneth Osgood and Andrew Frank (Gainesville: Univ. Press of Florida, 2010), 177–187.

55. Cartoons featured in *Time,* November 15 and 22, 1968.

56. Logevall ably defines "a strategy of coercive diplomacy" as one "in which a state employs threats or limited force to persuade an opponent to cease its aggression." See Logevall, *Choosing War,* 156.

57. Stephen Ambrose, *Nixon, Volume 1: The Education of a Politician, 1913–1962* (New York: Simon and Schuster, 1987), 29–32, 47–49.

58. Ibid., 127–128, 152–156; Conrad Black, *Richard Milhous Nixon: The Invincible Quest* (London: Quercus, 2007), 101, 148.

59. Handwritten notes on meeting, RN, "Agenda for Cabinet Meeting, June 5 1953," Pre-Presidential Series (hereafter PPS) 325:3–4, Richard Nixon Library Birthplace and Foundation (hereafter RNLBF); address, RN, February 24, 1954, PPS 208:14–4, RNLBF; letter, RN to William Bullitt, November 9, 1953, Laguna Niguel Series 364:2, RNLBF.

60. Letter, RN to Bullitt; handwritten notes, RN, May 1954, PPS 325:4–6, 55–69, RNLBF (emphasis in original).

61. Andrew Johns, *Vietnam's Second Front: Domestic Politics, the Republican Party, and the War* (Lexington: Univ. Press of Kentucky, 2010), 243–244.

62. Speech and handwritten notes on June 8, 1964, speech "A Win Policy for Southeast Asia," PPS 208:80:12, RNLBF; handwritten notes for Saigon press

backgrounder, 1965, PPS 347:7:12, RNLBF; column for North American Newspaper Alliance, RN, September 11, 1966, PPS 208:90:8, RNLBF; handwritten notes, circa 1965–1966, PPS 347:7:21, RNLBF.

63. On the paintings and Nixon's commitment, see Henry Brandon, *The Retreat of American Power* (New York: Doubleday, 1973), 325.

64. Publicly and privately, Nixon maintained that America should find some means of getting the Soviets and Chinese to reduce their aid to North Vietnam. For instance, see his 1968 discussion with Bui Diem, recounted in the *Jaws of History,* 237. See also Johannes Kadura, *The War After the War: The Struggle for Credibility during America's Exit from Vietnam* (Ithaca, N.Y.: Cornell Univ. Press, 2016), 38–42.

65. Robert Semple Jr., "Nixon Withholds His Peace Ideas," *New York Times,* March 11, 1968, 1.

66. Memo, Whalen to RN, February 3, 1968, PPS 208:102:21, RNLBF; Richard Whalen, *Catch the Falling Flag: A Republican's Challenge to His Party* (Boston: Houghton Mifflin, 1972), 82–83, 98, 128.

67. RN, interview for WKBK radio, March 3, 1968, folder "Nixon-Statements before the Presidency," box 21, Baroody Papers, GFL.

68. Robert Semple Jr., "Nixon Vows to End War with a 'New Leadership,'" *New York Times,* March 6, 1968, 1L.

69. For more on Laird, see Prentice, "From Hawk to Dawk: Congressman Melvin Laird and the Vietnam War, 1952–1968," in *The Cold War at Home and Abroad,* 36–63.

70. His childhood nickname, "Bom," did not help. For cartoonists' depictions and the nickname, see Van Atta, *With Honor,* 9–10, with the included cartoons.

71. Rowland Evans and Robert Novak, "House GOP Schism Puts Laird at Head of Pragmatic Minority," *Washington Post,* October 18, 1967, A17; Evans and Novak, "GOP Is Prepared to Counterattack Any Vietnamese Approach to NLF," *Washington Post,* September 7, 1967, A21.

72. "Laird Expects Nixon to Win Nomination," *New York Times,* January 5, 1968, 22; Rowland Evans and Robert Novak, *Nixon in the White House: The Frustration of Power* (New York: Random House, 1971), 76–77 (emphasis added); "Nixon Urges Rise in Allied Soldiers," *New York Times,* March 15, 1968, 26; Van Atta, *With Honor,* 126–128.

73. "Republican Platform, 1968," folder "Republican Platforms, 1964–1972," box A88, LP, GFL; Andrew Johns, "Doves among Hawks: Republican Opposition to the Vietnam War, 1964–1968," *Peace and Change* 31 (October 2006): 610–612; Dennis Wainstock, *The Turning Point: The 1968 United States Presidential Campaign* (Jefferson, N.C.: McFarland, 1988), 101–102.

74. RN quoted in Sandra Scanlon, "Every Way Out: Vietnam, American National Identity, and the 1968 Presidential Election," in *US Presidential Elections and Foreign Policy: Candidates, Campaigns, and Global Politics from FDR to Bill Clinton,* ed. Andrew Johnstone and Andrew Priest (Lexington: Univ. Press of Kentucky, 2017), 191.

Notes to Pages 30–33   201

75. Nixon misunderstood the origins of the Korean armistice, giving too much credit to Eisenhower and overlooking Chinese war weariness and the significance of Stalin's death. See Sheila Miyoshi Jager, *Brothers at War: The Unending Conflict in Korea* (New York: Norton, 2013).

76. Robert Semple Jr., "Nixon Withholds His Peace Ideas," *New York Times,* March 11, 1968, 1; Whalen, *Catch the Falling Flag,* 129.

77. Theodore White, *The Making of the President, 1968* (New York: Atheneum Publishers, 1969), 172–173.

2. Only the Strong Survive

1. Memo on inaugural address, Ray Price to RN, January 12, 1969, PPS 208:103:5, RNLBF.

2. RN, "Inaugural Address," January 20, 1969,in John Woolley and Gerhard Peters, *The American Presidency Project* [Santa Barbara: University of California (hosted), Gerhard Peters (database)] (hereafter *APP*), https://www.presidency.ucsb.edu/node/239549 (accessed July 26, 2021).

3. Nguyen, *Hanoi's War,* 131.

4. Having studied and researched both men, historian Pierre Asselin noted, "In Nixon, Le Duan would find his match. Just as the North Vietnamese leader was obsessed with victory as he defined it, so Nixon would seek peace only on his own terms. . . . Each was uncompromising on the matters dearest to him, less because he feared looking weak than because he was convinced he was right. . . . Le Duan and Richard Nixon were true believers—in themselves, and in their ability to eventually prevail in the titanic battle they were about to undertake." Asselin, *Vietnam's American War,* 172.

5. HAK, *White House Years* (Boston: Little, Brown, 1979), 261

6. Rogers quoted in Seymour Hersh, *The Price of Power: Kissinger in the Nixon White House* (New York: Summit Book, 1983), 32.

7. Evans and Novak, *Nixon in the White House,* 21–23.

8. Haldeman notes for December 3, 1968, box 36.18, White House Special Files (hereafter WHSF)-Returned Collection, Richard Nixon Presidential Library and Museum, Yorba Linda, California (hereafter RNPLM); Van Atta, *With Honor,* 4–5, 141–142.

9. RN, *RN: The Memoirs of Richard Nixon* (New York: Grossett and Dunlap), 1978, 289; HAK, *White House Years,* 31–33; note, W. M. Drower, "Mr. Melvin Laird," December 9, 1968, Ministry of Defence (hereafter DEFE) 13/890, TNA; draft note for undersecretaries meeting on December 13, T. R. M. Sewell, "Mr. Nixon's Cabinet," December 12, 1968, FCO 63/333, TNA; note, Patrick Dean to Paul Gore-Booth, "Mr. Melvin Laird," December 19, 1968, DEFE 13/890, TNA.

10. For instance, his militantly anticommunist book, *A House Divided: America's Strategy Gap* (1962), gave him legitimacy among the Republican Party's conservatives.

202 Notes to Pages 34–38

11. Van Atta, *With Honor,* 278–279.

12. On Kissinger's advice to the Nixon campaign, see Niall Ferguson, *Kissinger: 1923–1968: The Idealist* (New York, Penguin, 2015), 827–830.

13. Hersh, *Price of Power,* 13–14, 21; Roger Morris, *Uncertain Greatness: Henry Kissinger and American Foreign Policy* (New York: Harper and Row, 1977), 50–53.

14. Hersh, *Price of Power,* 12, 19; Dallek, *Nixon and Kissinger,* 81–84; Brigham, *Reckless,* 1–2, 5–7, 25.

15. Brigham, *Reckless,* 2; HAK, "Central Issues of American Foreign Policy," in *Agenda for the Nation: Papers on Domestic and Foreign Policy Issues,* ed. Kermit Gordon (Washington, D.C.: Brookings Institution, 1968), 612–613; memo, "President Nixon and the Department of State: A Program to Ensure Control of Key Personnel by the New President," November 11, 1968, box 1.28, HAK, RNPLM; memo, Herb Klein to RN, December 27, 1968, box 6.7, WHSF-Returned Collection, RNPLM; Jussi Hanhimaki, *The Flawed Architect: Henry Kissinger and American Foreign Policy* (New York: Oxford Univ. Press, 2004), 24. See also Ferguson, *Kissinger: 1923–1968,* 843–858.

16. Walter Isaacson, *Kissinger: A Biography* (New York: Simon and Schuster, 1992), 155; Morris, *Uncertain Greatness,* 77.

17. Gawthorpe, *To Build as Well as Destroy,* 119–122; Brigham, *Reckless,* 10.

18. Rogers quoted in Morris, *Uncertain Greatness,* 87.

19. Memo, Laird to HAK, January 9, 1969, box 1.32, HAK, RNPLM; Morris, *Uncertain Greatness,* 86–87; Hanhimaki, *Flawed Architect,* 24–25.

20. Looking back, Kissinger admitted, "Until the end of 1970 I was influential but not dominant. From then on, my role increased as Nixon sought to bypass the delays and sometimes opposition of departments." HAK, *White House Years,* 48.

21. Morris, *Uncertain Greatness,* 132, 135, 156; Hanhimaki, *Flawed Architect,* 24–25; Van Atta, *With Honor,* 153–154.

22. Morris, *Uncertain Greatness,* 153; memo, "Vietnam," October 31, 1968, box 3.9, HAK, RNPLM (emphasis in original); handwritten notes, unknown author (presumably RN), circa January 1969, box 6.13, WHSF-Returned Collection, RNPLM; memo, RN to HAK, January 8, 1969, box 1.37, WHSF-Returned Collection, RNPLM.

23. HAK, "The Viet Nam Negotiations," *Foreign Affairs* 47 (January 1969): 213–214, 218–219, 230, 233; notes of meeting, George Elsey, December 19, 1968, #184, folder "Van de Mark transcripts [2]," box 1, GEP, LBJPL.

24. Memorandum of conversation, December 19, 1968, box 2.3, HAK, RNPLM.

25. Notes, A. M. Palliser, "Notes on a Conversation with Dr. Henry Kissinger in New York on Friday, December 20, 1968," December 23, 1968, Prime Minister's Office 13/2097, TNA.

26. Kimball, *Nixon's Vietnam War,* 91; Brigham, *Reckless,* 26–27.

27. Memorandum on Vietnam Alternatives, HAK to RN, January 16, 1969, box H:019.5, NSC-IF, RNPLM.

28. Ibid.

29. Ibid.

30. See Kimball, *Nixon's Vietnam War*, 76ff.

31. Tom Wells, *The War Within: America's Battle over Vietnam* (Berkeley: Univ. of California Press, 1994), 287–288; interviews of Laird by Maurice Matloff and Alfred Goldberg, September 2 and October 29, 1986, folder "Laird-Oral History Interviews (1–2)," box D8, LP, GFL.

32. Laird, interview with author, April 10, 2007; Clark Clifford, *Counsel to the President: A Memoir* (New York: Random House, 1991), 603–604; minutes, R. Eugene Livesay, December 16, 1968 (#24), January 6, 1969 (#30), folder "Minutes of SoD Staff Meetings, Oct '68–Jan '69," box 18, Clark Clifford Papers (hereafter CCP), LBJPL; notes of meeting, George Elsey, January 16, 1969, #221, folder "Van de Mark transcripts [2]," box 1, GEP, LBJPL.

33. Van Atta, *With Honor*, 158–161; Clifford, *Counsel to the President*, 490–491; interview with Laird by James Reichley, March 31, 1978, folder "Foreign Policy Interviews, 1977-78: Laird, Melvin," box 1, A. James Reichley Interview Transcripts (1967) 1977-81, GFL; James Reichley, *Conservatives in an Age of Change: The Nixon and Ford Administrations* (Washington, D.C.: Brookings Institution, 1981), 110; notes of meeting, George Elsey, January 6, 1969, #223, folder "Van de Mark transcripts [2]," box 1, GEP, LBJPL.

34. RN, *No More Vietnams* (New York: Arbor House, 1985), 102–104; memorandum of conversation, Henry Cabot Lodge Jr., January 19, 1969, *FRUS, 1969–1976*, 6:2; Van Atta, *With Honor*, 157–158.

35. RN, *No More Vietnams*, 102–104.

36. Ibid., 112.

37. Johns, *Vietnam's Second Front*, 236–237, 242; Daniel Ellsberg, *Secrets: A Memoir of Vietnam and the Pentagon Papers* (New York: Viking, 2002), 230.

38. RN, *RN*, 366. See also Timothy Denevi, "The Striking Contradictions of Richard Nixon's Inauguration 50 Years Ago, as Observed by Hunter S. Thompson," *Time*, January 19, 2019.

39. *The Gallup Poll*, vol. 3, 1959–1971 (Wilmington, Del.: Scholarly Resources, 1999), 2173, 2179, 2181, 2189; Melvin Small, *Johnson, Nixon, and the Doves* (New Brunswick, N.J.: Rutgers Univ. Press, 1988), 130, 164; *Gallup Opinion Index* 43–45 (January–March 1969).

40. Hughes, *Fatal Politics*, 56. These numbers were provided to the president in August 1969.

41. Johns, *Vietnam's Second Front*, 236; minutes of National Security Meeting, January 25, 1969, *FRUS, 1969–1976*, 6:39.

42. Handwritten notes, unknown author (possibly RN), circa January 1969, RNPLM.

43. Joseph Fry, *The American South and the Vietnam War: Belligerence, Protest, and Agony in Dixie* (Lexington: Univ. Press of Kentucky, 2015), 253–256.

44. Reichley, *Conservatives in an Age of Change*, 79, 93; Robert David Johnson, *Congress and the Cold War* (New York: Cambridge Univ. Press, 2006), 105,

153–154; Small, *Johnson, Nixon, and the Doves,* 178–179; Johns, *Vietnam's Second Front,* 249.

45. J. William Fulbright, "For a New Order of Priorities at Home and Abroad," *Playboy,* July 1968.

46. Address at the Bohemian Club in San Francisco, Richard Nixon, July 29, 1967, *FRUS, 1969–1976,* 1:2–10; Edwin Reischauer, "Transpacific Relations," in *Agenda for the Nation,* 412–413; Brandon, *The Retreat of American Power,* 80–81. For a longer treatment of US credibility and Vietnam, see Fredrik Logevall, "Vietnam's Place in the Cold War: Some Reflections on the Domino Theory," in *The Most Dangerous Years: The Cold War, 1953–1975,* ed. Malcolm Muir and Mark Wilkinson (Lexington: Virginia Military Institute, 2005): 130–143.

47. RN, *RN,* 102; Johns, *Vietnam's Second Front,* 241–242; Kimball, *Nixon's Vietnam War,* 141–142.

48. Memo, HAK to RN, "Vietnam Situation and Options," early March 1969, box 98.7, NSC, RNPLM; telcon, RN and HAK, 10:45 a.m., March 8, 1969, box 1.4, HAK Telcons, RNPLM; telcon, Haldeman and HAK, 10:10 a.m., March 8, 1969, box 1.3, HAK, RNPLM; H. R. Haldeman, *The Haldeman Diaries: Inside the Nixon White House* (New York: Putnam's Sons, 1994), 38; Editorial Note, *FRUS, 1969–1976,* 6:11.

49. Memo, John Holdridge, January 23, 1969, folder "Briefing Papers 1969–1970," box 27, E-5408, RG 59, NAII.

50. HAK, *White House Years,* 261; minutes of National Security Meeting, January 25, 1969, *FRUS, 1969–1976,* 6:39–40; letter, Lodge to RN, February 12, 1969, *FRUS, 1969–1976,* 6:65–66; memo, RN to HAK, February 1, 1969, box 136.1, NSC, RNPLM.

51. Memorandum of conversation between Rogers and Harriman, January 21, 1969, *FRUS, 1969–1976,* 6:4.

52. Still, both Nixon and Laird expressed skepticism of the military's rosy view of the situation in Vietnam. The latter interjected, "I have heard these briefings each year and each year they get more optimistic and, therefore, I hope that we will be very careful in digesting the material which is put forth."

53. Minutes of National Security Meeting, January 25, 1969, *FRUS, 1969–1976,* 6:24, 26, 29, 36, 39 (full minutes contained in box H:109.1, NSC-IF, RNPLM); Robert McMahon, "The Politics and Geopolitics, of American Troop Withdrawals from Vietnam, 1968–1972," *Diplomatic History* 34, no. 3 (June 2010): 473.

54. Minutes of National Security Meeting, January 25, 1969, *FRUS, 1969–1976,* 6:39–40.

55. Alexander Haig Jr., *Inner Circles: How America Changed the World* (New York: Warner, 1992), 225–226.

56. Sven Kraemer quoted in Isaacson, *Kissinger,* 164.

57. Isaacson, *Kissinger,* 164–165; Haig, *Inner Circles,* 224; Hersh, *Price of Power,* 35.

Notes to Pages 46–50   205

58. Bui Diem to Thieu, January 25, 1969, Bui Diem Files (hereafter BDF), Vietnam War Oral History Project (hereafter VWOHP).

59. Bundy considered this message so sensitive that he made no carbon copies.

60. Memos, HAK to Rogers, January 28, 1969, and William Bundy to Rogers, January 29, 1969, folder "Miscellaneous Hold," box 1, E-5439, RG 59, NAII.

61. Daddis, *Withdrawal*, 46–47, 53–54, 63–66; memo, RN to HAK, February 1, 1969, box 136.1, NSC, RNPLM; Gawthorpe, *To Build as Well as Destroy*, 112, 115, 129–130.

62. Memorandum of meeting between HAK, Laird, and Wheeler, January 30, 1969, *FRUS*, 1969–1976, 6:44–46; HAK, *White House Years*, 241.

63. The offensive killed 4,500 civilians, destroyed 6,800 homes, and created another 27,500 refugees. See Daddis, *Withdrawal*, 93. Rather than testing Nixon, the North Vietnamese intended the offensive to inflict enough American casualties to increase public pressure on the White House to settle in Paris. See Veith, *Drawn Swords*, 343–345.

64. Kimball, *Nixon's Vietnam War*, 125, 127, 131; RN, *RN*, 380–381; memo, HAK to RN, February 19, 1969, *FRUS*, 1969–1976, 6:68–74; memo, HAK to Laird, February 22, 1969, *FRUS*, 1969–1976, 6:74–75.

65. Memo, Laird to RN, February 25, 1969, *FRUS*, 1969–1976, 6:77–78.

66. Memo, Haig to HAK, March 2, 1969, box 1007.5, NSC, RNPLM; memo, HAK to Laird, "Memorandum Enclosing Preliminary Draft of Potential Military Actions re Vietnam," March 3, 1969, box 1007.5, NSC, RNPLM.

67. Kimball, *Nixon's Vietnam War*, 133–134; telegram, Rogers to Lodge and Bunker, March 7, 1969, box 69.5, NSC, RNPLM; HAK, *White House Years*, 263–264; Haldeman, *Haldeman Diaries*, 37–38.

68. Memo, HAK to RN, "Reflections on De-escalation," March 8, 1969, box 91.2, NSC, RNPLM; telcon, RN and HAK, 6:25–7:10 p.m., March 8, 1969, box 1.4, HAK Telcons, RNPLM; memo, Wheeler to Laird, "Mining Plans for Haiphong," March 13, 1969, box 90.1, NSC, RNPLM.

69. On Nixon and Kissinger's deliberative approach to foreign affairs, see Daddis, *Withdrawal*, 50–53.

70. RN, *RN*, 381; Kimball, *Nixon's Vietnam War*, 132–133; memo, HAK to RN, "Breakfast Plan," March 16, 1969, box 98.5, NSC, RNPLM; telcons, RN and HAK, 10:45 a.m. and 6:25–7:10 p.m., March 8, 1969, box 1.4, HAK Telcons, RNPLM; Daddis, *Withdrawal*, 56.

71. Telcons, David Packard and HAK, 9:30 a.m., and RN and HAK, 6:25–7:10 p.m., March 8, 1969, box 1.4, HAK Telcons, RNPLM.

72. Kadura, *The War After the War*, 5, 26–27, 38–42; Melvin Laird et al., *The Nixon Doctrine: A Town Hall Meeting on National Security Policy Sponsored by the American Enterprise Institute Held at American Enterprise Institute, Washington, D.C.* (Washington, D.C.: American Enterprise Institute for Public Policy Research, 1972), 6–7.

73. Nixon's realism made him doubt the Soviets would cooperate. He told a group of US diplomats in Bangkok that summer, "If I were where they sit, I would

keep 'giving it to the US' in Vietnam." See memorandum of conversation, Bangkok, July 29, 1969, *FRUS, 1969–1976*, 6:320.

74. Nixon was correct about Hanoi's dependence on Sino-Soviet aid, though he misunderstood the complicated relationship among the three communist nations. He also exaggerated the Soviet and Chinese ability to influence Hanoi and their willingness to cut off aid to North Vietnam. On the Sino-Soviet split and the value of such aid, see Asselin, *Vietnam's American War,* 140.

75. Kimball, *Nixon's Vietnam War,* 50–51; Hanhimaki, *Flawed Architect,* 40–44; Chris Tudda, *A Cold War Turning Point: Nixon and China, 1969–1972* (Baton Rouge: Louisiana State Univ. Press, 2012).

76. Nixon and Kissinger outlined this "sort of carrot and stick approach" at the second NSC meeting. Minutes of NSC Meeting, January 25, 1969, box H:109.1, NSC-IF, RNPLM.

77. HAK, *White House Years,* 124; telcon, Dobrynin and HAK, 2:45 p.m., February 22, 1969, box 1.3, HAK Telcons, RNPLM; memo, HAK to RN, "Vietnam Situation and Options," early March 1969, box 98.7, NSC, RNPLM.

78. Nguyen, *Hanoi's War,* 163.

79. The Johnson administration had a similar debate in late 1967, with Wheeler urging the president to bomb Cambodia. Believing such an expansion of the war was contrary to their limited war strategy and impossible to hide from the public, LBJ rejected the proposal. See notes of meeting, December 5, 1967, *FRUS, 1964–1968,* 27:473ff.

80. Memo, Ivan Selin to Laird, May 13, 1969, #50, folder "Vietnam, Documents 47–50," box C32, LP, GFL.

81. Goodpaster quoted in Sorley, *Vietnam Chronicles,* 132; cable, Abrams to Goodpaster, March 22, 1969, box 65.7, NSC, RNPLM.

82. Memorandum for the Record, March 15, 1969, *FRUS, 1969–1976,* 6:120.

83. Kissinger's angst over public knowledge of the bombing returned as hints of it reached the press. His anger over what was an unexpectedly small public awareness and reaction led him to wiretap key American officials, including Laird and his military assistant, Robert Pursley. See Rick Perlstein, *Nixonland: The Rise of a President and the Fracturing of America* (New York: Scribner, 2008), 373–374.

84. Brigham, *Reckless,* 35–40; Hersh, *Price of Power,* 60, 121.

85. Memo, HAK to Rogers, March 18, 1969, folder "Personal Papers of William P. Rogers," box 3, E-5439, RG 59, NAII; Brigham, *Reckless,* 40–42.

3. My Way

1. Laird quoted in James Willbanks, *Abandoning Vietnam: How America Left and South Vietnam Lost Its War* (Lawrence: Univ. Press of Kansas, 2004), 15.

2. Reichley, *Conservatives in an Age of Change,* 110; Van Atta, *With Honor,* 150–152, 315–316.

Notes to Pages 54–56   207

3. Laird, letter to author, April 2, 2007; memo, Laird, "T-Day Planning and Force Redeployments from Southeast Asia," July 29, 1969, #84, folder "Vietnam, Documents 82–84," box C32, LP, GFL.

4. For instance, the Accelerated Pacification Campaign had placed an additional 1.6 million Vietnamese, roughly 10 percent of the population, into secure areas by February 1969. A PAVN report similarly estimated that the communists had forfeited the control of over a million people during the first six months of 1969. See Gawthorpe, *To Build as Well as Destroy*, 146–148, and Tran Trong Trung, *Tong Tu Lenh Vo Nguyen Giap Trong Nhung Nam De Quoc My Leo Thang Chien Tranh (1965–1969)* (Hanoi: National Political-Truth Publishing House, 2015), 471.

5. Memorandum of conversation, Thieu, Bunker, and Deputy Ambassador Samuel Berger, at Independence Palace, Saigon, March 21, 1969, box 78.7, NSC, RNPLM; Veith, *Drawn Swords*, 339–340; Buckley, "No One Can Be Sure What Thieu Is Thinking"; Nguyen and Schecter, *The Palace File*, 33.

6. Saigon opinion demanded renewed US bombing, though. For instance, editors at the *Saigon Post* on March 3 hoped Nixon would use American power to "render quick achievement of peace." Indeed, their prescription mirrored Kissinger's: "Perhaps it would be well to gradually commence new bombing raids on North Vietnam, giving some vital spot one massive dose of medicine this week increasing the dosage to two next week if nothing is jarred loose in Paris, and continuing to increase the applications until round-the-clock pounding is achieved." "If North Vietnam will not make it easy for the U.S. to finish this war and return her valiant sons to their homes, we think calling on America's reserve power is justified," they concluded.

7. Buckley, "No One Can Be Sure What Thieu Is Thinking"; Diem, *Jaws of History*, 257; Duc, *Saigon's Side*, 198, 213; memorandum of conversation, Independence Palace, March 21, 1969; press interview of Thieu, March 25, 1969, box 138.1, NSC, RNPLM; weekly roundups from Saigon, Roger Martin, "Political Round-Up," January 28, 1969, and March 11, 1969, FCO 15/1001, TNA; memo, Tran Chanh Thanh to Thieu and Prime Minister, "V/v tình- hình chính-trị tại Hoa-Kỳ trong 1 dl 1969," January 31, 1969, HS 16671, PTTVNCH, VNAC2; memo, GVN H.Q.P., "Những Nhận Xét Sau 6 Tuần Lễ Tại Washington," March 10, 1969, HS 959, PTT, VNAC2.

8. According to Nguyen Phu Duc, Laird refused to share his early planning with Vietnamese officials. "I don't know why [Thieu] kept announcing" potential withdrawals, he told them. "Let us handle U.S. opinion." See Nguyen Phu Duc, *Saigon's Side*, 191.

9. Memo, Trần-Văn-Phước, "Giải Thích Việc Quân Lực Việt-Nam Cộng-Hòa Sẽ Thay Thế Dần Quân Đội Hoa Kỳ," January 30, 1969, HS 17494, PTTVNCH, VNAC2; Diem, *Jaws of History*, 257; Nguyen Phu Duc, *Saigon's Side*, 198, 213; Cao Van Vien and Dong Van Khuyen, *Reflections on the Vietnam War* (Washington, D.C.: US Army Center of Military History, 1980), 316–317; dispatch, R. L. Harry (Saigon), "The Year Since the Tet Offensive of 1968," February 26, 1969, item

208 Notes to Pages 56–59

1950424 South East Asia, South Asia and East Asia despatches 1969, A4231, NAA; memorandum of conversation at Independence Palace, March 21, 1969; press interview of Thieu, March 25, 1969; weekly roundups from Saigon, Roger Martin, "Political Round-Up," January 28, 1969, and March 11, 1969, FCO 15/1001, TNA; "Laird Ends . . . ," *Vietnam Guardian,* March 12, 1969, 1, 6; editorial, "Ready, at Long Last," *Vietnam Guardian,* March 12, 1969, 1.

10. Memo, Laird to RN, "Trip to Vietnam and CINCPAC, March 5–12, 1969," March 13, 1969, box 70.13, NSC, RNPLM.

11. Nguyen, *Hanoi's War,* 129–131; Special National Intelligence Estimate, January 16, 1969, *FRUS,* 1969–1976, 6:1–2; Clemis, *The Control War,* 226; cable, Laird to MACV, February 17, 1969, folder "Modernization of RVNAF," box 4, A1-225, RG 472, NAII.

12. Phillip Davidson quoted in Sorley, *Vietnam Chronicles,* 138–139 (emphasis in original).

13. Memo, Laird to RN, "Trip to Vietnam and CINCPAC, March 5–12, 1969," March 13, 1969, box 70.13, NSC, RNPLM.

14. Jeffrey Clarke, *Advice and Support: The Final Years, 1965–1973* (Washington, D.C.: Government Printing Office, 1988), 347; Laird quoted in Sorley, *Vietnam Chronicles,* 140–141 (emphasis in original).

15. Laird, "Unforgettable Creighton Abrams," *Reader's Digest,* July 1976, 74.

16. Willbanks, *Abandoning Vietnam,* 14; Kimball, *Nixon's Vietnam War,* 137–138; Lewis Sorley, *Thunderbolt: General Creighton Abrams and the Army of His Times* (New York: Simon and Schuster, 1992), 259, 263; Laird, "Iraq: Learning the Lessons of Vietnam," *Foreign Affairs* 84 (2005): 22; Daddis, *Withdrawal,* 46–47; cable, Abrams to Goodpaster, March 22, 1969, box 65.7, NSC, RNPLM.

17. Laird, interview with author, June 21, 2007.

18. Douglas Selin, "Vietnamization: January to September 1969," folder "5/3/1984 Interview—Doug Selin," box D43, LP, GFL; memo, Laird to RN, "Trip to Vietnam and CINCPAC, March 5–12, 1969," March 13, 1969, box 70.13, NSC, RNPLM.

19. These were the same figures Thieu had suggested, belying the notion that the South Vietnamese were surprised by the pace of withdrawals in 1969.

20. Selin, "Vietnamization"; memo, Laird to RN, "Trip to Vietnam and CINCPAC, March 5–12, 1969."

21. Summary of Interagency Responses to NSSM 1, March 22, 1969, *FRUS,* 1969–1976, 6:131, 141; memo, Wheeler, March 20, 1969, folder "Vietnam Miscellaneous 1969," box 47, lot 70D207, RG 59 NAII.

22. American presidents preferred to make executive agreements with foreign nations rather than pursue formal treaties, which would require the Senate's cooperation, consent, and ultimately ratification. These commitments proliferated during the Cold War. Historian Andrew Johns noted that the United States had "signed 947 treaties and 4,359 executive agreements" by 1972. In 1954, the Senate failed (by one vote) to pass an amendment constraining executive agreements. The Senate For-

Notes to Pages 59–61   209

eign Relations Committee's scrutiny of commitments in the late 1960s reflected the ongoing debate over executive-legislative cooperation in foreign affairs. See Johns, "Declining the 'Invitation to Struggle': Congressional Complicity in the Rise of the Imperial Presidency," *Pacific Historical Review* 89, no. 1 (winter 2020): 114–115; Julian Zelizer, *Arsenal of Democracy: The Politics of National Security—From World War II to the War on Terrorism* (New York: Basic Books, 2010), 123–124.

23. Memo, "The Hill," to the Nixon Administration, 1969, folder "1969," box 17, Subseries 3 Committee Administration, Series 48 Foreign Relations Committee, JWFP; Randall Woods, *J. William Fulbright, Vietnam, and the Search for a Cold War Foreign Policy* (New York: Cambridge Univ. Press, 1998), 188–190; statement, Senator Symington, March 11, 1969, folder "FRC Subcommittees, Hearings, Studies, Investigations (Security Arrangements and Commitments), 1969," box 24:1, Subseries 6 Sub-Committees, Hearings, Studies, Investigations, 1961–1974, Series 48, Foreign Relations Committee, 1944–1974, JWFP; Johnson, *Congress and the Cold War*, 153–155.

24. Schwartz, *Henry Kissinger and American Power*, 77, 80, 133–136.

25. "What U.S. Should Do About Vietnam—Survey of Key Senators," *U.S. News and World Report*, February 10, 1969.

26. Robert Mann, *A Grand Delusion: America's Descent into Vietnam* (New York: Basic Books, 2001), 624; Rowland Evans and Robert Novak, "Secret Laird Plan Will Allow Early Troop Pullout," *Washington Post*, March 23, 1969.

27. Evans and Novak, *Nixon in the White House*, 83–84; address, Fulbright to Laird, March 21, 1969, folder "Published Statements and Speeches, January 21, 1968–December 22, 1970," box 2:3, Series 74, Published Statements and Speeches, 1943–1974, JWFP.

28. Senate Committee on Foreign Relations Hearing, briefing by Secretary Rogers, March 27, 1969, item 2121213005, folder 13, box 12, DPC: Unit 1—Assessment and Strategy, VCA.

29. Laird quoted in Wells, *The War Within*, 287–288; memo, circa April 1, 1969, folder "Department of Defense—Problems, 1969," box A67, LP, GFL; Johns, *Vietnam's Second Front*, 257.

30. Memo, Fulbright to RN, March 27, 1969, folder "The War in Vietnam—Memo Given to President," box 31:8, Series 72, Speeches Given Elsewhere, 1939–1976, JWFP; Mann, *A Grand Delusion*, 629; HAK, *White House Years*, 202, 288, 294.

31. Minutes of National Security Meeting, March 28, 1969, *FRUS*, 1969–1976, 6:169–170.

32. Although Laird gets credit for coining the term, "Vietnamised" and "Vietnamization" had been circulating in Saigon since late 1968.

33. Minutes of National Security Meeting, March 28, 1969, *FRUS*, 1969–1976, 6:169–170.

34. Ibid., 169.

35. National Security Decision Memorandum 9, RN, April 1, 1969, *FRUS*, 1969–1976, 6:179

210   Notes to Pages 61–65

36. Willard Webb, *The History of the Joint Chiefs of Staff: The Joint Chiefs of Staff and the War in Vietnam, 1969–1970* (Washington, D.C.: Office of the Chairman of the Joint Chiefs of Staff, 1976), 21.

37. Talking Points for RN, March 31, 1969, *FRUS,* 1969–1976, 6:178; memo, "Recommended Scenario," n.d., circa March 1969, box 1007.5, NSC, RNPLM; Webb, *The History of the Joint Chiefs of Staff,* 106.

38. Bundy, *A Tangled Web,* 66.

39. See Joseph Kraft, "Laird, Kissinger Approaches Affect President's Peace Plan," *Washington Post,* April 8, 1969.

40. Douglass Cater, *The Fourth Branch of Government* (New York: Houghton Mifflin, 1959), 125.

41. Van Atta, *With Honor,* 182–183. For instance, in the March 21 hearing, Laird told Fulbright, "If the peace talks in Paris fail this Administration has an alternative in place." Although the senator did not ask what he meant, that alternative was Vietnamization, and Laird indicated to a Fulbright aide that he would be willing to discuss it in private. See memo, Lee Williams to Fulbright, March 21, 1969, folder "1969," box 14:3, Subseries 4 Office Memos, Series 95 Office Files, JWFP.

42. Telcon, Rogers and HAK, 9:15 p.m., April 4, 1969, box 1.6, HAK Telcons, RNPLM; memo, RN, April 14, 1969, folder "Personal Papers of William P. Rogers," box 3, E-5439, RG 59, NAII.

43. Journalist Scottie Reston called Kissinger to confirm this development. He felt the White House would not sanction these reductions simply for budgetary reasons; it had to be a signal to either Hanoi or Saigon. See telcon, Scottie Reston and HAK, 3:45 p.m., April 3, 1969, box 1.6, HAK Telcons, RNPLM.

44. HAK, *Ending the Vietnam War: A History of America's Involvement in and Extrication from the Vietnam War* (New York: Simon and Schuster, 2003), 74; telcon, Elliot Richardson and HAK, 3:25 p.m., April 1, 1969, box 1.6, HAK Telcons, RNPLM; telcons, Laird and HAK, 3:45 p.m. and 4:25 p.m., April 1, 1969, box 1.6, HAK Telcons, RNPLM; Van Atta, *With Honor,* 184; Webb, *The History of the Joint Chiefs of Staff,* 61–68. On Abrams's use of airpower, see Daddis, *Withdrawal,* 42–43.

45. Memos, Rostow to LBJ, February 26 and March 1, 1969, "Intelligence Briefing 1/20.69 thru Mar. 1969," box 1, Post-Presidential Intelligence Briefings File, LBJPL.

46. Memo, HAK to RN, April 3, 1969, *FRUS,* 1969–1976, 6:180–183; Haldeman, *Haldeman Diaries,* 50.

47. Telcon, RN and HAK, 9:45 a.m., April 5, 1969, box 1.6, HAK Telcons, RNPLM; Haldeman, *Haldeman Diaries,* 50.

48. Memo, HAK to RN, April 15, 1969, *FRUS,* 1969–1976, 6:199–203.

49. Hersh, *Price of Power,* 69; Haldeman, *Haldeman Diaries,* 50–51; telcons, RN and HAK, 5:40 p.m., 6:30 p.m., April 15, 1969, box 1.7, HAK Telcons, RNPLM; telcon, Dr. Kraemer and HAK, 11:00 p.m., April 15, 1969, box 1.7, HAK Telcons, RNPLM; telcon, RN and HAK, 8:00 p.m., April 17, 1969, box 1.7, HAK Telcons, RNPLM; Haig, *Inner Circles,* 207.

Notes to Pages 65–70   211

50. RN, *RN,* 384.

51. Wells, *The War Within,* 293–294; Kirkpatrick, *1969,* 16–17; Terry Anderson, "Vietnam Is Here: The Antiwar Movement," in *The War that Never Ends,* 257; Bill Ayers quoted in Melvin Small, *At the Water's Edge: American Politics and the Vietnam War* (Chicago: Ivan R. Dee, 2005), 126.

52. For detailed information regarding the confrontation at Cornell, see Perlstein, *Nixonland,* 374–378.

53. Small, *At the Water's Edge,* 126, 151; Kirkpatrick, *1969,* 13, 79–82; Wells, *The War Within,* 294, 297; RN, *RN,* 398–399.

54. Wells, *War Within,* 306–308; memo, G. Sheehan, "Youth and Student Unrest," February 13, 1969, box 443.5, NSC, RNPLM; memo, "White House Conference on Youth," 1969, Harlow Subject File, box 14, WHSF:Staff Member and Office Files (hereafter SMOF), RNPLM.

55. Statement, RN, March 22, 1969, box 152, WHSF:SMOF, RNPLM.

56. Quoted in Wells, *The War Within,* 298–299 (emphasis added).

57. Perlstein, *Nixonland,* xii, 380–381; Eric Alterman and Kevin Mattson, *The Cause: The Fight for American Liberalism from Franklin Roosevelt to Barack Obama* (New York: Viking Penguin, 2012), 246–249.

58. Memo, John Freeman, "The Student Problems of the United States," September 29, 1969, FCO 7/1436, TNA; Van Atta, *With Honor,* 244; Wells, *The War Within,* 324; Mann, *Grand Delusion,* 633–634.

59. Packard had left his company, Hewlett-Packard, at Laird's behest.

60. Memo, David Packard, "RVNAF Phase II Plan for Improvements and Modernization (U)," April 28, 1969, #44, folder "Vietnam, Documents 43–46," box C32, LP, GFL; memos, S. Warren Nutter, "Weekly Progress Report on NSSM 36 (Period ending 24 April 1969)," April 28, 1969, #43, folder "Vietnam, Documents 43–46," box C32, LP, GFL; memo, S. Warren Nutter, "Weekly Progress Report on NSSM 36 (Period ending 8 May 1969)," May 9, 1969, #49, folder "Vietnam, Documents 47–50," box C32, LP, GFL; back channel message, HAK to Bunker, May 21, 1969, *FRUS,* 1969–1976, 6:226.

61. Dallek, *Nixon and Kissinger,* 127; Brigham, *Reckless,* 52.

62. Telcon, Rogers and HAK, 10:30 a.m., June 4, 1969, box 2.1, HAK Telcons, RNPLM.

63. Haldeman, *Haldeman Diaries,* 55; Editorial Note, *FRUS,* 1969–1976, 6:215–216; HAK, *White House Years,* 261, 270.

64. Memo, Laird to RN, May 13, 1969, box 76.2, NSC, RNPLM.

65. RN, "Address to the Nation on Vietnam," May 14, 1969, *APP,* https://www.presidency.ucsb.edu/node/239084 (accessed July 1, 2020).

66. Ibid.; Brigham, *Reckless,* 52–53; Dallek, *Nixon and Kissinger,* 129.

67. Selin, "Vietnamization," 18–19; Willbanks, *Abandoning Vietnam,* 44–45; David Broder, "Events of the Past 10 Days Have Shaken Administration," *Washington Post,* June 3, 1969, A19; memo, Lee Williams to Martin Agronsky, May 22, 1969, folder "Vietnam General Materials, 1969," box 45:2, Subseries 17 Vietnam—

(General Materials), Series 48 Foreign Relations Committee, JWFP; Kirkpatrick, *1969,* 95; "Gallup Poll Finds Gains for Nixon," *New York Times,* June 8, 1969, 11.

68. Sorley, *Vietnam Chronicles,* 184–186, 192 (emphasis in original); memo, Ivan Selin to Laird, May 13, 1969, #50, folder "Vietnam, Documents 47–50," box C32, LP, GFL.

69. "ARVN Replacing US Troops Near—Thieu," *Saigon Post,* April 13, 1969, 1; "President Underlines Readiness to Take on War Burden," *Vietnam Guardian,* April 18, 1969, 1, 6; back channel message, Bunker to HAK, May 21, 1969, *FRUS,* 1969–1976, 6:223–225; weekly roundup from Saigon, Roger Martin, "Political Round-Up," May 20, 1969, FCO 15/1001, TNA; speech, Thieu, "President Thieu's Six-Point Peace Plan," April 7, 1969, box 121.4, HAK, RNPLM.

70. Telegram #705, Bui Diem (Washington) to Thieu, May 7, 1969, HS 2162, PTT, VNAC2; telegram #702, Bui Diem (Washington) to Thieu and the Foreign Affairs Ministry, May 8, 1969, HS 602, PTT, VNAC2; Denis Warner, "Saigon Prepares to De-Americanize War," April 22, 1969, item 2121310018, folder 10, box 13, DPC: Unit 1—Assessment and Strategy, VCA; letter, Tran Van Don to Bui Diem, May 22, 1969, BDF, VWOHP; cable, Bailey (Australian High Commission, Ottawa), "Canadian Views on Vietnam," May 6, 1969, Item #7557933, Saigon-Vietnam-consultations, A4531, NAA; Nguyen, *Hanoi's War,* 140.

71. Laird interview with Tom Wells, May 21, 1986, LP, GFL; Selin, "Vietnamization," 19.

72. Back channel message, HAK to Bunker, May 21, 1969, *FRUS,* 1969–1976, 6:225–226; Haldeman, *Haldeman Diaries,* 59; Nguyen, *Hanoi's War,* 140.

73. See Kimball, *Nixon's Vietnam War,* 149–150; Anderson, *Vietnamization,* 33.

74. British Express News Supplement III, "Full Text of President Thieu's Press Conference (at the Grand Hotel on the Morning of June 3, 1969)," June 4, 1969, FCO 15/1033, TNA.

75. RN, "Address at the Air Force Academy Commencement Exercises in Colorado Springs, Colorado," June 4, 1969, *APP,* https://www.presidency.ucsb.edu /node/239334 (accessed July 26, 2021); William Safire, *Before the Fall: An Inside View of the Pre-Watergate White House* (New York: Doubleday, 1975), 137–141; telcon, RN and HAK, 12:30 p.m., May 29, 1969, box 1.10, HAK Telcons, RNPLM.

76. For Fulbright and neoisolationism in a broader context, see David Prentice, "J. William Fulbright and the Retreat of American Power: Anglo-Australian Views of Congress and U.S. Neo-Isolationism," in *The Legacy of J. William Fulbright: Policy, Power, and Ideology,* ed. David Snyder, Alessandro Brogi, and Giles Scott-Smith (Lexington: Univ. Press of Kentucky, 2019).

77. Letter, Fulbright to Tristram Coffin, June 6, 1969, folder "1969," box 9:3, Subseries 1 Foreign Relations Committee (General), Series 48, Foreign Relations Committee, 1944–1974, JWFP; transcript, *Issues and Answers,* June 22, 1969, folder "Issues and Answers," box 31:19, Series 72, Speeches Given Elsewhere, 1939–1976, JWFP; see also Woods, *Fulbright, Vietnam, and the Search for a Cold War Foreign Policy,* 193–194.

Notes to Pages 72–76   213

78. Their visit was remarkably brief. Thieu's consultations with President Johnson, like the one that occurred in Honolulu in 1968, spanned hours and days.

79. Memorandum of conversation, June 8, 1969, *FRUS, 1969–1976,* 6:248–249; Nguyen Phu Duc, *Saigon's Side,* 217–221.

80. RN and Thieu, remarks at Midway, June 8, 1969, WHCA-SR-P-690607, RNPLM.

81. *Gallup Opinion Index* 47–49 (May–July 1969); Hedrick Smith, "After the Midway Talks: Key to Troop-Reduction Tactics Lies in Hanoi's Response to Offers in Paris," *New York Times,* June 10, 1969, 16.

4. Going Up the Country

1. RN at May 15, 1969, NSC meeting, quoted in Editorial Note, *FRUS, 1969–1976,* 6:219; Safire, *Before the Fall,* 141.

2. RN, *RN,* 393.

3. "The Message of History's Biggest Happening," *Time,* August 29, 1969, 32–33; Kirkpatrick, *1969,* 171–190.

4. "Americans Too Anxious to Get Peace—Huong," *Saigon Post,* May 20, 1969, 1, 6; "NVT Off to Midway, House Warns against Concessions to Reds," *Saigon Post,* June 9, 1969, 1; *Vietnam Weekly,* June 9 through 15, 1969, folder "Vietnam Weekly," box 28, E-5414, RG 59, NAII; telegram, Bunker to Rogers, "South Vietnamese Reaction to Midway," June 1969, box 67.8, NSC, RNPLM; telegram, Saigon embassy, "Midway Meeting," June 13, 1969, item 7557958, Saigon—Vietnam—meeting between Presidents Thieu and Nixon at Midway June 1969, A4531, NAA; weekly roundup from Saigon, Roger Martin, "Political Round-Up," June 24, 1969, FCO 15/1001, TNA; telegram, R. L. Harry, "Viet-Nam Consultations," Saigon, June 4, 1969, item 7557958, Saigon—Vietnam—meeting between Presidents Thieu and Nixon at Midway June 1969, A4531, NAA.

5. Most but certainly not all: 52 percent of Saigon residents judged America "a reliable ally," while 20 percent "had no confidence in the U.S." In July, the *New York Times* reported apprehension among Saigon's upper and business classes as manifested in demand for exit visas and an avoidance of investments and projects that would take more than three years to break even. It attributed this flight to US withdrawal and coalition government fears. The Australian embassy in Saigon noted that at least one South Vietnamese general feared that Midway would encourage the communists to keep fighting until they "get hold of the South." Other officers worried that the RVNAF could not master US techniques at finding and eliminating communist forces, much less protect all South Vietnam. Others feared that corruption would undermine Vietnamization and that a lack of genuine loyalty would cause mass desertions after a settlement. See "U.S. Embassy Conducts Poll on Peace Issue," *Saigon Post,* July 29, 1969, and "Many South Vietnamese Leaving in Fear Over Outcome of the War," *New York Times,* July 18, 1969, as well as memo,

214   Notes to Pages 76–78

L. D. Thomson to Ambassador Harry, June 10, 1969, item #7557959, Saigon—Vietnam—troop reduction papers, A4531, NAA, and memo, The Military Situation in South Vietnam, July 9, 1969, #8j, "Intelligence Briefing July 1969 [2 of 2]," box 2, Post-Presidential Intelligence Briefings File, LBJPL.

6. See Nick Turse, *Kill Anything that Moves: The Real American War in Vietnam* (New York: Metropolitan Books, 2013), 207–215.

7. "VN Solons See Gains in Troop Replacement" and Tran Phong ("Focus on Vietnam"), "Coalition: Panacea or Hemlock?" *Saigon Post,* June 11, 1969, 1; memo, Political Developments in South Vietnam, June 9, 1969, #98, "Intelligence Briefing June 1969 [2 of 2]," box 1, Post-Presidential Intelligence Briefings File, LBJPL; telegram, Saigon embassy, "Reaction to Midway Meeting," June 11, 1969, item 7557958, Saigon—Vietnam—meeting between Presidents Thieu and Nixon at Midway June 1969, A4531, NAA; weekly roundup from Saigon, Roger Martin, "Political Round-Up," July 8, 1969, FCO 15/1001, TNA; Nguyen Phu Duc, *Saigon's Side,* 232; Robert Brigham, *ARVN: Life and Death in the South Vietnamese Army* (Lawrence: Univ. Press of Kansas, 2006), 99–100.

8. Telegram, Bunker to Rogers, "South Vietnamese Reaction to Midway," June 1969, box 67.8, NSC, RNPLM; weekly roundup from Saigon, Roger Martin, "Political Round-Up," June 10, 1969, FCO 15/1001, TNA; transcript, President Thieu Press Conference, June 9, 1969, box 78.7, NSC, RNPLM; telegram, Saigon embassy, "Reaction to Midway Meeting," June 11, 1969, item 7557958, Saigon—Vietnam—meeting between Presidents Thieu and Nixon at Midway June 1969, A4531, NAA; telegram, R. L. Harry, "Viet-Nam Consultations: The Midway Meeting," Saigon, June 12, 1969, item 7557958, Saigon—Vietnam—meeting between Presidents Thieu and Nixon at Midway June 1969, A4531, NAA; "RVN, US Closer Together in Anti-Red Fight—Thieu," *Saigon Post,* June 11, 1969, 1; telegram, Tait, Saigon, August 16, 1969, FCO 15/1009, TNA; diplomatic report, C. M. MacLehose to Secretary of State for Foreign and Commonwealth Affairs Stewart, "Valedictory Despatch," September 3, 1969, DEFE 11/696; dispatch no. 2, R. L. Harry, Saigon, August 21, 1969, A4231, NAA.

9. Memo, Clifford to LBJ, "Meeting with President Thieu and His Colleagues," circa July 16, 1968, #2a, "South Vietnam Trip, July 13–19, 1968: Memoranda to the President from Secretary Clifford," box 5, CCP, LBJPL; Gawthorpe, *To Build as Well as Destroy,* 164–175.

10. "President Thieu on Government's Main Efforts," *Vietnam Guardian,* May 26, 1969, 2; editorial, "Looking toward the Future," *Vietnam Guardian,* June 11, 1969, 1; "President Thieu: Land Reform Sharpest Weapon to Fight Reds," *Saigon Post,* June 28, 1969, 1; Cao Văn Thân, "Land Reform and Agricultural Development," in *The Republic of Vietnam, 1955–1975*; Gawthorpe, *To Build as Well as Destroy,* 128–143, 158–159; Veith, *Drawn Swords,* 375. On the Republic's plans and thinking on pacification, see memo, GVN, "Cảnh trạng chung quanh một cuộc ngưng Bắn," July 24, 1968, HS 1228, PTT, VNAC2; MACJ321 Fact Sheet, "Combined Campaign Plan, 1968, AB 143," May 22, 1968, HS 276, PTT, VNAC2; memo, Nguyen Van Huong (secretary to the President), "Tóm Tắt Buổi Họp-Đồng

Tổng-Trưởng Ngày5/11/1968," November 11, 1968, HS 39, PTT, VNAC2; Clemis, *The Control War,* 15–17, 67–71.

11. Thieu's proposal also called for respect of the DMZ, an end to the fighting, internationally supervised elections with the possibility of reunification, and the withdrawal of North Vietnamese forces from Laos, Cambodia, and South Vietnam. See Veith, *Drawn Swords,* 351.

12. Buckley, "No One Can Be Sure What Thieu Is Thinking"; "Ready to Join Private Talks in Paris—Thieu," *Saigon Post,* March 27, 1969, 1; telegram, GVN Ministry of Foreign Affairs to GVN embassies worldwide (Washington, Seoul, Canberra, Manila, Bangkok), May 3, 1969, HS 17494, PTTVNCH, VNAC2.

13. Letter, Bui Diem (Washington) to Thieu, June 28, 1969, HS 1665, PTT, VNAC2; handwritten letter, Bui Diem to Thieu, June 25, 1969, HS 776, PTT, VNAC2; Diem, *Jaws of History,* 262–266.

14. NLF leaders countered that America's demand for mutual withdrawal invented the concept of foreign enemy forces in South Vietnam because it obscured "the fact that 'Viet Nam is one.'" The NLF argued that a provisional coalition government should replace the Thieu regime and have sole responsibility for organizing elections. These elections could only occur after America and its allies departed. See "The Problem of Troop Withdrawal," *Nhan Dan,* June 1, 1969, and "The South Vietnamese People's Right to Self-Determination," *Nhan Dan,* June 6, 1969.

15. Speech, Thieu, July 11, 1969, box 121.4, HAK, RNPLM; FBIS Daily Report: Asia and Pacific, July 11, 1969, folder 9, box 5, DPC: Other Manuscripts—FBIS—Asia, VCA; "Thieu Offers Joint Polls Body with NLF," *Saigon Post,* July 12, 1969, 1.

16. "NVT Offer Hailed; Red Nod Doubtful," *Saigon Post,* July 12, 1969, 1; telegram, Tait, Saigon, August 16, 1969, FCO 15/1009, TNA; "Mixed Reaction: Saigon Bubbling Over New Peace Initiative," *Saigon Post,* July 13, 1969, 1; editorial, "Let the Leader Lead," *Vietnam Guardian,* July 14, 1969, 1, 6; "Peace Offer Anti-Red 'Assault Arm': Thieu," *Saigon Post,* July 23, 1969, 1.

17. Central Intelligence Bulletin, Directorate of Intelligence, "Vietnamization: Progress and Prospects," June 27, 1969, CIA-RDP79T00975A014000080001-7, CIA-Electronic Reading Room (hereafter ERR); "'No More Concessions,' House Warns President," *Saigon Post,* July 25, 1969, 1.

18. FBIS Daily Report: Asia and Pacific, July 29, 1969, folder 10, box 5, DPC: Other Manuscripts—FBIS—Asia, VCA.

19. Ibid.

20. Bunker quoted in Pike, *The Bunker Papers,* vol. 3, 713–714.

21. Cable, Australian embassy (Paris), August 1, 1969, item 7557959, Saigon—Vietnam—troop reduction papers, A4531, NAA; telegram no. 24, Gordon Philo, "Hanoi and American Public Opinion," Hanoi, May 12, 1969, FCO 15/1087, TNA (emphasis added); telegram, Paris embassy, "Viet-Nam," June 11, 1969, item 7557958, Saigon—Vietnam—meeting between Presidents Thieu and Nixon at Midway June 1969, A4531, NAA; telegram, FBIS, "Hanoi Comment on Midway," June 10, 1969, box 67.8, NSC, RNPLM.

216   Notes to Pages 81–82

22. "How the Vietcong Sees the War," Combined Document Exploitation Center (CDEC), April 12, 1969, item 2121413007, folder 13, box 14, DPC: Unit 1—Assessment and Strategy, VCA; FBIS Daily Report: Asia and Pacific, June 10, 1969, folder 7, box 5, DPC: Other Manuscripts—FBIS—Asia, VCA; Hai Cầu, "Schemes to Implement the Pacification Plan and the Dissension within the U.S. Government," CDEC, extract, June 14, 1969, item 2121402018, folder 2, box 14, DPC: Unit 1—Assessment and Strategy, VCA; Ho Chi Minh, "Appeal of President Ho Chi Minh on the Occasion of July 20," *Vietnam Courier* no. 226, July 21, 1969.

23. Asselin, *Vietnam's American War,* 172–174.

24. Memo, "Evidence of War Weariness in North Vietnam," June 11, 1969, FCO 15/1087, TNA; memo, CIA Directorate of Intelligence, "Stresses in North Vietnam," June 12, 1969, "Intelligence Briefing June 1969 [2 of 2]," box 1, Post-Presidential Intelligence Briefings File, LBJPL; Nguyen, *Hanoi's War,* 155–156.

25. Li Danhui, "The Sino-Soviet Dispute over Assistance for Vietnam's Anti-American War, 1965–1972," in *Behind the Bamboo Curtain: China, Vietnam, and the World beyond Asia,* ed. Priscilla Roberts (Washington, D.C.: Woodrow Wilson Center Press, 2006), 292, 302; Robert Brigham, "Vietnam at the Center: Patterns of Diplomacy and Resistance," in *International Perspectives on Vietnam,* ed. Lloyd Gardner and Ted Gittinger (College Station: Texas A&M Univ. Press, 2000), 124; Lien-Hang Nguyen, "Cold War Contradictions: Toward an International History of the Second Indochina War, 1969–1973," in *Making Sense of the Vietnam Wars: Local, National, and Transnational Perspectives,* ed. Mark Philip Bradley and Marilyn Young (New York: Oxford Univ. Press, 2008), 229; Military History Institute of Vietnam, *Victory in Vietnam: The Official History of the People's Army of Vietnam, 1954–1975,* trans. Merle Pribbenow (Lawrence: Univ. Press of Kansas, 2002), 244, 249–250; Asselin, *A Bitter Peace,* 20–21. On the magnitude of Chinese cuts in 1969, see Shao Xiao and Xiaoming Zhang, "Reassessment of Beijing's Economic and Military Aid to Hanoi's War, 1964–75," *Cold War History* 19, no. 4 (2019): 559.

26. The CIA noted most of these defectors were refugees or conscripts, not committed soldiers. Such defections still hurt communist efforts, but the agency judged that "the Communist political apparatus is still strong and active in much of the delta." See Central Intelligence Bulletin, "Vietnamization: Progress and Prospects," June 27, 1969, CIA-ERR.

27. Asselin, *Vietnam's American War,* 174–175.

28. Nguyen, *Hanoi's War,* 129–130.

29. Ibid., 130; Cheng Guan Ang, *Ending the Vietnam War: The Vietnamese Communists' Perspective* (New York: RoutledgeCurzon, 2004), 19–20.

30. Robert Brigham, *Guerrilla Diplomacy: The NLF's Foreign Relations and the Viet Nam War* (Ithaca, N.Y.: Cornell Univ. Press, 1999), 85–87; Ang, *Ending the Vietnam War,* 24; Nguyen, *Hanoi's War,* 140, 192; Asselin, *Vietnam's American War,* 175–177; Cabinet notes, South East Asian Department, "Item 2: Overseas Affairs Vietnam," June 12, 1969, FCO 15/1068, TNA.

Notes to Pages 83–86   217

31. Nguyen, *Hanoi's War,* 129–130; Ang, *Ending the Vietnam War,* 18, 22; Brigham, *Guerrilla Diplomacy,* 85; Clemis, *The Control War,* 212–215; telegram no. 24, Gordon Philo, "Hanoi and American Public Opinion," Hanoi, May 12, 1969, FCO 15/1087, TNA; memo, HAK to RN, "Morning Briefing Items," August 20, 1969, box 10.2, NSC, RNPLM.

32. "Study on the 1969 Spring-Summer Campaigns, SR 6, COSVN," CDEC, July 21, 1969, item 2121402030, folder 2, box 14, DPC: Unit 1—Assessment and Strategy, VCA (emphasis added); "Document No. 64—Summer 1969: A Viet Cong Study of the Situation and Prospects," CDEC, summer 1969, item 2121401006, folder 1, box 14, DPC: Unit 1—Assessment and Strategy, VCA; "Speech Delivered before a Conference of High Ranking Cadre at COSVN," CDEC, July 1969, item 2121401002, folder 1, box 14, DPC: Unit 1—Assessment and Strategy, VCA.

33. Anonymous veteran quoted in Cheng Guan Ang, *Ending the Vietnam War: The Vietnamese Communists' Perspective* (New York: RoutledgeCurzon, 2004), 137.

34. HAK, *Ending the Vietnam War,* 74; Haig, *Inner Circles,* 207–209; Hersh, *Price of Power,* 70, 73.

35. Haig, *Inner Circles,* 227.

36. Telcon, Laird and HAK, 2:10 p.m., April 16, 1969, box 1.7, HAK Telcons, RNPLM.

37. Memos, Dean Moor of the Operations Staff of the NSC to HAK, June 25, 1969, and July 1, 1969, *FRUS,* 1969–1976, 6:273, 282; memo, Morton Halperin and Dean Moor to HAK, July 8, 1969, *FRUS,* 1969–1976, 6:289.

38. Memo, HAK to RN, "Anti-Communist Prospects in South Vietnam," July 22, 1969, box 138.2, Country File—Vietnam, NSC, RNPLM.

39. Memorandum of conversation, June 26, 1969, 7–8:20 p.m., *FRUS,* 1969–1976, 6:272; letter, Bui Diem (Washington) to Thieu, June 28, 1969, HS 1665, PTT, VNAC2.

40. Memo, Richard Holbrooke to Tony Lake, June 21, 1969, box 1046.9, NSC, RNPLM.

41. Britain's ambassador in Saigon, C. M. MacLehose, provided a different take on Clifford's article. In a memo to Whitehall, he wrote, "In general, I found the article conveyed what I would call the 'businessman's' approach to foreign affairs. 'If you don't get a quick profit, get out' might sum it up." See memo, MacLehose (Saigon), July 1, 1969, FCO 15/1041, TNA.

42. Clifford, "A Viet Nam Reappraisal: The Personal History of One Man's View and How It Evolved," *Foreign Affairs* 47 (July 1969): 602–603, 613, 617, 619, 622.

43. RN, "The President's News Conference," June 19, 1969, *APP,* https://www.presidency.ucsb.edu/node/239481 (accessed June 3, 2022). As for the relationship between Nixon's faith in a quick termination of the war and his response to Clifford, see memorandum of conversation, Saigon, July 30, 1969, *FRUS,* 1969–1976, 6:324.

44. HAK, *White House Years,* 275.

218 Notes to Pages 87–90

45. Haldeman, *Haldeman Diaries,* 65.

46. Telegram, C. G. Woodward, "Vietnam—Midway Meeting," Washington D.C., June 13, 1969, item 7557958, Saigon—Vietnam—meeting between Presidents Thieu and Nixon at Midway June 1969, A4531, NAA.

47. Memo, HAK to RN, "South Vietnamese Combat Effectiveness," June 23, 1969, box 74.1, NSC, RNPLM; memo, HAK to RN, July 7, 1969, *FRUS, 1969–1976,* 6:286–288.

48. Haldeman, *Haldeman Diaries,* 69–70; telcons, Wheeler and HAK, 6:45 p.m., July 3, 1969, and 11:20 a.m., July 7, 1969, box 2.3, HAK Telcons, RNPLM.

49. HAK, *White House Years,* 284; memo, HAK to RN, October 2, 1969, *FRUS, 1969–1976,* 6:419; memo, Office of Chief of Naval Operations, "Duck Hook," July 20, 1969, box 98.1, NSC, RNPLM.

50. Nixon and Kissinger were also reopening the latter's previous back channel to Hanoi—Raymond Aubrac and Jean Sainteny—to deliver the ultimatum. See Brigham, *Reckless,* 57–59.

51. Editorial Note, *FRUS, 1969–1976,* 6:258; Intelligence Memorandum, "Stresses in North Vietnam," June 12, 1969, *FRUS, 1969–1976,* 6:259; telcon, Wheeler and HAK, 11:20 a.m., July 7, 1969, box 2.3, HAK Telcons, RNPLM.

52. Nixon, Laird, Rogers, Kissinger, Wheeler, Attorney General John Mitchell, and General Robert Cushman (Deputy CIA Director) attended this special session.

53. HAK, *White House Years,* 276; Richard Hunt, *Melvin Laird and the Foundation of the Post-Vietnam Military,* Secretaries of Defense Historical Series, vol. 7 (Washington, D.C.: Historical Office, Office of the Secretary of Defense, 2015), 112–113; Van Atta, *With Honor,* 204–205; Kimball, *Nixon's Vietnam War,* 151.

54. Sorley, *Thunderbolt,* 255.

55. Van Atta, *With Honor,* 204–205; telcon, Laird and HAK, 10:40 a.m., July 8, 1969, box 2.3, HAK Telcons, RNPLM (emphasis in original).

56. RN, "Letters of the President and President Ho Chi Minh of the Democratic Republic of Vietnam," *APP,* https://www.presidency.ucsb.edu/node/240029 (accessed July 26, 2021); Brigham, *Reckless,* 58–59.

57. Memo of conversation, Carl Marcy, July 29, 1969, folder "1969," box 17, Subseries 3 Committee Administration, Series 48 Foreign Relations Committee, JWFP; statement, Senator Symington, August 13, 1969, folder "FRC (Subcommittees, Hearings, Studies, Investigations (Security Arrangements and Commitments), 1969," box 24:1, Subseries 6 Sub-Committees, Hearings, Studies, Investigations, 1961–1974, Series 48, Foreign Relations Committee, 1944–1974, JWFP; announcement, Stuart Symington, "Plans of the Subcommittee on United States Security Agreements and Commitments Abroad," August 24, 1969, folder "1969—Sec. Agreements and Commitments," box 24:1, Subseries 6 Subcommittees, Series 48 Foreign Relations Committee, JWFP.

58. "President Nixon's Remarks at Congressional Breakfast with Remarks by Secretary Kennedy, Secretary Fowler, Secretary Rogers, Senator Mansfield, Con-

Notes to Pages 90–93   219

gressman Hale Boggs," July 22, 1969, WHCA-SR-P-690716, RNPLM. I am grateful to the anonymous *Diplomatic History* reviewer who brought this recording to my attention.

59. Ibid.

60. Ibid. On the "structures of peace," see Robert Litwak, *Détente and the Nixon Doctrine: American Foreign Policy and the Pursuit of Stability, 1969–1976* (New York: Cambridge Univ. Press, 1984). In a June 28 background briefing, Kissinger similarly described the upcoming trip as an effort to "lay the foundation for a 'post-Vietnam' South Asia policy in which American responsibilities and contributions can be redefined in the light of current realities." At the same time, the Romanian stop was to facilitate the birth of "an era of negotiation." See Background Briefing, June 28, 1969, #9-j, "Intelligence Briefing July 1969 [2 of 2]," box 2, Post-Presidential Intelligence Briefings File, LBJPL.

61. RN, *RN,* 394–395; RN, "Informal Remarks in Guam with Newsmen," July 25, 1969, *APP,* https://www.presidency.ucsb.edu/node/239667 (accessed July 26, 2021). See also memorandum of conversation, Bangkok, July 29, 1969, *FRUS, 1969–1976,* 6:317–320.

62. See Jeffrey Kimball, "The Nixon Doctrine: A Saga of Misunderstanding," *Presidential Studies Quarterly* 36, no. 1 (March 2006): 59–74. An advocate of the Nixon Doctrine, Laird argued it reflected "the basic philosophy underlying the conduct of both our foreign and national security affairs policies." See Laird et al., *The Nixon Doctrine.*

63. Haig, *Inner Circles,* 230. Kissinger's assistant John Holdridge noted that Nixon was "extremely tired at the time" of the Guam briefing and that the *New York Times* account "was more dramatic and stark in its terms . . . than the President's actual language warranted." Holdridge quoted in memo, Australian embassy (Washington), "President Nixon's Tour," August 10, 1969, item 3165068, A5882, NAA.

64. RN, "America and the World," in *The Nixon Yearbook 1968* (Nixon/Agnew Committee, 1968); campaign speech, RN, Omaha, Nebraska, May 6, 1968, *FRUS, 1969–1976,* 5:48–49; draft, Ray Price, "To Keep the Peace," October 17, 1968, PPS 208:101:14, RNLBF; radio broadcast, RN, "To Keep the Peace," October 19, 1968, PPS 208:101:14, RNLBF.

65. Nguyen Phu Duc, *Saigon's Side,* 225–226, 228–229; memorandum of conversation, Nixon, Thieu, et al., July 30, 1969, folder "Personal Papers of William P. Rogers," box 3, E-5439, RG 59, NAII; dispatch, Tait (Canadian Delegation to ICSC, Saigon) to External Affairs, "Interview with Pres Thieu," August 16, 1969, file 20-22-VIETS-2-1, part 36, vol. 9402, RG 25, LAC.

66. Ibid.; dispatch, Tait (Canadian Delegation to ICSC, Saigon) to External Affairs, "Vietnam: Pres Nixon's Visit to Saigon," August 6, 1969, file 20-22-VIETS-2-1, part 36, vol. 9402, RG 25, LAC.

67. "Text of Speech by Nixon" at Independence Palace reprinted in the *Saigon Post,* August 1, 1969, 1–2, 8.

220 Notes to Pages 94–97

68. Memo, Bui Quang Dinh to directors of news media, "Tổng Thống Hoa Kỳ R. Nixon viếng thăm Việt-Nam Cộng-Hòa," August 4, 1969, HS 1660, PTT, VNAC2; dispatch, Tait, "Vietnam: Pres Nixon's Visit to Saigon"; "Visit Regarded Notice to Reds," *Saigon Post,* July 31, 1969, 1; editorial, "Nixon's Act of Faith," *Vietnam Guardian,* August 1, 1969, 1; editorial, "The Ultimate Challenge," *Vietnam Guardian,* July 29, 1969, 1.

69. Richard Ruth, *In Buddha's Company: Thai Soldiers in the Vietnam War* (Honolulu: Univ. of Hawai'i Press, 2011), 2–4, 10–14; minutes of National Security Meeting, January 25, 1969, *FRUS,* 1969–1976, 6:24; memo, Mr. Littlejohn Cook, "President Nixon's Visit to Thailand," Thailand, August 12, 1969, FCO 15/798, TNA. Nixon also stopped in India and Pakistan, where he similarly clarified the new direction in US foreign policy. See memorandum of conversation, Washington, July 10, 1969, *FRUS,* 1969–1972, E-7: document 26; memorandum of conversation, New Delhi, July 31, 1969, *FRUS,* 1969–1972, E-7: document 29; memorandum of conversation, Lahore, August 1, 1969, *FRUS,* 1969–1972, E-7: document 31.

70. RN, *RN,* 395–396; memorandum of conversation, Bucharest, August 3, 1969, *FRUS,* 1969–1976, 29:448–455.

71. Logevall, *Choosing War,* 276–279.

72. Memo, FCO, for "British-American Parliamentary Group: Bermuda Conference: 17–20 March, The Future of Asia: Vietnam," March 5, 1969, FCO 15/792, TNA; dispatch, R. A. Burroughs, "Bilateral U.S./U.K. Planning Talks, Washington, 21 April, 1969," FCO 49/266, TNA; memo, C. S. R. Giffard, "Recent Developments in Soviet Policy in Asia," July 11, 1969, FCO 15/795, TNA; memo, C. M. MacLehose (Saigon), July 1, 1969, FCO 15/1041, TNA.

73. Cabinet briefing notes, South East Asian Department, "Vietnam," November 7, 12, and December 7, 1968, FCO 15/1067, TNA; Cabinet briefing note, South East Asian Department, "Item 2: Overseas Affairs Vietnam," March 5, 1969, FCO 15/1068, TNA.

74. Cabinet memo with comments, FCO Secretary Stewart, "Vietnam: An Assessment of the Present Position and, in particular, of the Probable Consequences of any Precipitate American Withdrawal," early January 1970, FCO 15/1095, TNA; draft letter, A. D. Brighty, early May 1969, FCO 15/1040, TNA; memo, C. M. MacLehose, "Call on Ambassador Bunker, 18 April," April 19, 1969, FCO 15/1040, TNA; diplomatic report, MacLehose to Secretary of State for Foreign and Commonwealth Affairs Stewart, "Valedictory Despatch," September 3, 1969, DEFE 11/696, TNA.

75. Prentice, "J. William Fulbright and the Retreat of American Power," 99–102.

76. Dispatch, Pat Dean, "Neo-Isolationism," Washington, July 16, 1968, FCO 7/778, TNA; report, Pat Dean to Mr. Stewart, "United States and British Foreign Policy," July 31, 1968, FCO 7/778, TNA; letter, John Freeman to Stewart, June 26, 1969, FCO 7/1427, TNA; John Freeman, "President's Difficulties," June 30, 1969, FCO 7/1420, TNA.

77. Records of talks between Wilson and RN, August 3, 1969, FCO 7/1428, TNA; memo, Harold Wilson, "The Prime Minister's Account of His Conversation

with President Nixon at Mildenhall on Sunday, August 3, 1969," FCO 15/1031, TNA; telcon, RN and HAK, 6:50 p.m., August 5, 1969, box 2.5, HAK Telcons, RNPLM.

78. Asselin, *Vietnam's American War,* 177–179. Historian Robert Brigham noted that Hanoi also wanted to determine if Nixon's real position was softer than his public rhetoric suggested. In Kissinger's eagerness to keep the secret talks going, he promised on August 4 that if the North Vietnamese kept the back channel open, "the United States will adjust its military activities to create the most favorable circumstances to arrive at a solution." This statement likely confirmed Hanoi's belief in American weakness and nullified the ultimatum's intended effect. See Brigham, *Reckless,* 61, 65.

79. Talking Points for HAK-NVN Secret Meeting, August 4, 1969, box 121.3, HAK, RNPLM; "Attachment: Memorandum of Conversation," HAK to RN, August 6, 1969, *FRUS,* 1969–1976, 6:332–333; letter, Lodge to HAK, August 9, 1969, *FRUS,* 1969–1976, 6:344–345, 348.

80. Lyndon Johnson had attempted the same in 1967 with his Citizens Committee for Peace with Freedom in Vietnam. See Sandra Scanlon, *The Pro-War Movement: Domestic Support for the Vietnam War and the Making of Modern American Conservatism* (Boston: Univ. of Massachusetts Press, 2013), 66–68.

81. *Gallup Opinion Index* 49–50 (July–August 1969); Kimball, *Nixon's Vietnam War,* 165–166; Perlstein, *Nixonland,* 421, 439; Chester Pach, "'Our Worst Enemy Seems to Be the Press': TV News, the Nixon Administration, and U.S. Troop Withdrawal from Vietnam, 1969–1973," *Diplomatic History* 34, no. 3 (June 2010): 555–556; Haldeman, *Haldeman Diaries,* 81–82; memo, John Brown to HAK; July 14, 1969, box 42, WHSF-Special Files, RNPLM.

82. Anthony Lake interview with James Reichley, October 28, 1977, folder "Foreign Policy Interviews, 1977-78: Lake, Anthony," box 1, A. James Reichley Interview Transcripts (1967) 1977-81, GFL; Kimball, *Nixon's Vietnam War,* 159; John Prados, *The Blood Road: The Ho Chi Minh Trail and the Vietnam War* (New York: John Wiley and Sons, 1999), 290–291; memo, Office of Chief of Naval Operations, "Duck Hook," July 20, 1969, box 98.1, NSC, RNPLM.

83. "Vietnam Policy Alternatives" (July 1969), attachment to memorandum, Morton Halperin to HAK, August 5, 1969, reproduced in Kimball, *The Vietnam War Files: Uncovering the Secret History of Nixon-Era Strategy* (Lawrence: Univ. Press of Kansas, 2004), 92–93.

84. Rogers quoted in Hersh, *Price of Power,* 41.

85. Van Atta, *With Honor,* 223–224; letter excerpt, Laird to HAK, sent to author by Laird on April 2, 2007; telcon, RN and HAK, 6:50 p.m., August 5, 1969, box 2.5, HAK Telcons, RNPLM; telcons, Laird and HAK, 10:20 a.m., August 9, 1969, and 9:30 a.m., August 18, 1969, box 2.5, HAK Telcons, RNPLM.

86. HAK, *White House Years,* 276; Selin, "Vietnamization," 20; Laird, "Improvement of the Vietnamese Forces and Vietnamization," August 21, 1969, folder "Vietnam (1)," box 26, Baroody Papers, GFL.

222 Notes to Pages 100–104

87. Sorley, *Vietnam Chronicles,* 230–233, 236–237, 244–245 (emphasis in original); record of conversation with Abrams, Mahoe to External Affairs, August 16, 1969, item 7557959, Saigon—Vietnam—troop reduction papers, A4531, NAA; memo, Wheeler to Laird, July 21, 1969, *FRUS,* 1969–1976, 6:308–315.

88. Memo, Laird to Wheeler, June 12, 1969, #67, "Vietnam, Documents 63–68," box C32, LP, GFL.

89. Memo, James Moffett to Sullivan, August 8, 1969, folder "POL 2—NSSM-36 Top Secret Vietnamizing the War, 1969–1970," box 8, E-5414, RG 59, NAII; memo, Laird to JCS, August 12, 1969, #87, "Vietnam, Documents 85–92," box C32, LP, GFL; telcon, Laird and HAK, 1:40 p.m., August 15, 1969, box 2.5, HAK Telcons, RNPLM.

90. Telcon, Laird and HAK, 11:30 a.m., August 19, 1969, box 2.5, HAK Telcons, RNPLM. Still, the White House delay surprised Pentagon officials. See cable, Australian embassy (Washington) to External Affairs, August 27, 1969, item 761742, Withdrawal of Australian Forces from Vietnam, series AWM122, Australia War Memorial, Canberra, Australia.

91. Neil Sheehan, "President Defers Decision on a Cut in Vietnam Force," *New York Times,* August 24, 1969, 1.

92. "Growing Doubts About Hanoi's Intentions," *Time,* September 5, 1969.

5. Come Together

1. On August 21, Nixon told South Korean president Park Chung Hee, "If I had been the President last November, I would not have halted the bombing. This is just between us; if there is no further progress in the Paris talks, we will re-evaluate the situation about October 15." Park responded that America's Asian allies would back the move but doubted US public opinion would welcome the escalation. Memorandum of conversation, "Talks between President Nixon and President Pak," WHSF:SMOF:President's Office Files, RNPLM.

2. HAK, *White House Years,* 288.

3. Haldeman, *Haldeman Diaries,* 83.

4. Sam Brown quoted in Wells, *The War Within,* 330; letter, Vietnam Moratorium Committee (signed Sam Brown, David Hawk, and David Mixner) to Fulbright, June 30, 1969, folder "U-Z," box 57:5, Subseries 18 Vietnam (correspondence), Series 48 Foreign Relations Committee, JWFP.

5. Telcon, RN and HAK, 1:30 p.m., September 2, 1969, box 2.6, HAK Telcons, RNPLM; telcon, Laird and HAK, 1:35 p.m., September 2, 1969, box 2.6, HAK Telcons, RNPLM; memo, addressed to Laird, "Phase 2 Redeployments from Vietnam," September 3, 1969, box 91.3, NSC, RNPLM.

6. Memo, Laird to RN, September 4, 1969, *FRUS,* 1969–1976, 6:358–362.

7. Memo, Laird to RN, June 2, 1969, 1969, *FRUS,* 1969–1976, 6:266.

Notes to Pages 104–108   223

8. Laird interview with Tom Wells (emphasis in original); memo, Laird to RN, September 4, 1969, *FRUS,* 1969–1976, 6:358, 362; memo, Wheeler to Laird, September 21, 1969, *FRUS,* 1969–1976, 6:311–315.

9. Dispatch, Tait (Canadian Delegation to ICSC, Saigon) to External Affairs, "Interview with Pres Thieu," August 16, 1969, file 20-22-VIETS-2-1, part 36, vol. 9402, RG 25, LAC.

10. Daddis, *Withdrawal,* 113.

11. Sorley, *Vietnam Chronicles,* 256–257 (emphasis in original); memo, Laird to RN, September 4, 1969, *FRUS,* 1969–1976, 6:360–362.

12. Hersh, *Price of Power,* 126; Morris, *Uncertain Greatness,* 163.

13. Memo, HAK to RN, "Analysis for Vietnam," September 5, 1969, box 91:1, NSC-Vietnam Special Files (hereafter VNSF), RNPLM. This memo would propose and lead to the creation of the Vietnam Special Studies Group to analyze the war and evidence of progress in Vietnam.

14. Memo, HAK to RN, "Our Present Course on Vietnam," September 10, 1969, box 70.14, NSC, RNPLM.

15. Kissinger was well aware of the risks of "a ceasefire/territorial accommodation approach" to negotiations and that a settlement along these lines "would be ambiguous and risky—if it turned sour we would be all the more responsible for engineering a fake peace. In short, we would repeat the Laos solution"—something neither Nixon nor Kissinger wanted. See memo, HAK to RN, September 11, 1969, *FRUS,* 1969–1976, 6:384–386.

16. Ibid., 376, 383–386, 388, 390 (emphasis in original); editor's footnote #3, *FRUS,* 1969–1976, 6:376.

17. See memo, Haig to HAK, "Items to Discuss with the President, Tuesday, September 9, 1969, 9:00 a.m.," September 9, 1969, box 334.6, NSC, RNPLM.

18. Minutes of National Security Meeting, September 12, 1969, *FRUS,* 1969–1976, 6:397–398.

19. Ibid., 398–399.

20. Ibid., 401–404.

21. Dallek, *Nixon and Kissinger,* 156; James McCarthy, "One Third of Kissinger Staff Has Quit," *Houston Chronicle,* October 19, 1969. One staffer told McCarthy, "Henry Kissinger is a one-man show. Some people just can't work with him." McCarthy reported that half of them resigned because of Kissinger's management style. The rest, many of them Democratic holdovers, departed over policy or political disagreements.

22. RN, "Statement on United States Troops in Vietnam," September 16, 1969, *APP,* https://www.presidency.ucsb.edu/node/239644 (accessed July 26, 2021).

23. Telcon, RN and HAK, 4:40 p.m., September 27, 1969, box 2.7, HAK Telcons, RNPLM.

24. Memo, Moorer to Laird, "Air and Naval Operations against North Vietnam," October 1, 1969 (revised October 7), box 123.1, NSC, RNPLM.

224 Notes to Pages 108–112

25. Memo, Tony Lake and Roger Morris, "Draft Memorandum to the President on Contingency Study," September 29, 1969, box 74.3, NSC, RNPLM.

26. Telcons, Laird and HAK, 5:05, 5:30, 5:50, and 6:58 p.m., September 30, 1969, box 2.7, HAK Telcons, RNPLM; memo, Buchanan to RN, September 18, 1969, box 74.3, NSC, RNPLM.

27. Scanlon, *The Pro-War Movement,* 47–51, 95–113; memo, Buchanan to RN, September 18, 1969; memo, Bryce Harlow to Lyn Nofziger, September 18, 1969, box 14, WHSF:SMOF, RNPLM.

28. RN, *RN,* 400; Rowland Evans and Robert Novak, "Nixon Is Talking About the War Just Like Johnson Used to Talk," *Washington Post,* October 8, 1969, A27; John Finney, "On Vietnam: Once Again a Sharp and Swelling Debate," *New York Times,* October 5, 1969, E1; "Nixon Quoted as Barring U.S. Defeat," *New York Times,* October 2, 1969, 18. Goldwater publicly proposed resuming the US bombing after November 1 if there had been no progress in Paris, though he was careful to say that it was his plan. At the same time, fifteen House members sent Nixon a public letter demanding "a sudden major escalation of the war with one aim—victory!" See *Time,* October 24, 1969, 17.

29. Haldeman notes for October 2, 1969, box 40.4, WHSF:SMOF, RNPLM.

30. Nick Cullather, "Bomb Them Back to the Stone Age: An Etymology," History News Network, https://historynewsnetwork.org/article/30347 (accessed January 20, 2021).https://historynewsnetwork.org/article/30347

31. Memos, HAK to RN, "Contingency Military Operations against North Vietnam," October 2, 1969, boxes 98.2 and 102.6, NSC, RNPLM (emphasis in original).

32. Ibid.

33. Ibid.

34. Ibid.; William Watts quoted in Wells, *War Within,* 357 (emphasis in original). Kissinger was likely with Nixon at Key Biscayne on October 3, giving them time to review the plan together. See Brigham, *Reckless,* 73.

35. Interestingly, Thieu was also aware that Kissinger had secretly met the North Vietnamese delegation in August. See Phan Cong Tam, "Testimony of a Senior Officer, South Vietnamese Central Intelligence Organization," in *Voices from the Second Republic of South Vietnam (1967–1975),* ed. K. W. Taylor (Ithaca, N.Y.: Cornell Southeast Asia Program Publications, 2014), 22.

36. See Van Atta, *With Honor,* 222–224.

37. Haldeman notes for October 2, 1969, RNPLM; Willbanks, *Abandoning Vietnam,* 62; speech, Laird, October 7, 1969, item 1702109 USA—Relations with Indo China, A1838, NAA.

38. Memo, Laird to RN, "Air and Naval Operations against North Vietnam," October 8, 1969, box 123.1, NSC, RNPLM; Laird interview with Wells.

39. Memo, Laurence Lynn Jr. to HAK, "JCS Concept Plan for Air and Naval Operations against North Vietnam," October 10, 1969, box 123.1, NSC, RNPLM; memo, HAK to RN, undated (before October 11, 1969), *FRUS,* 1969–1976, 6:447–450 (emphasis in original).

Notes to Pages 112–115   225

40. On the Moratorium and the Nixon administration, see Melvin Small, *Antiwarriors: The Vietnam War and the Battle for America's Hearts and Minds* (Wilmington, Del.: Scholarly Resources, 2002), 161–162.

41. Letter, Charles Percy to Fulbright, August 12, 1969, folder "ABM," box 24:5, Subseries 6 Subcommittees, Series 48 Foreign Relations Committee, JWFP; letter, Fulbright to Reuben Thomas, August 13, 1969, folder "ABM," box 24:5, Subseries 6 Subcommittees, Series 48 Foreign Relations Committee, JWFP.

42. "Military Cutbacks . . . ," *New York Times,* August 27, 1969, 42; HAK, *White House Years,* 396; telcons, Laird and HAK, 5:05, 5:30, 5:50, and 6:58 p.m., September 30, 1969, box 2.7, HAK Telcons, RNPLM.

43. In September, the stalwart Everett Dirksen (R-IL) died. Hugh Scott (R-PA) would replace Dirksen as Senate minority leader. Although Scott would support Nixon's foreign policy, his selection was evidence of the liberal Republican wing's power in 1969. Together, the Republican hawks' reticence and the liberals' strength confirmed that escalation in Vietnam would not be well-received in the Senate.

44. Address, Fulbright, "The War in Vietnam," September 25, 1969, folder "Vietnam, 1969," box 33:7, Series 5 Speeches and Articles, JWFP; letter, Frank Church and Mark Hatfield to Fulbright, October 7, 1969, folder "1969," box 45:3, Subseries 17 Vietnam (general), Series 48 Foreign Relations Committee, JWFP; Mann, *Grand Delusion,* 636–640; Wells, *War Within,* 365; statement, Senator Marlow Cook, September 19, 1969, folder "Commitment Resolution," box 28:2, Subseries 6 Subcommittees, Series 48 Foreign Relations Committee, JWFP; press release, Jacob K. Javits, October 14, 1969, folder "Vietnam General Materials, 1969," box 45:2, Subseries 17 Vietnam—(General Materials), Series 48 Foreign Relations Committee, JWFP; "Laird Blasts Loose-Lipped Congressmen," *Vietnam Guardian,* October 4, 1969.

45. Mann, *Grand Delusion,* 637; Woods, *Fulbright, Vietnam, and the Search for a Cold War Foreign Policy,* 205; address, Fulbright, "The War in Vietnam" (emphasis in original); speech, "The Vietnam Moratorium," Fulbright, October 1, 1969, folder "Senate Floor (The Vietnam Moratorium)," box 35:1, Series 71, Senate Floor Speeches, 1945–1974, JWFP; "Fulbright Calls U.S. Troop Cut 'Opiate,'" *Vietnam Guardian,* September 25, 1969, 1; "Fulbright Plans Hearings on Total Pullout Proposal," *Saigon Post,* October 9, 1969; transcript, *Newsmaker of the Week,* circa October 21, 1969, folder "News from Metromedia TV," box 31:22, Series 72, Speeches Given Elsewhere, 1939–1976, JWFP.

46. For more information on the trial, see Kirkpatrick, *1969,* 216–230.

47. Wells, *War Within,* 306–308, 347.

48. Ibid., 357–358, 366–370.

49. "U.S. War Deaths Are 95 for Week, Lowest in 2 Years," *New York Times,* October 3, 1969, 1.

50. RN, *RN,* 404; transcript, *Meet the Press,* October 12, 1969, folder "Meet the Press—NBC Sunday October 12, 1969," box 12, E-5439, RG 59, NAII.

226   Notes to Pages 115–119

51. Sorley, *Vietnam Chronicles,* 264–265, 274; memo, Moorer, "JCS Meeting with the President, Saturday, 11 October 1969," October 13, 1969, box 1008.1, NSC, RNPLM.

52. For typically inaccurate assessments, see Intelligence Information Cable, CIA, December 11, 1968, LBJPL; memo, John Holdridge to HAK, "CIA Study of the North Vietnamese Leadership," September 30, 1969, *FRUS, 1969–1976,* 6:416–418.

53. Asselin, *Vietnam's American War,* 251–252. Kissinger anticipated that Ho Chi Minh's death would not change North Vietnam's aims and that any movement in Paris would be to "stall us past our [November] deadline." See memo, HAK to RN, "Preliminary Analysis of the Significance of the Death of Ho Chi Minh," September 6, 1969, box 69.4, NSC, RNPLM; telcon, RN and HAK, 7:50 p.m., September 15, 1969, box 2.6, HAK Telcons, RNPLM.

54. Haldeman, *Haldeman Diaries,* 97–98 (emphasis in original); telcons, RN and HAK, 6:30–6:45 a.m., October 8, 1969, and 7:30 p.m., October 10, 1969, box 2.8, HAK Telcons, RNPLM. See also Morris, *Uncertain Greatness,* 165–166, Wells, *War Within,* 378, and Kimball, *Nixon's Vietnam War,* 169–173.

55. Memo, Moorer, "JCS Meeting with the President, Saturday, 11 October 1969," October 13, 1969, box 1008.1, NSC, RNPLM.

56. While in South Vietnam, Wheeler observed, "I gather [from Congress and the press], that we're hanging on over here by our teeth, barely able to stay in the stadium. . . . [When in actuality we] are dealing from a position of military strength. And I really *mean* military strength. . . . [Leaders in Washington] act and talk . . . as though the damned peace talks, or peace negotiations or whatever terminology you want to use in Paris, [as though] *we're* the guys that are doing the *suing.*" Wheeler quoted in Sorley, *Vietnam Chronicles,* 269. Later that month, Wheeler told Rostow that he was confident about military progress in Vietnam and that "the problem is in the U.S., not in Vietnam." See memo, Rostow to LBJ, October 31, 1968, #1, "Intelligence Briefing October 1969 [1 of 2]," box 2, Post-Presidential Intelligence Briefings File, LBJPL.

57. Memo, Moorer, "JCS Meeting with the President, Saturday, 11 October 1969."

58. Ibid. (emphasis in original).

59. Ibid.

60. Haldeman, *Haldeman Diaries,* 99–100; telcon, Laird and HAK, 8:45 a.m., October 13, 1969, box 2.8, HAK Telcons, RNPLM; Van Atta, *With Honor,* 218, 220. Robert Brigham noted that Nixon often worried about Kissinger's stability and judgment. See Brigham, *Reckless,* 75–76.

61. Small, *Antiwarriors,* 107, 110–111; *Time,* October 24, 1969, cover and 16–20.

62. See Van Atta, *With Honor,* 228; Wells, *War Within,* 372–373.

63. Small, *Antiwarriors,* 111; Gallup poll, "Vietnam: Question #8," 30 October—4 November 1969, in *The Gallup Poll,* 2222; Report #53, November 1969, *Gallup Opinion Index*; *Time,* October 17, 1969, 22. Only 31 percent of Americans labeled

Notes to Pages 119–120   227

themselves hawks, and only 30 percent opposed Goodell's legislation. Yet, in the wake of the Moratorium, 58 percent still approved of Nixon's handling of the war.

64. Laird recalled, "Nixon did it because of Soviet aid to North Vietnam—to alert them that he might do something. This was one of several examples of the Madman Theory. . . . He never used the term 'madman,' but he wanted adversaries to have the feeling that you could never put your finger on what he might do next. Nixon got this from Ike, who always felt that way." Quoted in William Burr and Jeffrey Kimball, "Nixon's Secret Nuclear Alert: Vietnam War Diplomacy and the Joint Chiefs of Staff Readiness Test, October 1969," *Cold War History* 3, no. 2 (January 2003): 129.

65. RN, *RN,* 399, 401, 403.

66. Burr and Kimball, "Nixon's Secret Nuclear Alert," 113–156; Scott Sagan and Jeremi Suri, "The Madman Nuclear Alert: Secrecy, Signaling, and Safety in October 1969," *International Security* 27, no. 4 (spring 2003): 150–183; memo, Haig to HAK, "Items to Discuss with the President, October 14," October 14, 1969, box 334.5, NSC, RNPLM; telcon, RN and HAK, 8:25 p.m., October 20, 1969, box 2.9, HAK Telcons, RNPLM; Editorial Note, *FRUS, 1969–1976,* 6:467–470; telcon, Laird and HAK, 2:30 p.m., October 23, 1969, box 2.10, HAK Telcons, RNPLM.

67. Hudson Institute, "Lessons from the Vietnam War," 1969, folder "Hudson Institute, 1969–1971 (1)," box A74, LP, GFL; Robert Thompson, *No Exit from Vietnam* (New York: McKay, 1969), 161, 192–193, 197–198; memo, HAK to RN, "Your Meeting with Sir Robert Thompson," October 16, 1969, box 42, WHSF-Special Files, RNPLM; memorandum of conversation, October 17, 1969, *FRUS, 1969– 1976,* 6:462–465. Thompson likely influenced Nixon's decision away from Duck Hook and toward Vietnamization. The president requested, presumably read, and discussed *No Exit from Vietnam* while he was in Key Biscayne earlier that month. For more on Thompson's role and his views on Vietnamization, see David Fitzgerald, "Sir Robert Thompson, Strategic Patience and Nixon's War in Vietnam," *Journal of Strategic Studies* 37, no. 6–7 (2014): 998–1026.

68. At the meeting, David Packard observed that they should "make the whole [study] 'Vietnamization'" since the strategy encompassed pacification, land and political reforms, economic aid, and the like.

69. Minutes, VSSG, October 20, 1969, folder "VSSG Meeting 12-20-69," box H-001, NSC-IF, RNPLM; memo, Roger Morris and Tony Lake to HAK, "Another Vietnam Option," October 21, 1969, box 1046.9, NSC, RNPLM (emphasis in original); memo, HAK to RN, "Assumptions Underlying Vietnamization," October 23, 1969, box 1046.5, NSC, RNPLM; memo, HAK to RN, October 30, 1969, *FRUS, 1969–1976,* 6:475–476.

70. Telcon, Laird and HAK, 5:15 p.m., October 23, 1969, box 2.10, HAK Telcons, RNPLM; memo, HAK to Laird, "North Vietnam Contingency Plan," October 24, 1969, box 123.1, NSC, RNPLM.

228   Notes to Pages 121–126

71. "Draft of a Presidential Speech," second draft, September 27, 1969, reproduced in Kimball, *The Vietnam War Files,* 106–107; Brigham, *Reckless,* 71; fourth draft of [original] November speech, October 2, 1969, box 98.2, NSC, RNPLM.

72. After October 11, White House drafts started over at "1" even though much of the content remained the same. See memo, Roger Morris and Tony Lake, October 12, 1969, box 1046.5, NSC, RNPLM; first draft of November 3 speech, October 12, 1969, box 79.2, NSC, RNPLM.

73. Fourth and tenth drafts of November 3 speech, respectively, October 15 and 20, 1969, box 79.1, NSC, RNPLM (emphasis in original).

74. RN, *RN,* 407–408; memo, Rogers to RN, October 23, 1969, folder "White House Correspondence 1969," box 4, E-5439, RG 59, NAII; memo, HAK to RN, "Suggestions for your November 3 Speech from Secretaries Laird and Rogers," October 24, 1969, boxes 78.3 and 79.5, NSC, RNPLM.

75. Memo, Laird to HAK, "Suggested Themes for President's November 3 Address," October 23, 1969, box 79.5, NSC, RNPLM (emphasis in original); Laird, "Memorandum for the President with enclosed draft," October 30, 1969, folder "Admin Strategy, 1969–1970 (1)," box A50, LP, GFL; telcon, RN and HAK, 11:33 p.m., November 3, 1969, box 3.1, HAK Telcons, RNPLM.

76. RN, "Address to the Nation on the War in Vietnam," November 3, 1969, *APP,* https://www.presidency.ucsb.edu/node/240027 (accessed July 26, 2021).

77. RN, *RN,* 405.

6. Give Me Just a Little More Time

1. Chalmers Roberts, "Nixon Wants to 'Win' in Vietnam," *Washington Post Outlook,* February 15, 1970.

2. RN, CBS interview conducted by Mike Wallace, October 8, 1968, PPS 208:100:6, RNLBF.

3. Haldeman, *Haldeman Diaries,* 102; Background Briefing (President's Vietnam Speech), HAK, November 3, 1969, box 98.3, NSC, RNPLM.

4. Nixon revealed as much in his memoirs: The speech's "impact came as a surprise to me; it was one thing to make a rhetorical appeal to the Silent Majority—it was another actually to hear from them." RN, *RN,* 409–410.

5. "Americans on the War: Divided, Glum, Unwilling to Quit," *Time,* October 31, 1969, 13–15.

6. Gallup poll, "Vietnam: Question #8," 30 October—4 November 1969, in *The Gallup Poll,* 2222.

7. Daddis, *Withdrawal,* 117.

8. Comparatively, 11 percent advocated sending *more* troops and stepping up the fighting, 19 percent wanted an immediate withdrawal, and 22 percent supported a plan to remove all US soldiers by the end of 1970. See *Gallup Opinion Index* #55 (January 1970).

Notes to Pages 126–128   229

9. *Gallup Opinion Index* #53–55 (November 1969–January 1970); Black, *The Invincible Quest,* 642; Mann, *Grand Delusion,* 652; Johns, *Vietnam's Second Front,* 273; Sorley, *A Better War,* 169; Haldeman, *Haldeman Diaries,* 105–106; memo, Dwight Chapin to Haldeman, "Re: Gallup Telephone Poll—the President's Speech," November 4, 1969, box 1008.4, NSC, RNPLM; telcon, Laird and HAK, 7:00 p.m., November 14, 1969, box 3.2, HAK Telcons, RNPLM.

10. For more on POW politics, see Scanlon, *The Pro-War Movement,* 226–239.

11. Johns, *Vietnam's Second Front,* 273; Haldeman, *Haldeman Diaries,* 106–108; Wells, *War Within,* 382–383, 388; telcon, Humphrey and HAK, 1:37 p.m., November 3, 1969, box 3.1, HAK Telcons, RNPLM; Arnold Offner, *Hubert Humphrey: The Conscience of the Country* (New Haven, Conn.: Yale Univ. Press, 2018), 341; memo, Rogers to RN, November 5, 1969, folder "White House Correspondence 1969," box 4, E-5439, RG 59, NAII.

12. Wells, *War Within,* 382; Background on November Moratorium, Bryce Harlow, November 1969, box 11.1, WHSF:SMOF, RNPLM; Scanlon, *The Pro-War Movement,* 125–128, 190–199.

13. Wells, *War Within,* 390–392, 395.

14. Ibid., 399; Black, *The Invincible Quest,* 639–641; Joseph Fry, "Unpopular Messengers: Student Opposition to the Vietnam War," in *The War that Never Ends,* 235.

15. Mann, *Grand Delusion,* 645–648; telcon, RN and HAK, 6:07 p.m., November 22, 1969, box 3.3, HAK Telcons, RNPLM.

16. See letters, Arthur Schlesinger Jr. to Fulbright (and his response), January 26, 1970, and January 30, 1970, folder "1970, 'S,'" box 61, Subseries 18 Vietnam (correspondence), Series 48 Foreign Relations Committee, JWFP. Both men, like other doves, wrongly believed Hanoi was "deeply interested in a negotiated settlement." Conversely, they felt that Nixon's emphasis on Vietnamization was based on "the new wave of military optimism."

17. Memo, H. G. Torbert Jr., November 10, 1969, folder "Welcome Home—the Under Secretary November 12, 1969," box 65, Lot 72D220, RG 59, NAII; memo, Bob Dockery to Fulbright, November 26, 1969, folder "Vietnam General Materials, 1969," box 45:3, Subseries 17 Vietnam—(General Materials), Series 48 Foreign Relations Committee, JWFP; letter, Fulbright to Tristram Coffin, November 8, 1969, folder "C," box 56:3, Subseries 18 Vietnam (correspondence), Series 48 Foreign Relations Committee, JWFP; Australian embassy (Washington), "Vietnam—Senate Foreign Relations Committee Hearings," February 18, 1970, item 555235, United States—Political—Congress-General Senate, A1838, NAA; memo, Political Research Division, Democratic National Committee, "Richard Nixon—One Year Later," December 19, 1969, folder "1969, 'July-December 1969,'" box 4:4, Subseries 1 President (the White House), Series 1, Office of the President, 1952–1974, JWFP.

18. Small, *At the Water's Edge,* 136, 147; James Reston, "Washington, D.C.: President Nixon's First Year," *New York Times,* December 31, 1969, 24; Editorial Note, *FRUS,* 1969–1976, 6:523.

230 Notes to Pages 129–131

19. Price quoted in Wells, *War Within,* 345; cable, Australian embassy (Washington), "Presidential News Conference," January 30, 1970, item 1728819 Withdrawal of Australian Forces from Vietnam, A1838, NAA.

20. Fry, *The American South and the Vietnam War,* 272; Julian Zelizer, "Congress and the Politics of Troop Withdrawal," *Diplomatic History* 34 (June 2010): 536; memo, Laird to RN, "Trip to Vietnam and CINCPAC, February 10–14, 1970," February 17, 1970, *FRUS, 1969–1976,* 6:579–593.

21. Johns, *Vietnam's Second Front,* 274.

22. See David Coleman, "Nixon's Presidential Approval Ratings," https://historyinpieces.com/research/nixon-approval-ratings (accessed July 28, 2020).

23. See the special forum, "The Politics of Troop Withdrawal," *Diplomatic History* 34, no. 3 (June 2010): 461–600.

24. For a discussion on November 3 as a turning point, see David Anderson, "No More Vietnams: Historians Debate the Policy Lessons of the Vietnam War," in *The War that Never Ends,* 27–28.

25. Dallek, *Nixon and Kissinger,* 130.

26. "'No Warlike Cabinet': Thieu Says National Peace Policy Stands," *Saigon Post,* August 28, 1969, 1.

27. Telegram, Bui Diem (Washington) to Thieu and the Foreign Affairs Ministry, July 16, 1969, HS 20529, PTTVNCH, VNAC2; minutes, Nguyen Van Huong, "Tóm Tắt Phiên Họp Hội- Đồng Tổng-Trưởng Ngày 15,9,1969," circa September 15, 1969, HS 80, PTT, VNAC2; Central Intelligence Bulletin, CIA, October 1, 1969, #9-t, "Intelligence Briefing October 1969 [2 of 2]," box 2, Post-Presidential Intelligence Briefings File, LBJPL; memo, Rostow to LBJ, October 17, 1969, #7, "Intelligence Briefing October 1969 [1 of 2]," box 2, Post-Presidential Intelligence Briefings File, LBJPL; telegram #2.802, Bui Diem (Washington) to Thieu, September 28, 1969, HS 2162, PTT, VNAC2; telegram, Bui Diem (Washington) to Thieu and the Foreign Affairs Ministry, October 3, 1969, HS 2162, PTT, VNAC2; telegram, Bui Diem (Washington) to Thieu and the Foreign Affairs Ministry, October 8, 1969, HS 16668, PTTVNCH, VNAC2; telegram, Bui Diem (Washington) to Thieu and the Foreign Affairs Ministry, October 14, 1969, HS 20529, PTTVNCH, VNAC2; memo, Trần-Văn-Lắm to the Prime Minister, "Về Hội-nghị quốc-gia đồng-minh cấp Tổng-Trưởng nhóm họp tại New York ngày 20 tháng 9 năm 1969," October 3, 1969, HS 296, PTT, VNAC2; telegram, Bui Diem (Washington) to Hoàng-Đức-Nhã, October 17, 1969, HS 2162, PTT, VNAC2 (emphasis in original).

28. "Complete U.S. Combat Withdrawal Announced," *Vietnam Guardian,* November 5, 1969, 1–2; "Nixon Policy Speech Draws Warm Praise: RVN Circles Rally Behind Stand," *Saigon Post,* November 6, 1969, 1, 8; FBIS Daily Reports: Asia and Pacific, November 6–7, 1969, folder 7, box 6, DPC: Other Manuscripts—FBIS—Asia, VCA; cable, CIA to White House Situation Room, "Comments of Hoang Duc Nha on President Thieu's View of the Internal Political Situation and on President Nixon's 4 November Speech," November 4, 1969, NSC-VNSF box 78:4,

Notes to Pages 131–132   231

RNPLM; telegram, Bui Diem (Washington) to Thieu and the Foreign Affairs Ministry, November 4, 1969, HS 2162, PTT, VNAC2; Diem book 267–271; memo, HAK to Agnew, "Your Visit to Saigon," late December 1969, box 81, NSC, RNPLM; editorials, "The Nixon Address (1)" and "The Nixon Speech (2)," *Vietnam Guardian,* November 6 and 17, 1969; memo, Nha [Mỹ] Châu, Lien Hiep Quoc, "Một Vài Nhận-Định Về Chính-Sách Của Hoa-Kỳ Đối Với Việt-Nam Trong Năm 1970," n.d. (early 1970), HS 20617, PTTVNCH, VNAC2.

29. Telegram, Australian embassy (Saigon), "American Troop Reductions," September 18, 1969, item 1702109 USA—Relations with Indo China, A1838, NAA; telegram, Australian embassy (Saigon), "Vietnam—Replacement of U.S. Troops," September 22, 1969, item 1702109 USA—Relations with Indo China, A1838, NAA; weekly roundup from Saigon, Roger Martin, "Political Round-Up," September 23, 1969, FCO 15/1001, TNA; telegram no. 602, British embassy (Saigon), "Reactions to President Nixon's Speech," November 6, 1969, FCO 15/1009, TNA; memo, HAK to Agnew, "Your Visit to Saigon," late December 1969, box 81, NSC, RNPLM; telegram no. 679, Moreton (Saigon), December 19, 1969, FCO 15/1093, TNA; editorial, "Difficult Days Ahead," *Vietnam Guardian,* October 13, 1969, 1; editorial, "It Is Later Than We May Think," *Vietnam Guardian,* November 3, 1969, 1.

30. Weekly roundup from Saigon, "Political Round-Up," October 28, 1969, FCO 15/1001; Diplomatic Report No.90/70, Ambassador in Viet-Nam J. O. Moreton to Secretary of State for Foreign and Commonwealth Affairs, "South Viet-Nam: Annual Review for 1969," January 23, 1970, DEFE 11/696, TNA; memo, Laird to RN, "Trip to Vietnam and CINCPAC, February 10–14, 1970"; GVN, "Study Document: Spring 1970: Spring of Certain Victory," January 1970, item 2121510033, folder 10, box 15, DPC: Unit 1—Assessment and Strategy, VCA.

31. Editorial, "Goodbye, 1969," *Vietnam Guardian,* December 30, 1969; Phu Si, "Vietnamese Reactions to America's 'Moratoriums,'" *Saigon Post,* January 1, 1970, 1; editorial, "We Hope . . . ," *Vietnam Guardian,* January 1, 1970, 1; Nguyen Ngoc Linh, "Food for Thought," *Saigon Post,* November 7, 1969, 1–2.

32. Thieu did stumble at times, though. On November 15, 1969, Thieu instructed the prime minister to prohibit officials from using Vietnamization as a noun in regard to the war and negotiations. He feared the term denied South Vietnamese agency and their contribution to the war. This order was leaked to the press, and the flap unfortunately reinforced American perceptions that he opposed the strategy and troop withdrawals. See Thieu, "V/V sử-dụng danh-từ 'Việt- Nam hòa'," November 15, 1969, HS 290, PTT, VNAC; Nguyễn-Văn-Vàng, "V/V dùng danh-từ 'Việt-Nam hòa'," November 20, 1969, HS 290, PTT, VNAC2; Herring, *America's Longest War,* 283–284.

33. Pike, *The Bunker Papers,* vol. 3, 745; telegram, Australian embassy (Saigon), "Viet-Nam—Statements by President Thieu," September 30, 1969, item 1702109 USA—Relations with Indo China, A1838, NAA; "Vietnam to Replace Most U.S. Combat Troops in 1970," *Vietnam Guardian,* October 7, 1969, 1, 6.

232 Notes to Pages 132–134

34. Saving telegram, Mr. Moreton, Saigon December 29, 1969, FCO 15/1009, TNA. On Thieu's rising confidence, see also dispatch, Tait (Canadian Delegation to ICSC, Saigon) to External Affairs, "Interview with Pres Thieu," August 16, 1969, file 20-22-VIETS-2-1, part 36, vol. 9402, RG 25, LAC. Similarly, Foreign Minister Tran Van Lam expressed "cautious optimism" about South Vietnamese military, economic, and political affairs. See dispatch, Hart (Canadian Delegation to ICSC, Saigon) to External Affairs, "Vietnam," December 11, 1969, file 20-22-VIETS-2-1, part 37, vol. 9402, RG 25, LAC.

35. Veith, *Drawn Swords*, 376.

36. A contemporaneous CIA study of Vietnamization found conflicting RVNAF officer attitudes about the strategy. They expressed "guarded optimism about the prospects of Vietnamization in their immediate areas of responsibility" and believed that with US air, artillery, and logistical support they could succeed. Yet, they understood that the American troop withdrawals were irreversible and that the war would continue indefinitely or until a major communist offensive finally toppled the Republic. Only one in ten thought the war would "fade away." See Intelligence Memorandum, Directorate of Intelligence, "Vietnamization: Progress and Prospects," January 23, 1970, CIA-RDP85T00875R001100090005-2, CIA-ERR.

37. Willard Webb, *The Joint Chiefs of Staff and the War in Vietnam, 1969–1970* (Washington, D.C.: Office of Joint History, 2002), 130; memo, T. J. Hanifen, January 7, 1970, folder "US Troop Withdrawal 1970," box 8, A1-136, RG 472, NAII; Major General Nguyen Duy Hinh, "Vietnamization and the Cease-Fire," in *The Vietnam War: An Assessment*, 754, 757; Van Ngan, "Progress in 'Vietnamizing' the War," *Saigon Post*, October 22, 1969; Dong Van Khuyen, *The RVNAF* (Washington, D.C.: US Army Center of Military History, 1980), 76, 143–144, 152–153, 195–197, 211–214, 276–277; Diem, *Jaws of History*, 284–285; Brigham, *ARVN*, 99–100.

38. Vietnamization encompassed both RVNAF improvement and pacification. "They were, in short, two faces of a single strategic coin," noted historian Martin Clemis. Clemis, *The Control War*, 192.

39. Memo, Nguyen Van Huong (secretary to the president), "Tóm Tắt Buổi Họp-Đồng Tổng-Trưởng Ngày 5/11/1968," November 11, 1968, HS 39, PTT, VNAC2; minutes, Nguyen Van Huong, "Tóm Tắt Phiên Họp Hội-Đồng Tổng-Trưởng Ngày 15,9,1969," circa September 15, 1969, HS 80, PTT, VNAC2; Clemis, *The Control War*, 92–93, 200, 230–236, 240–241; Brigadier General Tran Dinh Tho, "Pacification," in *The Vietnam War: An Assessment*, 219, 251, 257–259. On the return of refugees, historian George Veith noted, "Refugees, a perennial GVN punching bag, had dropped from an all-time high of 1.4 million people in February 1969 to around 350,000 by the end of the year." Veith, *Drawn Swords*, 375.

40. Veith, *Drawn Swords*, 388–390; Gawthorpe, *To Build as Well as Destroy*, 180–182; Cao Van Than, "Land Reform and Agricultural Developments, 1968–1975," in *The Republic of Vietnam, 1955–1975*, 47–55; Tran Quang Minh, "A Decade of Public Service: Nation-Building during the Interregnum and Second Republic (1964–75)," in *Voices from the Second Republic*, 53–63.

Notes to Pages 134–137   233

41. Up until the third tranche, Nixon's withdrawals had been in line with what Abrams proposed. The general wanted no more than 35,000 out in the December through April time frame, but Nixon went with 50,000. In early 1970, Abrams requested they postpone reductions, but Laird tried to hide Abrams's concerns from the president (see memo, Haig to RN, "Your Meeting with Secretary Laird at 3:00 p.m., Tuesday, March 31, 1970," March 31, 1970, box 1009.1, NSC, RNPLM). That said, Nixon's reductions were consistent with Thieu's expectations.

42. Sorley, *Vietnam Chronicles,* 307–311, 324, 329; Sorley, *A Better War,* 172–173, 189–190; Willbanks, *Abandoning Vietnam,* 57–58; Woods, *Fulbright, Vietnam, and the Search for a Cold War Foreign Policy,* 214.

43. Clemis, *The Control War,* 211–213; Daddis, *Withdrawal,* 70–71; Sorley, *Vietnam Chronicles,* 276, 287, 382, 388, 404–407 (emphasis in original); cable, Ambassador Mahoe (New Zealand embassy, Saigon), "Talk with Abrams," January 21, 1970, item 7557966 Saigon—Vietnamization, A4531, NAA; cable, R. L. Harry (Saigon), "Viet Nam Consultations," March 6, 1970, item 1728819 Withdrawal of Australian Forces from Vietnam, A1838, NAA.

44. Vann quoted in Sorley, *Vietnam Chronicles,* 354 (emphasis in original).

45. Memorandum of conversation, "Sir Robert Thompson's Report on Conditions in Vietnam," December 1, 1969, *FRUS,* 1969–1976, 6:499–505; Brian Crozier, "A Just Peace Now Possible in Vietnam," *Vietnam Guardian,* December 30, 1969, 2. David Fitzgerald argues that Thompson defined "victory" as strategic equilibrium between the North and the South. Vietnamization would "keep the home fires extinguished" in America and enable the South to survive. Privately, he imagined this process would take ten to fifteen years—an unreasonable time line given growing US congressional dissent. See Fitzgerald, "Sir Robert Thompson, Strategic Patience and Nixon's War in Vietnam," 1011–1013.

46. Gawthorpe, *To Build as Well as Destroy,* 146–148.

47. Memo, J.A. Thomson, November 11, 1969, FCO 15/1093, TNA; Second ANZUS Security Consultations (Washington), October 23, 1969, item 1727027 ANZUS-Official Consultations 1969, A1838, NAA; cable, Australian embassy (Washington), "ANZUS Officials Consultations: 23–24 October," October 25, 1969, item 1727027 ANZUS-Official Consultations 1969, A1838, NAA; "Westy, Laird Bar Views on War in Vietnam," December 3, 1969, item 2121501018, folder 1, box 15, DPC: Unit 1—Assessment and Strategy, VCA; memo, CIA, "Vietnamization: Progress, Problems, and Prospects," December 27, 1969, item 0410471010, folder 71, box 4, Central Intelligence Agency Collection, VCA; Intelligence Memorandum, Directorate of Intelligence, "Vietnamization: Progress and Prospects," January 23, 1970, CIA-ERR; Schmitz, *Richard Nixon and the Vietnam War,* 76–80.

48. Clemis, *The Control War,* 230–231; Daddis, *Withdrawal,* 69–72.

49. Gawthorpe, *To Build as Well as Destroy,* 125–126; memo, VSSG, "Allied Military Capability (Vietnamization)," circa December 1969, folder "VSSG Meeting 12-20-69," box H-001, NSC-IF, RNPLM; memo, VSSG, "The Situation in the Countryside," November 28, 1969, folder "VSSG Meeting 12-1-69," box H-001,

234 Notes to Pages 137–140

NSC-IF, RNPLM; memo, "HAK Talking Points: VSSG Meeting, December 1, 1969," folder "VSSG Meeting 12-1-69," box H-001, NSC-IF, RNPLM.

50. Memo, Laurence Lynn to HAK, "Vietnam Trip Report," March 2, 1970, folder "VSSG Meeting 3-3-70," box H-001, NSC-IF, RNPLM; Office of the Secretary of Defense, "Vietnamization: Consolidated RVNAF Improvement & Modernization Program," June 1970, box 92.1, NSC, RNPLM

51. See cable, Department of External Affairs to Australian embassy (Washington), February 21, 1970, item 555407 USA-Australia Relations Developments in US Policy Affecting Australia, A1838, NAA.

52. Memo, HAK to RN, "The Situation in the Countryside of South Vietnam," December 1969, folder "VSSG Meeting 1-14-70," box H-001, NSC-IF, RNPLM; memos, HAK to RN, "Reporting on Vietnamization," January 19, 1970, and "The Risks of Vietnamization," 1970, box 91.5, NSC, RNPLM; memo, HAK to RN, January 22, 1970, *FRUS, 1969–1976*, 6:537–540; memo, HAK to RN, January 31, 1970, *FRUS, 1969–1976*, 6:555–557; memo, Haig to HAK, "Contingency Plans for Air Strikes against North Vietnam," July 13, 1970, box 123.1, NSC, RNPLM.

53. Memo, Office of the Secretary of Defense, "Vietnamization: Consolidated RVNAF Improvement & Modernization Program," June 1970, box 92.1, NSC, RNPLM; telcon, Laird and HAK, 10:40 a.m., November 27, 1969, box 3.4, HAK Telcons, RNPLM.

54. Presidential Press Conference No. 8 Transcript; December 8, 1969, box 95.2, NSC, RNPLM.

55. Remarks of the President Regarding Vietnam, December 15, 1969, box 191, WHSF-Special Files, RNPLM; Records of Discussion between Wilson and RN, January 27, 1970, FCO 7/1820, TNA; RN handwritten note on memo from HAK to RN, January 31, 1970, *FRUS, 1969–1976*, 6:555–557 (emphasis in original); Kimball, *Nixon's Vietnam War,* 179–183.

56. Huong Nam, "Nixon's 'Vietnamization' Policy Is Doomed to Failure," *Vietnam Courier,* no. 252, January 19, 1970; "A Few Ideas of Muoi Khang," CDEC, December 7, 1969, item 212415002, folder 15, box 14, DPC: Unit 1—Assessment and Strategy, VCA; "Characteristics of the Situation," CDEC, December 1969, item 2121413004, folder 13, box 14, DPC: Unit 1—Assessment and Strategy, VCA.

57. Asselin, *Vietnam's American War,* 174–177; Asselin, *A Bitter Peace,* 25; Military History Institute of Vietnam, *Victory in Vietnam,* 247; Brigham, *Guerrilla Diplomacy,* 85, 93; Nguyen, *Hanoi's War,* 157–158.

58. Dispatch, Ambassador Ford (Canadian embassy, Moscow) to External Affairs, "Indochina," May 20, 1970, file 20-22-VIETS-2-1, part 38, vol. 9402, RG 25, LAC.

59. Asselin, *Vietnam's American War,* 179–184.

60. Hai Nguyen, "Memory and Motivation: Why the North Vietnamese Fought," conference paper presented at the Society for Military History 2014 Annual Meeting, April 4, 2014.

61. "Directive on Ideological Missions in the Coming Period, Unit 160, No. 242," CDEC, September 18, 1969, item 2121406023, folder 6, box 14, DPC: Unit 1—

Notes to Pages 140–142   235

Assessment and Strategy, VCA; Nguyen Ngoc Tien, "Directive Pertaining to Ideological Tasks for the Last Quarter of 1969," CDEC, October 1, 1969, item 2121408010, folder 8, box 14, DPC: Unit 1—Assessment and Strategy, VCA; "Remaining Erroneous Thoughts," CDEC, October 9, 1969, item 2121408015, folder 8, box 14, DPC: Unit 1—Assessment and Strategy, VCA; report, "Morale Deterioration, 9th VC Division, Headquarters, SVNLA," CDEC, November 10, 1969, item 2121411015, folder 11, box 14, DPC: Unit 1—Assessment and Strategy, VCA; "Characteristics of the Situation," CDEC, December 1969, item 2121413004, folder 13, box 14, DPC: Unit 1—Assessment and Strategy, VCA; "'Open Arms' Soon to Reach Takeoff Stage," *Vietnam Guardian,* November 27, 1969, 2, 4; "Lesson Plan on Resolution 9, COSVN," CDEC, November 14, 1969, item 2121408004, folder 8, box 14, DPC: Unit 1—Assessment and Strategy, VCA; "Directive 129 of COSVN," CDEC, November 8, 1969, item 212411012, folder 11, box 14, DPC: Unit 1—Assessment and Strategy, VCA; John Shaw, *The Cambodian Campaign: The 1970 Offensive and America's Vietnam War* (Lawrence: Univ. Press of Kansas, 2005), 20–21, 64.

62. "Remaining Erroneous Thoughts," VCA; Nguyen Ngoc Tien, "Directive Pertaining to Ideological Tasks for the Last Quarter of 1969," VCA; "Future Military Missions and Food and Ammunition Supply Difficulties, VC MR 7," CDEC, December 10, 1969, item 2121415008, folder 15, box 14, DPC: Unit 1—Assessment and Strategy, VCA.

63. DRVN Government, "Statement Regarding President Nixon's November 3, 1969 Address on the Viet Nam Problem," November 6, 1969, FCO 15/1087, TNA; Brian Jenkins, "Vietnamization: An American Strategy," December 16, 1969, item 2121415017, folder 15, box 14, DPC: Unit 1—Assessment and Strategy, VCA; "VC Intend to Force a Quick Withdrawal on U.S. Troops," CDEC, November 22, 1969, item 2121406017, folder 6, box 14, DPC: Unit 1—Assessment and Strategy, VCA.

64. Cabinet memo, FCO Secretary, "Vietnam: An Assessment of the Present Position and, in Particular, of the Probable Consequences of Any Precipitate American Withdrawal," early January, 1970, FCO 15/1095, TNA; memo, HAK to RN, "Special National Intelligence Estimate on Factors Affecting North Vietnam's Policy on the Vietnam War," February 18, 1970, *FRUS,* 1969–1976, 6:594–595; Special National Intelligence Estimate, CIA, "The Outlook from Hanoi: Factors Affecting North Vietnam Policy on the War in Vietnam," February 5, 1970, item 04112156002, folder 156, box 12, Central Intelligence Agency Collection, VCA; Nguyen, *Hanoi's War,* 157–158; Luu Van Loi and Nguyen Anh Vu, *Le Duc Tho-Kissinger Negotiations in Paris* (Hanoi: Gioi, 1996), 111–112.

65. General Vo Nguyen Giap, "South Vietnam Situation: An Assessment October 1969–February 1970," CDEC, 1970, item 2121513001, folder 13, box 15, DPC: Unit 1—Assessment and Strategy, VCA.

66. "NLF Yearend Assessment for 1969," CDEC, circa early 1970, item 2121413006, folder 13, box 14, DPC: Unit 1—Assessment and Strategy, VCA.

67. Memorandum of conversation, Paris February 21, 1970, 4:10 p.m., *FRUS,* 1969–1976, 6:615.

236 Notes to Pages 144–146

7. It's Too Late

1. Schmitz, *Richard Nixon and the Vietnam War,* 78–81.

2. Telcon, RN and HAK, 7:00 p.m., November 14, 1969, box 3.2, HAK Telcons, RNPLM; telcon, RN and HAK, 11:33 p.m., November 3, 1969, box 3.1, HAK Telcons, RNPLM; telcon, Laird and HAK, 3:50 p.m., November 21, 1969, box 3.3, HAK Telcons, RNPLM.

3. Address by Nixon on the CBS Radio Network, "A New Alignment for American Unity," May 16, 1968, in *Nixon Speaks Out.* For more on Nixon and this "new alignment," see James Loomis, "The Making of the Peacemaker: Domestic Politics of Nixon's 1972 Visit to China" (master's thesis, London School of Economics, 2020).

4. Fry, *The American South and the Vietnam War,* 253–263, 269–280.

5. Safire, *Before the Fall,* 180; Franz Schurmann, *The Foreign Politics of Richard Nixon: The Grand Design* (Berkeley: Univ. of California, 1987), 97, 134; Johns, *Vietnam's Second Front,* 282, 285; telcon, Laird and HAK, 3:50 p.m., November 21, 1969, box 3.3, HAK Telcons, RNPLM.

6. Laird acknowledged that, given the additional $2 billion per year needed to improve the RVNAF, Vietnamization would do little to trim the defense budget. See memo, Laird to RN, September 4, 1969, *FRUS,* 1969–1976, 6:364.

7. Mann, *Grand Delusion,* 647–650; Webb, *The History of the Joint Chiefs of Staff,* 61–68, 322, 373–374, 384, 393, 399; Zelizer, "Congress and the Politics of Troop Withdrawal," 536; David Schmitz, "Congress Must Draw the Line: Senator Frank Church and the Opposition to the Vietnam War and the Imperial Presidency," in *Vietnam and the American Political Tradition: The Politics of Dissent,* ed. Randall Woods (New York: Cambridge Univ. Press, 2003), 133–138.

8. Pierre Brocheux and Daniel Hémery, *Indochina: An Ambiguous Colonization, 1858–1954* (Berkeley: Univ. of California Press, 2009), 27; Fredrik Logevall, *Embers of War: The Fall of an Empire and the Making of America's Vietnam* (New York: Random House, 2012), 381–384.

9. Nguyen Phu Duc, *Saigon's Side,* 240–241.

10. Shaw, *The Cambodian Campaign,* 8–10; Nguyen, *Hanoi's War,* 158, 163–165; memo, Rostow to LBJ, October 17, 1969, #7, "Intelligence Briefing October 1969 [1 of 2]," box 2, Post-Presidential Intelligence Briefings File, LBJPL; memo, CIA Directorate of Intelligence, "Vietnamization: Progress and Prospects," January 23, 1970, #6-dd, "Intelligence Materials Jan. 1970," box 3, Post-Presidential Intelligence Briefings File, LBJPL.

11. Raymond Leos, "Cautious Rapprochement amid the Gathering Storm: Norodom Sihanouk and the United States, 1969" (paper presented at the Vietnam Center and Archive and Institute for Peace and Conflict joint conference on "1969: Vietnamization and the Year of Transition in the Vietnam War," Lubbock, Texas, April 27, 2019). Based on his research, Leos concluded, "Although there is strong evidence that some U.S. intelligence agencies and some in MACV were aware of the

Notes to Pages 146–150   237

coup plotters' plans, there is no evidence that the White House was involved in instigating the coup itself." For a longer history of Cambodia in the Cold War, see Paul Thomas Chamberlin, *The Cold War's Killing Fields: Rethinking the Long Peace* (New York: Harper, 2018), 299–320.

12. Kenton Clymer, *Troubled Relations: The United States and Cambodia since 1870* (Dekalb: Northern Illinois Univ. Press, 2007), 97–103.

13. For more on South Vietnamese thinking, see Veith, *Drawn Swords,* 402–403.

14. Memos, Haig to HAK, "Vietnam" and "General Abrams' and JCS Views on Vietnamization," April 8, 1970, box 1009.1, NSC, RNPLM; memo on Cambodian operations derived from MACV Plan of March 30, 1970, box 88.2, NSC-VNSF, RNPLM; Shaw, *The Cambodian Campaign,* 22; cable, RN to Bunker, April 27, 1970, box 88.4, NSC-VNSF, RNPLM; cable, Bunker to RN, April 27, 1970, box 88.4, NSC-VNSF, RNPLM; Brigham, *Reckless,* 112–114.

15. Schmitz, *Richard Nixon and the Vietnam War,* 83–89; Safire, *Before the Fall,* 183, 189; memo, RN to HAK, April 22, 1970, box 88.3, NSC-VNSF, RNPLM; memo, Laird to RN, "NSDM 57—Actions to Protect US Forces in South Vietnam," April 27, 1970, *FRUS,* 1969–1976, 6:896–897; memorandum of meeting, April 28, 1970, *FRUS,* 1969–1976, 6:905; Daddis, *Withdrawal,* 120–126.

16. Daddis, *Withdrawal,* 121–123; memo, RN to HAK, April 22, 1970, RNPLM; Safire, *Before the Fall,* 182–183; RN, "Address to the Nation on the Situation in Southeast Asia," April 30, 1970, *APP,* https://www.presidency.ucsb.edu/node/239701 (accessed July 26, 2021).

17. Safire, *Before the Fall,* 193–194; memo and briefing book, HAK to RN, "Your May 5 Meetings with Congressional Committees," May 4, 1970, folder "Cambodia: Pres 5 May MTGs/Congressional Committees [1970]," box 585, NSC, RNPLM (emphasis in original).

18. Daddis, *Withdrawal,* 129; Fry, "Unpopular Messengers," 235–238; Brigham, *Reckless,* 117.

19. Shaw, *The Cambodian Campaign,* 153–160, 167; Sorley, *Vietnam Chronicles,* 412, 415, 423–424; Daddis, *Withdrawal,* 130–132; Veith, *Drawn Swords,* 404–405.

20. Fry, *The American South and the Vietnam War,* 269–274; Julian Zelizer, "How Congress Got Us Out of Vietnam," *The American Prospect,* March 2007.

21. Telcon, RN and HAK, 6:07 p.m., November 22, 1969, box 3.3, HAK Telcons, RNPLM; Donald Ritchie, "Advice and Dissent: Mike Mansfield and the Vietnam War," and Robert Schulzinger, "Richard Nixon, Congress, and the War in Vietnam, 1969–1974," in *Vietnam and the American Political Tradition,* 196–201, 282–294; Mann, *Grand Delusion,* 659; transcript, CBS News, *Face the Nation,* May 17, 1970, item 555235, United States—Political—Congress-General Senate, A1838, NAA.

22. Sorley, *Vietnam Chronicles,* 445–446 (emphasis in original).

23. Memo, Tom Huston to Harlow, Ehrlichman, Haldeman, William Timmons, and HAK, "The Assault on the Constitutional Powers of the Presidency,"

238 Notes to Pages 150–152

May 23, 1970, folder "Foreign Policy," box 10, WHCF:SMOF:Bryce Harlow, RNPLM; VSSG Report on Vietnamization, circa May 1970, folder "VSSG Meeting May 19, 1970 [2 of 2]," box H-001, NSC-IF, RNPLM; memo, HAK, "Background Paper on Vietnamization Economic Problems," circa May 1970, folder "VSSG Meeting May 19, 1970 [2 of 2]," box H-001, NSC-IF, RNPLM; memo, HAK to RN, "The Risks of Vietnamization," 1970, box 91.5, NSC, RNPLM; memo, HAK to RN, "Issues for the May 31 Meeting," May 1970, box 585.5, NSC, RNPLM.

24. RN quoted in Safire, *Before the Fall*, 195.

25. In August 1969, Thieu supported US reductions down to 300,000 or so. He argued then, "To ask SVN to take on the whole job in these circumstances would be to place an intolerable strain on its capacity to develop economically and socially." See Dispatch, Tait (Canadian Delegation to ICSC, Saigon) to External Affairs, "Interview with Pres Thieu," August 16, 1969, file 20-22-VIETS-2-1, part 36, vol. 9402, RG 25, LAC. In April 1970, Thieu still desired a residual presence and worried Nixon might quicken withdrawals (Rowland Evans and Robert Novak, "Thieu Fears Pace of U.S. Troop Pullout May Invite New Communist Offensive," *Washington Post*, April 1970). Thereafter, Thieu steadily lowered his expectations. By mid-1971, he understood American military forces would be gone by 1973. See dispatch, R. D. Jackson (Canadian Delegation to ICSC, Saigon), "Vietnam: President Thieu on PRC and DRVN," August 17, 1971, file 20-NVIET-1-3-S VIET part 2, vol. 8923, RG 25, LAC.

26. Memo, Laird to RN, "The Defense Budget—Fiscal Year 1971 and Beyond," circa May 31, 1970, folder "Cambodia/Vietnam 31 May 70 Meeting," box 585.5, NSC, RNPLM; memo, HAK to RN, "Memorandum from the Secretary of Defense Outlining Budgetary Problems," May 31, 1970, folder "Cambodia/Vietnam 31 May 70 Meeting," box 585.5, NSC, RNPLM; memo, HAK to Haig, "U.S. Troop Levels in SVN," August 23, 1970, box 1009.1, NSC, RNPLM; Herring, *America's Longest War*, 182.

27. George Herring, "Nixon's 'Laotian Gamble': Lam Son 719 as a Turning Point in the Vietnam War," *Army History*, no. 119 (spring 2021): 7.

28. Memo, Bob Dockery to Fulbright, "Telegrams Received on the Cambodian Issue," May 1, 1970, folder "1970," box 14:4, Subseries 4 Office Memos, Series 95 Office Files, JWFP.

29. Scanlon, *The Pro-War Movement*, 185–190, 202–208; Fry, *The American South and the Vietnam War*, 237–239, 320; Hughes, *Fatal Politics*, 12, 218.

30. Editorial, "Dangerous Game," *Vietnam Guardian*, January 23, 1970, 1.

31. Scanlon, *The Pro-War Movement*, 236–241.

32. "Financial Situation in Vietnam," *Saigon Post*, July 19, 1969; FBIS Daily Report: Asia and Pacific, July 29, 1969, folder 10, box 5, DPC: Other Manuscripts—FBIS—Asia, VCA; Simon Toner, "Imagining Taiwan: The Nixon Administration, the Developmental States, and South Vietnam's Search for Economic Viability, 1969–1975," *Diplomatic History* 41, no. 4 (September 2017): 774–784.

33. FBIS Daily Report: Asia and Pacific, July 29, 1969, folder 10, box 5, DPC: Other Manuscripts—FBIS—Asia, VCA; minutes, Nguyen Van Huong, "Tóm Tắt

Phiên Họp Hội-Đồng Tổng-Trưởng Ngày 15,9,1969," circa September 15, 1969, HS 80, PTT, VNAC2.

34. "Anti-Huong Move Explained," *Saigon Post,* July 4, 1969; "Huong Gives Way: New Cabinet Expected Next Week," *Saigon Post,* August 24, 1969; "'No Warlike Cabinet': Thieu Says National Peace Policy Stands," *Saigon Post,* August 28, 1969; Fear, "Saigon Goes Global," 449–450; Veith, *Drawn Swords,* 368–371.

35. Nguyen Duc Cuong, "Building a Market Economy during Wartime," in *Voices from the Second Republic,* 110; Veith, *Drawn Swords,* 380–383; FBIS Daily Report: Asia and Pacific, November 3, 1969, folder 7, box 6, DPC: Other Manuscripts—FBIS—Asia, VCA.

36. Toner, "Imagining Taiwan," 785–786; "Austerity Taxes Spur Flurry of Protests," *Saigon Post,* October 27, 1969, 1; "House Stages Anti-Tax Walkout," *Vietnam Guardian,* October 28, 1969, 1, 6; Nguyen Duy Lieu, "More Austerity Measures Coming," *Saigon Post,* October 30, 1969, 1; Wendell Merick, "Behind Optimism about Vietnam," *U.S. News and World Report,* December 1, 1969. See also Phạm Kim Ngọc, "Reform or Collapse: Economic Challenges during Vietnamization," in *The Republic of Vietnam, 1955–1975.*

37. Tran Ngoc Chau, *Vietnam Labyrinth,* 325–336, 358; Veith, *Drawn Swords,* 383–384; memo, "Political Developments in South Vietnam," January 16, 1970, "Intelligence Materials Jan. 1970," box 3, Post-Presidential Intelligence Briefings File, LBJPL.

38. Veith, *Drawn Swords,* 385–386; memos, "Political Developments in South Vietnam," January 16 and 18, 1970, "Intelligence Materials Jan. 1970," box 3, Post-Presidential Intelligence Briefings File, LBJPL.

39. Veith, *Drawn Swords,* 395–396.

40. Toner, "Imagining Taiwan," 774–775, 784–788, 796–797; memo, CIA, "An Appraisal of the Internal Unrest in Vietnam as of 7 May 1970," May 7, 1970, item 0410470003, folder 70, box 4, Central Intelligence Agency Collection, VCA.

41. Nguyen Duc Cuong, "Building a Market Economy during Wartime," 96, 100; Toner, "Imagining Taiwan," 787; memo, GVN (illegible author) to Thieu, "V/v tiếp kiến Ông J. Mendenhall," September 8, 1969, HS 1665, PTT, VNAC2.

42. Dispatch, Hart (Canadian Delegation to ICSC, Saigon) to External Affairs, "Vietnam—Laird-Wheeler Visit," February 19, 1970, file 20-22-VIETS-2-1, part 37, vol. 9402, RG 25, LAC; Diem, *Jaws of History,* 274–277; Margaret Kilgore, "Thieu Presses for More Aid, Laird Receptive to Proposals," *Saigon Post,* February 15, 1970; telegram, Bui Diem (Washington) to Thieu, November 10, 1969, HS 2162, PTT, VNAC2; letter, Bui Diem (Washington) to Thieu, January 24, 1970, HS 602, PTT, VNAC2; report, Bui Diem to Thieu, May 27, 1970, BDF, VWOHP; memo, Hoa-Thịnh-Đốn, "Viện-Trợ Kinh-Tế Và Giúp đỡ Thực-Phẩm Và Nhà Cho Quân-Lực Việt-Nam Cộng-Hòa," May 27, 1970, HS 588, PTT, VNAC2.

43. Memo, GVN, "Vấn-Đề Ôn-Định Và Phát-Triển Kinh-Tế Trong Giai-Đoạn Việt-Nam- Hóa Chiến-Tranh," circa early 1970, HS 2457, PTT, VNAC2; handwritten note from within GVN Ministry of Economy, circa mid-1970, HS 588, PTT,

240   Notes to Pages 155–160

VNAC2; telegram Nguyen Phu Duc to Bui Diem (Washington), June 15, 1970, HS 588, PTT, VNAC2; memo, GVN, "Chương-Trình Ổn-Định Kinh-Tế," n.d. (circa early 1970), HS 2185, PTT, VNAC2.

44. Ibid.

45. On foreign investment in the period, see memo, Rogers to RN, December 8, 1969, folder "NATO Ministerial Meeting, Brussels and Visits to Bonn and Paris 12/2–8/68," box 13, E-5439, RG 59, NAII; memo, C. M. James (Saigon), "French Policy towards South Vietnam," September 14, 1970, FCO 15/1349, TNA; memo, C. M. James (Saigon), "France and Vietnam," November 19, 1970, FCO 15/1349, TNA.

46. Nguyen Duc Cuong, "Coping with Changes and War, Building a Foundation for Growth," in *The Republic of Vietnam, 1955–1975,* 19–20; Phạm Kim Ngọc, "Reform or Collapse: Economic Challenges during Vietnamization," in *The Republic of Vietnam, 1955–1975,* 36–43; Veith, *Drawn Swords,* 394–399.

47. Ngoc quoted in Veith, *Drawn Swords,* 400.

48. Thieu quoted in Nguyen Duy Lieu, "More Austerity Measures Coming."

49. Memo, CIA, "The Political Base of the Saigon Government," October 7, 1969, item 04114188005, folder 188, box 14, Central Intelligence Agency Collection, VCA; memo, R. L. Harry (Saigon), "The Political Scene in Viet-Nam," April 29, 1970, item 4963063, South East Asia, South Asia and East Asia despatches 1970, A4231, NAA; Fear, "Saigon Goes Global," 449–450; Fear, "The Ambiguous Legacy of Ngo Dinh Diem," 48–49; Toner, "Imagining Taiwan," 775.

50. Nguyen, *Hanoi's War,* 158, 163–165; memorandum of conversation, Bangkok, July 29, 1969, *FRUS, 1969–1976,* 6:317–318; Shaw, *The Cambodian Campaign,* 27, 103–104 (emphasis in original); "'Vietnamization' Means Not to End the War But to Drag It On," *Vietnam Courier,* no. 259, March 9, 1970.

51. Brigham, *Reckless,* 136–138; Daddis, *Withdrawal,* 169–170.

52. Schmitz, "Congress Must Draw the Line," 133–138.

53. Daddis, *Withdrawal,* 170–171; Herring, "Nixon's 'Laotian Gamble,'" 9–10; Schmitz, *Richard Nixon and the Vietnam War,* 119; Anderson, *Vietnamization,* 77; Brigham, *Reckless,* 138–140

54. Veith, *Drawn Swords,* 425–426; Andrew Wiest, *Vietnam's Forgotten Army: Heroism and Betrayal in the ARVN* (New York: New York Univ. Press, 2008), 203–205, 209.

55. Brigham, *Reckless,* 141.

56. Veith, *Drawn Swords,* 424–425.

57. Herring, "Nixon's 'Laotian Gamble,'" 11–12; Nguyen Phu Duc, *Saigon's Side,* 253–259.

58. Wiest, *Vietnam's Forgotten Army,* 206–209; Herring, "Nixon's 'Laotian Gamble,'" 12–13.

59. This American assistance came at a high cost: "Two hundred fifty-three Americans were listed as killed in action or missing, with an additional 1,149 wounded," noted historian George Herring. Herring, "Nixon's 'Laotian Gamble,'" 14.

Notes to Pages 160–162   241

60. Wiest, *Vietnam's Forgotten Army*, 214–217; Brigham, *Reckless*, 144; Herring, "Nixon's 'Laotian Gamble,'" 14.

61. Schmitz, *Richard Nixon and the Vietnam War*, 120–121; Brigham, *Reckless*, 145; Veith, *Drawn Swords*, 428.

62. Wiest, *Vietnam's Forgotten Army*, 223; Herring, "Nixon's 'Laotian Gamble,'" 15; Daddis, *Withdrawal*, 170–171; Veith, *Drawn Swords*, 427–428; Willbanks, *Abandoning Vietnam*, 109–115, 124–125; Nguyen Phu Duc, *Saigon's Side*, 253–259; Willbanks, *A Raid Too Far: Operation Lam Son 719 and Vietnamization in Laos* (College Station: Texas A&M Univ. Press, 2014), 178–180.

63. Wiest, *Vietnam's Forgotten Army*, 224–227.

64. Brigham, *Reckless*, 146–147; Herring, "Nixon's 'Laotian Gamble,'" 15–17; Johns, *Vietnam's Second Front*, 294–295.

65. Veith, *Drawn Swords*, 427–429; Wiest, *Vietnam's Forgotten Army*, 224–227.

66. Francis Epplin, "Vietnam, My Story, Our Story, and Freedom to Choose," unpublished manuscript in author's possession (2020), 111–112. They also conducted "a bitter little war" against allied firebases near the DMZ that summer, overrunning and wiping out at least one South Vietnamese outpost. See Craig Whitney, "A Bitter Little War Raging Just Below the DMZ," *New York Times*, August 20, 1971.

67. Nguyen, *Hanoi's War*, 228; Veith, *Drawn Swords*, 429–430; Asselin, *Vietnam's American War*, 184–185.

68. Too often, those who maintain that the allies had essentially won the conflict after the Tet Offensive—the so-called better war advocates—end the pacification story here, shifting their attention to the big war of 1972. As the evidence indicated, the battle for the countryside (the control war) was far from won in 1971.

69. Clemis, *The Control War*, 96, 104–115, 130–133, 246; memo, CIA, "Protracted War and Decisive Victory: Communist Doctrine and Strategy in South Vietnam," December 20, 1969, item 04116207002, folder 207, box 16, Central Intelligence Agency Collection, VCA; Report, "The Military Situation in South Vietnam," June 12, 1970, #2d, "Intelligence Materials June 1970 [2 of 3]," box 5, Post-Presidential Intelligence Briefings File, LBJPL; Kevin Boylan, "The Red Queen's Race: Operation Washington Green and Pacification in Binh Dinh Province, 1969–70," *Journal of Military History* 73, no. 4 (October 2009): 1208–1225; Boylan, "Goodnight Saigon: American Provincial Advisors' Final Impressions of the Vietnam War," *Journal of Military History* 78, no. 1 (January 2014): 242, 249, 262, 265–268; Jeffrey Race, *War Comes to Long An: Revolutionary Conflict in a Vietnamese Province*, 1st paperback ed. (Berkeley: Univ. of California Press, 1973), 211–212, 270; Gawthorpe, *To Build as Well as Destroy*, 146–148.

70. Veith, *Drawn Swords*, 436–438.

71. Again, the resemblance is striking: Thieu, the provincial son of a minor merchant and fisherman, who was beneath cosmopolitan Saigon, and Nixon, the son of a Californian grocer, excluded and mocked by Washington's elite.

72. Gawthorpe, *To Build as Well as Destroy*, 122–127, 139–143, 162, 173–174, 182–184; Clemis, *The Control War*, 122–129, 162, 300–302.

242   Notes to Pages 163–165

73. Memo, Canadian Delegation to ICSC (Saigon) to the Undersecretary of State for External Affairs, "Presidential Election Bill," December 30, 1970, file 20-VIETS-19 part 1, vol. 9377, RG 25, LAC; dispatch, New Zealand embassy (Saigon) to Wellington, "Presidential Candidates," February 15, 1971, file 20-VIETS-19 part 1, vol. 9377, RG 25, LAC; memo, Canadian Delegation to ICSC (Saigon) to the Undersecretary of State for External Affairs, "The Vietnamese Presidential Elections," May 17, 1971, file 20-VIETS-19 part 1, vol. 9377, RG 25, LAC; memo, R. D. Jackson (Canadian Delegation to ICSC, Saigon) to the Undersecretary of State for External Affairs, "Presidential Election Law and Possible Repercussions," July 21, 1971, file 20-VIETS-19 part 1, vol. 9377, RG 25, LAC; dispatch, New Zealand embassy (Saigon) to Wellington, "Political Affairs," August 5, 1971, file 20-VIETS-19 part 1, vol. 9377, RG 25, LAC; Fear, "Saigon Goes Global," 450; Fear, "The Ambiguous Legacy of Ngo Dinh Diem," 49–54.

74. Veith, *Drawn Swords,* 439–444; dispatch, New Zealand embassy (Saigon) to Wellington, "Final Part of Two Parts," August 23, 1971, file 20-VIETS-19 part 2, vol. 9377, RG 25, LAC.

75. Dispatch, New Zealand embassy (Saigon) to Wellington, "Political Affairs," August 6, 1971, file 20-VIETS-19 part 1, vol. 9377, RG 25, LAC; dispatch, New Zealand embassy (Saigon) to Wellington, "Political Affairs," August 7, 1971, file 20-VIETS-19 part 1, vol. 9377, RG 25, LAC; dispatch, New Zealand embassy (Saigon) to Wellington, "Political Affairs," October 9, 1971, file 20-VIETS-19 part 3, vol. 9377, RG 25, LAC; dispatch, New Zealand embassy (Saigon) to Wellington, "Political Affairs," August 28, 1971, file 20-VIETS-19 part 2, vol. 9377, RG 25, LAC.

76. Veith, *Drawn Swords,* 444; Fear, "The 1971 Presidential Election and the Twilight of the Republican Vietnam," paper presented at the University of Oregon's International Workshop on Studying Republican Vietnam: Issues, Challenges, and Prospects, October 2019.

77. Fear, "The 1971 Presidential Election and the Twilight of the Republican Vietnam." On Lam Son 719 as a "turning point," see Herring, "Nixon's 'Laotian Gamble,'" 17–18.

78. Herring, *America's Longest War,* 299–300; Fry, *The American South and the Vietnam War,* 324–332; John Stennis, "We Have to Seek a Middle Ground," *U.S. News and World Report,* June 28, 1971; letter, Stennis to Fulbright, July 7, 1971, folder "1971," box 10:2, Subseries 1 FRC (General), Series 48 Foreign Relations Committee, JWFP; memo, RN to Laird and Rogers, August 30, 1971, folder "1971," box 18:1, Subseries 3 Committee Administration, Series 48 Foreign Relations Committee, JWFP; Diem, book, 287–294; memo, Trần-Kim-Phượng to the Prime Minister, "Tu-chính án Mansfield," July 7, 1971, HS 17494, PTTVNCH, VNAC2; Fear, "Saigon Goes Global," 450–451.

79. In 1971, neoisolationism remained an ever-present concern for Nixon (as it was for his predecessor). See letter, LBJ to RN, June 1, 1971, "Henry A. Kissinger," box 88, Post-Presidential, LBJPL.

80. Memo, HAK to RN, "Alternative Vietnam Strategies," July 20, 1970, box 91.4, NSC, RNPLM.

81. Brigham, *Reckless,* 150–151, 197; Kadura, *The War After the War,* 1–4, 13–15. See also memo, HAK to RN, September 18, 1971, *FRUS, 1969–1976,* 7:918–928. As both Brigham and Kadura affirm, Kissinger's acceptance of a decent interval came later. For his part, Nixon was always restive about any decent interval strategy.

82. On Thieu's and Nixon's optimism, see dispatch, commissioner (Canadian Delegation to ICSC, Saigon), "National Day of the Republic of Vietnam—Conversation with President Thieu," November 10, 1970, file 20-NVIET-1-3-S VIET part 2, vol. 8923, RG 25, LAC; records of discussion between Prime Minister Heath and RN at Camp David, December 18, 1970, FCO 15/1118, TNA; Peregrine Worsthorne, "The President Is Playing to Win in Southeast Asia," *Sunday Telegraph,* April 4, 1971.

83. Kadura, *The War after the War,* 1–4; Anderson, *Vietnamization,* 85.

84. Martin Clemis believes that this concession was in part a product of Nixon's confidence that pacification and Vietnamization were working. See Clemis, *The Control War,* 184–187.

85. Brigham, *Reckless,* 83–84, 148–159.

86. Kadura, *The War after the War,* 38–42; Tudda, *A Cold War Turning Point,* 206–207.

87. Fear, "Saigon Goes Global," 441–445; dispatch, R. D. Jackson and Canadian Delegation to ICSC (Saigon) to Under-Secretary of State for External Affairs, "South VietNamese Reaction to President Nixon's Proposed Visit to Peking," August 5, 1971, file 20-USA-3-Viet (S) part 2, vol. 8929, RG 25, LAC; dispatch, R. D. Jackson (Canadian Delegation to ICSC, Saigon), "Vietnam: President Thieu on PRC and DRVN," August 17, 1971, file 20-NVIET-1-3-S VIET part 2, vol. 8923, RG 25, LAC; Nguyen, *Hanoi's War,* 195–196; Asselin, *Vietnam's American War,* 186–191.

88. RN quoted in Douglas Brinkley and Luke Nichter, eds., *The Nixon Tapes, 1971–1972* (New York: Houghton Mifflin Harcourt, 2014), 622.

8. Alone Again, Naturally

1. RN, "Address to the Nation Making Public a Plan for Peace in Vietnam," January 25, 1972, *APP,* https://www.presidency.ucsb.edu/node/254597 (accessed October 2, 2020)

2. Herring, *America's Longest War,* 182.

3. Schwartz, *Henry Kissinger and American Power,* 6.

4. Asselin, *Vietnam's American War,* 191–193. Hanoi committed fourteen divisions (some 125,000 men) to the South during the offensive, with three of these crossing the DMZ on March 30, which was a violation of the 1968 bombing halt understanding. See Veith, *Drawn Swords,* 461–463.

244 Notes to Pages 169–174

5. Black, *The Invincible Quest*, 798. One telephone survey found 70 percent of Americans supported Nixon's bombing, with a similar percentage believing it was imperative the United States not be defeated in Vietnam. Survey contained in dispatch, Canadian embassy (Washington), "Vietnam: The President's Speech," May 1972, file 20-USA-3-Viet (S) part 3, vol. 8929, RG 25, LAC.

6. Brigham, *Reckless*, 171, 174, 185–186; Schwartz, *Henry Kissinger and American Power*, 168–170, 173–179; Asselin, *Vietnam's American War*, 194–196.

7. Daddis, *Withdrawal*, 183–189; Fear, "Saigon Goes Global," 450; Toner, "Imagining Taiwan," 774–775, 792–796; Clemis, *The Control War*, 257–261; Tuong Vu and Sean Fear, "Nation Building in South Vietnam: Vietnamese Perspectives," in *The Republic of Vietnam, 1955–1975*, 6.

8. Both MACV and South Vietnamese officials knew in 1972 that the RVNAF were outgunned. For instance, the Soviet 130 mm heavy artillery had a far greater range than anything the allies had on the ground. American light antitank weapons enabled ARVN troops to destroy enemy armor, but as with much Vietnamization-era equipment and modernization, more would be needed in the future. See Anderson, *Vietnamization*, 89–90; Nguyen Phu Duc, *Saigon's Side*, 279–281.

9. Schwartz, *Henry Kissinger and American Power*, 168–169; Brigham, *Reckless*, 180.

10. Laird et al., *The Nixon Doctrine*, 64–65.

11. Herring, *America's Longest War*, 182.

12. Dispatch, Canadian embassy (Washington) to External Affairs, "USA Election: Nixon the Anti-War Candidate?," September 29, 1972, file 20-USA-19 part 3, vol. 9377, RG 25, LAC; Hughes, *Fatal Politics*, xi, 138–142.

13. Letter excerpt, Laird to HAK, sent to author April 2, 2007

14. Asselin, *Vietnam's American War*, 187, 194–199; Brigham, *Reckless*, 190–195; Schwartz, *Henry Kissinger and American Power*, 193–194.

15. Asselin, *Vietnam's American War*, 199–202.

16. Ibid., 202–204, 206; Berman *No Peace, No Honor*, 215–216.

17. Veith, *Drawn Swords*, 475–476.

18. Ibid., 476–480; Schwartz, *Henry Kissinger and American Power*, 196–200, 207–208.

19. Asselin, *Vietnam's American War*, 198–199, 206–213.

20. Ibid., 208.

21. Kadura, *The War After the War*, 11–12, 16–23; Schwartz, *Henry Kissinger and American Power*, 467; Veith, *Drawn Swords*, 481–482.

22. Dispatch, Hart (Canadian Delegation to ICSC, Saigon) to External Affairs, "Views of President Thieu," May 28, 1971, file 20-VIETS-19 part 1, vol. 9377, RG 25, LAC.

23. Nguyen and Schecter, *The Palace File*, 153–154, 353; Veith, *Drawn Swords*, 472, 477.

24. Bundy, *A Tangled Web*, 362; Hughes, *Fatal Politics*, 155–158; memorandum of conversation at San Clemente, February 10, 1973, *FRUS*, 1969–1976, E-12: doc-

Notes to Pages 174–178   245

ument #1; draft memo, RN to Rogers, Richardson, Assistant to the President for Legislative Affairs Timmons, and Kissinger, March 10, 1973, *FRUS, 1969–1976*, 35:31–32.

25. Quoted in Daddis, *Withdrawal*, 142.

26. David Halberstam, "The Vietnamization of America," *Playboy*, January 1971.

27. Lam Quang Thi, *The Twenty-Five Year Century: A South Vietnamese General Remembers the Indochina War to the Fall of Saigon* (Denton: Univ. of North Texas Press, 2001), 278, 290.

28. Kadura, *The War after the War*, 5–7, 52–82; Johns, *Vietnam's Second Front*, 286–294, 311–321; Mann, *Grand Delusion*, 711–712, 716–718; Schulzinger, "Richard Nixon, Congress, and the War in Vietnam, 1969–1974," 294–300; Schmitz, *Richard Nixon and the Vietnam War*, 117–118, 140–143; Asselin, *A Bitter Peace*, 187–189; Hughes, *Fatal Politics*, 163–170.

29. Daddis, *Withdrawal*, 78; Kadura, *The War after the War*, 94; Clemis, *The Control War*, 281–283.

30. Minutes of WSAG Meeting, "Cambodia," October 2, 1973, *FRUS*, 1969–1976, 10:437–445; see also minutes of October 2, 1973 WSAG meeting, Jeanne Davis, "Cambodia," October 9, 1973, WSAG, Minutes of Meetings, NSC-IF, RNPLM.

31. Minutes of September 20, 1973 WSAG meeting, Jeanne Davis, "Cambodia," October 5, 1973, WSAG, Minutes of Meetings, NSC-IF, RNPLM.

32. George Veith, *Black April: The Fall of South Vietnam, 1973–75* (New York: Encounter Books, 2012), 55–57; minutes of WSAG, January 25, 1974, *FRUS*, 1969–1976, 10:507ff.

33. Barbara Keys, *Reclaiming American Virtue: The Human Rights Revolution of the 1970s* (Cambridge, Mass.: Harvard Univ. Press, 2014), 133–165; Veith, *Drawn Swords*, 449.

34. Asselin, *Vietnam's American War*, 213–214, 220–224; Veith, *Drawn Swords*, 486–489.

35. Veith, *Black April*, 58–63, 82–85, 111–112 (emphasis in original).

36. Several essays in *The Republic of Vietnam, 1955–1975* provide Vietnamese perspectives on this period and their sense of contingent economic success.

37. Toner, "Imagining Taiwan," 792–796; Veith, *Black April*, 49–50, 54–55; Veith, *Drawn Swords*, 501–506.

38. On South Vietnamese identity, see Nu-Anh Tran, "South Vietnamese Identity, American Intervention, and the Newspaper *Chinh Luan* [Political Discussion], 1965–1969," *Journal of Vietnamese Studies* 1, nos.1–2 (February/August 2006): 169–209.

39. Fear, "The Ambiguous Legacy of Ngo Dinh Diem," 54; Gawthorpe, *To Build as Well as Destroy*, 160–162; Veith, *Drawn Swords*, 515–533.

40. PAVN estimates vary, but historian David Anderson noted that in 1973 North Vietnam had 170,000 regulars in the South and an additional 100,000 just across the border in Cambodia and Laos. See Anderson, *Vietnamization*, 97. The Paris Peace Accords were supposed to limit the resupply of these forces (and remove

246   Notes to Pages 178–188

those soldiers in Laos and Cambodia). Kissinger understood Hanoi was unlikely to abide by either of those provisions. See Schwartz, *Henry Kissinger and American Power*, 208–209.

41. Veith, *Drawn Swords*, 535–554; Nguyen Phu Duc, *Saigon's Side*, 405, 416; Anderson, *Vietnamization*, 39–42, 99, 106–107; Clemis, *The Control War*, 279–283; Ronald Spector, *After Tet: The Bloodiest Year in Vietnam* (New York: Free Press, 1993), xvii, 313–314; Willbanks, *Abandoning Vietnam*, 283–284, 287; Sorley, *A Better War*, 373.

42. Danhui, "The Sino-Soviet Dispute," 304–305; Shen Zhihua, "Sino-U.S. Reconciliation and China's Vietnam Policy," in Roberts, *Behind the Bamboo Curtain*, 355.

43. Asselin, *Vietnam's American War*, 220–233; Anderson, *Vietnamization*, 116–123; Veith, *Black April*, 6–7.

Conclusion

1. See Kadura, *The War after the War*, 8; Clemis, *The Control War*, 26.

2. Hughes, *Fatal Politics*, 180.

3. Nguyen, *Hanoi's War*, 192; Diem, *Jaws of History*, 237.

4. Tran Van Don, *Our Endless War*, 341.

5. Safire, *Before the Fall*, 203–212.

6. Logevall, "A Delicate Balance: John Sherman Cooper and the Republican Opposition to the Vietnam War," in *Vietnam and the American Political Tradition*, 237. For more on American credibility and the difficulties of withdrawal, see Logevall, "Vietnam's Place in the Cold War: Some Reflections on the Domino Theory," 130–143.

7. RN, *No More Vietnams*, 101–104.

8. Logevall, *Choosing War*, 378–379.

9. "President Thieu Raps 'Destructive' Regimes," *Vietnam Guardian*, July 23, 1969, 1, 6; "All US Combat Units' Pullout Risky—Thieu," *Saigon Post*, January 11, 1970, 1.

10. Kadura, *The War after the War*, 57.

11. Asselin, *Vietnam's American War*, 168, 177–179, 197–198, 207.

12. Ken Hughes, "Fatal Politics: Nixon's Political Timetable for Withdrawing from Vietnam," *Diplomatic History* 38, no. 3 (June 2014): 504–506.

13. Kadura, *The War after the War*, 18–23.

14. Memo, Nha [Mỹ] Châu, Lien Hiep Quoc, "Một Vài Nhận-Định Về Chính-Sách Của Hoa-Kỳ Đối Với Việt-Nam Trong Năm 1970," n.d. (early 1970), HS 20617, PTTVNCH, VNAC2; "All US Combat Units' Pullout Risky—Thieu," Saigon Post, January 11, 1970. See also Veith, Drawn Swords.

15. Immediately after Saigon's 1975 fall, South Vietnamese dignitaries blamed the United States for abandoning their country. Even still, they acknowledged more

Notes to Page 188   247

American aid and airpower would have been unlikely to save South Vietnam. See Hosmer, Kellen, and Jenkins, *The Fall of South Vietnam,* 9–10, 14, 257.

16. Military historian James Willbanks adds that Vietnamization was too closely modeled after US military doctrine. See Willbanks, *Abandoning Vietnam,* 277–288.

17. Australia and other allies would follow America out and prepare for South Vietnam's presumed, though still contingent, fall. By late 1970, Australian officials were using the phrase "decent interval" to describe one of the possible outcomes. See R. L. Harry (Saigon), "Australian Interests and Role in Viet-Nam," December 3, 1970, item 4963063, South East Asia, South Asia and East Asia despatches 1970, A4231, NAA; memo, Defence Committee, "Strategic Basis of Australian Defence Policy," March 1971, item 3188732, The Strategic Basis of Australian Defence Policy—1971, A5619, NAA.

18. Quoted in "Transcript of Broadcast with Walter Cronkite Inaugurating a CBS Television News Program," September 2, 1963, *APP,* https://www.presidency.ucsb.edu/node/237355 (accessed July 26, 2021).

19. Address, Fulbright, "The Price of Empire," August 8, 1967, reprinted in *Concern* (October 1967), in folder "1967–1969," box 23:4, Subseries 5 Articles by JWF, Series 78 Press, 1943–1974, JWFP.

Bibliography

Primary Sources

Archives
Australia War Memorial. Canberra, Australia.
    AWM122, Joint Staff File
CIA Electronic Reading Room.
Gerald R. Ford Library. Ann Arbor, Michigan.
    William J. Baroody Jr. Papers
    Melvin R. Laird Papers
    A. James Reichley Research Interviews
Lyndon Baines Johnson Presidential Library. Austin, Texas.
    Cabinet Papers
    Clark Clifford Papers
    George M. Elsey Papers
    National Security Files
    Special Files
    Paul C. Warnke Files
    Post-Presidential Files
Library and Archives Canada. Ottawa, Canada.
    Ministerial Group 26, Prime Minister's Office
    Record Group 25, External Affairs
Miller Center, University of Virginia, Charlottesville, Virginia.
    Presidential Recordings Program
National Archives II. College Park, Maryland.
    Record Group 59, General Records of the Department of State
    Record Group 472, Records of the U.S. Forces in Southeast Asia
National Archives of Australia. Canberra, Australia.
    A1838, A4231, Department of External Affairs
    A4531, Australian Embassy, Saigon

250 Bibliography

A5869, A5882, Department of the Cabinet Office
A7942, Department of Defence
M3787, Subject Files of John Grey Gorton
Richard M. Nixon Library. Yorba Linda, California.
H. R. Haldeman Collection
Henry A. Kissinger Office Files Collection
Laguna Niguel Series
NSC Files
Pre-Presidential Series
White House Communications Agency Sound Recordings Collection
White House Special Files
The National Archives. Kew, England.
Ministry of Defence
Foreign and Commonwealth Office
Prime Minister's Office
University Libraries Special Collections. University of Arkansas. Fayetteville, Arkansas.
J. William Fulbright Papers
Vietnam Center and Archive at Texas Tech University. Lubbock, Texas.
Central Intelligence Agency Collection
Douglas Pike Collection
Vietnam Center Collection
Vietnam National Archives Center II. Ho Chi Minh City, Vietnam.
Hôi đồng An ninh phát triển, 1969–1975
Phủ Tổng thống Đệ nhị Cộng hòa, 1967–1975
Phủ Thủ Tướng Việt-Nam Cộng hòa, 1954–1975
Vietnam War Oral History Project.
Bui Diem Files

Government Publications

U.S. Department of State. *Foreign Relations of the United States, 1964–1968*. Vol. 5, *Vietnam, 1967*. Washington, D.C.: Government Printing Office, 2002.

———. *Foreign Relations of the United States, 1964–1968*. Vol. 27, *Mainland Southeast Asia; Regional Affairs*. Washington, D.C.: Government Printing Office, 2000.

———. *Foreign Relations of the United States, 1969–1976*. Vol. 1, *Foundations of Foreign Policy, 1969–1972*. Washington, D.C.: Government Printing Office, 2003.

———. *Foreign Relations of the United States, 1969–1976*. Vol. 6, *Vietnam, January 1969–July 1970*. Washington, D.C.: Government Printing Office, 2006.

———. *Foreign Relations of the United States, 1969–1976*. Vol. 7, *Vietnam, July 1970–January 1972*. Washington, D.C.: Government Printing Office, 2010.

Bibliography   251

Interviews

Baroody, William J., Jr. Interview with A. James Reichley, n.d. A. James Reichley Interview Transcripts, (1967) 1977–81, Gerald R. Ford Library.

Lake, Anthony. Interview with A. James Reichley, October 28, 1977. A. James Reichley Interview Transcripts, (1967) 1977–81, Gerald R. Ford Library.

Laird, Melvin. Telephone interviews by author. April 10, June 25, and November 24, 2007.

———. Interview with Maurice Matloff and Alfred Goldberg, September 2, 1986. Melvin Laird Papers, Gerald R. Ford Library.

———. Interview with Tom Wells, May 21, 1986. Melvin Laird Papers, Gerald R. Ford Library.

Memoirs and Autobiographies

Bui Diem. *In the Jaws of History.* Boston: Houghton Mifflin, 1987.

Cao Van Vien and Dong Van Khuyen. *Reflections on the Vietnam War.* Washington, D.C.: US Army Center of Military History, 1980.

Ellsberg, Daniel. *Secrets: A Memoir of Vietnam and the Pentagon Papers.* New York: Viking, 2002.

Haig, Alexander, Jr. *Inner Circles: How America Changed the World.* New York: Warner Books, 1992.

Haldeman, H. R. *The Haldeman Diaries.* New York: G. P. Putnam's Sons, 1994.

Hosmer, Stephen, Konrad Kellen, and Brian Jenkins. *The Fall of South Vietnam: Statements by Vietnamese Military and Civilian Leaders.* New York: Crane, Russak, 1980.

Johnson, Lyndon Baines. *The Vantage Point: Perspectives of the Presidency, 1963–1969.* New York: Holt, Rinehart, and Winston, 1971.

Kissinger, Henry. *Ending the Vietnam War: A History of America's Involvement in and Extrication from the Vietnam War.* New York: Simon and Schuster, 2003.

———. "The Viet Nam Negotiations." *Foreign Affairs* 47 (January 1969): 211–234.

———. *White House Years.* Boston: Little, Brown, 1979.

Laird, Melvin. *A House Divided: America's Strategy Gap.* Chicago: Henry Regnery, 1962.

———. "Iraq: Learning the Lessons of Vietnam." *Foreign Affairs* 84 (2005): 22–43.

———. "Unforgettable Creighton Abrams." *Reader's Digest,* July 1976.

Laird, Melvin, et al. *The Nixon Doctrine: A Town Hall Meeting on National Security Policy Sponsored by the American Enterprise Institute Held at American Enterprise Institute, Washington, D.C.* Washington, D.C.: American Enterprise Institute for Public Policy Research, 1972.

Nixon, Richard. *No More Vietnams.* New York: Arbor House, 1985.

———. *RN: The Memoirs of Richard Nixon.* New York: Grossett and Dunlap, 1978.

Nguyen Cao Ky. *Twenty Years and Twenty Days.* New York: Stein and Day, 1976.

Nguyen Phu Duc. *The Viet-Nam Peace Negotiations, Saigon's Side of the Story.* Christiansburg, Va.: Dalley Book Service, 2005.

250 Bibliography

Nguyen Tien Hung, and Jerrold Schecter. *The Palace File*. New York: Harper and Row, 1986.

Safire, William. *Before the Fall: An Inside View of the Pre-Watergate White House*. New York: Doubleday, 1975.

Sorley, Lewis, ed. *The Vietnam War: An Assessment by South Vietnam's Generals*. Lubbock: Texas Tech Univ. Press, 2010.

Taylor, K. W., ed. *Voices from the Second Republic of South Vietnam (1967–1975)*. Ithaca, N.Y.: Cornell Southeast Asia Program Publications, 2014.

Tran Ngoc Chau. *Vietnam Labyrinth: Allies, Enemies, and Why the U.S. Lost the War*. Lubbock: Texas Tech Univ. Press, 2012

Tran Van Don. *Our Endless War: Inside Vietnam*. San Rafael, Calif.: Presidio, 1978.

Vu, Tuong, and Sean Fear, eds. *The Republic of Vietnam, 1955–1975: Vietnamese Perspectives on Nation Building*. Ithaca, N.Y.: Cornell Univ. Press, 2019.

Whalen, Richard. *Catch the Falling Flag: A Republican's Challenge to His Party*. Boston: Houghton Mifflin, 1972.

Other Published Documents

Beschloss, Michael R. *Reaching for Glory: Lyndon Johnson's Secret White House Tapes, 1964–1965*. New York: Touchstone, 2002.

———. *Taking Charge: The Johnson White House Tapes, 1963–1964*. New York: Simon and Schuster, 1997.

Brinkley, Douglas, and Luke Nichter, eds. *The Nixon Tapes, 1971–1972*. New York: Houghton Mifflin Harcourt, 2014.

Kimball, Jeffrey. *The Vietnam War Files: Uncovering the Secret History of Nixon-Era Strategy*. Lawrence: Univ. Press of Kansas, 2004.

Nixon Speaks Out: Major Speeches and Statements by Richard M. Nixon in the Presidential Campaign of 1968. New York: Nixon-Agnew Campaign Committee, 1968.

Pike, Douglas, ed. *The Bunker Papers: Reports to the President from Vietnam, 1967–1973*. 3 vols. Berkeley: Univ. of California Press, 1990.

Sorley, Lewis, ed. *Vietnam Chronicles: The Abrams Tapes, 1968–1972*. Lubbock: Texas Tech Univ. Press, 2004.

Secondary Works

Alterman, Eric, and Kevin Mattson. *The Cause: The Fight for American Liberalism from Franklin Roosevelt to Barack Obama*. New York: Viking Penguin, 2012.

Ambrose, Stephen. *Nixon, Volume 1: The Education of a Politician, 1913–1962*. New York: Simon and Schuster, 1987.

———. *Nixon, Volume 2: The Triumph of a Politician, 1962–1972*. New York: Simon and Schuster, 1989.

Anderson, David. *Vietnamization: Politics, Strategy, Legacy*. New York: Rowman and Littlefield, 2020.

Bibliography 253

Anderson, David, and John Ernst, eds. *The War that Never Ends: New Perspectives on the Vietnam War.* Lexington: Univ. Press of Kentucky, 2007.

Ang, Cheng Guan. *Ending the Vietnam War: The Vietnamese Communists' Perspective.* New York: RoutledgeCurzon, 2004.

———. *The Vietnam War from the Other Side: The Vietnamese Communists' Perspective.* New York: RoutledgeCurzon, 2002.

Asselin, Pierre. *A Bitter Peace: Washington, Hanoi, and the Making of the Paris Agreement.* Chapel Hill: Univ. of North Carolina Press, 2002.

———. *Vietnam's American War.* New York: Cambridge Univ. Press, 2018.

Berman, Larry. *No Peace, No Honor: Nixon, Kissinger, and Betrayal in Vietnam.* New York: Free Press, 2001.

Black, Conrad. *Richard Milhous Nixon: The Invincible Quest.* London: Quercus, 2007.

Boylan, Kevin. "Goodnight Saigon: American Provincial Advisors' Final Impressions of the Vietnam War." *Journal of Military History* 78, no.1 (January 2014): 233–270.

———. "The Red Queen's Race: Operation Washington Green and Pacification in Binh Dinh Province, 1969–70." *Journal of Military History* 73, no. 4 (October 2009): 1195–1230.

Bradley, Mark Philip, and Marilyn Young, eds. *Making Sense of the Vietnam Wars: Local, National, and Transnational Perspectives.* New York: Oxford Univ. Press, 2008.

Brigham, Robert. *ARVN: Life and Death in the South Vietnamese Army.* Lawrence: Univ. Press of Kansas, 2006.

———. *Guerrilla Diplomacy: The NLF's Foreign Relations and the Viet Nam War.* Ithaca, N.Y.: Cornell Univ. Press, 1999.

———. *Reckless: Henry Kissinger and the Tragedy of Vietnam.* New York: PublicAffairs, 2018.

Bundy, William. *A Tangled Web: The Making of Foreign Policy in the Nixon Administration.* New York: Hill and Wang, 1998.

Clarke, Jeffrey J. *Advice and Support: The Final Years, 1965–1973.* Washington, D.C.: Government Printing Office, 1988.

Clemis, Martin. *The Control War: The Struggle for South Vietnam, 1968–1975.* Norman: Univ. of Oklahoma Press, 2018.

Daddis, Gregory. *Withdrawal: Reassessing America's Final Years in Vietnam.* New York: Oxford Univ. Press, 2017.

Dallek, Robert. *Nixon and Kissinger: Partners in Power.* New York: Harper Collins, 2007.

Dong Van Khuyen. *The RVNAF.* Washington, D.C.: US Army Center of Military History, 1980.

Evans, Rowland, Jr., and Robert D. Novak. *Nixon in the White House: The Frustration of Power.* New York: Random House, 1971.

Fear, Sean. "The Ambiguous Legacy of Ngo Dinh Diem in South Vietnam's Second Republic (1967–1975)." *Journal of Vietnamese Studies* 11, no. 1 (2016): 1–75.

———. "Saigon Goes Global: South Vietnam's Quest for International Legitimacy in the Age of Détente." *Diplomatic History* 42, no. 3 (June 2018): 428–455.

Ferguson, Niall. *Kissinger: 1923–1968: The Idealist.* New York, Penguin, 2015.

Fitzgerald, David. "Sir Robert Thompson, Strategic Patience and Nixon's War in Vietnam." *Journal of Strategic Studies* 37, no. 6–7 (2014): 998–1026.

Fry, Joseph. *The American South and the Vietnam War: Belligerence, Protest, and Agony in Dixie.* Lexington: Univ. Press of Kentucky, 2015.

Gaiduk, Ilya V. *The Soviet Union and the Vietnam War.* Chicago: Ivan R. Dee, 1996.

Gardner, Lloyd. *Pay Any Price: Lyndon Johnson and the Wars for Vietnam.* Chicago: Ivan R. Dee, 1995.

Gawthorpe, Andrew. *To Build as Well as Destroy: American Nation Building in South Vietnam.* Ithaca, N.Y.: Cornell Univ. Press, 2018.

Hanhimäki, Jussi. *The Flawed Architect: Henry Kissinger and American Foreign Policy.* New York: Oxford Univ. Press, 2004.

Herring, George. *America's Longest War: The United States and Vietnam, 1950–1975,* 4th ed. New York: McGraw Hill, 2002.

———. "Nixon's 'Laotian Gamble': Lam Son 719 as a Turning Point in the Vietnam War." *Army History* no. 119 (spring 2021): 6–19.

Hersh, Seymour. *The Price of Power: Kissinger in the Nixon White House.* New York: Summit, 1983.

Hughes, Ken. *Fatal Politics: The Nixon Tapes, the Vietnam War, and the Casualties of Reelection.* Charlottesville: Univ. of Virginia Press, 2015.

Hunt, Richard. *Melvin Laird and the Foundation of the Post-Vietnam Military.* Secretaries of Defense Historical Series, vol. 7. Washington, D.C.: Historical Office, Office of the Secretary of Defense, 2015.

Isaacson, Walter. *Kissinger: A Biography.* New York: Simon and Schuster, 1992.

Johns, Andrew. "Doves among Hawks: Republican Opposition to the Vietnam War, 1964–1968." *Peace and Change* 31 (October 2006): 585–628.

———. *Vietnam's Second Front: Domestic Politics, the Republican Party, and the War.* Lexington: Univ. Press of Kentucky, 2010.

Johnson, Robert David. *Congress and the Cold War.* New York: Cambridge Univ. Press, 2006.

Kadura, Johannes. *The War After the War: The Struggle for Credibility during America's Exit from Vietnam.* Ithaca, N.Y.: Cornell Univ. Press, 2016.

Kimball, Jeffrey. "The Nixon Doctrine: A Saga of Misunderstanding." *Presidential Studies Quarterly* 36 (March 2006): 59–74.

———. *Nixon's Vietnam War.* Lawrence: Univ. Press of Kansas, 1998.

Kirkpatrick, Rob. *1969: The Year Everything Changed.* New York: Skyhorse Publishing, 2009.

Litwak, Robert. *Détente and the Nixon Doctrine: American Foreign Policy and the Pursuit of Stability, 1969–1976.* New York: Cambridge Univ. Press, 1986.

Logevall, Fredrik. *Choosing War: The Lost Chance for Peace and the Escalation of War in Vietnam.* Berkeley: Univ. of California Press, 1999.

Bibliography 255

———. "Vietnam's Place in the Cold War: Some Reflections on the Domino Theory." In *The Most Dangerous Years: The Cold War, 1953–1975,* ed. Malcolm Muir and Mark Wilkinson. Lexington, Va.: Virginia Military Institute, 2005.

Logevall, Fredrik, and Andrew Preston, eds. *Nixon in the World: American Foreign Relations, 1969–1977.* New York: Oxford Univ. Press, 2008.

Luu Van Loi and Nguyen Anh Vu. *Le Duc Tho-Kissinger Negotiations in Paris.* Hanoi, Vietnam: Gioi, 1996.

Mann, Robert. *A Grand Delusion: America's Descent into Vietnam.* New York: Basic Books, 2001.

Military History Institute of Vietnam. *Victory in Vietnam: The Official History of the People's Army of Vietnam, 1954–1975.* Translated by Merle L. Pribbenow. Lawrence: Univ. Press of Kansas, 2002.

Morris, Roger. *Uncertain Greatness: Henry Kissinger and American Foreign Policy.* New York: Harper and Row, 1977.

Nguyen, Lien-Hang. *Hanoi's War: An International History of the War for Peace in Vietnam.* Chapel Hill: Univ. of North Carolina Press, 2012.

Perlstein, Rick. *Nixonland: The Rise of a President and the Fracturing of America.* New York: Scribner, 2008.

Prados, John. *The Blood Road: The Ho Chi Minh Trail and the Vietnam War.* New York: John Wiley and Sons, 1999.

Reichley, A. James. *Conservatives in an Age of Change: The Nixon and Ford Administrations.* Washington, D.C.: Brookings Institution, 1981.

Ruth, Richard. *In Buddha's Company: Thai Soldiers in the Vietnam War.* Honolulu: Univ. of Hawai'i Press, 2011.

Scanlon, Sandra. "Every Way Out: Vietnam, American National Identity, and the 1968 Presidential Election." In *US Presidential Elections and Foreign Policy: Candidates, Campaigns, and Global Politics from FDR to Bill Clinton,* ed. Andrew Johnstone and Andrew Priest. Lexington: Univ. Press of Kentucky, 2017.

———. *The Pro-War Movement: Domestic Support for the Vietnam War and the Making of Modern American Conservatism.* Boston: Univ. of Massachusetts Press, 2013.

Schaffer, Howard. *Ellsworth Bunker: Global Troubleshooter, Vietnam Hawk.* Chapel Hill: Univ. of North Carolina Press, 2003.

Schmitz, David. *Richard Nixon and the Vietnam War: The End of the American Century.* New York: Rowman and Littlefield, 2014.

Schwartz, Thomas. *Henry Kissinger and American Power: A Political Biography.* New York, Hill and Wang, 2020.

Shaw, John. *The Cambodian Campaign: The 1970 Offensive and America's Vietnam War.* Lawrence: Univ. Press of Kansas, 2005.

Small, Melvin. *Antiwarriors: The Vietnam War and the Battle for America's Hearts and Minds.* Wilmington, Del.: Scholarly Resources, 2002.

———. *At the Water's Edge: American Politics and the Vietnam War.* Chicago: Ivan R. Dee, 2005.

Sorley, Lewis. *A Better War: The Unexamined Victories and Final Tragedy of America's Last Years in Vietnam*. New York: Harcourt Brace, 1999.

———. *Thunderbolt: General Creighton Abrams and the Army of His Times*. New York: Simon and Schuster, 1992.

Suri, Jeremi. *Power and Protest: Global Revolution and the Rise of Détente*. Cambridge, Mass.: Harvard Univ. Press, 2003.

Toner, Simon. "Imagining Taiwan: The Nixon Administration, the Developmental States, and South Vietnam's Search for Economic Viability, 1969–1975." *Diplomatic History* 41, no. 4 (September 2017): 772–798.

Tudda, Chris. *A Cold War Turning Point: Nixon and China, 1969–1972*. Baton Rouge: Louisiana State Univ. Press, 2012.

Van Atta, Dale. *With Honor: Melvin Laird in War, Peace, and Politics*. Madison: Univ. of Wisconsin Press, 2008.

Veith, George. *Black April: The Fall of South Vietnam, 1973–75*. New York: Encounter Books, 2012.

———. *Drawn Swords in a Distant Land: South Vietnam's Shattered Dreams*. New York: Encounter Books, 2021.

Webb, Willard. *The History of the Joint Chiefs of Staff: The Joint Chiefs of Staff and the War in Vietnam, 1969–1970*. Washington, D.C.: Office of the Chairman of the Joint Chiefs of Staff, 1976.

Wells, Tom. *The War Within: America's Battle over Vietnam*. Berkeley: Univ. of California Press, 1994.

Wiest, Andrew. *Vietnam's Forgotten Army: Heroism and Betrayal in the ARVN*. New York: New York Univ. Press, 2008.

Willbanks, James. *Abandoning Vietnam: How America Left and South Vietnam Lost Its War*. Lawrence: Univ. Press of Kansas, 2004.

———. *A Raid Too Far: Operation Lam Son 719 and Vietnamization in Laos*. College Station: Texas A&M Univ. Press, 2014.

Woods, Randall. *J. William Fulbright, Vietnam, and the Search for a Cold War Foreign Policy*. New York: Cambridge Univ. Press, 1998.

———. *LBJ: Architect of American Ambition*. New York: Free Press, 2006.

———, ed. *Vietnam and the American Political Tradition: The Politics of Dissent*. New York: Cambridge Univ. Press, 2003.

Zhai, Qiang. *China and the Vietnam Wars, 1950–1975*. Chapel Hill: Univ. of North Carolina Press, 2000.

Index

ABM (anti-ballistic missile) system, 59, 112, 185

Abrams, General Creighton, 18, 19, 51, 54, 56, 89; on the Cambodian incursion, 148; on "cut-and-try" approach to withdrawals, 115; escalation questioned by, 107; on failure of Lam Son 719 operation, 160; on Operation Arc Light, 63; optimism of, 134; pace of troop withdrawals and, 146; reduction in troop withdrawals and, 103; South Vietnamese forces criticized by, 134–135; on South Vietnamese reliance on US firepower, 171; Vietnamization and, 57, 71, 99–100

Accelerated Pacification Campaign (1968–1969), 46

Acheson, Dean, 126–127

Agnew, Spiro, 112, 126

airpower, US, 2, 29, 30, 102, 171, 180

American bombing of North Vietnam, 11, 13, 27, 45, 49, 55, 79, 92, 95, 102; Christmas bombing [Linebacker II] (1972), 172–173, 174; communists' ability to withstand, 108; Johnson's halt of, 14, 15, 20, 21, 22, 23, 147; Operation Linebacker, 169; renewed and expanded, 172; resumption of, 38, 97, 141, 142; reticence to continue (post-1972), 175. *See also* Duck Hook, Operation

antiwar movement, 5, 22, 31, 66–67, 102, 103, 126; radicalization of, 127; revived by Nixon's invasion of Cambodia, 143

Apollo XI astronauts, 89, 91

Arc Light, Operation, 63

ARVN (Army of the Republic of Vietnam), 12, 28, 36, 135, 140, 186; in Cambodia, 148, 157; de-escalation and, 38; improvement program of, 57, 58, 62, 85; modernization of, 19; morale of, 161; strength and size of, 55, 105, 133; territorial forces and, 77; Vietnamization and, 29, 165. *See also* RVNAF (Republic of Vietnam Armed Forces)

Asselin, Pierre, 5, 82, 115, 173

Ayers, Bill, 65

Binh, Madame (Nguyen Thi Binh), 82

Boggs, Hale, 90

Brezhnev, Leonid, 161

Brinkley, Alan, 23

Brocheux, Pierre, 145

Brown, Sam, 103

Buckley, Kevin, 55

Buddhists, 13, 154

Bui Diem, 6, 16–17, 18, 70, 78, 131, 155, 164; Kissinger and, 46; on post-Midway optimism in South Vietnam, 85; State Department criticism of Thieu and, 78; on Thieu as "prisoner of the palace," 156

Bundy, William, 46, 61

Bunker, Ellsworth, 13, 18, 163; on the American home front, 23; on troop withdrawals, 19, 80

bureaucracy, 32, 45, 64; Nixon's hatred of, 34

258 Index

Cambodia, 2, 5, 47, 102; clandestine bombing of, 51, 52, 65, 84, 92, 119, 140, 175; communist border sanctuaries in, 27, 145; expansion of war into, 49, 141, 143, 172, 181, 184–185; in the French colonial empire, 145; Nixon's invasion as a grave error, 143–151; North Vietnamese supply lines in, 48, 50; South Vietnamese forces in, 143, 148, 150, 157

Cao Van Than, 134

Catholics, Vietnamese, 13, 154

Ceausescu, Nicolae, 94, 95

Chambers, Whittaker, 72

Chiang Kai-shek, 156

China, People's Republic of, 40, 95, 161, 179; opening to, 33; secret diplomacy of Nixon/Kissinger with, 166, 167; split with Soviet Union, 50, 81, 140; superpower diplomacy and, 181

Church, Senator Frank, 113, 148

CIA (Central Intelligence Agency), 11, 14, 44, 46, 81, 88; Laird's Vietnam Task Force and, 54; on Operation Duck Hook, 112; on progress of Vietnamization, 136; on strength of NLF, 162

civil rights movement, 10, 22, 25, 181

Clements, William, 176, 177

Clemis, Martin, 162

Clifford, Clark, 19, 39–40, 46, 54, 56, 86

Colby, William, 77, 134

Cold War, 9, 50, 110, 165, 167, 184; consequences of failure in Vietnam, 49; fracturing consensus about, 42; Truman's policies and, 25

Columbia University, student occupations at, 23

communism, 25–26, 50, 142

Congress, US, 2, 10, 40, 63, 89–90, 102; budget for war restricted by, 145; Democratic critics of Nixon administration, 69–70; dissent against the war in, 5; doves in, 144; hawks in, 109; response to Cambodian incursion, 148–149; Senate Foreign Relations Committee, 58, 90, 128, 134; troop withdrawals and, 74, 187; turn against the war, 16–17, 127–128, 129; Vietnamization and, 113

conservative movement, 5, 7, 144

Cooper, Senator John, 148

Cooper-Church amendment, 129, 149, 158

Cornell University, armed occupation at (1969), 65–66

COSVN (Central Office of South Vietnam), 20, 82, 83, 142

Cronkite, Walter, 188

Cushman, Robert, 88

Daddis, Gregory, 5, 49

Dallek, Robert, 69, 130

Davidson, Phillip, 56, 57

de-Americanization, 15, 16, 19, 20, 29, 30; American public opinion and, 41; bombing of Laos and Cambodia, 51; Congress and, 58–60; Laird and, 40; mutual withdrawal scenario, 54; Nixon's election and, 43; as path toward de-escalation, 44; Republican Party convention (1968), 36; Thieu's embrace of, 181. *See also* Vietnamization

Defense Department, US, 33, 39, 164; Laird's Vietnam Task Force and, 54; Nixon/Kissinger "quiet coup" and, 35; Vietnamization and, 99. *See also* Pentagon

Dellinger, David, 114

Democratic Party, 16, 25, 27, 182; cease-fire proposal of, 69; congressional critics of Nixon administration, 69–70; doves in, 24; Southern Democrats' support for the war, 144; violence at National Convention (Chicago, 1968), 23, 65, 114

détente, Soviet–American, 8, 33, 50, 64, 81, 91, 185; "choking warfare" of, 172; escalation as potential threat to, 110; peace negotiations over Vietnam and, 165–167

Dewey Canyon, Operation, 46

Dewey Canyon II, Operation, 158

Diem (Ngo Dinh Diem), 6, 11, 12, 186

Index 259

diplomacy, 14, 22, 29, 186; "consequential diplomacy," 34; containment of communism and, 50; North Vietnamese strategy, 85–86, 142; peace talks and theater of, 17; superpower diplomacy, 181; "triangular," 166

DMZ (Demilitarized Zone), 63, 119, 147, 162, 169

Dobrynin, Anatoly, 48, 50, 64, 88, 119, 128

domino theory, 96

Drawn Swords (Veith), 6

Duck Hook, Operation, 5, 87–88, 98–99, 105, 120, 125, 183; abandonment of, 112, 113, 117, 121, 123, 138, 146, 184; congressional conservatives and, 109; debate over, 102; generals' doubts about, 103, 115; intended as blow to North Vietnamese morale, 110–112; Pruning Knife, 98, 108

Dulles, John Foster, 49

Eisenhower, Dwight, 3, 9, 32, 92, 164, 188; armistice in Korea and, 30; French war in Indochina and, 26

Ellsberg, Daniel, 37

escalation, 32, 88, 93; anticipated collapse of North Vietnam and, 38; efficacy questioned by generals, 107; "go for broke" strategy, 102; military preparations for, 98; Paris peace talks and, 100–101; as path to "peace with honor," 108; "political reality" in conflict with, 182; as prerequisite to Vietnamization, 51; US domestic constraints on, 40

Evans, Rowland, 59

Fear, Sean, 164, 170

Ford, Gerald, 33

France, 3, 186; colonial empire of, 145; defeat at Dien Bien Phu, 145; French Indochina, 26; "yellowing" strategy in the First Indochina War, 82

Fulbright, Senator J. William, 24, 42, 128, 150, 182; constraint on presidential power and, 58–59; as "neo-isolationist,"

72; Nixon's private meeting with, 60; on price of empire, 188; Vietnamization opposed by, 113–114

Gawthorpe, Andrew, 77

Geneva accords, 26

gold standard, end to, 90

Goldwater, Senator Barry, 43, 109

Goodell, Senator Charles, 113

Goodpaster, General Andrew, 51

Gulf of Tonkin Resolution, 113, 149

GVN (Government of Vietnam), 10, 16, 55, 85, 137; Chieu Hoi (Open Arms) program, 140; possible collapse of, 104

Habib, Philip, 61, 106

Hai Cầu, 81

Haig, Alexander, 35, 48, 91, 99

Haiphong harbor, mining of, 49, 88

Halberstam, David, 175

Haldeman, H. R., 38, 43, 86, 87, 102, 109, 125

Halperin, Morton, 85

Harlow, Bryce, 109

Harriman, W. Averell, 44

Hatfield, Senator Mark, 113

Hayden, Tom, 114

"hearts and minds" rhetoric, 17

Helms, Richard, 44–45

Hémery, Daniel, 145

Ho Chi Minh, 10, 11, 22, 39, 89; death of, 115, 140; response to Vietnamization, 81

Ho Chi Minh Trail, 50, 145, 157, 158

Hoffman, Abbie, 114

Holbrooke, Richard, 85, 86

Holdridge, John, 44

home front, American, 22–25, 31, 65–67, 71, 80–81, 109–110; "Days of Rage," 114; erosion of support for war among moderates, 112; "hard hat" riots in New York City, 150; Kent State students shot by National Guard, 148; Nixon's "silent majority" speech and, 129; popular music of 1960s and 1970s, 40, 53, 75, 126, 167, 168; youth culture and counterculture, 76

Hope, Bob, 127
Hughes, Ken, 180
Hughes, Thomas, 3, 21
Humphrey, Hubert, 16, 20, 126, 182

Indochina War, First, 82
inflation, in US economy, 90
isolationism, 37, 42, 96

Jackson, Senator Henry "Scoop," 33
Javits, Senator Jacob, 113, 134
JCS (Joint Chiefs of Staff), 45, 48, 71, 103, 104, 112; expansion of war into Laos and, 157–158; pace of troop withdrawals and, 150
Jenkins, Brian, 141
Johns, Andrew, 129
Johnson, Lyndon Baines (LBJ), 1, 9, 32, 46, 93, 140, 188; Americanization of the war, 27, 29, 144; domestic policies of, 10; escalation of war, 11, 171; final months in office, 21–22; on getting into and out of war, 3; halt in bombings, 15, 20, 21; media representation of, 24; negotiations with the North, 14; peace talks started by, 2; Pentagon Papers and, 164; State Department and, 35
journalists, 24, 118

Kadura, Johannes, 165–166
Kennedy, Senator Edward, 69–70
Kennedy, John F. (JFK), 3, 9, 124, 164, 188; electoral victory over Nixon, 27; number of troops sent to Vietnam, 11
Kimball, Jeffrey, 91
King, Martin Luther, Jr., 22
Kissinger, Henry, 2, 4, 31, 36, 176–177; Cambodian operations and, 47, 51, 64, 146; coercive diplomacy of, 38, 49, 63–64; Duck Hook and, 110–112; go-for-broke strategy and, 84, 88, 102; hawkish views of, 37; Laird's rivalry with, 34, 40, 62–63, 84–85, 89, 103–109, 184; National Security Study Memorandum (NSSM) 1 and, 46; "negotiated victory" concept of, 37, 41; on Nixon's "silent majority" speech, 125;

at Paris peace talks, 142, 166; "quiet coup" and, 35; secret meetings with North Vietnamese negotiators, 97; troop withdrawals and, 68, 86; ultimatum to North Vietnam, 89, 115, 118, 120; Vietnamization criticized by, 83, 87, 105–106, 107, 120, 137–138, 165
Komer, Robert, 134
Korea, North, 64–65, 84
Korea, South, 53, 91, 152
Korean War, 26, 28, 30
Ky (Nguyen Cao Ky), General, 6, 12, 79, 161, 163

Laird, Melvin, 1, 3–4, 33–34, 52, 83–84, 161; on American public opinion, 39, 60, 100, 112; on antiwar movement, 103–104; Cambodian incursion opposed by, 147, 148; on Congress and the war, 113; de-escalation supported by, 31; defense budget cut by, 144; draft lottery proposed by, 67; Duck Hook and, 111, 112, 116; influence in the Republican Party, 33; on insufficiency of air power alone, 171; Kissinger's rivalry with, 34, 40, 62–63, 84–85, 89, 103–109, 184; military strikes in Cambodia and, 47; Operation Duck Hook and, 98, 103; Paris peace talks and, 99; public opinion lobbied by, 36; role in shaping Nixon's policy, 4; shifting policy views of, 28–29; tensions with Nixon and Kissinger, 62–63; tours of Vietnam, 54–57, 154–155; troop withdrawals and, 150. See also Vietnamization, Laird and
Lake, Anthony, 85, 98, 108, 110, 119, 120
Lam (Hoang Xuan Lam), General, 159
Lam Son 719, battle of, 157–162, 163, 164, 165, 166
Laos, 2, 11, 38, 102, 129; communist border sanctuaries in, 27, 145; expansion of war into, 141, 172; in the French colonial empire, 145; North Vietnamese supply lines in, 48, 50; South Vietnamese forces in, 143, 148, 158–159; strategic importance to Hanoi, 159; US bombing in, 11, 51, 84, 92

Index 261

Le Duan, 11, 14, 32, 81, 157, 174; Christmas bombing and, 173; determination of, 142; Easter Offensive and, 169; increasingly aggressive actions of, 177; Lam Son 719 battle and, 159, 161; national reunification as goal of, 11, 142, 157, 167, 185–186; negotiating position at Paris peace talks, 172; optimism in the face of difficulties, 139; as real ruler of North Vietnam, 115; "talking while fighting" strategy of, 82
Le Duc Tho, 82, 142, 172
Lee Kuan Yew, 37
Leos, Raymond, 146
Linebacker, Operation, 169
linkage, 30
Lodge, Henry Cabot, Jr., 40, 44, 80
Logevall, Fredrik, 182
Lon Nol, General, 146, 147
Lynn, Laurence, 137, 138

MACV (US Military Assistance Command, Vietnam), 18, 19, 51, 99, 115, 137; Cambodian incursion supported by, 146; expansion of war into Laos and, 157–158; optimism of, 134; Vietnamization and, 56–57, 105
Mansfield, Senator Mike, 128, 149, 176
Mao Zedong, 166
McCarthy, Senator Eugene, 23
McCarthy, Senator Joe, 72
McGovern, Senator George, 59
McGrory, Mary, 42
McNamara, Robert, 39, 54
Mekong Delta, 46, 82, 133
Menu, Operation, 49, 50–51, 65, 146
Midway Island, Nixon–Thieu meeting on (1969), 71–73, 74, 77, 78, 83, 95, 155, 185
Minh (Duong Van ["Big"] Minh), 163
Mitchell, John, 88
Moor, Dean, 85
Moorer, Admiral Thomas, 98, 99, 108, 172
Moratorium to End the War in Vietnam (October 15, 1969), 102, 103, 114, 121, 127; division of American public

opinion and, 125–126; media coverage of, 118–119; role in killing Operation Duck Hook, 112; South Vietnamese officials' views of, 130, 132. *See also* antiwar movement
Moreton, J. O., 132
Morris, Roger, 34, 35, 66, 108, 110, 120
My Lai massacre (1968), 127

National Assembly, of South Vietnam, 13, 15, 77, 164; economic consequences of Vietnamization and, 152–154; "Land to the Tiller" reform, 133–134; "Program Law" and, 156; support for Vietnamization, 131; Thieu alienated from, 152; Thieu's offer to negotiate with NLF and, 79
NATO (North Atlantic Treaty Organization), 96, 113
neoisolationism, 8, 72, 96
Ngoc (Pham Kim Ngoc), 153, 156, 157
Nguyen, Hai, 140
Nguyen, Lien-Hang, 32, 115
Nguyen Duc Cuong, 154
Nguyen Ngoc Linh, 132
Nixon, Richard: administration of, 32–40; antiwar movement and, 144; Breakfast Plan of, 51; circumstances inherited by, 9, 10; coercive diplomacy of, 2, 4, 25, 49, 62; Democratic-dominated Congress and, 42; détente and, 8, 91; diplomatic travels of, 89–94; Duck Hook and, 115–116, 138; election victory over Humphrey, 16, 128; between escalation and withdrawal, 40; expansion of war into Cambodia, 49, 64, 84, 140, 143, 181, 184–185; family background and political career of, 25–26; Guam speech, 74, 89, 91, 93; history of Vietnam policy and, 25–30; inaugural address (1969), 31; Johnson criticized by, 28; lack of options available to end the war, 181–186; landslide reelection (1972), 168–169, 171, 174; "Madman Theory" of, 38–39, 50; media representation of, 24–25; Paris peace talks and, 68–69, 168;

"peace with honor" goal of, 4, 30, 43, 125, 171, 180, 184; personalized political style of, 144, 147; presidential trips to Moscow and Beijing (1972), 168, 169; public opinion and, 43; rise of conservative movement and, 7, 144; on the "silent center," 23, 67; "silent majority" speech (November 3, 1969), 120–129, 130, 131, 141, 144; Thieu's meeting with, 70–73; troop withdrawals and, 1, 7, 20, 138; ultimatum to North Vietnam, 89, 115, 118, 119; as vice president, 26; Vietnam War strategy of, 44–52; war inheritance left by Johnson, 21–22. *See also* Vietnamization; Watergate scandal

Nixon Doctrine, 74, 89, 91, 96, 122, 149

NLF [National Liberation Front] (Viet Cong), 10, 14, 27, 55, 58, 92; calls for accommodation with, 153; land reforms/redistribution of, 133; level of popular support in the South, 20; losses sustained from Tet Offensive, 136; media coverage of, 18; morale of, 140; pacification program and, 135, 162; peace negotiations and, 15, 17, 44, 68; Provisional Revolutionary Government formed by, 76; sanctuary in Mekong Delta, 82; strength decimated by Tet Offensive, 22; Thieu's concessions on participation of, 78–79; Vietnamization and, 83, 100, 139–141

No Exit from Vietnam (Thompson, 1969), 119

North Vietnam. *See* Vietnam, Democratic Republic of [DRV] (North Vietnam)

Novak, Robert, 59

NSC (National Security Council), 35, 44, 45, 85, 88; de-Americanization and, 60; review of options for war strategy, 106–107

nuclear weapons, 48, 59, 108, 110

NVA (North Vietnamese Army), 54, 85, 87, 136, 145. *See also* PAVN (People's Army of Vietnam)

oil shock (1973), 178

pacification, 18, 19, 61, 77, 92, 133; Accelerated Pacification Campaign (1968–1969), 46; communists' failure to disrupt, 139; faltering momentum of, 137; Kissinger's strategy and, 36; politics in South Vietnam and, 162–165; post-Tet Offensive, 56; in Red River Delta, 12; US troop withdrawals and, 57; Vietnamization and, 104

Packard, David, 67–68

Paris peace talks, 13, 15, 17, 68–69, 72, 96, 122; American concessions at, 44; American head of, 40; American public opinion and, 55; China's opposition to, 140; Peace Accords (1973), 168, 173, 175, 176, 186; stalled progress at, 107; US troop withdrawals and, 39, 45, 141

Park Chung Hee, 156

Pathet Lao (Laotian communist organization), 157

PAVN (People's Army of Vietnam), 14, 57, 58, 70, 77, 135, 186; in Cambodia, 146; in Easter Offensive, 169, 170; heavy arms of, 159, 161, 169, 171; in Lam Son 719 battle, 159, 160, 165; presence in South Vietnam, 173; South Vietnam's ability to fight against, 105; Vietnamization and, 83, 100, 139. *See also* NVA (North Vietnamese Army)

Pell, Senator Claiborne, 60

Pentagon, 33, 39, 46, 176; journalists and, 24; Laird and, 36; Vietnamization and, 67–68. *See also* Defense Department, US

Pentagon Papers, 164

Perot, Ross, 126

PF (Popular Forces), of South Vietnam, 77, 133

Philo, Gordon, 80

Poor People's Campaign, 22

POWs (prisoners of war), American, 126, 149, 151, 172, 173, 175

PRG (Provisional Revolutionary Government), 82

Price, Ray, 66, 92, 129

PSDF (Popular Self-Defense Forces), of South Vietnam, 77, 134, 135
Pursley, Robert, 54

Quan doi Nhan dan (PAVN newspaper), 20–21

racism, 23
RAND Corporation, 37, 45
Red River Delta, 12
Republican Party (GOP), 29, 33, 41, 126; National Convention (1968), 36; shift of American South toward, 7
Resor, Stanley, 149
RF (Regional Forces), of South Vietnam, 77, 133
Richardson, Elliot, 45, 135–136
riots, in American cities, 22–23
Rockefeller, Nelson, 34
Rogers, William P., 31–32, 35–36, 46, 87, 106; cut out of loop by Nixon and Kissinger, 48, 50, 51–52; Operation Duck Hook and, 98; Paris peace talks and, 44, 99; peace plan of, 68; Senate doves and, 60; on troop withdrawals, 45
Roosevelt, Franklin, 186
Rostow, Walt, 63
Rubin, Jerry, 114
Rusk, Dean, 21, 46
Ruth, Richard, 94
RVNAF (Republic of Vietnam Armed Forces), 15, 27, 53, 72, 100, 131; expansion of, 152; improvement program of, 144–145; inability to keep fighting (1974–1975), 177–178, 179; in Laos and Cambodia, 143; modernization of, 56; morale of, 133; strength and confidence of, 115; uncertain improvement of, 137; Vietnamization and, 76, 81; Wheeler's optimism about, 116. *See also* ARVN (Army of the Republic of Vietnam)

Safire, William, 147
SALT (strategic arms limitation talks), 64, 110
Schlesinger, Arthur, Jr., 128

Scott, Hugh, 161
SDS (Students for a Democratic Society), 65, 66
Seale, Bobby, 114
Sequoia (presidential yacht), meeting on, 88, 89, 99
Shaw, John, 157
Sheehan, Neil, 100–101
Sihanouk, Prince Norodom, 146
"silent majority," 132, 145, 169, 173; Cambodian incursion and limits of, 184; counterdemonstrations against the second Moratorium and, 127; Nixon's speech about (Nov. 3, 1969), 120–129, 130, 131, 141, 144; Vietnamization and, 138, 151
Simon, Bob, 170
Sino-Soviet split, 50, 81, 140
Small, Melvin, 118
South Vietnam. *See* Vietnam, Republic of [RVN] (South Vietnam)
Soviet Union, 33, 40, 49, 90–91, 95, 179; arms control talks with, 64; increase in military aid to North Vietnam, 161; Nixon's summit in Moscow (1972), 169; Soviet assets as possible targets in Duck Hook, 110–111; split with China, 50, 81, 140; superpower diplomacy and, 181. *See also* détente, Soviet–American
Speedy Express, Operation, 46
State Department, US, 21, 33, 46, 51, 64, 97; Bureau of Intelligence and Research, 3; escalation opposed in, 46; Nixon/Kissinger "quiet coup" and, 35; Nixon's distrust of, 68; opposition to Nixon within, 34; Thieu criticized by, 78
Stennis, Senator John, 164
Suri, Jeremi, 22

Taiwan, 152
Tet Offensive (1968), 2, 6, 13, 23, 28, 83, 153; American public opinion and, 24, 27, 42; communist losses during, 14, 20; resiliency of South Vietnam and, 85, 132; US optimism following, 44
Thailand, 91, 94, 129

264   Index

Thieu (Nguyen Van Thieu), 2, 3, 16, 97, 113, 155, 174; de-Americanization embraced by, 181; defeat and resignation of, 179; family background and early career of, 11–12; foreign diplomats and, 7; Lam Son 719 battle and, 158–161; land reform and, 134; "Long Haul, Low Cost" strategy of, 85, 186–187; military's relationship with, 12–13; missteps of, 7, 85, 163, 178, 187–188; "New Opportunities" campaign, 55; Nixon's Cambodian incursion and, 146, 148; Nixon's Midway meeting with, 70–73; offer to negotiate with NLF, 78–79; optimism about victory, 130, 132–133, 139, 143; overconfidence of, 152; peace negotiations and, 15, 76, 173; "Program Law" and, 156; reelection campaign, 163–164; response to Easter Offensive, 170; rural reform and, 77–78; secrecy and caution of, 12; "three pillars" strategy of, 18; tours of countryside, 162; US troop withdrawals and, 105, 182; Vietnamization and, 6, 18, 54–55, 70, 92, 99

Third World, 26, 92
Thompson, Sir Robert, 119, 135, 138
Tran Ngoc Chau, 153–154, 156
Tran Quy Phong, 79
Tran Thien Khiem, General, 153
Tran Van Don, General, 6, 70, 154, 181
Tran Van Huong, 55–56, 76, 152–153
Tran Van Tuyen, 154
troop withdrawals, 1, 4, 6, 15, 18, 120, 184; American public opinion and, 106, 119; ARVN improvements and, 61, 62; as coda to tougher measures, 44; communist negotiating demand for, 68, 97; "cut-and-try" approach to, 100, 115; element of time and, 41; irreversibility of, 86, 87; Kissinger's strategy options and, 37–38; mutual withdrawal scenario, 19, 35, 54, 57, 86, 165, 166, 186; Nixon's announcements (1969–1972), 170; pace of, 146, 150; pacification and, 57; as a pillar of Vietnamization, 39; postponement of, 100–101; as "salted

peanuts" to public opinion, 106, 119, 158, 170; South Vietnamese officials' view of, 6, 131; troop strength figures, 9, 150, 151, 168; US domestic pressures and, 74. *See also* Vietnamization

Truman, Harry, 3, 9, 25, 164, 188
Truong Nhu Tang, 139

Ut, Nick, 170

Van Atta, Dale, 111
Vann, John Paul, 135
Van Ngan, 133
Veith, George, 6, 177
Viet Cong. *See* NLF [National Liberation Front] (Viet Cong)
Viet Minh, 12, 26
Vietnam, Democratic Republic of [DRV] (North Vietnam), 4, 28; American escalation and, 38; domestic problems of, 81; Easter Offensive [*Nguyen Hue*] (1972), 169–171, 172; forces built up in Laos and Cambodia, 144–145, 157, 159; naval blockade of, 27; Nixon's war assessed by, 139–142; Sino-Soviet split and, 50, 81, 140; threatened destruction of, 52, 75, 102; US elections and politics followed by, 20; victorious military machine of, 179; Vietnamization anticipated by, 5, 82
Vietnam, Republic of [RVN] (South Vietnam): American intervention on behalf of, 1; collapse of, 2, 8, 60, 130, 179, 180; drying up of US economic and military aid, 176; economic consequences of Vietnamized war, 143, 152–156, 187; formation of, 26–27; human rights abuses of, 177; legitimacy undermined by 1971 election, 165; military draft in, 15; Nixon's visit to, 92–94; pacification and politics in, 162–165; right to self-determination of, 108; Second Republic (1967–1975), 11, 13, 78, 95, 168, 178; survival of, 3, 4, 27, 47, 96, 131, 143, 152, 165, 166, 187; US abandonment of, 7, 69, 121, 182; US bombing sorties in, 63, 113. *See also*

Index   265

ARVN (Army of the Republic of Vietnam); GVN (Government of Vietnam); National Assembly
Vietnam Courier (North Vietnamese newspaper), 20, 157
Vietnamese National Army (French-created force), 12
Vietnam Guardian (newspaper), 94, 131, 132, 151
Vietnamization: American public opinion and, 76, 97–98, 107, 126, 128–129, 139; British view of, 95–96; Cambodian incursion and, 149; collapse of, 178; communist assessments of, 139–142; congressional critics of, 113; as cover for US retreat, 6; Duck Hook as alternative to, 111; economic consequences of, 143, 152–156, 187; end of American presence in Vietnam and, 4; escalation as prerequisite to, 51; as fraud perpetrated by Nixon, 180; as gradual and unilateral de-escalation, 84, 87; "indigenization," 81; Kissinger's criticism of, 105–106; Lam Son 719, 157–162; leaked to reporters, 62–63; "long haul" strategy, 74, 85, 144, 186–187; Nixon Doctrine and, 122; North Vietnamese view of, 80; pace of, 104, 106, 146, 155–156; as political panacea, 124–129; promoted in Saigon and Washington, 54–62; as "race against time," 75–83, 106, 141; seen as foreordained, 1, 2, 4; shift from escalation to, 120; "silent majority" speech and, 122–123; as successful strategy, 130–139; three tests of (1972), 168–175; twin pillars of, 39; as unilateral US withdrawal, 120; US troop withdrawals and, 67–73; "war and peace Vietnamization," 17. *See also* de-Americanization; troop withdrawals
Vietnamization, Laird and, 1, 54, 56–62, 75, 84–85, 103; as best course in domestic context, 180; conscription issue and, 67; domestic public pressures and, 100, 105; escalation as alternative opposed by Laird, 5, 73; generals'

assessments and, 115; Laird's definition of Vietnamization, 53; Nixon's "silent majority" speech and, 122, 123; South Vietnamese leadership and, 131–132; union members addressed about Vietnamization, 111–112; on Vietnamization as path to victory, 136
Vietnam Moratorium Committee, 103
"Viet Nam Negotiations, The" (Kissinger, 1969), 36
Vietnam's American War (Asselin), 5
Vietnam Special Studies Group (VSSG), 120, 137, 138, 149
Vietnam War: American casualties, 22, 44, 88, 114–115, 128, 141; Americanization of, 1, 2, 144, 154, 186; as America's longest twentieth-century war, 1; division of American public opinion over, 23–24, 41; "Hamburger Hill" battle (1969), 69; historiography of, 5, 180; Lam Son 719 battle, 157–162, 163, 164, 165, 166; military draft in United States, 67; search for American exit from, 3–8. *See also* Tet Offensive
Vo Nguyen Giap, General, 142
Vu, Tuong, 170

Wallace, George, 23, 182
Warner, Dennis, 70
Warnke, Paul, 39, 54
Watergate scandal, 2–3, 7, 175, 176, 180
Watts, William, 114, 119
Wells, Tom, 66, 114
Westmoreland, General William, 18, 23, 56, 67
Wheeler, General Earle, 47, 49, 58, 88, 115; Duck Hook criticized by, 116; escalation questioned by, 107; troop withdrawals and, 104
White, Theodore, 30
Williams, Lee, 69
Wilson, Harold, 89, 95, 96
World War II, 8
Wright, Ian, 162

Xuan Thuy, 82

Studies in Conflict, Diplomacy, and Peace

Series Editors: George C. Herring, Andrew L. Johns, and Kathryn C. Statler

This series focuses on key moments of conflict, diplomacy, and peace from the eighteenth century to the present to explore their wider significance in the development of US foreign relations. The series editors welcome new research in the form of original monographs, interpretive studies, biographies, and anthologies from historians, political scientists, journalists, and policymakers. A primary goal of the series is to examine the United States' engagement with the world, its evolving role in the international arena, and the ways in which the state, nonstate actors, individuals, and ideas have shaped and continue to influence history, both at home and abroad.

Advisory Board Members

David Anderson, California State University, Monterey Bay
Laura Belmonte, Oklahoma State University
Robert Brigham, Vassar College
Paul Chamberlin, Columbia University
Jessica Chapman, Williams College
Frank Costigliola, University of Connecticut
Michael C. Desch, University of Notre Dame
Kurk Dorsey, University of New Hampshire
John Ernst, Morehead State University
Joseph A. Fry, University of Nevada, Las Vegas
Ann Heiss, Kent State University
Sheyda Jahanbani, University of Kansas
Mark Lawrence, University of Texas
Mitchell Lerner, Ohio State University
Kyle Longley, LBJ Presidential Library
Robert McMahon, Ohio State University
Michaela Hoenicke Moore, University of Iowa
Lien-Hang T. Nguyen, Columbia University
Jason Parker, Texas A&M University
Andrew Preston, Cambridge University
Thomas Schwartz, Vanderbilt University
Salim Yaqub, University of California, Santa Barbara

Books in the Series

Truman, Congress, and Korea: The Politics of America's First Undeclared War
Larry Blomstedt

The Legacy of J. William Fulbright: Policy, Power, and Ideology
Edited by Alessandro Brogi, Giles Scott-Smith, and David J. Snyder

The Gulf: The Bush Presidencies and the Middle East
Michael F. Cairo

Remaking the World: Decolonization and the Cold War
Jessica M. Chapman

Reagan and the World: Leadership and National Security, 1981–1989
Edited by Bradley Lynn Coleman and Kyle Longley

A Diplomatic Meeting: Reagan, Thatcher, and the Art of Summitry
James Cooper

American Justice in Taiwan: The 1957 Riots and Cold War Foreign Policy
Stephen G. Craft

Soccer Diplomacy: International Relations and Football since 1914
Edited by Heather L. Dichter

Diplomatic Games: Sport, Statecraft, and International Relations since 1945
Edited by Heather L. Dichter and Andrew L. Johns

Nothing Less Than War: A New History of America's Entry into World War I
Justus D. Doenecke

Aid under Fire: Nation Building and the Vietnam War
Jessica Elkind

Enemies to Allies: Cold War Germany and American Memory
Brian C. Etheridge

Grounded: The Case for Abolishing the United States Air Force
Robert M. Farley

Foreign Friends: Syngman Rhee, American Exceptionalism, and the Division of Korea
David P. Fields

The Myth of Triumphalism: Rethinking President Reagan's Cold War Legacy
Beth A. Fischer

The American South and the Vietnam War: Belligerence, Protest, and Agony in Dixie
Joseph A. Fry

Lincoln, Seward, and US Foreign Relations in the Civil War Era
Joseph A. Fry

The Turkish Arms Embargo: Drugs, Ethnic Lobbies, and US Domestic Politics
James F. Goode

Obama at War: Congress and the Imperial Presidency
Ryan C. Hendrickson

Fourteen Points for the Twenty-First Century: A Renewed Appeal for Cooperative Internationalism
Edited by Richard H. Immerman and Jeffrey A. Engel

The Cold War at Home and Abroad: Domestic Politics and US Foreign Policy since 1945
Edited by Andrew L. Johns and Mitchell B. Lerner

US Presidential Elections and Foreign Policy: Candidates, Campaigns, and Global Politics from FDR to Bill Clinton
Edited by Andrew Johnstone and Andrew Priest

Paving the Way for Reagan: The Influence of Conservative Media on US Foreign Policy
Laurence R. Jurdem

The Conversion of Senator Arthur H. Vandenberg: From Isolation to International Engagement
Lawrence S. Kaplan

Harold Stassen: Eisenhower, the Cold War, and the Pursuit of Nuclear Disarmament
Lawrence S. Kaplan

America's Israel: The US Congress and American-Israeli Relations, 1967–1975
Kenneth Kolander

JFK and de Gaulle: How America and France Failed in Vietnam, 1961–1963
Sean J. McLaughlin

Nixon's Back Channel to Moscow: Confidential Diplomacy and Détente
Richard A. Moss

Breaking Protocol: America's First Female Ambassadors, 1933–1964
Philip Nash

Peacemakers: American Leadership and the End of Genocide in the Balkans
James W. Pardew

The Currents of War: A New History of American-Japanese Relations, 1899–1941
Sidney Pash

Unwilling to Quit: The Long Unwinding of American Involvement in Vietnam
David L. Prentice

Eisenhower and Cambodia: Diplomacy, Covert Action, and the Origins of the Second Indochina War
William J. Rust

So Much to Lose: John F. Kennedy and American Policy in Laos
William J. Rust

The Sailor: Franklin D. Roosevelt and the Transformation of American Foreign Policy
David F. Schmitz

Foreign Policy at the Periphery: The Shifting Margins of US International Relations since World War II
Edited by Bevan Sewell and Maria Ryan

Lincoln Gordon: Architect of Cold War Foreign Policy
Bruce L. R. Smith

Thomas C. Mann: President Johnson, the Cold War, and the Restructuring of Latin American Foreign Policy
Thomas Tunstall Allcock